MICROSOFT® QUICK PROGRAMMER'S TOOLBOX

MICROSOFT® QUICKBASIC PROGRAMMER'S TOOLBOX

JOHN CLARK CRAIG

PUBLISHED BY
Microsoft Press
A Division of Microsoft Corporation
16011 NE 36th Way, Box 97017, Redmond, Washington 98073-9717

Copyright © 1988 by John Clark Craig
All rights reserved. No part of the contents of this book may
be reproduced or transmitted in any form or by any means without
the written permission of the publisher.

Library of Congress Cataloging in Publication Data
Craig, John Clark.
  The Microsoft QuickBASIC programmer's toolbox.
  1. BASIC (Computer program language)   2. Microsoft QuickBASIC
(Computer program)   I. Title.
  QA76.73.B3C7   1988   005.13'3   88-5115
  ISBN 1-55615-127-6

Printed and bound in the United States of America.

  2 3 4 5 6 7 8 9   MLML   3 2 1 0 9 8

Distributed to the book trade in the
United States by Harper & Row.

Distributed to the book trade in
Canada by General Publishing Company, Ltd.

Distributed to the book trade outside the
United States and Canada by Penguin Books Ltd.

Penguin Books Ltd., Harmondsworth, Middlesex, England
Penguin Books Australia Ltd., Ringwood, Victoria, Australia
Penguin Books N.Z. Ltd., 182–190 Wairau Road, Auckland 10, New Zealand

British Cataloging in Publication Data available

Project Editor: Suzanne Viescas   **Manuscript Editor:** Michele Tomiak   **Technical Editor:** Jon Harshaw

*This book is dedicated with love to
the three most important people in my life:*

Jeanie, Jennifer, and Adam.

SPECIAL OFFER

Companion Disks to MICROSOFT QUICKBASIC PROGRAMMER'S TOOLBOX

Microsoft Press has created Companion Disks to MICROSOFT QUICKBASIC PROGRAMMER'S TOOLBOX, available in either 5.25-inch (2-disk set) or 3.5-inch (1-disk set) format.

The Companion Disks contain the QuickBASIC toolboxes and programs listed in this book plus all the functions and subprograms—more than 250 routines. An additional program, INTRODEM.BAS, is included to showcase the capability and power of some of the toolboxes. In all, more than 17,000 lines of code are on the disks! These disks are an essential resource for anyone who wants to forgo the drudgery of typing in the listings (and save the time required to find and correct those inevitable typing errors) and begin to use these powerful QuickBASIC toolbox routines immediately.

If you have questions about the files on the disk, please write to: QuickBASIC Toolbox Editor, Microsoft Press, 16011 NE 36th Way, Box 97017, Redmond, WA 98073-9717.

The Companion Disks to MICROSOFT QUICKBASIC PROGRAMMER'S TOOLBOX are available only from Microsoft Press. To order, use the special reply card bound in the back of the book. If the card has already been used, please send $19.95, plus sales tax if applicable (CA residents 5% plus local option tax, CT 7.5%, FL 6%, MA 5%, MN 6%, MO 4.225%, NY 4% plus local option tax, WA State 7.8%) and $2.50 per disk for domestic postage and handling, $6.00 per disk for foreign orders, to: Microsoft Press, Attn: Companion Disk Offer, 21919 20th Ave S.E., Box 3011, Bothell, WA 98041-3011. Please specify 5.25-inch or 3.5-inch format. Payment must be in U.S. funds. You may pay by check or money order (payable to Microsoft Press) or by American Express, VISA, or MasterCard; please include both your credit card number and the expiration date. All domestic orders are shipped 2nd day air upon receipt of order by Microsoft.

If any of these disks prove defective, please send the defective disk(s) along with your packing slip to: Microsoft Press, Consumer Sales, 16011 NE 36th Way, Box 97017, Redmond, WA 98073-9717.

CONTENTS

PART I: GETTING STARTED

QUICKBASIC AND TOOLBOXES 3
    Advantages of Structured Programming 3
    The Toolboxes in This Book 4

MINICAL.BAS—A COMPLETE PROGRAM 5
    Modular Source-Code Editing 5
    Building a Quick Library 6
    Creating the Source Code for MINICAL 6
    Compiling and Running as an Executable (.EXE) Program 17

PART II: QUICKBASIC TOOLBOXES AND PROGRAMS

USING QUICKBASIC TOOLBOXES 21
    Special Requirements 21
    QuickBASIC *vs* Executable Files 24

ATTRIB 27
BIN2HEX 30
BIOSCALL 33
BITS 47
CALENDAR 55
CARTESIA 78
CIPHER 84
COLORS 91
COMPLEX 98
DOLLARS 113
DOSCALLS 117
EDIT 148
ERROR 169
FIGETPUT 173
FILEINFO 177
FRACTION 186
GAMES 198

HEX2BIN   210
JUSTIFY   212
KEYS   217
LOOK   221
MONTH   226
MOUSGCRS   229
MOUSSUBS   241
MOUSTCRS   275
OBJECT   281
PARSE   293
PROBSTAT   298
QBFMT   305
QBTREE   314
QCAL   319
QCALMATH   330
RANDOMS   353
STDOUT   365
STRINGS   378
TRIANGLE   406
WINDOWS   413
WORDCOUN   427

PART III: MIXED-LANGUAGE TOOLBOXES

USING MIXED-LANGUAGE TOOLBOXES   433
    Near and Far Addressing   433
    Passing Variables   434
    Creating Mixed-Language Toolboxes   435

CDEMO1.BAS AND CTOOLS1.C   440
CDEMO2.BAS AND CTOOLS2.C   456

PART IV: APPENDIXES

APPENDIX A   Requirements for Running Toolboxes/Programs   479
APPENDIX B   Functions-to-Modules Cross Reference   485
APPENDIX C   Subprograms-to-Modules Cross Reference   490
APPENDIX D   Hexadecimal Format (.OBJ) Files   494
APPENDIX E   Line-Drawing Characters   497

PART I

GETTING STARTED

QUICKBASIC AND TOOLBOXES

Thanks to Microsoft QuickBASIC 4.0, BASIC has finally grown into a flexible, full-featured, and powerful programming language. By thumbing through this book and glancing at the program listings, you'll see that BASIC isn't what it used to be. Microsoft QuickBASIC is easier to read, has a faster learning curve, and gives you the power to quickly create sophisticated programs that would have been difficult, if not impossible, with traditional BASIC.

A key difference between traditional BASIC and QuickBASIC is that QuickBASIC allows structured programming, an important feature that makes large programs easier to create and maintain.

Advantages of Structured Programming

With early versions of BASIC, a program was written and executed as a single block of program lines. Inexperienced programmers writing large programs could unknowingly create "spaghetti code" (programs that make frequent and improper use of GOTO statements) making them generally difficult to follow and maintain.

A key feature of QuickBASIC is its ability to let you create structured programs—large programs constructed of small, individual program modules. Instead of having to create and work with a large (and often overwhelming) single block of code, the QuickBASIC programmer need only construct the program modules, which are in turn constructed from procedures called subprograms and functions. Each of these procedures performs a specific, well-defined task. By concentrating on the functionality of a single procedure, the programmer is freed from having to worry about other parts of the program and can devote full concentration to the task at hand. It's been proven that programmers can develop complex programs more quickly and accurately using this modular approach.

An additional advantage to structured programming is that these modules and procedures can be organized and saved in such a way that they can be reused with other programs—avoiding duplication of effort from one programming project to another. By grouping modules with complementary functionality, a programmer can easily create "toolboxes" of useful routines that can, over time, make large programming projects progress quickly because major portions of the program are already written.

After construction, a module can also be organized into a Quick Library, which is a file saved on disk in a special format. You can then load Quick Libraries with the QuickBASIC program, effectively adding the routines in the Quick Library to the ones built into QuickBASIC.

The Toolboxes in This Book

If you are using (or even thinking of using) QuickBASIC, this book will be a valuable reference. If you're only starting out and learning QuickBASIC as a first language, you'll find the book immediately useful for learning by example. If you're a seasoned, professional programmer using QuickBASIC as a software development system, you'll find the routines in this book to be valuable extensions to the QuickBASIC language.

Part I provides step-by-step instructions for constructing a complete, working program called MINICAL. Beginning programmers in particular will find this tutorial helpful. Part II contains all the QuickBASIC toolboxes and begins with a brief section that explains how to load and run them. Part III describes the use of mixed-language toolboxes and contains several examples. Finally, five appendixes contain information on the requirements for running the toolboxes, cross references to functions and subprograms, and additional important information.

If you're an experienced programmer, you may want to skip ahead to Part II and start using some of the toolboxes. If you're new to QuickBASIC, turn now to the next section. You'll create two modules containing functions and subprograms and use them to build a Quick Library. Once you've learned the steps needed to create your own programs and your own Quick Library, you can use the modules in Parts II and III of this book, as well as modules of your own, to create even more Quick Libraries. You'll soon have powerful toolboxes that you can use to build programs quickly.

MINICAL.BAS—
A COMPLETE
PROGRAM

In this section we will start from scratch and build a complete, working program. We'll construct the program, build a Quick Library to extend the QuickBASIC language, and build a stand-alone, executable program.

Before we begin, let's take a quick look at the capabilities of the QuickBASIC programming environment and at some of the major concepts involved. The sample program in this section is made up of two separate modules, each consisting of several subprograms and functions. Let's look at how QuickBASIC handles each of these.

Modular Source-Code Editing

One of the new features of Microsoft QuickBASIC 4.0 is the way that you review and edit programs from within the QuickBASIC environment. If you've programmed in QuickBASIC, perhaps you've noticed that a program comprising several subprograms and functions can't be shown and edited all in one piece on the screen. If you haven't yet programmed in QuickBASIC, you need only know at this point that you select one subprogram or function from a list of currently loaded subprograms and functions as the one you want to view and edit. All the other routines are hidden from view. This might seem strange at first, but after working on a few programs, you'll begin to appreciate the power that this modular editing provides.

A second major advance in QuickBASIC 4.0 is its ability to load into memory more than one source-code file at a time. This opens the door to creating collections of subprograms and functions, stored in separate source-code files by subject, that several different programs can load and use independently.

The important concepts about these new features can be summarized in this way: A program can be made up of one or more source-code files (modules), and each source-code file can be made up of one or more subprograms or functions. You can load several of these source files into the QuickBASIC environment simultaneously, and all modules can work together to make a complete program. Although you can display and edit only one portion of a source file at a time, it's easy to jump from one portion to another while editing a program.

Building a Quick Library

Wouldn't it be nice to create new QuickBASIC statements and functions that you could add to the language in such a way that they'd be available for your use every time you fired up QuickBASIC? That's what Quick Libraries can do for you!

For example, suppose you use hyperbolic functions in almost every program you write. You could create these functions in a source-code file to be loaded into memory along with each main program you write, or you could create a Quick Library so that these functions load at the same time you load QuickBASIC. To build a Quick Library, you would simply load the hyperbolic function source-code file and select the appropriate menu choices from the Run menu.

Creating the Source Code for MINICAL

Let's walk through the creation of a complete programming project, step by step, to get your feet wet. Fire up your computer and follow along to get the maximum benefit. The MINICAL program performs five functions: addition, subtraction, multiplication, division, and square root. The program is simple in scope, yet it has most of the major components of much larger software projects.

Before we start coding, let's look at how the program should run once we get it built. The MINICAL program uses Reverse Polish Notation (RPN) for input. Using RPN simplifies the programming considerably because it eliminates the coding necessary to rearrange those math commands enshrouded in parentheses.

Using RPN, you enter numbers first, followed by the operators. For example, to add 3 and 4, you would enter:

3 4 +

(We'll show how these numbers are actually entered later in the section.) To add 1 and 2 and then multiply the result by 3, you would enter:

```
1 2 + 3 *
```

MINICAL uses double-precision numbers, so you can enter any type of integer or floating-point numeric values. Results are displayed using as many as 16 digits. For example, to divide 1.2 by −3.45, you would enter:

```
1.2 -3.45 /
```

and the display would read:

```
Result... -.3478260869565217
```

NOTE: Because a computer keyboard does not have × and ÷ keys, an asterisk (*) is used for multiplication and a forward slash (/) is used for division.

By the way, MINICAL uses a structure called a stack to hold the numbers and the operators while performing the calculations. (Technically, the structure used in MINICAL only mimics a traditional stack, but for discussion purposes it can be thought of as a stack.) A stack is a sequential series of memory locations set aside to hold a number of separate items—in this case, the numbers and operators provided by the user. RPN is used for specifying numbers and operators primarily because of the existence of the stack—the RPN syntax is ideal for stack-based calculations. The alternative method, parsing, involves "reading" the equation entered by the user, rearranging and selecting the separate elements, and acting on them. This latter method involves much more coding.

The stack in MINICAL can hold as many as 20 values plus the associated operators. You can enter numbers as explained above, or you can enter all numbers and then the operators. For example, to add the numbers 1 through 5, you can enter either of these two command lines:

```
1 2 + 3 + 4 + 5 +
1 2 3 4 5 + + + +
```

The MINIMATH Module

This project consists of two parts: the MINIMATH module and the MINICAL module. Let's begin with MINIMATH.

If you haven't done so yet, at the system prompt type *QB* and press Enter to start QuickBASIC. Type in the title block on the following page.

```
' ****************************************************
' **   Name:          MINIMATH                      **
' **   Type:          Toolbox                       **
' **   Module:        MINIMATH.BAS                  **
' **   Language:      Microsoft QuickBASIC 4.00     **
' ****************************************************
'
' Collection of math subprograms for the MINICAL
' program.
```

At this point, it's convenient to tell QuickBASIC this module's name. Pull down the File menu and choose Save As. Type the filename *MINIMATH,* and press the Enter key or move your mouse pointer to the OK box and click the left mouse button. The file is then saved to disk, and you're ready to continue entering more of the program. Note that if you omit the .BAS extension, as you did here, QuickBASIC automatically adds it for you.

This first module will be made up of the five subprograms that perform the math functions. First, let's create the Add subprogram. Pull down the Edit menu and choose New SUB. When you're asked for the name of the subprogram, respond with Add. QuickBASIC then creates the first and last lines of your new subprogram:

```
SUB Add
END SUB
```

Note that QuickBASIC also adjusts the editing window so that only the Add subprogram is displayed, allowing you to concentrate on this subprogram only. (You'll greatly appreciate this feature later on, when your programming projects become larger.) The next step is to add comment information before the first line of the subprogram and to insert the "guts" of the subprogram between the two lines displayed by QuickBASIC.

Start by adding comments. Move the cursor to the first character of the first line of the subprogram and press Enter. When you do, a dialog box appears with the message *Blank lines not allowed before SUB/FUNCTION line. Is remark OK?* Since a remark (comment) is what you want, choose OK. QuickBASIC then inserts a blank line preceded by a ' character for the comment. After you type the first comment line (taken from the lines on the following page) and press Enter, the dialog box appears again. Click OK and then type the next comment line.

Use the lines below to build the Add subprogram. Note the locations of the SUB Add and END SUB lines, and note that you need to append items to the SUB Add line. Also note that some lines are indented: Although this indention is not required, it is good programming style to indent subordinate lines so that the program is easier to read and relationships between lines are visually apparent. When you're done, your Add subprogram should look exactly like this:

```
' ****************************************************
' **   Name:         Add                            **
' **   Type:         Subprogram                     **
' **   Module:       MINIMATH.BAS                   **
' **   Language:     Microsoft QuickBASIC 4.00      **
' ****************************************************
'
' Performs addition for the MINICAL program.
'
  SUB Add (stack#(), ptr%) STATIC
      ptr% = ptr% - 1
      IF ptr% THEN
          stack#(ptr%) = stack#(ptr%) + stack#(ptr% + 1)
      END IF
  END SUB
```

You can save your work at any point. (It's a good idea to back up your work often to prevent losing your work in case of a power failure or other disaster.) Do so now by pulling down the File menu and choosing Save All.

You're well on your way now! You will create and edit the other four math subprograms (shown on pages 11-12) in the same way.

Here's a tip that can speed up the process. Notice that the initial comment lines for each of the five subprograms are nearly identical. So, instead of retyping each one, you'll copy the lines you typed in for the Add subprogram and paste them into the other subprograms. Let's do that now.

First, set up the new subprograms. For the Subtract subprogram, choose New SUB from the Edit menu, enter the name *Subtract*, and press Enter. After the two lines of the Subtract subprogram are displayed, repeat the New SUB process for the Multiply, Divide, and SquareRoot subprograms. Be sure you type the subprogram names as shown here— each starts with a capital letter, and no space is allowed in the subprogram name SquareRoot.

GETTING STARTED

Next, make a copy of the comment lines in the Add subprogram. Pull down the View menu and choose SUBS. QuickBASIC displays a list of all subprogram names you entered. Here's where the power of QuickBASIC is really apparent: Using the SUBS command, you can jump to any subprogram for editing by simply selecting the name of the desired subprogram. You do this by double-clicking on the desired subprogram name with your mouse or by using the cursor movement keys followed by the Enter key. For now, choose Add.

To copy the comment lines, move the cursor to the first character of the first comment line, and then (using the keyboard) hold down either Shift key and press the Down arrow key until all comment lines are highlighted; or (using the mouse) move the mouse pointer to the location of the cursor, hold down the left mouse button, and drag down until all comment lines are highlighted. Finally, choose Copy from the Edit menu to copy the highlighted lines to the Clipboard.

Next, copy those lines into the four other subprograms. Choose SUBS from the View menu to again display a list of subprograms. Select Subtract, move the cursor to the first character of the first line, pull down the Edit menu, and choose Paste. The lines copied from the Add subprogram should appear. (If they don't or if you get a dialog box telling you that blank lines can't appear before a subprogram, go back to the Add subprogram and repeat the Edit-Copy process. Remember to copy only comment lines—those preceded by a ' character.)

Select the remaining subprogram names in the same way, and repeat the Edit-Paste process. You don't have to repeat the Copy operation, because an item copied to the Clipboard stays there until something else is copied to the Clipboard or until you quit QuickBASIC. When you're done, go back to each subprogram. Edit the comment lines and enter the program lines as you did for the Add subprogram. Be sure to choose Save All from the File menu after completing each subprogram. Also, be sure to go back and review your work—the ability to view each subprogram separately using the SUBS option on the View menu makes this important task easier and your program clearer to read. Your results should match the four subprograms on the following two pages.

NOTE: Don't forget to edit the comments! Remember—the comments you pasted in were the comments for the Add subprogram. You must change the name in each comment block and the information on the line below the block to reflect the subprogram the comments identify.

The following is the Subtract subprogram:

```
' **************************************************
' **  Name:           Subtract                    **
' **  Type:           Subprogram                  **
' **  Module:         MINIMATH.BAS                **
' **  Language:       Microsoft QuickBASIC 4.00   **
' **************************************************
'
' Performs subtraction for the MINICAL program.
'
  SUB Subtract (stack#(), ptr%) STATIC
      ptr% = ptr% - 1
      IF ptr% THEN
          stack#(ptr%) = stack#(ptr%) - stack#(ptr% + 1)
      END IF
  END SUB
```

The following is the Multiply subprogram:

```
' **************************************************
' **  Name:           Multiply                    **
' **  Type:           Subprogram                  **
' **  Module:         MINIMATH.BAS                **
' **  Language:       Microsoft QuickBASIC 4.00   **
' **************************************************
'
' Performs multiplication for the MINICAL program.
'
  SUB Multiply (stack#(), ptr%) STATIC
      ptr% = ptr% - 1
      IF ptr% THEN
          stack#(ptr%) = stack#(ptr%) * stack#(ptr% + 1)
      END IF
  END SUB
```

The following is the Divide subprogram:

```
' **************************************************
' **  Name:           Divide                      **
' **  Type:           Subprogram                  **
' **  Module:         MINIMATH.BAS                **
' **  Language:       Microsoft QuickBASIC 4.00   **
' **************************************************
```

(continued)

continued

```
' Performs division for the MINICAL program.
'
  SUB Divide (stack#(), ptr%) STATIC
      ptr% = ptr% - 1
      IF ptr% THEN
          stack#(ptr%) = stack#(ptr%) / stack#(ptr% + 1)
      END IF
  END SUB
```

The following is the SquareRoot subprogram:

```
' ****************************************************
' **   Name:         SquareRoot                     **
' **   Type:         Subprogram                     **
' **   Module:       MINIMATH.BAS                   **
' **   Language:     Microsoft QuickBASIC 4.00      **
' ****************************************************
'
' Determines square root for the MINICAL program.
'
  SUB SquareRoot (stack#(), ptr%) STATIC
      stack#(ptr%) = SQR(stack#(ptr%))
  END SUB
```

This completes the first part of the MINICAL program. The subprograms you created and saved as MINIMATH form the heart of MINICAL because they perform the actual calculations. The next part involves creating MINICAL itself. MINICAL performs the overhead work—taking the numbers the user wants to calculate, passing them to the appropriate subprograms in MINIMATH, and displaying the result.

The MINICAL Module

From here, you can proceed in one of two ways. Because both MINIMATH and MINICAL are small, you can build the MINICAL program entirely in memory by creating a second module named MINICAL. (You do this by choosing Create File from the File menu, accepting the default choice of Module, and then choosing OK.) Or you can turn MINIMATH into a Quick Library and load it with the QuickBASIC system so that it becomes an extension to the language. We'll use the second method to see how easy it is to use this advanced QuickBASIC feature.

To create a Quick Library, pull down the Run menu and choose Make Library. You'll be asked to name the library. MINIMATH will be fine, because QuickBASIC automatically appends a default extension of .QLB for the Quick Library and .LIB for the normal library it also builds. After you type *MINIMATH*, choose Make Library. (You can ignore the other options in the dialog box for now.) When completed, QuickBASIC will have created two new files in the current directory: MINIMATH.QLB and MINIMATH.LIB.

Now quit QuickBASIC so that you can restart it and load the new Quick Library with it. To do this, pull down the File menu and choose Exit. Then start QuickBASIC from the system prompt by entering:

```
QB /L MINIMATH
```

You'll see no obvious sign that anything is different, but a very exciting event has actually taken place! Your QuickBASIC has been extended. It's now more than it used to be. The subprograms in MINIMATH are part of the QuickBASIC language, ready to be used like many of the other QuickBASIC keywords. In fact, because you can optionally use the CALL keyword when calling subprograms, these new subprograms will appear much like new keywords in QuickBASIC.

Proceed with the rest of the program now so that you can try out the new, extended QuickBASIC. Be sure QuickBASIC is loaded, as described earlier, with the MINIMATH Quick Library as part of the system. Then type in the following program, MINICAL.BAS:

```
' ****************************************************
' **   Name:         MINICAL                        **
' **   Type:         Program                        **
' **   Module:       MINICAL.BAS                    **
' **   Language:     Microsoft QuickBASIC 4.00      **
' ****************************************************

' Functions
  DECLARE FUNCTION NextParameter$ (cmd$)

' Subprograms
  DECLARE SUB Process (cmd$, stack#(), ptr%)
  DECLARE SUB DisplayStack (stack#(), ptr%)
  DECLARE SUB Add (stack#(), ptr%)
  DECLARE SUB Subtract (stack#(), ptr%)
  DECLARE SUB Multiply (stack#(), ptr%)
  DECLARE SUB Divide (stack#(), ptr%)
  DECLARE SUB SquareRoot (stack#(), ptr%)
```

(continued)

continued

```
' Get the command line
  cmd$ = COMMAND$

' Create a pseudo stack
  DIM stack#(1 TO 20)
  ptr% = 0

' Process each part of the command line
  DO UNTIL cmd$ = ""
      parm$ = NextParameter$(cmd$)
      Process parm$, stack#(), ptr%
      IF ptr% < 1 THEN
          PRINT "Not enough stack values"
          SYSTEM
      END IF
  LOOP

' Display results
  DisplayStack stack#(), ptr%

' All done
  END
```

This is the main part of the MINICAL program, where all the action begins. Note the first two lines in the DO-LOOP structure, the ones that read *parm$ = NextParameter$(cmd$)* and *Process parm$, stack#(), ptr%*. The first line calls the user-defined function named NextParameter$, and the second line calls the user-defined subprogram named Process. (No, you haven't defined them yet. That's next on the list of tasks to do.) Notice that the keyword CALL was not used to call the Process subprogram. You can use CALL if desired, but there's no need to anymore. Because of the way QuickBASIC deals with subprograms, the Process subprogram that you'll create shortly will be more like part of the QuickBASIC system, rather than part of the program, because you can't list it or modify it while this portion of the program is on the screen. You also don't have to think about it or recompile it! Your creative energies are free to tackle the next higher level of the program's complexity.

Once you've entered the main program's lines, it's again time to save this module to disk. Select Save As from the File menu and enter the filename *MINICAL*.

You still have a few pieces of coding to do before you can try the program. To create the one function of this program, select New Function from the Edit menu. Type in the function name NextParameter$, and press the Enter key. Creating and editing functions are really no different from creating and editing subprograms. In fact, the only major difference between a function and a subprogram is that a function returns a value to be used in a calculation or assigned to a QuickBASIC variable. Subprograms return values only through passed variables. Follow the same steps you used to create the subprograms in MINIMATH to create the function NextParameter$:

```
' ****************************************************
' **   Name:         NextParameter$                 **
' **   Type:         Function                       **
' **   Module:       MINICAL.BAS                    **
' **   Language:     Microsoft QuickBASIC 4.00      **
' ****************************************************
'
' Extracts parameters from the front of the
' command line. Parameters are groups of any
' characters separated by spaces.

FUNCTION NextParameter$ (cmd$) STATIC
    parm$ = ""
    DO WHILE LEFT$(cmd$, 1) <> " " AND cmd$ <> ""
        parm$ = parm$ + LEFT$(cmd$, 1)
        cmd$ = MID$(cmd$, 2)
    LOOP
    DO WHILE LEFT$(cmd$, 1) = " " AND cmd$ <> ""
        cmd$ = MID$(cmd$, 2)
    LOOP
    NextParameter$ = parm$
END FUNCTION
```

Now create and edit the following two subprograms as part of the MINICAL module.

Create the subprogram DisplayStack:

```
' ****************************************************
' **   Name:         DisplayStack                   **
' **   Type:         Subprogram                     **
' **   Module:       MINICAL.BAS                    **
' **   Language:     Microsoft QuickBASIC 4.00      **
' ****************************************************
'
' Displays anything left on the stack when MINICAL
' finishes processing the command line.
```

(continued)

continued

```
SUB DisplayStack (stack#(), ptr%) STATIC
    PRINT
    IF ptr% > 1 THEN
        PRINT "Stack... ",
    ELSE
        PRINT "Result... ",
    END IF
    FOR i% = 1 TO ptr%
        PRINT stack#(i%),
    NEXT i%
    PRINT
END SUB
```

Next create the subprogram Process:

```
' **************************************************
' **   Name:         Process                      **
' **   Type:         Subprogram                   **
' **   Module:       MINICAL.BAS                  **
' **   Language:     Microsoft QuickBASIC 4.00    **
' **************************************************
'
' Processes each command parameter for the MINICAL
' program.
'
SUB Process (parm$, stack#(), ptr%) STATIC
    SELECT CASE parm$
    CASE "+"
        Add stack#(), ptr%
    CASE "-"
        Subtract stack#(), ptr%
    CASE "*"
        Multiply stack#(), ptr%
    CASE "/"
        Divide stack#(), ptr%
    CASE "SQR"
        SquareRoot stack#(), ptr%
    CASE ELSE
        ptr% = ptr% + 1
        stack#(ptr%) = VAL(parm$)
    END SELECT
END SUB
```

Be sure you save your efforts on disk by selecting Save All from the File menu.

You've done it! One last detail remains, however. This program reads the command line and assumes that numbers and operators were typed in following the name of the program at the system prompt. Fortunately, QuickBASIC provides a mechanism to let you type in a command line, even though you're currently going to be running the program in memory from the QuickBASIC system. From the Run menu select Modify COMMAND$. You'll be asked to enter a new command line. Enter this for the first try:

```
3 4 +
```

Everything should be in place now, so try running the program. Select Start from the Run menu. If all is well, you'll see the following:

```
Result... 7
```

If all is not well, you'll probably find yourself staring at an error message from QuickBASIC, describing an error that's probably the indirect result of a typographical error. If so, double-check your typing, and rebuild the library if the problem was in the MINIMATH module.

Once you get the program working, take a little time to try different command line parameters. See what happens if several numbers are placed on the stack but not enough operators are given to reduce the stack to a final result. For example, try entering:

```
3 4 5 6 7 + *
```

Also, find out what happens if not enough numbers are on the stack. For example, enter:

```
3 4 + *
```

Compiling and Running as an Executable (.EXE) Program

Finally, to see how you can create programs that you can run from MS-DOS, select Make EXE File from the Run menu. You can create two types of .EXE files. The first type results in a smaller MINICAL.EXE file, but it requires access to the QuickBASIC file named BRUN40.EXE at runtime. The second type results in a larger MINICAL.EXE file that stands completely on its own. When you select Make EXE File from the Run menu, you are prompted to select the type of .EXE file you want to create. Try it both ways. Take a look at the resulting file sizes, and note that the BRUN40.EXE file must be accessible in the current directory or in a place defined by the MS-DOS PATH setting. (Your QuickBASIC manual discusses this subject in more detail.)

Either way, running the MINICAL.EXE program from the system prompt uses the command line in the way that COMMAND$ expects. For example, to subtract 5 from 17, enter the following at the system prompt:

```
MINICAL 17 5 -
```

While building MINICAL, you've learned how easy it is to create toolboxes of your own or to edit existing toolboxes. Turn now to Part II of this book. Be sure to read the first section, which explains how to use the QuickBASIC toolboxes. Then choose a toolbox that interests you, and have fun.

PART II

QUICKBASIC TOOLBOXES AND PROGRAMS

USING QUICKBASIC TOOLBOXES

The toolboxes in Part II cover a wide range of topics and are presented alphabetically by subject. Each is designed to be loaded and called by user-written application software. You can run the demo module that begins each toolbox to illustrate the routines within the toolbox, you can ignore the demo module and use the routines as they are written, or you can restructure the routines so that they meet your application requirements.

The toolboxes and utility programs do not require any knowledge of previously presented toolboxes, so you can run them in any order. Try them all at least once, and review the code as you run them. You'll find unique techniques and programming concepts in most of the listings. You'll also find that these toolbox routines, along with your own creations, will be useful in your future programming projects.

Many of the utility programs use command line input or the COMMAND$ variable from within QuickBASIC to pass values or parameters to the program. Others (those using toolboxes from different programs) might require an associated .MAK file. A few programs require color and graphics capability, and others require a mouse. Check the comments at the beginning of each listing or Appendix A to determine environmental and running requirements for each toolbox and utility program.

Special Requirements

The following toolboxes require that the MIXED.QLB Quick Library be loaded into memory with QuickBASIC: BIOSCALL, CDEMO1, CDEMO2, COLORS, DOSCALLS, FILEINFO, MOUSGCRS, MOUSSUBS, MOUSTCRS, QBTREE, STDOUT, and WINDOWS. MIXED.QLB consists of a handful of subprograms and functions written in assembly language and in Microsoft QuickC. (The assembly-language and C source listings for MIXED.QLB are in Part III.)

Although MIXED.QLB isn't required by all toolboxes in this book, it's a good idea to load it each time you start QuickBASIC to use the toolboxes in this book. Toolboxes that do not require its presence will not be affected if MIXED.QLB is loaded.

Below are instructions for creating MIXED.QLB, which was written in Microsoft QuickC and assembly language to demonstrate how other languages can be used with QuickBASIC. It is beyond the scope of this book to explain in detail mixed-language programming concepts, so simply follow the steps presented here to create MIXED.QLB. In Part III of the book, you will have the opportunity to try some examples of mixed-language programs.

Creating MIXED.QLB

If you own Microsoft QuickC, the first step is to compile an object-code file for CTOOLS1.C and CTOOLS2.C.

You can load the C source-code files from the companion disk if you have purchased it, or you can type them in yourself. You will find CTOOLS1.C on page 445, and CTOOLS2.C on page 462. Once you have these files, enter the following commands at the system prompt to compile the CTOOLS1.C and CTOOLS2.C source-code files to create object-code files:

```
QCL /Ox /AM /Gs /c CTOOLS1.C
QCL /Ox /AM /Gs /c CTOOLS2.C
```

NOTE: If you don't have QuickC, you can still create MIXED.QLB. Compile the assembly-language source-code files as explained below. You will then be able to run all toolboxes in this book except CDEMO1 and CDEMO2.

If you have version 5.0 or later of the Microsoft Macro Assembler, load the assembly-language source-code files from the companion disk or type them in. MOUSE.ASM is on page 437 and CASEMAP.ASM is on page 436. The third assembly-language file, INTRPT.ASM, is part of QuickBASIC itself and can be found on the disk that comes with the program. Then, enter the following commands at the system prompt to compile the source-code files into object-code files:

```
MASM MOUSE;
MASM CASEMAP;
MASM INTRPT;
```

If you have an earlier version of the Microsoft Macro Assembler, follow the guidelines in your QuickBASIC documentation to replace the .MODEL directives with appropriate statements.

If you don't have the Microsoft Macro Assembler, you can use HEX2BIN (on pages 210 and 211) to convert the MOUSE.HEX, CASEMAP.HEX, and INTRPT.HEX files into object-code files. The hexadecimal character files are listed in Appendix D.

Once you've created the object-code files, you can build the MIXED library files to use with QuickBASIC. (Note that two files will be created: MIXED.QLB and MIXED.LIB. MIXED.QLB will be loaded with the QuickBASIC program because it is needed by some toolboxes; MIXED.LIB will be used for creating stand-alone programs that can be executed directly from MS-DOS.) The following commands accomplish this task:

```
LINK /Q INTRPT+MOUSE+CASEMAP+CTOOLS1+CTOOLS2,MIXED.QLB,,BQLB40.LIB;
DEL MIXED.LIB
LIB MIXED.LIB+INTRPT+MOUSE+CASEMAP+CTOOLS1+CTOOLS2;
```

NOTE: If you don't have QuickC, remember that you cannot run CDEMO1 and CDEMO2; therefore, you must delete +CTOOLS1 and +CTOOLS2 from the above commands.

If you have a problem, the cause might be that the necessary files can't be located. Try moving all the files and programs into the current directory, including the programs LINK.EXE and LIB.EXE; the QuickBASIC library file, BQLB40.LIB; and, if you have Quick C, MLIBCE.LIB.

Finally, after the MIXED.QLB and MIXED.LIB files are successfully created, enter the following lines to create a file named Q.BAT:

```
COPY CON Q.BAT
QB /L MIXED.QLB
^Z
```

NOTE: The ^Z is obtained by pressing F6 or Ctrl-Z.

Using this batch file automates the loading process so that MIXED.QLB loads along with QuickBASIC. To use it, type *Q* and press the Enter key at the system prompt.

Using a .MAK File

Those toolboxes that consist of more than one module require a .MAK file. When you save a program consisting of more than one module, QuickBASIC automatically creates a .MAK file so that it knows where to locate each module the next time it loads the program. If the .MAK file is not available, or if you must create a new .MAK file, you must load each module from within QuickBASIC by selecting Load File from the File menu, selecting the module to load, and then repeating the process for each additional module. After loading all the modules, choose Save All from the File menu and QuickBASIC creates the new .MAK file. Appendix A lists all toolboxes and required .MAK files.

QuickBASIC *vs* Executable Files

You can run the demo modules and utility programs from within the QuickBASIC environment by selecting the applicable source-code file, or you can compile the code and create files to execute directly from MS-DOS. Source-code files are those with the .BAS file extension. Executable files are created from .BAS files from within the QuickBASIC environment and are saved with a .EXE file extension. All toolbox and utility programs on the companion diskettes are .BAS files. The steps necessary for loading and running the programs and toolboxes are simple.

Running Programs from the QuickBASIC Environment

Check your QuickBASIC manual, "Learning and Using Microsoft QuickBASIC," for starting QuickBASIC on your system. When the program starts, you are ready to load and run a demo module or utility program. Using the keyboard, the steps are:

1. Press the Alt key and then *F* to display the File menu.

2. Press *O* to choose the Open Program command.

3. Select the demo module or program from the list of .BAS files shown. If the file is not shown, you must set the path to the drive and directory where the file resides. First, type the correct path in the File Name box and press Enter to display the .BAS files in that path. Then type the name of the file you want to load, or use the Tab key to move to the list box and

use the arrow keys to select the filename you want and press Enter. Filenames are displayed in all lowercase, directory names in all uppercase. You can also select directory names, including the parent(..) directory, in the list box until the .BAS files you want are displayed.

4. If command line parameters are required for execution, press Alt and then *R* to pull down the Run menu, and then press *C* to choose the Modify COMMAND$ option. Type the value(s) or input parameter(s) separated by spaces in the dialog box provided, and press the Enter key. You are now ready to execute the program and can do so by pressing Alt-*R* again and then *S* (or in this case Enter because the option is already highlighted) to choose the Start option.

NOTE: Each listing contains a USAGE line within the comments to let you know when user input is expected and in what format. Parameters might be other filenames, numeric values, alphanumeric characters, math functions, drive designators, paths to directories and subdirectories, or symbols. You can also find parameters in Appendix A.

5. If no command line parameters are required, simply press Alt-*R* and then *S* to start the selected module. (You can also press Shift-F5 to start.)

These steps are basically the same for systems using a mouse device. Instead of pressing the Alt key, however, you move the mouse pointer to the desired menu names, menu options, and dialog box fields and press the left mouse button to make dialog box selections and execute menu commands.

If you receive no response or the program doesn't seem to work correctly, look up the module in Appendix A and check that .MAK files, libraries (including MIXED.QLB), color graphics requirements, and so on are resident and that the paths to them are properly set.

Running Programs as Executable Files

Some of the utility programs, especially those expecting command line variable input, are more conveniently run as stand-alone executable files (.EXE). If you plan to develop commercial or public domain software, the .EXE format is usually preferable.

Before you can run the toolboxes and utility programs directly from MS-DOS, you must first compile a .BAS file or files using a special option to create a .EXE file. Two options are available for compiling programs. The first option is to compile the source code into a stand-alone .EXE file that runs by itself when executed from MS-DOS. The file, however, will be quite large, even if it is a simple application or module. The second option is to create a .EXE file that requires another file, BRUN40.EXE, to be in the same drive and directory at runtime (when you execute the program). The resulting compiled program file will be much smaller, but BRUN40.EXE must always accompany the executable file.

To create a stand-alone executable file from within QuickBASIC, follow the steps below. Refer to your QuickBASIC manual for instructions on how to create other .EXE files from within the QuickBASIC environment or from MS-DOS using BC.EXE.

1. Load the file using steps 1 through 3 above in "Running Programs from the QuickBASIC Environment."

2. Press Alt-*R* to display the Run Menu.

3. Press *X* (Make EXE File).

4. Press Alt-*A* to select the Stand-Alone .EXE File option. (This method produces a file with the same filename as the .BAS file but appends the .EXE file extension. To change the filename, type over the displayed name before pressing Alt-*A*.)

5. Press *E* to choose the Make EXE and Exit command.

QuickBASIC then creates the executable file, the QuickBASIC program is terminated, and you return to the system prompt. To verify that the file exists, type *DIR* and press Enter, and look for that program's filename with a .EXE extension.

To run the program as a stand-alone .EXE file, type the filename (without the .EXE extension) from the system prompt. Type any command line values or input parameters after the filename, with spaces between the filename and parameters. The program or toolbox module begins executing as soon as you press the Enter key.

ATTRIB

The ATTRIB program generates a table showing combinations of text-mode character attributes, including all combinations of foreground and background colors. Only the blink attribute isn't demonstrated, but it is described at the head of the table. Use this program as a utility program. Compile it as a stand-alone executable program, and run it to decide what colors to use in your own programs.

The sole purpose of the ATTRIB main program is to call the single subprogram, also named Attrib. Actually, the program has only enough supporting module-level code to demonstrate the subprogram.

The Attrib subprogram may be called by other programs, either by loading the entire ATTRIB module into memory or by copying only the Attrib subprogram into another module. Refer to the MOUSTCRS program for an example.

Program Module: ATTRIB

```
' ***************************************************
' **   Name:          ATTRIB                       **
' **   Type:          Program                      **
' **   Module:        ATTRIB.BAS                   **
' **   Language:      Microsoft QuickBASIC 4.00    **
' ***************************************************
'
' Displays all combinations of text mode character
' attributes on the screen for review.
'
' USAGE:          No command line parameters
' REQUIREMENTS:   CGA
' .MAK FILE:      (none)
' FUNCTIONS:      (none)
' PARAMETERS:     (none)
' VARIABLES:      (none)
  DECLARE SUB Attrib ()
```

(continued)

continued

```
' Call the subprogram
  Attrib

' All done
  END
```

Subprogram: Attrib

Creates the color attribute table on the screen for the ATTRIB module. Sixteen foreground and eight background color attributes are available in the default SCREEN 0 text mode, not counting the blink attribute for the foreground color. This subprogram displays all 128 combinations in a way that makes it easy to see which numbers result in which colors.

```
' *****************************************
' **   Name:            Attrib                       **
' **   Type:            Subprogram                   **
' **   Module:          ATTRIB.BAS                   **
' **   Language:        Microsoft QuickBASIC 4.00    **
' *****************************************
'
' Displays table of color attributes for text mode.
'
' EXAMPLE OF USE:   Attrib
' PARAMETERS:       (none)
' VARIABLES:        bgd%        Background number for COLOR statement
'                   fgd%        Foreground number for COLOR statement
' MODULE LEVEL
'   DECLARATIONS:               DECLARE SUB Attrib ()
'
SUB Attrib STATIC
    SCREEN 0
    CLS
    PRINT "Attributes for the COLOR statement in text mode (SCREEN 0)."
    PRINT "Add 16 to the foreground to cause the character to blink."
    FOR bgd% = 0 TO 7
        COLOR bgd% XOR 7, bgd%
        PRINT
```

(continued)

continued

```
            PRINT "Background%"; STR$(bgd%),
            PRINT "Foreground%    ..."; SPACE$(41)
            FOR fgd% = 0 TO 15
                COLOR fgd%, bgd%
                PRINT STR$(fgd%); " ";
            NEXT fgd%
    NEXT bgd%
    COLOR 7, 0
    PRINT
END SUB
```

BIN2HEX

The BIN2HEX program is a utility that creates hexadecimal format files showing the contents of a given binary file. In this book, its most useful purpose is in displaying the contents of .OBJ files created by the Microsoft Macro Assembler. This enables you to create the necessary files for using the assembly-language routines in this book, even if you don't have the Macro Assembler.

The program reads bytes of the input file using binary mode, converts each to a two-character hexadecimal string, and then formats the output by blocking the hexadecimal numbers into two groups of eight bytes per line. The output file can be listed or printed and can easily be transferred over a modem using conventional ASCII protocol.

The HEX2BIN program performs the opposite function of this program, converting a hexadecimal listing back to a binary file.

You will find several assembly-language subprograms in Part III of this book, and Microsoft provides two assembly listings with the QuickBASIC language. The suggested method of creating the .OBJ files from these listings is to use the Microsoft Macro Assembler, version 5.0. However, if you don't have the Macro Assembler, type in the hexadecimal files using the QuickBASIC Document editing capability, and then run the HEX2BIN program to convert each to the required .OBJ file.

To use BIN2HEX, type the input filename and output filename on the command line when you run the program. For example, to convert MOUSE.OBJ to the hexadecimal listing MOUSE.HEX, enter these two command line parameters:

```
MOUSE.OBJ MOUSE.HEX
```

Be sure to use the full filename, including the extension. Separate filenames with spaces, as shown, or with commas if preferred.

The BIN2HEX program was used to create the hexadecimal listings in Appendix D.

Also review the HEX2BIN program for more information on using these routines.

Program Module: BIN2HEX

```
' *************************************************
' **   Name:           BIN2HEX                   **
' **   Type:           Program                   **
' **   Module:         BIN2HEX.BAS               **
' **   Language:       Microsoft QuickBASIC 4.00 **
' *************************************************
'
' Reads in any file and writes out a hexadecimal format file
' suitable for rebuilding the original file using the HEX2BIN
' program.
'
' USAGE:         BIN2HEX inFileName.ext outFileName.ext
' .MAK FILE:     BIN2HEX.BAS
'                PARSE.BAS
' PARAMETERS:    inFileName   Name of file to be duplicated in hexadecimal
'                             format
'                outFileName  Name of hexadecimal format file to be created
' VARIABLES:     cmd$         Working copy of the command line
'                inFile$      Name of input file
'                outFile$     Name of output file
'                byte$        Buffer for binary file access
'                i&           Index to each byte of input file
'                h$           Pair of hexadecimal characters representing
'                             each byte


    DECLARE SUB ParseWord (a$, sep$, word$)

' Initialization
    CLS
    PRINT "BIN2HEX "; COMMAND$
    PRINT

' Get the input and output filenames from the command line
    cmd$ = COMMAND$
    ParseWord cmd$, " ,", inFile$
    ParseWord cmd$, " ,", outFile$

' Verify that both filenames were given
    IF outFile$ = "" THEN
        PRINT
        PRINT "Usage: BIN2HEX inFileName outFileName"
        SYSTEM
    END IF
```

(continued)

continued

```
' Open the input file
  OPEN inFile$ FOR BINARY AS #1 LEN = 1
  IF LOF(1) = 0 THEN
      CLOSE #1
      KILL inFile$
      PRINT
      PRINT "File not found - "; inFile$
      SYSTEM
  END IF

' Open the output file
  OPEN outFile$ FOR OUTPUT AS #2

' Process each byte of the file
  byte$ = SPACE$(1)
  FOR i& = 1 TO LOF(1)
      GET #1, , byte$
      h$ = RIGHT$("0" + HEX$(ASC(byte$)), 2)
      PRINT #2, h$; SPACE$(1);
      IF i& = LOF(1) THEN
          PRINT #2, ""
      ELSEIF i& MOD 16 = 0 THEN
          PRINT #2, ""
      ELSEIF i& MOD 8 = 0 THEN
          PRINT #2, "- ";
      END IF
  NEXT i&

' Clean up and quit
  CLOSE
  END
```

BIOSCALL

The BIOSCALL toolbox provides a collection of utility BIOS system calls.

Several useful routines and data tables are in your computer's BIOS ROM (Basic Input/Output Services, Read Only Memory), ready to be tapped into by your QuickBASIC programs. This toolbox of routines provides a sampler of the most useful interrupt calls that return the information provided by BIOS. With QuickBASIC, it's easy to access the BIOS ROM.

The module-level code provides demonstrations of the available subprograms when BIOSCALL is the designated main program. Later, load the BIOSCALL module along with any program you're developing when you need any information provided by the subprograms.

Be aware that whenever you use the BIOSCALL toolbox, the mixed-language subprograms Interrupt and InterruptX must be accessible. Refer to "Using QuickBASIC Toolboxes" on page 21 for instructions on creating and loading the Quick Library MIXED.QLB with the QuickBASIC system.

The Scroll subprogram, demonstrated first, prints a block of fifteen lines of uppercase characters on the screen. The first line is filled with As, the second with Bs, and so on. Each line is also printed in a different color scheme to make it easier to see exactly which characters are scrolled. The Scroll subprogram scrolls the rectangular area (from row 2, column 3 to row 6, column 16) up 3 lines. The attribute byte is set to green foreground on blue background, the same as the attribute byte at row 2, column 3. Study the displayed result, and notice that the lines moved up three rows and that the three blank lines show the blue background.

The Equipment subprogram determines the computer equipment settings as maintained by BIOS. A short table is displayed, listing the availability or count of the printers, the game adapter, the serial I/O ports, the floppy disk drives, and the math coprocessor. Also displayed is the initial video state at boot-up time.

VideoState, the next subprogram demonstrated, determines the current video state. The current video mode, number of text columns, and current active video page are displayed.

Finally, GetShiftStates displays a table of the shift keys and shift states. This table is continuously updated until you press the Enter key, allowing you to try out the various shift keys. For example, press the left and right shift keys, singly or together, and notice how the state of each is monitored independently.

In the demo module, two subprograms, PrintScreen and Reboot, are commented out, as the actions they take are a bit extreme. To demo these subprograms, remove the apostrophes in front of these statements, which you'll find near the end of the module-level code. Don't forget that once you reboot, everything currently in memory is erased, and you'll be starting fresh.

For more information on the available BIOS calls, refer to the technical reference manual for your computer.

Name	Type	Description
BIOSCALL.BAS		Demo module
Equipment	Sub	Equipment/hardware information
GetShiftStates	Sub	Shift key states
PrintScreen	Sub	Screen dump
ReBoot	Sub	System reboot
Scroll	Sub	Moves text in designated area of screen
VideoState	Sub	Mode, col, and page display of current state

Demo Module: BIOSCALL

```
' *******************************************
' **   Name:         BIOSCALL               **
' **   Type:         Toolbox                **
' **   Module:       BIOSCALL.BAS           **
' **   Language:     Microsoft QuickBASIC 4.00  **
' *******************************************
'
' Demonstrates several interrupt calls to the ROM BIOS.
'
' USAGE: No command line parameters
' REQUIREMENTS:    MIXED.QLB/.LIB
' .MAK FILE:       (none)
' PARAMETERS:      (none)
```

(continued)

continued

```
' VARIABLES:      i%          Loop index for creating lines to scroll
'                 equip       Structure of type EquipmentType
'                 mode%       Video mode returned by VideoState
'                 columns%    Video columns returned by VideoState
'                 page%       Video page returned by VideoState
'                 shift       Structure of type ShiftType


' Constants
  CONST FALSE = 0
  CONST TRUE = NOT FALSE

' Declare the Type structures
  TYPE RegType
       ax    AS INTEGER
       bx    AS INTEGER
       cx    AS INTEGER
       dx    AS INTEGER
       Bp    AS INTEGER
       si    AS INTEGER
       di    AS INTEGER
       flags AS INTEGER
  END TYPE

  TYPE RegTypeX
       ax    AS INTEGER
       bx    AS INTEGER
       cx    AS INTEGER
       dx    AS INTEGER
       Bp    AS INTEGER
       si    AS INTEGER
       di    AS INTEGER
       flags AS INTEGER
       ds    AS INTEGER
       es    AS INTEGER
  END TYPE

  TYPE EquipmentType
       printers      AS INTEGER
       gameAdapter   AS INTEGER
       serial        AS INTEGER
       floppies      AS INTEGER
       initialVideo  AS INTEGER
       coprocessor   AS INTEGER
  END TYPE
```

(continued)

continued

```
    TYPE ShiftType
        right            AS INTEGER
        left             AS INTEGER
        ctrl             AS INTEGER
        alt              AS INTEGER
        scrollLockState  AS INTEGER
        numLockState     AS INTEGER
        capsLockState    AS INTEGER
        insertState      AS INTEGER
    END TYPE

    DECLARE SUB Interrupt (intnum%, inreg AS RegType, outreg AS RegType)
    DECLARE SUB InterruptX (intnum%, inreg AS RegTypeX, outreg AS RegTypeX)
    DECLARE SUB PrintScreen ()
    DECLARE SUB Scroll (row1%, col1%, row2%, col2%, lines%, attribute%)
    DECLARE SUB Equipment (equip AS EquipmentType)
    DECLARE SUB VideoState (mode%, columns%, page%)
    DECLARE SUB GetShiftStates (shift AS ShiftType)
    DECLARE SUB ReBoot ()

' Demonstrate the Scroll subprogram
    CLS
    FOR i% = 1 TO 15
        COLOR i%, i% - 1
        PRINT STRING$(25, i% + 64)
    NEXT i%
    COLOR 7, 0
    PRINT
    PRINT "Press <Enter> to scroll part of the screen"
    DO
    LOOP UNTIL INKEY$ = CHR$(13)
    Scroll 2, 3, 6, 16, 3, SCREEN(2, 3, 1)

' Wait for user before continuing
    PRINT
    PRINT "Press any key to continue"
    DO
    LOOP UNTIL INKEY$ <> ""
    CLS

' Determine the equipment information
    DIM equip AS EquipmentType
    Equipment equip
    PRINT "Printers:", equip.printers
    PRINT "Game adapter:", equip.gameAdapter
```

(continued)

continued

```
        PRINT "Serial IO:", equip.serial
        PRINT "Floppies:", equip.floppies
        PRINT "Video:", equip.initialVideo
        PRINT "Coprocessor:", equip.coprocessor

    ' Determine the current video state
        PRINT
        VideoState mode%, columns%, page%
        PRINT "Video mode:", mode%
        PRINT "Text columns:", columns%
        PRINT "Video page:", page%

    ' Wait for user before continuing
        PRINT
        PRINT "Press any key to continue"
        DO
        LOOP UNTIL INKEY$ <> ""

    ' Demonstrate the shift key states
        CLS
        PRINT "(Press shift keys, then <Enter> to continue...)"
        DIM shift AS ShiftType
        DO
            LOCATE 4, 1
            PRINT "Shift states:"
            GetShiftStates shift
            PRINT
            PRINT "Left shift:", shift.left
            PRINT "Right shift:", shift.right
            PRINT "Ctrl:", shift.ctrl
            PRINT "Alt:", shift.alt
            PRINT "Scroll Lock:", shift.scrollLockState
            PRINT "Num Lock:", shift.numLockState
            PRINT "Caps Lock:", shift.capsLockState
            PRINT "Insert:", shift.insertState
        LOOP UNTIL INKEY$ = CHR$(13)

    ' Uncomment the following line to cause a screen dump to printer....
    ' PrintScreen

    ' Uncomment the following line only if you want to reboot....
    ' ReBoot

        END
```

Subprogram: Equipment

Returns information about the available computer hardware by calling the BIOS service at interrupt 11H, which returns bit patterns indicating the equipment configuration. The definition of the data structure named EquipmentType lists the items that this call can determine.

This subprogram allows your program to decide how to handle input and output chores. As one example, the user can be prompted to *Remove the first disk and insert the second* or to *Insert the second disk in drive B*, depending on whether the computer has one or two floppy disk drives available.

```
' ***************************************************
' **   Name:        Equipment                      **
' **   Type:        Subprogram                     **
' **   Module:      BIOSCALL.BAS                   **
' **   Language:    Microsoft QuickBASIC 4.00      **
' ***************************************************
'
' Returns equipment configuration information from BIOS.
'
' EXAMPLE OF USE:  Equipment equip
' PARAMETERS:      equip      Structure of type EquipmentType
' VARIABLES:       reg        Structure of type RegType
' MODULE LEVEL
'   DECLARATIONS:  TYPE RegType
'                      ax    AS INTEGER
'                      bx    AS INTEGER
'                      cx    AS INTEGER
'                      dx    AS INTEGER
'                      Bp    AS INTEGER
'                      si    AS INTEGER
'                      di    AS INTEGER
'                      flags AS INTEGER
'                  END TYPE
'
'                  TYPE EquipmentType
'                      printers      AS INTEGER
'                      gameAdapter   AS INTEGER
'                      serial        AS INTEGER
'                      floppies      AS INTEGER
'                      initialVideo  AS INTEGER
'                      coprocessor   AS INTEGER
'                  END TYPE
'
```

(continued)

continued

```
'       DECLARE SUB Interrupt (intnum%, inreg AS RegType, outreg AS RegType)
'       DECLARE SUB Equipment (equip AS EquipmentType)
'
    SUB Equipment (equip AS EquipmentType) STATIC
        DIM reg AS RegType
        Interrupt &H11, reg, reg
        equip.printers = (reg.ax AND &HC000&) \ 16384
        equip.gameAdapter = (reg.ax AND &H1000) \ 4096
        equip.serial = (reg.ax AND &HE00) \ 512
        equip.floppies = (reg.ax AND &HC0) \ 64 + 1
        equip.initialVideo = (reg.ax AND &H30) \ 16
        equip.coprocessor = (reg.ax AND 2) \ 2
    END SUB
```

Subprogram: GetShiftStates

Returns the state of each shift key at the moment the subprogram is called and the current shift key states.

The left Shift, right Shift, Ctrl, and Alt keys return a *1* in the appropriate structure variables if they are pressed at the moment this subprogram is called. If not pressed, a *0* is returned instead.

This subprogram can also monitor the four shift states. If active, the Scroll Lock, Num Lock, Caps Lock, and Insert states return a value of *1* in the appropriate variable. If your keyboard has lights indicating the current states of these shift keys, this subprogram returns a *1* whenever a light is on and a *0* when the light is off.

```
' ******************************************
' **   Name:          GetShiftStates       **
' **   Type:          Subprogram           **
' **   Module:        BIOSCALL.BAS         **
' **   Language:      Microsoft QuickBASIC 4.00   **
' ******************************************
'
' Returns state of the various shift keys.
'
' EXAMPLE OF USE:  GetShiftStates shift
' PARAMETERS:      shift      Structure of type ShiftType
' VARIABLES:       reg        Structure of type RegType
```

(continued)

continued

```
' MODULE LEVEL
'    DECLARATIONS:  TYPE RegType
'                       ax    AS INTEGER
'                       bx    AS INTEGER
'                       cx    AS INTEGER
'                       dx    AS INTEGER
'                       Bp    AS INTEGER
'                       si    AS INTEGER
'                       di    AS INTEGER
'                       flags AS INTEGER
'                   END TYPE
'
'                   TYPE ShiftType
'                       right           AS INTEGER
'                       left            AS INTEGER
'                       ctrl            AS INTEGER
'                       alt             AS INTEGER
'                       scrollLockState AS INTEGER
'                       numLockState    AS INTEGER
'                       capsLockState   AS INTEGER
'                       insertState     AS INTEGER
'                   END TYPE
'
'    DECLARE SUB Interrupt (intnum%, inreg AS RegType, outreg AS RegType)
'    DECLARE SUB GetShiftStates (shift AS ShiftType)
'
SUB GetShiftStates (shift AS ShiftType) STATIC
    DIM reg AS RegType
    reg.ax = &H200
    Interrupt &H16, reg, reg
    shift.right = reg.ax AND 1
    shift.left = (reg.ax AND 2) \ 2
    shift.ctrl = (reg.ax AND 4) \ 4
    shift.alt = (reg.ax AND 8) \ 8
    shift.scrollLockState = (reg.ax AND 16) \ 16
    shift.numLockState = (reg.ax AND 32) \ 32
    shift.capsLockState = (reg.ax AND 64) \ 64
    shift.insertState = (reg.ax AND 128) \ 128
END SUB
```

Subprogram: PrintScreen

Performs exactly the same screen-to-printer dump that occurs when the Shift-Print Screen keys are pressed.

Whenever you press the Shift-Print Screen keys, the operating system performs an interrupt 5 to activate the BIOS-level code for performing the screen dump. With the PrintScreen subprogram, you can program such a screen dump at any point in the operation of a running program without requiring user intervention.

Because the screen dump BIOS routine is interrupt driven, any changes to the screen dump code are automatically taken into account. For example, if your computer loads and patches in an improved version of the screen dump at boot-up time, this subprogram activates the new routine with no problem. That's one of the nice features of the interrupt mechanism provided by the 8086 family of computers.

```
' **************************************************
' **   Name:         PrintScreen                   **
' **   Type:         Subprogram                    **
' **   Module:       BIOSCALL.BAS                  **
' **   Language:     Microsoft QuickBASIC 4.00     **
' **************************************************
'
' Activates interrupt 5 to cause a dump of the
' screen's contents to the printer.
'
' EXAMPLE OF USE:  PrintScreen
' PARAMETERS:      (none)
' VARIABLES:       reg         Structure of type RegType
' MODULE LEVEL
'   DECLARATIONS:  TYPE RegType
'                    ax    AS INTEGER
'                    bx    AS INTEGER
'                    cx    AS INTEGER
'                    dx    AS INTEGER
'                    Bp    AS INTEGER
'                    si    AS INTEGER
'                    di    AS INTEGER
'                    flags AS INTEGER
'                  END TYPE
'
'     DECLARE SUB Interrupt (intnum%, inreg AS RegType, outreg AS RegType)
'     DECLARE SUB PrintScreen ()
'
  SUB PrintScreen STATIC
    DIM reg AS RegType
    Interrupt 5, reg, reg
  END SUB
```

Subprogram: ReBoot

Causes the system to reboot. Depending on the computer and its configuration, this reboot won't always work perfectly. Be sure to test the subprogram carefully for your specific circumstances if you plan to use it on a routine basis.

Perhaps the best and safest use for this subprogram is as an escape route for unauthorized access to software, because rebooting can frustrate attempts to overcome copy protection schemes. For example, try rebooting after a user fails a password check for the third time or if an unauthorized copy of a program is detected.

```
' ***********************************************
' **   Name:          ReBoot                   **
' **   Type:          Subprogram               **
' **   Module:        BIOSCALL.BAS             **
' **   Language:      Microsoft QuickBASIC 4.00 **
' ***********************************************
'
' Causes the computer to reboot.
'
' EXAMPLE OF USE:  ReBoot
' PARAMETERS:      (none)
' VARIABLES:       reg        Structure of type RegType
' MODULE LEVEL
'   DECLARATIONS:  TYPE RegType
'                       ax    AS INTEGER
'                       bx    AS INTEGER
'                       cx    AS INTEGER
'                       dx    AS INTEGER
'                       Bp    AS INTEGER
'                       si    AS INTEGER
'                       di    AS INTEGER
'                       flags AS INTEGER
'                  END TYPE
'
'     DECLARE SUB Interrupt (intnum%, inreg AS RegType, outreg AS RegType)
'     DECLARE SUB ReBoot ()
'
SUB ReBoot STATIC
    DIM reg AS RegType
    Interrupt &H19, reg, reg
END SUB
```

Subprogram: Scroll

Provides a quick scroll of text lines in a rectangular area of the display. The BIOS video interrupt 10H is set up to scroll. You place the correct parameters in the processor registers, and the BIOS code does the rest.

Six parameters are passed to this subprogram. The first four define the upper left and lower right corners of the area to be scrolled. These coordinates refer to text-mode character locations, with the upper left corner of the screen defined as row 1, column 1. The lower right corner of the screen is defined as row 25, column 80 for 80-column text mode, or row 25, column 40 for 40-column text mode.

The last two parameters provide the line count and the color attribute. If the line count is a positive number, the lines scroll up by the indicated number of rows, leaving blank lines at the bottom of the scrolled area. If the line count is negative, the lines scroll down. The blank lines are filled with space characters, and the color attribute is set by the attribute byte passed in the sixth parameter.

Usually this subprogram is used to scroll text one line at a time, such as when displaying the contents of a long file using the MS-DOS TYPE command. A handy feature is the subprogram's ability to completely clear any or all of the screen, setting the background color at the same time. To do this, pass a line count of 0. The BIOS routine will fill the entire rectangular area with spaces, much faster than if you were to PRINT the same number of space strings.

```
' ***************************************************
' **   Name:          Scroll                       **
' **   Type:          Subprogram                   **
' **   Module:        BIOSCALL.BAS                 **
' **   Language:      Microsoft QuickBASIC 4.00    **
' ***************************************************
'
' Scrolls the screen in the rectangular area defined
' by the row and col parameters.  Positive line count
' moves the lines up, leaving blank lines at bottom;
' negative line count moves the lines down.
'
' EXAMPLE OF USE:   Scroll row1%, col1%, row2%, col2%, lines%, attr%
' PARAMETERS:       row1%    Upper left character row defining rectangular
'                            scroll area
```

(continued)

continued

```
'                       col1     Upper left character column defining rectangular
'                                scroll area
'                       row2%    Lower right character row defining rectangular
'                                scroll area
'                       col2%    Lower right character column defining
'                                rectangular scroll area
'                       lines%   Number of character lines to scroll
'                       attr%    Color attribute byte to be used in new text
'                                lines scrolled onto the screen
' VARIABLES:            reg      Structure of type RegType
' MODULE LEVEL
'   DECLARATIONS: TYPE RegType
'                       ax   AS INTEGER
'                       bx   AS INTEGER
'                       cx   AS INTEGER
'                       dx   AS INTEGER
'                       Bp   AS INTEGER
'                       si   AS INTEGER
'                       di   AS INTEGER
'                       flags AS INTEGER
'                 END TYPE
'     DECLARE SUB Interrupt (intnum%, inreg AS RegType, outreg AS RegType)
'     DECLARE SUB Scroll (row1%, col1%, row2%, col2%, lines%, attribute%)
'
  SUB Scroll (row1%, col1%, row2%, col2%, lines%, attribute%) STATIC
      DIM reg AS RegType
      IF lines% > 0 THEN
          reg.ax = &H600 + lines% MOD 256
      ELSE
          reg.ax = &H700 + ABS(lines%) MOD 256
      END IF
      reg.bx = (attribute% * 256&) AND &HFF00
      reg.cx = (row1% - 1) * 256 + col1% - 1
      reg.dx = (row2% - 1) * 256 + col2% - 1
      Interrupt &H10, reg, reg
  END SUB
```

Subprogram: VideoState

Returns the current mode, the number of columns, and the page of the display.

This subprogram returns information about the current video mode. The mode% parameter returned by the ROM BIOS is different from the number used in the SCREEN statement to set a video mode. The two parameters do correlate, however, and the following table provides a useful comparison:

SCREEN Mode	WIDTH	Mode% (from VideoState)
0	40	1
0	80	3
1	40	4
2	80	6
7	40	13
8	80	14
9	80	16
10	80	15
11	80	17
12	80	18
13	40	19

The column% parameter is always 40 or 80, depending on the current SCREEN and WIDTH settings.

The page% parameter is the currently active page number as set by the SCREEN statement. The default is page 0, and the maximum active page number is a function of the current screen mode. See the SCREEN statement in your QuickBASIC documentation for more information about active and virtual pages as set by the SCREEN statement.

```
' *************************************************
' ** Name:         VideoState                    **
' ** Type:         Subprogram                    **
' ** Module:       BIOSCALL.BAS                  **
' ** Language:     Microsoft QuickBASIC 4.00     **
' *************************************************
```

(continued)

continued

```
' Determines the current video mode parameters.
'
' EXAMPLE OF USE:   VideoState mode%, columns%, page%
' PARAMETERS:       mode%      Current video mode
'                   columns%   Current number of text columns
'                   page%      Current active display page
' VARIABLES:        reg        Structure of type RegType
' MODULE LEVEL
'   DECLARATIONS:   TYPE RegType
'                     ax    AS INTEGER
'                     bx    AS INTEGER
'                     cx    AS INTEGER
'                     dx    AS INTEGER
'                     Bp    AS INTEGER
'                     si    AS INTEGER
'                     di    AS INTEGER
'                     flags AS INTEGER
'                   END TYPE
'
'     DECLARE SUB Interrupt (intnum%, inreg AS RegType, outreg AS RegType)
'     DECLARE SUB VideoState (mode%, columns%, page%)
'
   SUB VideoState (mode%, columns%, page%) STATIC
       DIM reg AS RegType
       reg.ax = &HF00
       Interrupt &H10, reg, reg
       mode% = reg.ax AND &HFF
       columns% = (CLNG(reg.ax) AND &HFF00) \ 256
       page% = (CLNG(reg.bx) AND &HFF00) \ 256
   END SUB
```

BITS

The BITS toolbox provides four bit manipulation routines. The Bin2BinStr$ and BinStr2Bin% functions convert integer numbers to and from binary string representations. This action is similar to that of the QuickBASIC HEX$, OCT$, and VAL functions, except that the conversions deal with base 2 representations.

The BitGet and BitPut subprograms let you store and retrieve single bits from any location in any string. Up to 32767 bits can be accessed in a single string, which results in a string of 4096 bytes. These subprograms would be useful for data acquisition and process control applications involving a large number of contact closures. The famous sieve of Eratosthenes for finding prime numbers is used to demonstrate these two subprograms. Prime numbers from 1 through 1000 are found and printed by keeping track of a string of bits, each representing an integer from 1 through 1000.

You can change the value of max% in this demonstration to find prime numbers up to about 10937. Larger values of max% will cause overflow, but by reprogramming the variables involved, you can probably find even bigger primes.

Name	Type	Description
BITS.BAS		Demo module
Bin2BinStr$	Func	Integer to 16-character binary string
BinStr2Bin%	Func	16-character binary string to integer
BitGet	Sub	Value from any bit position in a string
BitPut	Sub	Sets or clears bit at location in a string

Demo Module: BITS

```
' **************************************************
' **   Name:          BITS                        **
' **   Type:          Toolbox                     **
' **   Module:        BITS.BAS                    **
' **   Language:      Microsoft QuickBASIC 4.00   **
' **************************************************
```

(continued)

QUICKBASIC TOOLBOXES AND PROGRAMS

continued

```
' Demonstrates the bit manipulation functions
' and subprograms.
'
' USAGE: No command line parameters
' .MAK FILE:       (none)
' PARAMETERS:      (none)
' VARIABLES:       max%       Upper limit for the prime number generator
'                  b$         Bit string for finding prime numbers
'                  n%         Loop index for sieve of Eratosthenes
'                  bit%       Bit retrieved from b$
'                  i%         Bit loop index
'                  q$         The double quote character


' Functions
  DECLARE FUNCTION BinStr2Bin% (b$)
  DECLARE FUNCTION Bin2BinStr$ (b%)

' Subprograms
  DECLARE SUB BitGet (a$, bitIndex%, bit%)
  DECLARE SUB BitPut (b$, bitIndex%, bit%)

' Prime numbers less than max%, using bit fields in B$
  CLS
  max% = 1000
  PRINT "Primes up to"; max%; "using BitGet and BitPut for sieve..."
  PRINT
  PRINT 1; 2;
  b$ = STRING$(max% \ 8 + 1, 0)
  FOR n% = 3 TO max% STEP 2
      BitGet b$, n%, bit%
      IF bit% = 0 THEN
          PRINT n%;
          FOR i% = 3 * n% TO max% STEP n% + n%
              BitPut b$, i%, 1
          NEXT i%
      END IF
  NEXT n%
  PRINT

' Demonstration of the Bin2BinStr$ function
  PRINT
  PRINT "Bin2BinStr$(12345) = "; Bin2BinStr$(12345)
```

(continued)

continued

```
' Demonstration of the BinStr2Bin% function
  PRINT
  q$ = CHR$(34)
  PRINT "BinStr2Bin%("; q$; "1001011"; q$; ") = ";
  PRINT BinStr2Bin%("1001011")

' That's all
  END
```

Function: Bin2BinStr$

Returns a 16-character binary representation of an integer value. This function is similar to QuickBASIC's HEX$ and OCT$ functions, except that the conversion base is 2 instead of 16 or 8, and that 16 characters are always returned. For example, Bin2BinStr$(7) returns *0000000000000111*, and Bin2BinStr$(-1) returns *1111111111111111*.

You can easily remove leading zeros in the 16-character string by using the LtrimSet$ function, as shown in the STRINGS module:

```
bin$ = LtrimSet$(bin$, "0")
```

```
' ***********************************************
' **   Name:          Bin2BinStr$              **
' **   Type:          Function                 **
' **   Module:        BITS.BAS                 **
' **   Language:      Microsoft QuickBASIC 4.00 **
' ***********************************************
'
' Returns a string of sixteen "0" and "1" characters
' that represent the binary value of b%.
'
' EXAMPLE OF USE:   PRINT Bin2BinStr$(b%)
' PARAMETERS:       b%         Integer number
' VARIABLES:        t$         Working string space for forming
'                                      binary string
'                   b%         Integer number
'                   mask%      Bit isolation mask
'                   i%         Looping index
```

(continued)

continued

```
' MODULE LEVEL
'   DECLARATIONS:  DECLARE FUNCTION Bin2BinStr$ (b%)
'
  FUNCTION Bin2BinStr$ (b%) STATIC
      t$ = STRING$(16, "0")
      IF b% THEN
          IF b% < 0 THEN
              MID$(t$, 1, 1) = "1"
          END IF
          mask% = &H4000
          FOR i% = 2 TO 16
              IF b% AND mask% THEN
                  MID$(t$, i%, 1) = "1"
              END IF
              mask% = mask% \ 2
          NEXT i%
      END IF
      Bin2BinStr$ = t$
  END FUNCTION
```

Function: BinStr2Bin%

Returns the integer represented by a string of up to 16 0s and 1s. For example, BinStr2Bin%("111") returns 7; BinStr2Bin%("000101") returns 5.

If the string has more than 16 characters, only the rightmost 16 are used. Any character other than 1 is treated as 0.

```
' ***************************************************
' **  Name:          BinStr2Bin%                   **
' **  Type:          Function                      **
' **  Module:        BITS.BAS                      **
' **  Language:      Microsoft QuickBASIC 4.00     **
' ***************************************************
'
' Returns the integer represented by a string of up
' to 16 "0" and "1" characters.
'
' EXAMPLE OF USE:   PRINT BinStr2Bin%(b$)
' PARAMETERS:       b$          Binary representation string
```

(continued)

continued

```
'   VARIABLES:      bin%       Working variable for finding value
'                   t$         Working copy of b$
'                   mask%      Bit mask for forming value
'                   i%         Looping index
'   MODULE LEVEL
'     DECLARATIONS: DECLARE FUNCTION BinStr2Bin% (b$)
'
    FUNCTION BinStr2Bin% (b$) STATIC
        bin% = 0
        t$ = RIGHT$(STRING$(16, "0") + b$, 16)
        IF LEFT$(t$, 1) = "1" THEN
            bin% = &H8000
        END IF
        mask% = &H4000
        FOR i% = 2 TO 16
            IF MID$(t$, i%, 1) = "1" THEN
                bin% = bin% OR mask%
            END IF
            mask% = mask% \ 2
        NEXT i%
        BinStr2Bin% = bin%
    END FUNCTION
```

Subprogram: BitGet

Returns a bit value extracted from any bit position in a string. The bits are numbered consecutively, starting with bit 1 in the most significant bit position of the first byte of the string. Bit 8 is the least significant bit of this same byte, bit 9 is the most significant bit of the second byte, and so on. This subprogram can access up to 32767 bits, in which case the string must be 4096 bytes in length. For example:

```
                         A              B              C
a$ = "A B C"       0 1 0 0 0 0 0 1   0 1 0 0 0 0 1 0   0 1 0 0 0 0 1 1
                   ↕           ↕     ↕                 ↕
                  bit1        bit5   bit9              bit17

BitGet (a$, 17, bit%) ... bit% = 0
BitGet (a$, 18, bit%) ... bit% = 1
```

The BitPut subprogram lets you set the bits in a string as desired.

```
' ****************************************************
' **  Name:           BitGet                        **
' **  Type:           Subprogram                    **
' **  Module:         BITS.BAS                      **
' **  Language:       Microsoft QuickBASIC 4.00     **
' ****************************************************
'
' Extracts the bit at bitIndex% into a$ and returns
' either 0 or 1 in bit%.  The value of bitIndex%
' can range from 1 to 8 * LEN(a$).
'
' EXAMPLE OF USE:   BitGet a$, bitIndex%, bit%
' PARAMETERS:       a$          String where bit is stored
'                   bitIndex%   Bit position in string
'                   bit%        Extracted bit value, 0 or 1
' VARIABLES:        byte%       Byte location in string of the bit
'                   mask%       Bit isolation mask for given bit
' MODULE LEVEL
'   DECLARATIONS:   DECLARE SUB BitGet (a$, bitIndex%, bit%)
'
   SUB BitGet (a$, bitIndex%, bit%) STATIC
      byte% = (bitIndex% - 1) \ 8 + 1
      SELECT CASE bitIndex% MOD 8
      CASE 1
         mask% = 128
      CASE 2
         mask% = 64
      CASE 3
         mask% = 32
      CASE 4
         mask% = 16
      CASE 5
         mask% = 8
      CASE 6
         mask% = 4
      CASE 7
         mask% = 2
      CASE 0
         mask% = 1
      END SELECT
```

(continued)

continued

```
        IF ASC(MID$(a$, byte%, 1)) AND mask% THEN
            bit% = 1
        ELSE
            bit% = 0
        END IF
END SUB
```

Subprogram: BitPut

Sets or clears a single bit at any bit location in a string. The string can be up to 4096 bytes in length, allowing access of up to 32767 bits. Bits are numbered from left to right; the most significant bit of the first byte is bit 1, the least significant bit of the first byte is bit 8, the most significant bit of the second byte is bit 9, and so on. You can use the BitGet subprogram to get the bit values from the string as necessary. To initialize a string to all zeros or ones, use the STRING$ function. For example, STRING$(4096, 0) returns a string of 32767 cleared bits, and STRING$(4096, 255) returns a string of 32767 set bits.

```
' **************************************************
' **   Name:         BitPut                       **
' **   Type:         Subprogram                   **
' **   Module:       BITS.BAS                     **
' **   Language:     Microsoft QuickBASIC 4.00    **
' **************************************************
'
' If bit% is non-zero, then the bit at bitIndex% into
' a$ is set to 1; otherwise, it's set to 0. The value
' of bitIndex% can range from 1 to 8 * LEN(a$).
'
' EXAMPLE OF USE:   BitPut a$, bitIndex%, bit%
' PARAMETERS:       a$          String containing the bits
'                   bitIndex%   Index to the bit of concern
'                   bit%        Value of bit (1 to set, 0 to clear)
' VARIABLES:        bytePtr%    Pointer to the byte position in the string
'                   mask%       Bit isolation mask
'                   byteNow%    Current numeric value of string byte
' MODULE LEVEL
'   DECLARATIONS:   DECLARE SUB BitPut (b$, bitIndex%, bit%)
```

(continued)

continued

```
    SUB BitPut (a$, bitIndex%, bit%) STATIC
        bytePtr% = bitIndex% \ 8 + 1
        SELECT CASE bitIndex% MOD 8
        CASE 1
            mask% = 128
        CASE 2
            mask% = 64
        CASE 3
            mask% = 32
        CASE 4
            mask% = 16
        CASE 5
            mask% = 8
        CASE 6
            mask% = 4
        CASE 7
            mask% = 2
        CASE 0
            mask% = 1
            bytePtr% = bytePtr% - 1
        END SELECT
        byteNow% = ASC(MID$(a$, bytePtr%, 1))
        IF byteNow% AND mask% THEN
            IF bit% = 0 THEN
                MID$(a$, bytePtr%, 1) = CHR$(byteNow% XOR mask%)
            END IF
        ELSE
            IF bit% THEN
                MID$(a$, bytePtr%, 1) = CHR$(byteNow% XOR mask%)
            END IF
        END IF
    END SUB
```

CALENDAR

The CALENDAR toolbox is a collection of easy-to-use functions and subprograms for date and time conversions and calculations. See the MONTH program for an example of how this module can be loaded as a toolbox for use by another main program.

Wherever possible, dates and times are passed in a string format identical to that used by the QuickBASIC DATE$ and TIME$ functions. This makes the required parameters easier to remember and makes it possible to define many of the routines as functions that would otherwise have to be defined as subprograms. For example, the Julian2Date$ function returns a date in the string format mentioned. Alternative approaches would require defining three functions (one for returning the year, one for the month, and one for the day) or defining a subprogram that returned the three numbers in the parameter list. Returning dates in this string format also eliminates output numeric formatting because the string is ready to be printed as is.

The Julian day number is an astronomical convention that allows dates to be cataloged by a single, large integer. A useful feature of the Julian day number is that a simple subtraction can calculate the number of days between any two dates. Leap years and the strange pattern of days in the various months make this calculation difficult when dealing with the usual month, day, and year numbers. The Date2Julian& and Julian2Date$ conversion functions take care of all the details for you, making calendar calculations a breeze. Other functions return the day of the week, day of the year, day of the century, name of each month, and other related details—just about everything you ever wanted to know, but were afraid to ask, about dates and time.

The calculations are usually accurate for dates from 1583 to the indefinite future, although some functions generate errors for dates between 1583 and 1599 if the calculations involve earlier dates. For example, consider how the DayOfTheCentury& function would attempt to calculate the day of the century for July 4, 1599. First, the function calculates the Julian day number for 07-04-1599 and then it attempts to subtract from that the Julian day number for the last day of the previous century. Because 12-31-1499 is earlier than 1583, the function will not work correctly.

Name	Type	Description
CALENDAR.BAS		Demo module
CheckDate%	Func	Validates date with return of TRUE/FALSE
Date2Day%	Func	Day of month number from date string
Date2Julian&	Func	Julian day number for a given date
Date2Month%	Func	Month number from date string
Date2Year%	Func	Year number from date string
DayOfTheCentury&	Func	Day of the given century
DayOfTheWeek$	Func	Name of day of the week for given date
DayOfTheYear%	Func	Day of the year (1 through 366) for given date
DaysBetweenDates&	Func	Number of days between two dates
HMS2Time$	Func	Time string for given hour, minute, and second
Julian2Date$	Func	Date string from given Julian day number
MDY2Date$	Func	Date string from given month, day, and year
MonthName$	Func	Name of month for a given date
OneMonthCalendar	Sub	One-month calendar for given date
Second2Date$	Func	Seconds from last of 1979 to date given
Second2Time$	Func	Time of day from seconds since last of 1979
Time2Hour%	Func	Hour number from time string
Time2Minute%	Func	Minute number from time string
Time2Second%	Func	Seconds number from time string
TimeDate2Second&	Func	Seconds from last of 1979 from date/time

Demo Module: CALENDAR

```
' **************************************************
' **  Name:         CALENDAR                      **
' **  Type:         Toolbox                       **
' **  Module:       CALENDAR.BAS                  **
' **  Language:     Microsoft QuickBASIC 4.00     **
' **************************************************
'
' USAGE: No command line parameters
' .MAK FILE:       (none)
' PARAMETERS:      (none)
' VARIABLES:       month%    Month for demonstration
'                  day%      Day for demonstration
'                  year%     Year for demonstration
'                  dat$      Date for demonstration
'                  j&        Julian day number
'                  tim$      System time right now
'                  hour%     Hour right now
'                  minute%   Minute right now
'                  second%   Second right now
'                  sec&      Seconds since last second of 1979

  CONST FALSE = 0
  CONST TRUE = NOT FALSE

' Functions
  DECLARE FUNCTION CheckDate% (dat$)
  DECLARE FUNCTION Date2Day% (dat$)
  DECLARE FUNCTION Date2Julian& (dat$)
  DECLARE FUNCTION Date2Month% (dat$)
  DECLARE FUNCTION Date2Year% (dat$)
  DECLARE FUNCTION DayOfTheCentury& (dat$)
  DECLARE FUNCTION DayOfTheWeek$ (dat$)
  DECLARE FUNCTION DayOfTheYear% (dat$)
  DECLARE FUNCTION DaysBetweenDates& (dat1$, dat2$)
  DECLARE FUNCTION HMS2Time$ (hour%, minute%, second%)
  DECLARE FUNCTION Julian2Date$ (julian&)
  DECLARE FUNCTION MDY2Date$ (month%, day%, year%)
  DECLARE FUNCTION MonthName$ (dat$)
  DECLARE FUNCTION Second2Date$ (second&)
  DECLARE FUNCTION Second2Time$ (second&)
```

(continued)

continued

```
        DECLARE FUNCTION Time2Hour% (tim$)
        DECLARE FUNCTION Time2Minute% (tim$)
        DECLARE FUNCTION Time2Second% (tim$)
        DECLARE FUNCTION TimeDate2Second& (tim$, dat$)

' Subprograms
        DECLARE SUB OneMonthCalendar (dat$, row%, col%)

' Let's choose the fourth of July for the demonstration
        CLS
        PRINT "All about the fourth of July for this year..."
        month% = 7
        day% = 4
        year% = Date2Year%(DATE$)

' Demonstrate the conversion to dat$
        PRINT
        dat$ = MDY2Date$(month%, day%, year%)
        PRINT "QuickBASIC string format for this date is "; dat$

' Check the validity of this date
        IF CheckDate%(dat$) = FALSE THEN
            PRINT "The date you entered is faulty... " + dat$
            SYSTEM
        END IF

' Day of the week and name of the month
        PRINT "The day of the week is "; DayOfTheWeek$(dat$); "."

' Astronomical Julian day number
        j& = Date2Julian&(dat$)
        PRINT "The Julian day number is"; j&

' Conversion of Julian number to date
        PRINT "Date for the given Julian number is "; Julian2Date$(j&); "."

' Convert the date string to numbers
        PRINT "The month, day, and year numbers are ";
        PRINT Date2Month%(dat$); ","; Date2Day%(dat$); ","; Date2Year%(dat$)

' The month name
        PRINT "The month name is "; MonthName$(dat$)

' Day of the year
        PRINT "The day of the year is"; DayOfTheYear%(dat$)
```

(continued)

continued

```
' Day of the century
  PRINT "The day of the century is"; DayOfTheCentury&(dat$)

' Days from right now
  IF Date2Julian&(dat$) < Date2Julian&(DATE$) THEN
      PRINT "That was"; DaysBetweenDates&(dat$, DATE$); "days ago."
  ELSEIF Date2Julian&(dat$) > Date2Julian&(DATE$) THEN
      PRINT "That is"; DaysBetweenDates&(dat$, DATE$); "days from now."
  ELSE
      PRINT "The date you entered is today's date."
  END IF

' Print a one-month calendar
  OneMonthCalendar dat$, 14, 25

' Wait for user
  LOCATE 23, 1
  PRINT "Press any key to continue"
  DO
  LOOP UNTIL INKEY$ <> ""
  CLS

' Demonstrate extracting hour, minute, and second from tim$
  dat$ = DATE$
  tim$ = TIME$
  hour% = Time2Hour%(tim$)
  minute% = Time2Minute%(tim$)
  second% = Time2Second%(tim$)
  PRINT "The date today... "; dat$
  PRINT "The time now   ... "; tim$
  PRINT "The hour, minute, and second numbers are ";
  PRINT hour%; ","; minute%; ","; second%

' Now put it all back together again
  PRINT "Time string created from hour, minute, and second is ";
  PRINT HMS2Time$(hour%, minute%, second%)

' Seconds since end of 1979
  dat$ = DATE$
  PRINT "The number of seconds since the last second of 1979 is";
  sec& = TimeDate2Second&(tim$, dat$)
  PRINT sec&
  PRINT "From this number we can extract the date and time..."
  PRINT Second2Date$(sec&); " and "; Second2Time$(sec&); "."
```

Function: CheckDate%

Returns *TRUE* if date is valid or *FALSE* if date is faulty.

Was February 29, 1726, a real date? The CheckDate% function quickly finds the answer to this question. If the date checks out as valid, a value of *TRUE* (non-zero) is returned. If the date is faulty, a value of *FALSE* (0) is returned.

This function is useful in any program that prompts the user to enter a date. A quick check can be made of the entered date, and the user can be asked to repeat the input if the entered date is faulty.

```
' ****************************************************
' **   Name:          CheckDate%                    **
' **   Type:          Function                      **
' **   Module:        CALENDAR.BAS                  **
' **   Language:      Microsoft QuickBASIC 4.00     **
' ****************************************************
'
' Returns TRUE if the given date represents a real
' date or FALSE if the date is in error.
'
' EXAMPLE OF USE:   test% = CheckDate%(dat$)
' PARAMETERS:       dat$      Date to be checked
' VARIABLES:        julian&   Julian day number for the date
'                   test$     Date string for given Julian day number
' MODULE LEVEL
'   DECLARATIONS:   CONST FALSE = 0
'                   CONST TRUE = NOT FALSE
'
'                   DECLARE FUNCTION CheckDate% (dat$)
'                   DECLARE FUNCTION Date2Julian& (dat$)
'                   DECLARE FUNCTION Julian2Date$ (julian&)

FUNCTION CheckDate% (dat$) STATIC
    julian& = Date2Julian&(dat$)
    test$ = Julian2Date$(julian&)
    IF dat$ = test$ THEN
        CheckDate% = TRUE
    ELSE
        CheckDate% = FALSE
    END IF
END FUNCTION
```

Function: Date2Day%

Extracts the day number from a date string that is in the standard format *MM-DD-YYYY*.

```
' **************************************************
' **   Name:         Date2Day%                    **
' **   Type:         Function                     **
' **   Module:       CALENDAR.BAS                 **
' **   Language:     Microsoft QuickBASIC 4.00    **
' **************************************************
'
' Returns the day number given a date in the
' QuickBASIC string format MM-DD-YYYY.
'
' EXAMPLE OF USE:    day% = Date2Day%(dat$)
' PARAMETERS:        dat$        Date of concern
' VARIABLES:         (none)
' MODULE LEVEL
'   DECLARATIONS:    DECLARE FUNCTION Date2Day% (dat$)
'
  FUNCTION Date2Day% (dat$) STATIC
      Date2Day% = VAL(MID$(dat$, 4, 2))
  END FUNCTION
```

Function: Date2Julian&

Returns the Julian day number for a given date. This function and the related function Julian2Date$ are at the heart of many of the other functions in this toolbox. This function calculates the astronomical Julian day number for any date from January 1, 1583, into the indefinite future, accounting for leap years and century adjustments.

The main advantage of converting dates to long integer numbers is in being able to easily calculate the number of days between dates and the day of the week for any date. Further, if you need to store a large number of dates in a disk file, storing them as four-byte, long integers is more efficient than storing them in the longer string format or as separate integers representing the month, day, and year.

```
' **************************************************
' **   Name:         Date2Julian&                  **
' **   Type:         Function                      **
' **   Module:       CALENDAR.BAS                  **
' **   Language:     Microsoft QuickBASIC 4.00     **
' **************************************************
'
' Returns the astronomical Julian day number given a
' date in the QuickBASIC string format MM-DD-YYYY.
'
' EXAMPLE OF USE:   j& = Date2Julian&(dat$)
' PARAMETERS:       dat$      Date of concern
' VARIABLES:        month%    Month number for given date
'                   day%      Day number for given date
'                   year%     Year number for given date
'                   ta&       First term of the Julian day number calculation
'                   tb&       Second term of the Julian day number calculation
'                   tc&       Third term of the Julian day number calculation
' MODULE LEVEL
'   DECLARATIONS:   DECLARE FUNCTION Date2Day% (dat$)
'                   DECLARE FUNCTION Date2Julian& (dat$)
'                   DECLARE FUNCTION Date2Month% (dat$)
'                   DECLARE FUNCTION Date2Year% (dat$)
'
FUNCTION Date2Julian& (dat$) STATIC
    month% = Date2Month%(dat$)
    day% = Date2Day%(dat$)
    year% = Date2Year%(dat$)
    IF year% < 1583 THEN
        PRINT "Date2Julian: Year is less than 1583"
        SYSTEM
    END IF
    IF month% > 2 THEN
        month% = month% - 3
    ELSE
        month% = month% + 9
        year% = year% - 1
    END IF
    ta& = 146097 * (year% \ 100) \ 4
    tb& = 1461& * (year% MOD 100) \ 4
    tc& = (153 * month% + 2) \ 5 + day% + 1721119
    Date2Julian& = ta& + tb& + tc&
END FUNCTION
```

Function: Date2Month%

Extracts the month number from a date string that is in the standard format *MM-DD-YYYY*.

```
' **************************************************
' **   Name:         Date2Month%                   **
' **   Type:         Function                      **
' **   Module:       CALENDAR.BAS                  **
' **   Language:     Microsoft QuickBASIC 4.00     **
' **************************************************
'
' Returns the month number given a date in the
' QuickBASIC string format MM-DD-YYYY.
'
' EXAMPLE OF USE:   month% = Date2Month%(dat$)
' PARAMETERS:       dat$         Date of concern
' VARIABLES:        (none)
' MODULE LEVEL
'   DECLARATIONS:   DECLARE FUNCTION Date2Month% (dat$)
'
  FUNCTION Date2Month% (dat$) STATIC
      Date2Month% = VAL(MID$(dat$, 1, 2))
  END FUNCTION
```

Function: Date2Year%

Extracts the year number from a date string that is in the standard format *MM-DD-YYYY*.

```
' **************************************************
' **   Name:         Date2Year%                    **
' **   Type:         Function                      **
' **   Module:       CALENDAR.BAS                  **
' **   Language:     Microsoft QuickBASIC 4.00     **
' **************************************************
'
' Returns the year number given a date in the
' QuickBASIC string format MM-DD-YYYY.
```

(continued)

continued

```
' EXAMPLE OF USE:   year% = Date2Year%(dat$)
' PARAMETERS:       dat$        Date of concern
' VARIABLES:        (none)
' MODULE LEVEL
'   DECLARATIONS:   DECLARE FUNCTION Date2Year% (dat$)
'
  FUNCTION Date2Year% (dat$) STATIC
      Date2Year% = VAL(MID$(dat$, 7))
  END FUNCTION
```

Function: DayOfTheCentury&

Returns the day of the given century. Each century has more than 32767 days, requiring this function to be declared as returning a long integer result.

Dates before 01-01-1600 generate an error. See page 55 for an explanation.

```
' *********************************************
' **   Name:         DayOfTheCentury%         **
' **   Type:         Function                 **
' **   Module:       CALENDAR.BAS             **
' **   Language:     Microsoft QuickBASIC 4.00 **
' *********************************************
'
' Returns the number of the day of the century.
'
' EXAMPLE OF USE:   cDay& = DayOfTheCentury&(dat$)
' PARAMETERS:       dat$        Date of concern
' VARIABLES:        year%       Year for given date
'                   dat1$       Date for last day of previous century
' MODULE LEVEL
'   DECLARATIONS:   DECLARE FUNCTION DayOfTheCentury& (dat$)
'
  FUNCTION DayOfTheCentury& (dat$)
      year% = Date2Year%(dat$)
      dat1$ = MDY2Date$(12, 31, year% - (year% MOD 100) - 1)
      DayOfTheCentury& = DaysBetweenDates&(dat1$, dat$)
  END FUNCTION
```

Function: DayOfTheWeek$

Finds the name of the day of the week for any date. In displaying calendar calculation results, it's often desirable to be able to print the name of the day of the week. This function lets you conveniently do so.

```
' ****************************************************
' **   Name:         DayOfTheWeek$                   **
' **   Type:         Function                        **
' **   Module:       CALENDAR.BAS                    **
' **   Language:     Microsoft QuickBASIC 4.00       **
' ****************************************************
'
' Returns a string stating the day of the week.
' Input is a date expressed in the QuickBASIC string
' format MM-DD-YYYY.
'
' EXAMPLE OF USE: PRINT "The day of the week is "; DayOfTheWeek$(dat$)
' PARAMETERS:     dat$       Date of concern
' VARIABLES:      (none)
' MODULE LEVEL
'   DECLARATIONS: DECLARE FUNCTION DayOfTheWeek$ (dat$)

FUNCTION DayOfTheWeek$ (dat$) STATIC
    SELECT CASE Date2Julian&(dat$) MOD 7
    CASE 0
        DayOfTheWeek$ = "Monday"
    CASE 1
        DayOfTheWeek$ = "Tuesday"
    CASE 2
        DayOfTheWeek$ = "Wednesday"
    CASE 3
        DayOfTheWeek$ = "Thursday"
    CASE 4
        DayOfTheWeek$ = "Friday"
    CASE 5
        DayOfTheWeek$ = "Saturday"
    CASE 6
        DayOfTheWeek$ = "Sunday"
    END SELECT
END FUNCTION
```

Function: DayOfTheYear%

Returns a number in the range 1 through 366, indicating the day of the year for the given date, by subtracting the Julian day number for the last day of the previous year from that of the given date. This calculation generates an error if the date is before January 1, 1584.

```
' *************************************************
' **   Name:          DayOfTheYear%              **
' **   Type:          Function                   **
' **   Module:        CALENDAR.BAS               **
' **   Language:      Microsoft QuickBASIC 4.00  **
' *************************************************
'
' Returns the number of the day of the year (1-366).
'
' EXAMPLE OF USE:   PRINT "The day of the year is"; DayOfTheYear%(dat$)
' PARAMETERS:       dat$       Date of concern
' VARIABLES:        dat1$      Date of last day of previous year
' MODULE LEVEL
'   DECLARATIONS:   DECLARE FUNCTION DayOfTheYear% (dat$)
'
FUNCTION DayOfTheYear% (dat$) STATIC
    dat1$ = MDY2Date$(12, 31, Date2Year%(dat$) - 1)
    DayOfTheYear% = DaysBetweenDates&(dat1$, dat$)
END FUNCTION
```

Function: DaysBetweenDates&

Returns the number of days between two dates by subtracting the Julian day numbers of the dates. The absolute value of the difference is returned, so the first date can be earlier or later than the second. The number of days returned will always be a positive value.

```
' *************************************************
' **   Name:          DaysBetweenDates&          **
' **   Type:          Function                   **
' **   Module:        CALENDAR.BAS               **
' **   Language:      Microsoft QuickBASIC 4.00  **
' *************************************************
```

(continued)

continued

```
' Returns the number of days between any two dates.
'
' EXAMPLE OF USE:   days& = DaysBetweenDates&(dat1$, dat2$)
' PARAMETERS:       dat1$       First date
'                   dat2$       Second date
' VARIABLES:        (none)
' MODULE LEVEL
'   DECLARATIONS:   DECLARE FUNCTION DaysBetweenDates& (dat1$, dat2$)
'
  FUNCTION DaysBetweenDates& (dat1$, dat2$) STATIC
      DaysBetweenDates& = ABS(Date2Julian&(dat1$) - Date2Julian&(dat2$))
  END FUNCTION
```

Function: HMS2Time$

Given hour, minute, and second numbers, returns a time string, in the same format as the string returned by QuickBASIC's TIME$ function. For example, HMS2Time$(23, 59, 59) returns *23:59:59*.

```
' **************************************************
' **   Name:         HMS2Time$                     **
' **   Type:         Function                      **
' **   Module:       CALENDAR.BAS                  **
' **   Language:     Microsoft QuickBASIC 4.00     **
' **************************************************
'
' Returns the time in the QuickBASIC string format
' HH:MM:SS given hour%, minute%, and second%.
'
' EXAMPLE OF USE:   PRINT HMS2Time$(hour%, minute%, second%)
' PARAMETERS:       hour%       Hour number
'                   minute%     Minutes number
'                   second%     Seconds number
' VARIABLES:        t$          Workspace for building the time string
' MODULE LEVEL
'   DECLARATIONS:   DECLARE FUNCTION HMS2Time$ (hour%, minute%, second%)
'
  FUNCTION HMS2Time$ (hour%, minute%, second%) STATIC
      t$ = RIGHT$("0" + MID$(STR$(hour%), 2), 2) + ":"
      t$ = t$ + RIGHT$("0" + MID$(STR$(minute%), 2), 2) + ":"
      HMS2Time$ = t$ + RIGHT$("0" + MID$(STR$(second%), 2), 2)
  END FUNCTION
```

Function: Julian2Date$

Converts a Julian day number to a date. The smallest long integer number that can be passed to this function without generating an error is 2299239, the Julian number for the date 01-01-1583.

```
' *************************************************
' **    Name:           Julian2Date$              **
' **    Type:           Function                  **
' **    Module:         CALENDAR.BAS              **
' **    Language:       Microsoft QuickBASIC 4.00 **
' *************************************************
'
' Returns a date in the QuickBASIC string format
' MM-DD-YYYY as calculated from a Julian day number.
'
' EXAMPLE OF USE:
'       PRINT "Date for the given Julian number is ";Julian2Date$(j&)
' PARAMETERS:      j&        Julian day number
' VARIABLES:       x&        Temporary calculation variable
'                  y&        Temporary calculation variable
'                  d&        Day number in long integer form
'                  m&        Month number before adjustment
'                  month%    Month number
'                  year%     Year number
'                  day%      Day number
' MODULE LEVEL
'   DECLARATIONS:  DECLARE FUNCTION Julian2Date$ (julian&)
'
  FUNCTION Julian2Date$ (julian&) STATIC

      x& = 4 * julian& - 6884477
      y& = (x& \ 146097) * 100
      d& = (x& MOD 146097) \ 4

      x& = 4 * d& + 3
      y& = (x& \ 1461) + y&
      d& = (x& MOD 1461) \ 4 + 1

      x& = 5 * d& - 3
      m& = x& \ 153 + 1
      d& = (x& MOD 153) \ 5 + 1
```

(continued)

continued

```
        IF m& < 11 THEN
            month% = m& + 2
        ELSE
            month% = m& - 10
        END IF
        day% = d&
        year% = y& + m& \ 11

        dat$ = MDY2Date$(month%, day%, year%)
        Julian2Date$ = dat$

    END FUNCTION
```

Function: MDY2Date$

Creates a date string from the numeric values of month, day, and year for a given date. The string format is the same as that returned by the QuickBASIC DATE$ function, *MM-DD-YYYY*.

```
' **************************************************
' **   Name:          MDY2Date$                    **
' **   Type:          Function                     **
' **   Module:        CALENDAR.BAS                 **
' **   Language:      Microsoft QuickBASIC 4.00    **
' **************************************************
'
' Converts month%, day%, and year% to a date string
' in the QuickBASIC string format MM-DD-YYYY.
'
' EXAMPLE OF USE:    dat$ = MDY2Date$(month%, day%, year%)
' PARAMETERS:        month%     Month for the date
'                    day%       Day of the month
'                    year%      Year number
' VARIABLES:         y$         Temporary year string
'                    m$         Temporary month string
'                    d$         Temporary day string
' MODULE LEVEL
'   DECLARATIONS:    DECLARE FUNCTION MDY2Date$ (month%, day%, year%)
```

(continued)

continued

```
    FUNCTION MDY2Date$ (month%, day%, year%) STATIC
        y$ = RIGHT$("000" + MID$(STR$(year%), 2), 4)
        m$ = RIGHT$("0" + MID$(STR$(month%), 2), 2)
        d$ = RIGHT$("0" + MID$(STR$(day%), 2), 2)
        MDY2Date$ = m$ + "-" + d$ + "-" + y$
    END FUNCTION
```

Function: MonthName$

Returns the name of the month for a given date. If the passed date string has the wrong number of characters, the returned name defaults to *MM-DD-YYYY* to remind you of the required format for date strings. If the string is the right length but the first two characters don't represent a valid month number, *?MonthName?* is returned.

```
' *************************************************
' **   Name:         MonthName$                  **
' **   Type:         Function                    **
' **   Module:       CALENDAR.BAS                **
' **   Language:     Microsoft QuickBASIC 4.00   **
' *************************************************
'
' Returns a string stating the month as indicated
' in dat$ (QuickBASIC string format MM-DD-YYYY).
'
' EXAMPLE OF USE:   PRINT MonthName$(dat$)
' PARAMETERS:       dat$        Date of concern
' VARIABLES:        (none)
' MODULE LEVEL
'    DECLARATIONS:  DECLARE FUNCTION MonthName$ (dat$)
'
    FUNCTION MonthName$ (dat$) STATIC

        IF LEN(dat$) <> 10 THEN
            dat$ = "MM-DD-YYYY"
        END IF

        SELECT CASE LEFT$(dat$, 2)
        CASE "01"
            MonthName$ = "January"
        CASE "02"
            MonthName$ = "February"
```

(continued)

continued

```
            CASE "03"
                MonthName$ = "March"
            CASE "04"
                MonthName$ = "April"
            CASE "05"
                MonthName$ = "May"
            CASE "06"
                MonthName$ = "June"
            CASE "07"
                MonthName$ = "July"
            CASE "08"
                MonthName$ = "August"
            CASE "09"
                MonthName$ = "September"
            CASE "10"
                MonthName$ = "October"
            CASE "11"
                MonthName$ = "November"
            CASE "12"
                MonthName$ = "December"
            CASE ELSE
                MonthName$ = "?MonthName?"
        END SELECT

END FUNCTION
```

Subprogram: OneMonthCalendar

Uses several functions from the CALENDAR toolbox to print a small, one-month calendar at any location on the screen. The stand-alone program named MONTH provides a good demonstration of this subprogram at work.

```
' *************************************************
' **   Name:        OneMonthCalendar            **
' **   Type:        Subprogram                  **
' **   Module:      CALENDAR.BAS                **
' **   Language:    Microsoft QuickBASIC 4.00   **
' *************************************************
'
' Prints a small, one-month calendar at the row%
' and col% indicated.
```

(continued)

continued

```
' EXAMPLE OF USE:    OneMonthCalendar dat$, row%, col%
' PARAMETERS:    dat$       Date of concern
'                row%       Screen row for upper left corner of calendar
'                col%       Screen column for upper left corner of calendar
' VARIABLES:     mname$     Name of given month
'                month%     Month number
'                day%       Day number
'                year%      Year number
'                dat1$      Date for first of the given month
'                j&         Julian day number for each day of the month
'                heading$   Title line for calendar
'                wa%        Day of the week for each day of the month
'                rowloc%    Row for printing each day number
' MODULE LEVEL
'   DECLARATIONS:   DECLARE SUB OneMonthCalendar (dat$, row%, col%)
'
  SUB OneMonthCalendar (dat$, row%, col%) STATIC
      mname$ = MonthName$(dat$)
      LOCATE row%, col% + 12 - LEN(mname$) \ 2
      PRINT mname$; ","; Date2Year%(dat$)
      month% = Date2Month%(dat$)
      day% = 1
      year% = Date2Year%(dat$)
      dat1$ = MDY2Date$(month%, day%, year%)
      j& = Date2Julian&(dat1$)
      heading$ = " Sun Mon Tue Wed Thu Fri Sat"
      wa% = INSTR(heading$, LEFT$(DayOfTheWeek$(dat1$), 3)) \ 4
      LOCATE row% + 1, col%
      PRINT heading$
      rowloc% = row% + 2
      LOCATE rowloc%, col% + 4 * wa%
      DO
          PRINT USING "####"; day%;
          IF wa% = 6 THEN
              rowloc% = rowloc% + 1
              LOCATE rowloc%, col%
          END IF
          wa% = (wa% + 1) MOD 7
          j& = j& + 1
          day% = Date2Day%(Julian2Date$(j&))
      LOOP UNTIL day% = 1
      PRINT
  END SUB
```

Function: Second2Date$

Returns a date string given the number of seconds since the last second of 1979. The number of seconds is limited to the range of positive long integers (1 to 2147483647). Given the largest possible long integer, the function returns the date *01-19-2048*.

Related functions are Second2Time$ and TimeDate2Second&. The Second2Time$ function finds the time string for a given second, and the TimeDate2Second$ function finds the seconds since 1979 for a given date and time.

```
' *************************************************
' **   Name:         Second2Date$                  **
' **   Type:         Function                      **
' **   Module:       CALENDAR.BAS                  **
' **   Language:     Microsoft QuickBASIC 4.00     **
' *************************************************
'
' Returns the date in the QuickBASIC string format
' MM-DD-YYYY given a number of seconds since the
' last second of 1979.  Use Second2Time$ to find
' the time of day at the indicated second.
'
' EXAMPLE OF USE:  dat$ = Second2Date$(second&)
' PARAMETERS:      second&   Number of seconds since the last second of 1979
' VARIABLES:       days&     Julian day number of the date
' MODULE LEVEL
'   DECLARATIONS:  DECLARE FUNCTION Second2Date$ (second&)
'
  FUNCTION Second2Date$ (second&) STATIC
      days& = second& \ 86400 + 2444240
      Second2Date$ = Julian2Date$(days&)
  END FUNCTION
```

Function: Second2Time$

Returns a time string given the number of seconds since the last second of 1979.

Related functions are Second2Date$ and TimeDate2Second&. The Second2Date$ function finds the date string for a given second, and the TimeDate2Second$ function finds the seconds since 1979 for a given date and time.

```
' *************************************************
' ** Name:          Second2Time$                **
' ** Type:          Function                    **
' ** Module:        CALENDAR.BAS                **
' ** Language:      Microsoft QuickBASIC 4.00   **
' *************************************************
'
' Returns the time in the QuickBASIC string format
' HH:MM:SS given the number of seconds since the
' last second of 1979.  Use Second2Date$ to find
' the date at the indicated second.
'
' EXAMPLE OF USE:   tim$ = Second2Time$(second&)
' PARAMETERS:       second&    Number of seconds since the last second of 1979
' VARIABLES:        time&      Number of seconds in current day
'                   second%    Current second of the minute
'                   minute%    Current minute of the hour
'                   hour%      Current hour of the day
' MODULE LEVEL
'   DECLARATIONS:   DECLARE FUNCTION Second2Time$ (second&)
'
FUNCTION Second2Time$ (second&) STATIC
    IF second& > 0 THEN
        time& = second& MOD 86400
        second% = time& MOD 60
        time& = time& \ 60
        minute% = time& MOD 60
        hour% = time& \ 60
        Second2Time$ = HMS2Time$(hour%, minute%, second%)
    ELSE
        Second2Time$ = "HH:MM:SS"
    END IF
END FUNCTION
```

Function: Time2Hour%

Extracts the numeric value of the hour from a time string if in the standard TIME$ format *HH:MM:SS*.

```
' ****************************************************
' **    Name:         Time2Hour%                    **
' **    Type:         Function                      **
' **    Module:       CALENDAR.BAS                  **
' **    Language:     Microsoft QuickBASIC 4.00     **
' ****************************************************
'
' Returns the hour number as indicated in a time
' string in the format HH:MM:SS.
'
' EXAMPLE OF USE:   hour% = Time2Hour%(tim$)
' PARAMETERS:       tim$         Time of concern
' VARIABLES:        (none)
' MODULE LEVEL
'   DECLARATIONS:   DECLARE FUNCTION Time2Hour% (tim$)

FUNCTION Time2Hour% (tim$) STATIC
    Time2Hour% = VAL(LEFT$(tim$, 2))
END FUNCTION
```

Function: Time2Minute%

Extracts the numeric value of the hour from a time string that is in the standard TIME$ format *HH:MM:SS*.

```
' ****************************************************
' **    Name:         Time2Minute%                  **
' **    Type:         Function                      **
' **    Module:       CALENDAR.BAS                  **
' **    Language:     Microsoft QuickBASIC 4.00     **
' ****************************************************
'
' Returns the minute number as indicated in a time
' string in the format HH:MM:SS.
'
' EXAMPLE OF USE:   minute% = Time2Minute%(tim$)
```

(continued)

continued

```
' PARAMETERS:      tim$       Time of concern
' VARIABLES:       (none)
' MODULE LEVEL
'   DECLARATIONS:  DECLARE FUNCTION Time2Minute% (tim$)
'
  FUNCTION Time2Minute% (tim$) STATIC
      Time2Minute% = VAL(MID$(tim$, 4, 2))
  END FUNCTION
```

Function: Time2Second%

Extracts the numeric value of the seconds from a time string that is in the standard TIME$ format *HH:MM:SS*.

```
' *********************************************
' **  Name:       Time2Second%              **
' **  Type:       Function                  **
' **  Module:     CALENDAR.BAS              **
' **  Language:   Microsoft QuickBASIC 4.00 **
' *********************************************
'
' Returns the second number as indicated in a time
' string in the format HH:MM:SS.
'
' EXAMPLE OF USE:  second% = Time2Second%(tim$)
' PARAMETERS:      tim$       Time of concern
' VARIABLES:       (none)
' MODULE LEVEL
'   DECLARATIONS:  DECLARE FUNCTION Time2Second% (tim$)
'
  FUNCTION Time2Second% (tim$) STATIC
      Time2Second% = VAL(MID$(tim$, 7))
  END FUNCTION
```

Function: TimeDate2Second&

Returns the number of seconds since the last second of 1979 given any date and time between the first second of 1980 and a moment in the year 2048.

The largest positive long integer that can be stored in four bytes using two's complement notation is 2147483647. From the arbitrary point in time at the start of 1980, counting in seconds reaches this largest possible positive integer at 03:14:07 on 01-19-2048.

One advantage of converting date and time to a number of seconds is that this long integer is more compact; this is an advantage, for example, when a large number of dates and times must be recorded in a disk file. Event logging, data acquisition, and business transaction time stamping are examples of the use of this type of subprogram.

```
' **************************************************
' **   Name:         TimeDate2Second&              **
' **   Type:         Function                      **
' **   Module:       CALENDAR.BAS                  **
' **   Language:     Microsoft QuickBASIC 4.00     **
' **************************************************
'
' Returns the number of seconds since the last
' second of 1979.  If the date is not in the years
' 1980 to 2047, an error message is output.
'
' EXAMPLE OF USE:   sec& = TimeDate2Second&(tim$, dat$)
' PARAMETERS:       tim$      Time of concern
'                   dat$      Date of concern
' VARIABLES:        days&     Days since 12-31-1979
'                   hour%     Hour of the day
'                   minute%   Minute of the hour
'                   second%   Second of the minute
'                   secs&     Working number of total seconds
' MODULE LEVEL
'   DECLARATIONS:   DECLARE FUNCTION TimeDate2Second& (tim$, dat$)
'
FUNCTION TimeDate2Second& (tim$, dat$) STATIC
    days& = Date2Julian&(dat$) - 2444240
    hour% = VAL(LEFT$(tim$, 2))
    minute% = VAL(MID$(tim$, 4, 2))
    second% = VAL(RIGHT$(tim$, 2))
    secs& = CLNG(hour%) * 3600 + minute% * 60 + second%
    IF days& >= 0 AND days& < 24857 THEN
        TimeDate2Second& = days& * 86400 + secs&
    ELSE
        PRINT "TimeDate2Second: Not in range 1980 to 2047"
        SYSTEM
    END IF
END FUNCTION
```

CARTESIA

The CARTESIA toolbox contains two subprograms and two functions that convert between Cartesian and polar coordinates. The program first prompts you to enter x and y values defining a point on the Cartesian plane and then prints the equivalent coordinate in polar notation.

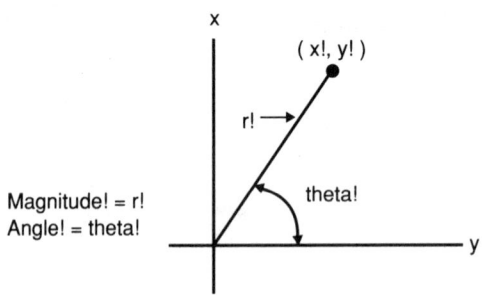

Magnitude! = r!
Angle! = theta!

All of the variables in this module are defined as single-precision, floating-point values. If you need greater precision, globally change all exclamation point characters to pound sign characters. You'll also want to change the CONST PI statement in the Angle! function to provide a double-precision value for PI.

Name	Type	Description
CARTESIA.BAS		Demo module
Angle!	Func	Angle between X axis and line to x, y point
Magnitude!	Func	Distance from origin to x, y point
Pol2Rec	Sub	Polar to Cartesian conversion
Rec2Pol	Sub	Cartesian to polar conversion

Demo Module: CARTESIA

```
' **************************************************
' **   Name:         CARTESIA                     **
' **   Type:         Toolbox                      **
' **   Module:       CARTESIA.BAS                 **
' **   Language:     Microsoft QuickBASIC 4.00    **
' **************************************************
'
' Demonstrates a set of functions and subprograms
' dealing with Cartesian coordinates.
'
' USAGE:          No command line parameters
' .MAK FILE:      (none)
' PARAMETERS:     (none)
' VARIABLES:      x!     X value of Cartesian coordinate
'                 y!     Y value of Cartesian coordinate
'                 r!     Polar notation distance from origin
'                 theta! Polar notation angle from X axis

DECLARE FUNCTION Angle! (x!, y!)
DECLARE FUNCTION Magnitude! (x!, y!)

DECLARE SUB Pol2Rec (r!, theta!, x!, y!)
DECLARE SUB Rec2Pol (x!, y!, r!, theta!)

CLS
INPUT "Enter X  ", x!
INPUT "Enter Y  ", y!
PRINT
PRINT "Magnitude!(x!, y!)", Magnitude!(x!, y!)
PRINT "Angle!(x!, y!)", Angle!(x!, y!)
PRINT
Rec2Pol x!, y!, r!, theta!
PRINT "Rec2Pol", , r!; theta!
Pol2Rec r!, theta!, x!, y!
PRINT "Pol2Rec", , x!; y!
```

Function: Angle!

Returns the angle from the origin to a given Cartesian coordinate, measured from the positive X axis. The angle, expressed in radians, is returned in the range -PI < Angle! <= +PI.

This function has a good example of an IF-ELSEIF-ELSE-ENDIF structured statement. Notice that even though this function contains quite a few statements, the routine quickly skips over the unnecessary instructions. These tests let the function cover all the special case situations, such as when the coordinate falls on one or both axes.

```
' *****************************************************
' **   Name:          Angle!                         **
' **   Type:          Function                       **
' **   Module:        CARTESIA.BAS                   **
' **   Language:      Microsoft QuickBASIC 4.00      **
' *****************************************************
'
' Returns the angle (in radians) between the X axis
' and the line from the origin to the point x!,y!
'
' EXAMPLE OF USE:   a! = Angle!(x!, y!)
' PARAMETERS:       x!          X part of the Cartesian coordinate
'                   y!          Y part of the Cartesian coordinate
' VARIABLES:        (none)
' MODULE LEVEL
'   DECLARATIONS:   DECLARE FUNCTION Angle! (x!, y!)
'
FUNCTION Angle! (x!, y!) STATIC

   CONST PI = 3.141593
   CONST HALFPI = PI / 2

   IF x! = 0! THEN
       IF y! > 0! THEN
           Angle! = HALFPI
       ELSEIF y! < 0! THEN
           Angle! = -HALFPI
       ELSE
           Angle! = 0!
       END IF
   ELSEIF y! = 0! THEN
       IF x! < 0! THEN
           Angle! = PI
       ELSE
```

(continued)

continued

```
            Angle! = 0!
        END IF
    ELSE
        IF x! < 0! THEN
            IF y! > 0! THEN
                Angle! = ATN(y! / x!) + PI
            ELSE
                Angle! = ATN(y! / x!) - PI
            END IF
        ELSE
            Angle! = ATN(y! / x!)
        END IF
    END IF

END FUNCTION
```

Function: Magnitude!

Returns the distance from the origin to a given Cartesian coordinate.
This function, together with the Angle! function, provides the calculations that perform rectangular to polar coordinate conversions. They are both called by the Rec2Pol subprogram.

```
' **************************************************
' **   Name:          Magnitude!                  **
' **   Type:          Function                    **
' **   Module:        CARTESIA.BAS                **
' **   Language:      Microsoft QuickBASIC 4.00   **
' **************************************************
'
' Returns the distance from the origin to the
' point x!,y!
'
' EXAMPLE OF USE:  r! = Magnitude!(x!, y!)
' PARAMETERS:      x!         X part of the Cartesian coordinate
'                  y!         Y part of the Cartesian coordinate
' VARIABLES:       (none)
' MODULE LEVEL
'   DECLARATIONS:  DECLARE FUNCTION Magnitude! (x!, y!)
'
FUNCTION Magnitude! (x!, y!) STATIC
    Magnitude! = SQR(x! * x! + y! * y!)
END FUNCTION
```

Subprogram: Pol2Rec

Converts a polar notation point (magnitude, angle) to its equivalent (x, y) Cartesian coordinates. The conversion assumes that theta! is expressed in radians and uses the built-in QuickBASIC functions for finding the sine and cosine of this angle.

```
' *************************************************
' ** Name:          Pol2rec                      **
' ** Type:          Subprogram                   **
' ** Module:        CARTESIA.BAS                 **
' ** Language:      Microsoft QuickBASIC 4.00    **
' *************************************************
'
' Converts polar coordinates to Cartesian notation.
'
' EXAMPLE OF USE:   Pol2Rec r!, theta!, x!, y!
' PARAMETERS:       r!          Distance of point from the origin
'                   theta!      Angle of point from the X axis
'                   x!          X coordinate of the point
'                   y!          Y coordinate of the point
' VARIABLES:        (none)
' MODULE LEVEL
'   DECLARATIONS:   DECLARE SUB Pol2Rec (r!, theta!, x!, y!)
'
  SUB Pol2Rec (r!, theta!, x!, y!) STATIC
      x! = r! * COS(theta!)
      y! = r! * SIN(theta!)
  END SUB
```

Subprogram: Rec2Pol

Converts a point expressed as a Cartesian coordinate pair (x, y) to the equivalent polar notation (magnitude, angle). The Angle! and Magnitude! functions within this toolbox perform the calculations for this conversion.

```
' *************************************************
' ** Name:          Rec2pol                      **
' ** Type:          Subprogram                   **
' ** Module:        CARTESIA.BAS                 **
' ** Language:      Microsoft QuickBASIC 4.00    **
' *************************************************
```

(continued)

continued

```
' Converts Cartesian coordinates to polar notation.
'
' EXAMPLE OF USE:   Rec2Pol x!, y!, r!, theta!
' PARAMETERS:       x!        X coordinate of the point
'                   y!        Y coordinate of the point
'                   r!        Distance of point from the origin
'                   theta!    Angle of point from the X axis
' VARIABLES:        (none)
' MODULE LEVEL
'   DECLARATIONS:   DECLARE FUNCTION Angle! (x!, y!)
'                   DECLARE FUNCTION Magnitude! (x!, y!)
'                   DECLARE SUB Rec2Pol (x!, y!, r!, theta!)
'
    SUB Rec2Pol (x!, y!, r!, theta!) STATIC
        r! = Magnitude!(x!, y!)
        theta! = Angle!(x!, y!)
    END SUB
```

CIPHER

The CIPHER program securely ciphers and deciphers any file. You probably have some files or data that you'd prefer to keep secret, such as personal financial information or proprietary business matters. Several packages on the market let you keep your files secure from prying eyes, but they do it at some expense. This program does it quickly and simply.

For each byte in the file to be ciphered, the program generates a pseudorandom byte in the range 0 through 255. The pseudorandom byte and the file byte are combined using the QuickBASIC XOR function, and the byte in the file is replaced with this result. To decipher the file, use the CIPHER program to process the file a second time, using exactly the same key. XOR then returns the file to its original state.

The bytes in the ciphered file will appear to be as random as the seqtuence of pseudorandom bytes generated for this process. The RandInteger function generates the bytes, which makes the number of possible pseudorandom sequences astronomical. Without knowing the key string used to initialize this sequence, a person could probably not break the cipher. This points out an important fact about the security of this technique: The ciphered file is only as secure as the key you select. Let's see how you can choose a secure key.

First, the "don'ts": Don't use simple, obvious keys such as your name, initials, names of family members or pets, addresses, phone numbers, and the like. Don't use the same key repeatedly. Don't record the keys in an easy-to-find place, such as in a batch file containing CIPHER commands. And don't forget to keep track of your key in some safe way. You won't be able to get your file back if you forget the key!

There are several ways to generate your own keys in a safe, secure manner. Be creative! For example, you might choose your own private "magic number" that you can easily remember and use it to define a key. If your number is 17, you could use the first 17 characters of line 17, page 17, in your favorite novel. Another technique is to create a common phrase that's easy to remember yet contains deliberately misspelled words or an odd combination of upper- and lowercase characters—3 blined MiSe, for example. Don't get too carried away with your creativity, though, and end up with something you can't remember. Changing even one character in the key will generate an entirely different sequence of pseudorandom bytes.

The CIPHER program has a unique feature built into it to help generate new words that you can use as keys. Instead of typing the filename and key string on the command line that invokes the CIPHER program, type CIPHER /NEWKEY and press the Enter key. The program will generate nine pseudorandom words, created by randomly selecting characters from sets of consonants and vowels in a way that makes most of them readable.

When you use the /NEWKEY command line option, a unique set of new words is generated for every possible clock tick in the life of your computer. In the module-level code of CIPHER.BAS is the statement *RandShuffle DATE$ + TIME$ + STR$(TIMER)*, which initializes the random number generator when you give the /NEWKEY option. The key string for the initialization is formed by combining the date, time, and timer information into a string of about 27 characters.

Eighteen times each second your computer updates its internal clock. The TIMER function returns a different value each time this happens, and the date and time are unique for every possible second of each day. As a result, the key string that initializes the random number generator will always be unique, and it's safe to say you'll never see the same group of nine words repeated.

If you have a large number of files that you'd like to cipher, you can automate the process. Create a batch file containing CIPHER command lines, complete with filenames and keys. Keep this batch file ciphered at all times, except when you want to use it to cipher or decipher the group of files listed in the commands. This way, the only key you must remember is the one for unlocking the batch command file.

To try out the CIPHER program, follow these steps. Create a small, readable file using the Document mode of the QuickBASIC editor, and save it as TEST.TXT. Verify the file contents by typing TYPE TEST.TXT. Now, to cipher the file, run CIPHER with the command line TEST.TXT ABC. When CIPHER is finished, the file will be unreadable, and entering TYPE TEST.TXT will result in strange characters on your screen. To decipher the file, once again run CIPHER with the same command line: TEST.TXT ABC. Be sure to enter the key string ("ABC" in this case) exactly the same as you did when the file was ciphered. Finally, type out the file to verify that it was correctly deciphered.

QUICKBASIC TOOLBOXES AND PROGRAMS

Name	Type	Description
CIPHER.BAS		Program module
NewWord$	Func	Creates pseudorandom new word
ProcesX	Sub	Enciphers string by XORing bytes

Program Module: CIPHER

```
' *************************************************
' **  Name:        CIPHER                        **
' **  Type:        Program                       **
' **  Module:      CIPHER.BAS                    **
' **  Language:    Microsoft QuickBASIC 4.00     **
' *************************************************
'
' USAGE:       CIPHER  filename.ext key    or    CIPHER /NEWKEY
' .MAK FILE:   CIPHER.BAS
'              RANDOMS.BAS
' PARAMETERS:  filename      Name of file to be ciphered or deciphered
'              key           String of one or more words used as the
'                            cipher key
' VARIABLES:   cmd$          Working copy of COMMAND$
'              i%            Loop index
'              firstSpace%   Location in command line of first character
'              fileName$     Name of file to be processed
'              key$          String to be used as cipher key
'              fileLength&   Length of file to be processed
'              a$            Workspace for groups of bytes from the file
'              count%        Number of groups of bytes to be processed
'              j&            Location in file of each group of bytes

' Constants
  CONST BYTES = 1000&

' Functions
  DECLARE FUNCTION NewWord$ ()
  DECLARE FUNCTION Rand& ()
  DECLARE FUNCTION RandInteger% (a%, b%)

' Subprograms
  DECLARE SUB RandShuffle (key$)
  DECLARE SUB ProcesX (a$)
```

(continued)

continued

```
' Initialization
CLS
PRINT "CIPHER "; COMMAND$
PRINT

' Grab the command line parameters
cmd$ = COMMAND$

' If no command line parameters, then tell user what's needed
IF cmd$ = "" THEN
    PRINT
    PRINT "Usage:   CIPHER /NEWKEY"
    PRINT "(or)     CIPHER filename key-string"
    PRINT
    SYSTEM
END IF

' If /NEWKEY option, generate a few new words, and then quit
IF INSTR(cmd$, "/NEWKEY") THEN

    ' Clear the screen and describe the output
    CLS
    PRINT "Randomly created words that can be used as cipher keys..."
    PRINT
    RandShuffle DATE$ + TIME$ + STR$(TIMER)
    FOR i% = 1 TO 9
        PRINT NewWord$; " ";
    NEXT i%
    PRINT
    SYSTEM
END IF

' Get the filename from the command line
cmd$ = cmd$ + " "
firstSpace% = INSTR(cmd$, " ")
fileName$ = LEFT$(cmd$, firstSpace% - 1)

' Grab the rest of the command line as the cipher key
key$ = LTRIM$(MID$(cmd$, firstSpace% + 1))

' Prepare the pseudorandom numbers using the key for shuffling
RandShuffle key$
```

(continued)

continued

```
' Open up the file
  OPEN fileName$ FOR BINARY AS #1
  fileLength& = LOF(1)

' Process the file in manageable pieces
  a$ = SPACE$(BYTES)
  count% = fileLength& \ BYTES

' Loop through the file
  FOR i% = 0 TO count%
      j& = i% * BYTES + 1
      IF i% = count% THEN
          a$ = SPACE$(fileLength& - BYTES * count%)
      END IF
      GET #1, j&, a$
      ProcesX a$
      PUT #1, j&, a$
  NEXT i%

' All done
  SYSTEM
```

Function: NewWord$

Creates a pseudorandom, new "word" by randomly selecting appropriate consonants and vowels to form one to three syllables. These words can be useful as passwords, cipher keys, or new product names.

```
' *************************************************
' **   Name:         NewWord$                    **
' **   Type:         Function                    **
' **   Module:       CIPHER.BAS                  **
' **   Language:     Microsoft QuickBASIC 4.00   **
' *************************************************
'
' Returns a pseudorandom word of a possibly
' speakable form.
'
' EXAMPLE OF USE: PRINT NewWord$
' PARAMETERS:    (none)
' VARIABLES:     vowel$     String constant listing the set of vowels
'                consonant$ String constant listing the set of consonants
```

(continued)

```
'                      syllables%  Random number of syllables for the new word
'                      i%          Loop index for creating each syllable
'                      t$          Temporary work string for forming the new word
' MODULE LEVEL
'   DECLARATIONS: DECLARE FUNCTION NewWord$ ()
'
  FUNCTION NewWord$ STATIC
      CONST vowel$ = "aeiou"
      CONST consonant$ = "bcdfghjklmnpqrstvwxyz"
      syllables% = Rand& MOD 3 + 1
      FOR i% = 1 TO syllables%
          t$ = t$ + MID$(consonant$, RandInteger%(1, 21), 1)
          IF i% = 1 THEN
              t$ = UCASE$(t$)
          END IF
          t$ = t$ + MID$(vowel$, RandInteger%(1, 5), 1)
      NEXT i%
      IF Rand& MOD 2 THEN
          t$ = t$ + MID$(consonant$, RandInteger%(1, 21), 1)
      END IF
      NewWord$ = t$
      t$ = ""
  END FUNCTION
```

Subprogram: ProcesX

Enciphers a string by XORing the bytes with a sequence of pseudorandom bytes. The bytes are generated as pseudorandom integers in the range 0 through 255 by the RandInteger% function.

If you initialize the random number generator with the same sequence and process the ciphered string a second time with this subprogram, the original string will result. The CIPHER program allows deciphering in this way by simply requiring that the ciphered file be "ciphered" a second time with the same key.

```
' **************************************************
' **   Name:          ProcesX                     **
' **   Type:          Subprogram                  **
' **   Module:        CIPHER.BAS                  **
' **   Language:      Microsoft QuickBASIC 4.00   **
' **************************************************
```

(continued)

continued

```
' Enciphers a string by XORing with pseudorandom bytes.
'
' EXAMPLE OF USE:    ProcesX a$
' PARAMETERS:        a$         String to be ciphered
' VARIABLES:         i%         Index into the string
'                    byte%      Numeric value of each string character
' MODULE LEVEL
'   DECLARATIONS:    DECLARE SUB ProcesX (a$)
'
  SUB ProcesX (a$) STATIC
      FOR i% = 1 TO LEN(a$)
          byte% = ASC(MID$(a$, i%, 1)) XOR RandInteger%(0, 255)
          MID$(a$, i%, 1) = CHR$(byte%)
      NEXT i%
  END SUB
```

COLORS

The COLORS program provides a handy utility for interactively selecting colors from the 262,144 available in the VGA and MCGA graphics modes. To run this program, you must have a mouse and VGA or MCGA graphics capability.

The program is easy to use. Simply click on any of the three color bars to set the intensity of that color. The ellipse on the left side of the screen shows the color shade you selected, and the long integer value at the top of the screen shows the numeric value to use with the PALETTE statement for setting this same color in other programs. When you're ready to quit, click on the X at the lower left corner of the screen.

You can run this program from the QuickBASIC environment, but to make it an easily accessible utility, it's probably better to compile it and create a stand-alone .EXE program module.

Name	Type	Description
COLORS.BAS		Program module
Shade&	Func	Color value from given red, green, and blue

Program Module: COLORS

```
' **************************************************
' **   Name:         COLORS                       **
' **   Type:         Program                      **
' **   Module:       COLORS.BAS                   **
' **   Language:     Microsoft QuickBASIC 4.00    **
' **************************************************
'
' Provides interactive selection of a color shade.
'
' USAGE:          No command line parameters
' REQUIREMENTS:   VGA or MCGA
'                 MIXED.QLB/.LIB
'                 Mouse
```

(continued)

continued

```
' .MAK FILE:      COLORS.BAS
'                 BITS.BAS
'                 MOUSSUBS.BAS
' PARAMETERS:     (none)
' VARIABLES:      red!            Intensity of red, from 0 to 1
'                 green!          Intensity of green, from 0 to 1
'                 blue!           Intensity of blue, from 0 to 1
'                 mask$           Mouse graphics cursor definition string
'                 xHot%           Mouse cursor hot spot X location
'                 yHot%           Mouse cursor hot spot Y location
'                 cursor$         Mouse cursor binary definition string
'                 fill%           Color bar height calculation
'                 x%              Color bar horizontal left edge
'                 x2%             Color bar horizontal right edge
'                 y%              Color bar vertical top edge
'                 y2%             Color bar vertical bottom edge
'                 leftButton%     State of left mouse button
'                 rightButton%    State of right mouse button
'                 xMouse%         Horizontal mouse location
'                 yMouse%         Vertical mouse location
'                 clickFlag%      Toggle for left mouse button state
'                 xM%             Modified mouse horizontal location
'                 quitFlag%       Signal to end program


' Logical constants
  CONST FALSE = 0
  CONST TRUE = NOT FALSE

' Constants
  CONST REDPAL = 1
  CONST BLUEPAL = 2
  CONST GREENPAL = 3
  CONST TESTPAL = 4
  CONST WHITEPAL = 5
  CONST BARPAL = 6
  CONST DX = 15
  CONST DY = 150
  CONST RX = 180
  CONST RY = 30
  CONST GX = RX + DX + DX
  CONST GY = RY
  CONST BX = GX + DX + DX
  CONST BY = RY
```

(continued)

continued

```
' Functions
  DECLARE FUNCTION Shade& (red!, green!, blue!)

' Subprograms
  DECLARE SUB MouseHide ()
  DECLARE SUB MouseMaskTranslate (mask$, xHot%, yHot%, cursor$)
  DECLARE SUB MouseSetGcursor (cursor$)
  DECLARE SUB MouseShow ()
  DECLARE SUB Cursleft (mask$, xHot%, yHot%)
  DECLARE SUB MouseNow (leftButton%, rightButton%, xMouse%, yMouse%)

' Set 256 color mode
  SCREEN 13

' Set first three colors as pure red, green, blue
  PALETTE REDPAL, Shade&(1!, 0!, 0!)
  PALETTE GREENPAL, Shade&(0!, 1!, 0!)
  PALETTE BLUEPAL, Shade&(0!, 0!, 1!)

' Set a pure white color choice
  PALETTE WHITEPAL, Shade&(1!, 1!, 1!)

' Set bar background color
  PALETTE BARPAL, Shade&(0!, 0!, 0!)

' Set background to light gray
  PALETTE 0, Shade&(.4, .4, .4)

' Start each intensity at midscale
  red! = .5
  green! = .5
  blue! = .5

' Set starting shade
  PALETTE TESTPAL, Shade&(red!, green!, blue!)

' Create ellipse of circle to show current shade selected
  CIRCLE (70, 100), 80, TESTPAL, , , 1.4
  PAINT (70, 100), TESTPAL

' Create the three color bars
  LINE (RX, RY)-(RX + DX, RY + DY), WHITEPAL, B
  LINE (GX, GY)-(GX + DX, GY + DY), WHITEPAL, B
  LINE (BX, BY)-(BX + DX, BY + DY), WHITEPAL, B
```

(continued)

continued

```
' Mark place to quit by clicking
  LOCATE 25, 1
  PRINT "(X) "; CHR$(27); " Quit";

' Make the left arrow mouse cursor
  Cursleft mask$, xHot%, yHot%
  MouseMaskTranslate mask$, xHot%, yHot%, cursor$
  MouseSetGcursor cursor$

' Main loop
  DO

    ' Put title and current shade number at top
      LOCATE 1, 1
      PRINT "COLOR CHOOSER"; TAB(22);
      PRINT USING "##########"; Shade&(red!, green!, blue!)

    ' Fill in the red color bar
      fill% = red! * (DY - 3) + 1
      x% = RX + 1
      x2% = RX + DX
      y% = RY + 1
      y2% = RY + DY
      LINE (x%, y%)-(x2% - 1, y2% - fill% - 1), BARPAL, BF
      LINE (x%, y2% - fill%)-(x2% - 1, y2% - 1), REDPAL, BF

    ' Fill in the green color bar
      fill% = green! * (DY - 3) + 1
      x% = GX + 1
      x2% = GX + DX
      y% = GY + 1
      y2% = GY + DY
      LINE (x%, y%)-(x2% - 1, y2% - fill% - 1), BARPAL, BF
      LINE (x%, y2% - fill%)-(x2% - 1, y2% - 1), GREENPAL, BF

    ' Fill in the blue color bar
      fill% = blue! * (DY - 3) + 1
      x% = BX + 1
      x2% = BX + DX
      y% = BY + 1
      y2% = BY + DY
      LINE (x%, y%)-(x2% - 1, y2% - fill% - 1), BARPAL, BF
      LINE (x%, y2% - fill%)-(x2% - 1, y2% - 1), BLUEPAL, BF
```

(continued)

continued

```
' Change the shade of the ellipse
  PALETTE TESTPAL, Shade&(red!, green!, blue!)

' Refresh mouse cursor
  MouseShow

' Wait for fresh mouse left button click
  DO
      MouseNow leftButton%, rightButton%, xMouse%, yMouse%
      IF leftButton% = FALSE THEN
          clickFlag% = FALSE
      END IF
      IF clickFlag% THEN
          leftButton% = 0
      END IF
  LOOP UNTIL leftButton%

' Hide mouse and set parameters
  MouseHide
  clickFlag% = TRUE
  xM% = xMouse% \ 2

' Is mouse in the "Quit" area?
  IF xMouse% < 45 AND yMouse% > 190 THEN
      quitFlag% = TRUE
  END IF

' Is mouse at the right height to be in a bar?
  IF yMouse% > RY - 2 AND yMouse% < RY + DY + 2 THEN

     ' Is mouse in the red bar?
       IF xM% > RX AND xM% < RX + DX THEN
           red! = 1! - (yMouse% - RY) / DY
           IF red! < 0 THEN
               red! = 0
           ELSEIF red! > 1 THEN
               red! = 1
           END IF
       END IF

     ' Is mouse in the green bar?
       IF xM% > GX AND xM% < GX + DX THEN
           green! = 1! - (yMouse% - RY) / DY
```

(continued)

continued

```
            IF green! < 0 THEN
                green! = 0
            ELSEIF green! > 1 THEN
                green! = 1
            END IF
        END IF

        ' Is mouse in the blue bar?
        IF xM% > BX AND xM% < BX + DX THEN
            blue! = 1! - (yMouse% - RY) / DY
            IF blue! < 0 THEN
                blue! = 0
            ELSEIF blue! > 1 THEN
                blue! = 1
            END IF
        END IF

    END IF

LOOP UNTIL quitFlag%

SCREEN 0
WIDTH 80
CLS
END
```

Function: Shade&

Returns the long integer number for a given shade of color.

This is the only function the COLORS utility provides, but it's useful when programming the VGA and MCGA SCREEN modes 11, 12, and 13. You can use the long integer value returned in a PALETTE statement for setting a color attribute to one of 262,144 color choices.

Three single-precision numbers are passed to this routine, representing the desired intensities of the red, green, and blue colors. These numbers must be in the range 0.0 through 1.0. Shade&(1!, 0!, 0!), for example, returns the long integer value for bright red; Shade&(.5, .5, .5) returns a number for medium gray.

The best way to see the results of setting the three colors to various intensity levels is by running the COLORS program.

```
' **************************************************
' **   Name:           Shade&                      **
' **   Type:           Function                    **
' **   Module:         COLORS.BAS                  **
' **   Language:       Microsoft QuickBASIC 4.00   **
' **************************************************
'
' Returns the long integer color number given red,
' green, and blue intensity numbers in the range
' 0 through 1.
'
' EXAMPLE OF USE:   PALETTE 1, Shade&(red!, green!, blue!)
' PARAMETERS:       red!        Intensity of red, from 0 to 1
'                   green!      Intensity of green, from 0 to 1
'                   blue!       Intensity of blue, from 0 to 1
' VARIABLES:        r&          Red amount
'                   g&          Green amount
'                   b&          Blue amount
' MODULE LEVEL
'   DECLARATIONS:   DECLARE FUNCTION Shade& (red!, green!, blue!)
'
    FUNCTION Shade& (red!, green!, blue!) STATIC
        r& = red! * 63!
        g& = green! * 63!
        b& = blue! * 63!
        Shade& = r& + g& * 256& + b& * 65536
    END FUNCTION
```

COMPLEX

The COMPLEX toolbox provides a collection of subprograms for working with complex numbers. The QuickBASIC TYPE definition statement is ideal for declaring variables to be of type Complex, as shown. The variables a, b, and c each comprise a pair of single-precision numbers representing the real and imaginary parts of a complex number. These variables are passed to and from the subprograms as easily as if they were simple numeric values.

Complex numbers are expressed as the sum of a real and an imaginary number. Usually you show a complex number by writing the real number, followed immediately by a plus or minus sign, the imaginary number, and a small letter "i" or "j," which represents the square root of −1 and indicates the imaginary numeric component of the complex number.

In this program, complex numbers are entered and displayed in a similar format. You use parentheses to surround each complex number. This sample run of COMPLEX shows typical input and output complex-number formats:

```
Enter first complex number   ? (4-5i)
(4-5i)

ComplexExp                   (15.48743+52.35549i)
ComplexLog                   1.856786-.8960554i
ComplexReciprocal            9.756097E-02+.1219512i
ComplexSqr                   2.280693-1.096158i

Enter second complex number  ? (3+4i)
(3+4i)

ComplexAdd                   (7-1i)
ComplexSub                   (1-9i)
ComplexMul                   (32+1i)
ComplexDiv                   (-.32-1.24i)
ComplexPower                 (251.4394-9454.315i)
ComplexRoot                  (.9952651-.4262131i)


Press any key to continue
```

Name	Type	Description
COMPLEX.BAS		Demo module
Complex2String	Sub	String representation of a complex number
ComplexAdd	Sub	Adds two complex numbers
ComplexDiv	Sub	Divides two complex numbers
ComplexExp	Sub	Exponential function of a complex number
ComplexLog	Sub	Natural log of a complex number
ComplexMul	Sub	Multiplies two complex numbers
ComplexPower	Sub	Complex number raised to a complex number
ComplexReciprocal	Sub	Reciprocal of a complex number
ComplexRoot	Sub	Complex root of a complex number
ComplexSqr	Sub	Square root of a complex number
ComplexSub	Sub	Subtracts two complex numbers
String2Complex	Sub	Converts string to complex variable

Demo Module: COMPLEX

```
' *************************************************
' ** Name:        COMPLEX                        **
' ** Type:        Toolbox                        **
' ** Module:      COMPLEX.BAS                    **
' ** Language:    Microsoft QuickBASIC 4.00      **
' *************************************************
'
' Demonstrates a set of complex number functions and
' subprograms.
'
' USAGE:        No command line parameters
' .MAK FILE:    COMPLEX.BAS
'               CARTESIA.BAS
' PARAMETERS:   (none)
```

(continued)

continued

```
' VARIABLES:    a       Variable of type Complex
'               b       Variable of type Complex
'               c       Variable of type Complex
'               x$      String representation of a complex number
'               y$      String representation of a complex number
'               z$      String representation of a complex number

TYPE Complex
    r AS SINGLE
    i AS SINGLE
END TYPE

' Subprograms
DECLARE SUB ComplexSub (a AS Complex, b AS Complex, c AS Complex)
DECLARE SUB ComplexSqr (a AS Complex, c AS Complex)
DECLARE SUB ComplexRoot (a AS Complex, b AS Complex, c AS Complex)
DECLARE SUB ComplexReciprocal (a AS Complex, c AS Complex)
DECLARE SUB ComplexAdd (a AS Complex, b AS Complex, c AS Complex)
DECLARE SUB ComplexLog (a AS Complex, c AS Complex)
DECLARE SUB ComplexPower (a AS Complex, b AS Complex, c AS Complex)
DECLARE SUB Complex2String (a AS Complex, x$)
DECLARE SUB String2Complex (x$, a AS Complex)
DECLARE SUB ComplexDiv (a AS Complex, b AS Complex, c AS Complex)
DECLARE SUB ComplexExp (a AS Complex, c AS Complex)
DECLARE SUB ComplexMul (a AS Complex, b AS Complex, c AS Complex)
DECLARE SUB Rec2pol (x!, y!, r!, theta!)

DIM a AS Complex, b AS Complex, c AS Complex

CLS
INPUT "Enter first complex number  "; x$
String2Complex x$, a
Complex2String a, x$
PRINT x$
PRINT

ComplexExp a, c
Complex2String c, z$
PRINT "ComplexExp", , z$
```

(continued)

continued

```
    ComplexLog a, c
    Complex2String c, z$
    PRINT "ComplexLog", , z$

    ComplexReciprocal a, c
    Complex2String c, z$
    PRINT "ComplexReciprocal", z$

    ComplexSqr a, c
    Complex2String c, z$
    PRINT "ComplexSqr", , z$

    PRINT
    INPUT "Enter second complex number "; y$
    String2Complex y$, b
    Complex2String b, y$
    PRINT y$
    PRINT

    ComplexAdd a, b, c
    Complex2String c, z$
    PRINT "ComplexAdd", , z$

    ComplexSub a, b, c
    Complex2String c, z$
    PRINT "ComplexSub", , z$

    ComplexMul a, b, c
    Complex2String c, z$
    PRINT "ComplexMul", , z$

    ComplexDiv a, b, c
    Complex2String c, z$
    PRINT "ComplexDiv", , z$

    ComplexPower a, b, c
    Complex2String c, z$
    PRINT "ComplexPower", , z$

    ComplexRoot a, b, c
    Complex2String c, z$
    PRINT "ComplexRoot", , z$
```

Subprogram: Complex2String

Creates a string representation of a complex number suitable for printing or displaying the results of complex number calculations. The string consists of two numbers enclosed in parentheses and separated by either a plus or minus sign, with the second number followed by a lowercase "i" to indicate the imaginary component. The length of this string result will vary, depending on the numeric values of the real and imaginary parts.

All results displayed by the demonstrations are formatted using this subprogram.

```
' *****************************************
' **   Name:        Complex2String          **
' **   Type:        Subprogram              **
' **   Module:      COMPLEX.BAS             **
' **   Language:    Microsoft QuickBASIC 4.00 **
' *****************************************
'
' Makes a string representation of a complex number.
'
' EXAMPLE OF USE:   Complex2String a, x$
' PARAMETERS:       a           Complex number variable (type Complex)
'                   x$          String representation of the complex number
' VARIABLES:        r$          Working string, real part
'                   i$          Working string, imaginary part
' MODULE LEVEL
'   DECLARATIONS:   TYPE Complex
'                     r AS SINGLE
'                     i AS SINGLE
'                   END TYPE
'
'                   DECLARE SUB Complex2String (a AS Complex, x$)
'
SUB Complex2String (a AS Complex, x$) STATIC

    ' Form the left part of the string
    IF a.r < 0 THEN
        r$ = "(" + STR$(a.r)
    ELSE
        r$ = "(" + MID$(STR$(a.r), 2)
    END IF
```

(continued)

continued

```
    ' Form the right part of the string
    IF a.i < 0 THEN
        i$ = STR$(a.i)
    ELSE
        i$ = "+" + MID$(STR$(a.i), 2)
    END IF

    ' The whole is more complex than the sum of the parts
    x$ = r$ + i$ + "i)"

END SUB
```

Subprogram: ComplexAdd

Calculates the sum of two complex numbers. Complex number a is added to complex number b, and the result is placed in the variable c.

```
' *****************************************
' **   Name:         ComplexAdd            **
' **   Type:         Subprogram            **
' **   Module:       COMPLEX.BAS           **
' **   Language:     Microsoft QuickBASIC 4.00  **
' *****************************************
'
' Adds two complex numbers.
'
' EXAMPLE OF USE:  ComplexAdd a, b, c
' PARAMETERS:      a           First complex number for the addition
'                  b           Second complex number for the addition
'                  c           Result of the complex number addition
' VARIABLES:       (none)
' MODULE LEVEL
'   DECLARATIONS:  TYPE Complex
'                      r AS SINGLE
'                      i AS SINGLE
'                  END TYPE
'
'          DECLARE SUB ComplexAdd (a AS Complex, b AS Complex, c AS Complex)
'
  SUB ComplexAdd (a AS Complex, b AS Complex, c AS Complex) STATIC
      c.r = a.r + b.r
      c.i = a.i + b.i
  END SUB
```

Subprogram: ComplexDiv

Calculates the result of dividing one complex number by another. The result of a/b is placed in the variable c.

```
' *********************************************
' ** Name:         ComplexDiv                **
' ** Type:         Subprogram                **
' ** Module:       COMPLEX.BAS               **
' ** Language:     Microsoft QuickBASIC 4.00 **
' *********************************************
'
' Divides two complex numbers.
'
' EXAMPLE OF USE:  ComplexDiv a, b, c
' PARAMETERS:      a          First complex number for the division
'                  b          Second complex number for the division
'                  c          Result of the complex number division a/b
' VARIABLES:       (none)
' MODULE LEVEL
'   DECLARATIONS:  TYPE Complex
'                     r AS SINGLE
'                     i AS SINGLE
'                  END TYPE
'
'       DECLARE SUB ComplexDiv (a AS Complex, b AS Complex, c AS Complex)
'
  SUB ComplexDiv (a AS Complex, b AS Complex, c AS Complex) STATIC
    t! = b.r * b.r + b.i * b.i
    c.r = (a.r * b.r + a.i * b.i) / t!
    c.i = (a.i * b.r - a.r * b.i) / t!
  END SUB
```

Subprogram: ComplexExp

Calculates the exponential function of a complex number a. The result is placed in the variable c.

```
' *********************************************
' ** Name:         ComplexExp                **
' ** Type:         Subprogram                **
' ** Module:       COMPLEX.BAS               **
' ** Language:     Microsoft QuickBASIC 4.00 **
' *********************************************
```

(continued)

continued

```
' Calculates the exponential function of a complex number.
'
' EXAMPLE OF USE:  ComplexExp a, c
' PARAMETERS:      a         Complex number argument
'                  c         Complex result of the calculations
' VARIABLES:       t!        Temporary working value
' MODULE LEVEL
'   DECLARATIONS:  TYPE Complex
'                     r AS SINGLE
'                     i AS SINGLE
'                  END TYPE
'
'                  DECLARE SUB ComplexExp (a AS Complex, c AS Complex)
'
  SUB ComplexExp (a AS Complex, c AS Complex) STATIC
      t! = EXP(a.r)
      c.r = t! * COS(a.i)
      c.i = t! * SIN(a.i)
  END SUB
```

Subprogram: ComplexLog

Calculates the complex logarithm of a complex number a. The result is placed in the variable c.

```
' *************************************************
' **   Name:       ComplexLog                    **
' **   Type:       Subprogram                    **
' **   Module:     COMPLEX.BAS                   **
' **   Language:   Microsoft QuickBASIC 4.00     **
' *************************************************
'
' Calculates the log of a complex number.
'
' EXAMPLE OF USE:  ComplexLog a, c
' PARAMETERS:      a         Complex number argument
'                  c         Complex result of the calculations
' VARIABLES:       r!        Magnitude of complex number a
'                  theta!    Angle of complex number a
' MODULE LEVEL
'   DECLARATIONS:  TYPE Complex
'                     r AS SINGLE
'                     i AS SINGLE
'                  END TYPE
```

(continued)

continued

```
'                    DECLARE SUB ComplexLog (a AS Complex, c AS Complex)
'                    DECLARE SUB Rec2pol (x!, y!, r!, theta!)
'
SUB ComplexLog (a AS Complex, c AS Complex) STATIC
    CALL Rec2pol(a.r, a.i, r!, theta!)
    IF r! <> 0! THEN
        c.r = LOG(r!)
        c.i = theta!
    ELSE
        ERROR 5
    END IF
END SUB
```

Subprogram: ComplexMul

Calculates the product of two complex numbers. Complex variables a and b are multiplied, and the result is placed in the variable c.

```
' **************************************************
' **   Name:         ComplexMul                    **
' **   Type:         Subprogram                    **
' **   Module:       COMPLEX.BAS                   **
' **   Language:     Microsoft QuickBASIC 4.00     **
' **************************************************
'
' Multiplies two complex numbers.
'
' EXAMPLE OF USE:  ComplexMul a, b, c
' PARAMETERS:      a          First complex number for the multiplication
'                  b          Second complex number for the multiplication
'                  c          Result of the complex number multiplication
' VARIABLES:       (none)
' MODULE LEVEL
'   DECLARATIONS:  TYPE Complex
'                    r AS SINGLE
'                    i AS SINGLE
'                  END TYPE
'
'          DECLARE SUB ComplexMul (a AS Complex, b AS Complex, c AS Complex)
SUB ComplexMul (a AS Complex, b AS Complex, c AS Complex) STATIC
    c.r = a.r * b.r - a.i * b.i
    c.i = a.r * b.i + a.i * b.r
END SUB
```

Subprogram: ComplexPower

Calculates the result of raising one complex number to the power of another. The result of raising a to the power of b is then placed in the variable c.

Notice that this subprogram calls several others. If you extract this routine for use in another program module, be sure to extract the other subprograms as well.

```
' **************************************************
' **   Name:         ComplexPower                  **
' **   Type:         Subprogram                    **
' **   Module:       COMPLEX.BAS                   **
' **   Language:     Microsoft QuickBASIC 4.00     **
' **************************************************
'
' Calculates a complex number raised to a complex number.
'
' EXAMPLE OF USE:    ComplexPower a, b, c
' PARAMETERS:        a          Complex number to be raised to a power
'                    b          Complex number to raise a to
'                    c          Result of a raised to the power of b
' VARIABLES:         t1         Structure of type Complex
'                    t2         Structure of type Complex
' MODULE LEVEL
'   DECLARATIONS:    TYPE Complex
'                        r AS SINGLE
'                        i AS SINGLE
'                    END TYPE
'
'     DECLARE SUB ComplexPower (a AS Complex, b AS Complex, c AS Complex)
'     DECLARE SUB ComplexExp (a AS Complex, c AS Complex)
'     DECLARE SUB ComplexLog (a AS Complex, c AS Complex)
'     DECLARE SUB ComplexMul (a AS Complex, b AS Complex, c AS Complex)

SUB ComplexPower (a AS Complex, b AS Complex, c AS Complex) STATIC
    DIM t1 AS Complex, t2 AS Complex
    IF a.r <> 0! OR a.i <> 0! THEN
        CALL ComplexLog(a, t1)
        CALL ComplexMul(t1, b, t2)
        CALL ComplexExp(t2, c)
    ELSE
        ERROR 5
    END IF
END SUB
```

Subprogram: ComplexReciprocal

Calculates the reciprocal of a complex number by dividing the complex number (1+0i) by the complex number a. The result is placed in the variable c.

```
' **************************************************
' **   Name:        ComplexReciprocal             **
' **   Type:        Subprogram                    **
' **   Module:      COMPLEX.BAS                   **
' **   Language:    Microsoft QuickBASIC 4.00     **
' **************************************************
'
' Calculates the reciprocal of a complex number.
'
' EXAMPLE OF USE:  ComplexReciprocal a, c
' PARAMETERS:      a           Complex number to be processed
'                  c           Result of calculating 1/a
' VARIABLES:       t           Structure of type Complex
' MODULE LEVEL
'   DECLARATIONS:  TYPE Complex
'                    r AS SINGLE
'                    i AS SINGLE
'                  END TYPE
'
'       DECLARE SUB ComplexReciprocal (a AS Complex, c AS Complex)
'       DECLARE SUB ComplexDiv (a AS Complex, b AS Complex, c AS Complex)

SUB ComplexReciprocal (a AS Complex, c AS Complex) STATIC
    DIM t AS Complex
    t.r = 1!
    t.i = 0
    ComplexDiv t, a, c
END SUB
```

Subprogram: ComplexRoot

Calculates the complex root of a complex number. The ComplexReciprocal and ComplexPower subprograms are called by this subprogram. These routines allow the root to be found by raising a to the power of 1/b.

```
' ***************************************************
' ** Name:         ComplexRoot                    **
' ** Type:         Subprogram                     **
' ** Module:       COMPLEX.BAS                    **
' ** Language:     Microsoft QuickBASIC 4.00      **
' ***************************************************
'
' Calculates the complex root of a complex number.
'
' EXAMPLE OF USE:  ComplexRoot a, b, c
' PARAMETERS:      a            First complex number
'                  b            Complex number root
'                  c            Result of finding the bth root of a
' VARIABLES:       t            Structure of type Complex
' MODULE LEVEL
'   DECLARATIONS:  TYPE Complex
'                    r AS SINGLE
'                    i AS SINGLE
'                  END TYPE
'
    DECLARE SUB ComplexRoot (a AS Complex, b AS Complex, c AS Complex)
    DECLARE SUB ComplexReciprocal (a AS Complex, c AS Complex)
    DECLARE SUB ComplexPower (a AS Complex, b AS Complex, c AS Complex)
'
  SUB ComplexRoot (a AS Complex, b AS Complex, c AS Complex) STATIC
      DIM t AS Complex
      IF b.r <> 0! OR b.i <> 0! THEN
          CALL ComplexReciprocal(b, t)
          CALL ComplexPower(a, t, c)
      ELSE
          ERROR 5
      END IF
  END SUB
```

Subprogram: ComplexSqr

Calculates the complex square root of a complex number. The square root of a is placed in the variable c.

```
' ***************************************************
' ** Name:         ComplexSqr                     **
' ** Type:         Subprogram                     **
' ** Module:       COMPLEX.BAS                    **
' ** Language:     Microsoft QuickBASIC 4.00      **
' ***************************************************
```

(continued)

continued

```
' Calculates the square root of a complex number.
'
' EXAMPLE OF USE: ComplexSqr a, c
' PARAMETERS:    a          Complex number argument
'                c          Result of finding the square root of a
' VARIABLES:     r!         Magnitude of complex number a
'                theta!     Angle of complex number a
'                rs!        Square root of r!
'                h!         One half of theta!
' MODULE LEVEL
'   DECLARATIONS: TYPE Complex
'                   r AS SINGLE
'                   i AS SINGLE
'                 END TYPE
'
'                 DECLARE SUB ComplexSqr (a AS Complex, c AS Complex)

SUB ComplexSqr (a AS Complex, c AS Complex) STATIC
    CALL Rec2pol(a.r, a.i, r!, theta!)
    rs! = SQR(r!)
    h! = theta! / 2!
    c.r = rs! * COS(h!)
    c.i = rs! * SIN(h!)
END SUB
```

Subprogram: ComplexSub

Calculates the difference between two complex numbers. The result of subtracting b from a is returned in the variable c.

```
' ***************************************************
' **  Name:         ComplexSub                     **
' **  Type:         Subprogram                     **
' **  Module:       COMPLEX.BAS                    **
' **  Language:     Microsoft QuickBASIC 4.00      **
' ***************************************************
'
' Subtracts two complex numbers.
'
' EXAMPLE OF USE: ComplexSub a, b, c
' PARAMETERS:    a          First complex number
'                b          Second Complex number
'                c          Result of subtracting b from a
```

(continued)

continued

```
' VARIABLES:        (none)
' MODULE LEVEL
'   DECLARATIONS:   TYPE Complex
'                       r AS SINGLE
'                       i AS SINGLE
'                   END TYPE
'
'        DECLARE SUB ComplexSub (a AS Complex, b AS Complex, c AS Complex)
'
    SUB ComplexSub (a AS Complex, b AS Complex, c AS Complex) STATIC
        c.r = a.r - b.r
        c.i = a.i - b.i
    END SUB
```

Subprogram: String2Complex

Converts a string representation of a complex number to a complex number variable of type Complex. This routine is useful for converting user input of a complex number to a complex variable.

In general, the string should be in the same format as that produced by the Complex2String function. However, there is some flexibility to allow for variations in the way a user might type in complex numbers. For example, the "i" character indicates the imaginary part of a complex number, but a "j" will also be recognized. Also, parentheses around the numbers are optional.

```
' **************************************************
' **   Name:        String2Complex                **
' **   Type:        Subprogram                    **
' **   Module:      COMPLEX.BAS                   **
' **   Language:    Microsoft QuickBASIC 4.00     **
' **************************************************
'
' Converts a string representation of a complex
' number to a type Complex variable.
'
' EXAMPLE OF USE:  String2Complex x$, a
' PARAMETERS:      x$         String representation of a complex number
'                  a          Complex number structure of type Complex
' VARIABLES:       j%         Index to first numerical character
'                  i%         Pointer to the "i" or "j" character
'                  k%         Pointer to start of imaginary part
' MODULE LEVEL
'   DECLARATIONS:  TYPE Complex
'                      r AS SINGLE
```

(continued)

continued

```
                     i AS SINGLE
                 END TYPE

                 _DECLARE SUB Complex2String (x$, a AS Complex)

SUB String2Complex (x$, a AS Complex) STATIC

   ' Real part starts just after left parenthesis
     j% = INSTR(x$, "(") + 1

   ' Step forward to find start of number
     DO UNTIL INSTR("+-0123456789", MID$(x$, j%, 1)) OR j% > LEN(x$)
         j% = j% + 1
     LOOP

   ' Imaginary part ends at the "i" or "j"
     i% = INSTR(LCASE$(x$), "i")
     IF INSTR(LCASE$(x$), "j") > i% THEN
         i% = INSTR(LCASE$(x$), "j")
     END IF

   ' Step back to find start of imaginary part
     FOR k% = i% TO 1 STEP -1
         IF INSTR("+-", MID$(x$, k%, 1)) THEN
             EXIT FOR
         END IF
     NEXT k%

   ' Error if pointers don't make sense
     IF j% = 0 OR j% > LEN(x$) THEN
         PRINT "Error: String2Complex - unrecognizable string format"
         SYSTEM
     END IF

   ' Grab the real part
     a.r = VAL(MID$(x$, j%))

   ' Grab the imaginary part
     IF k% > j% THEN
         a.i = VAL(MID$(x$, k%))
     ELSEIF k% = j% THEN
         a.r = 0
         a.i = VAL(MID$(x$, j%))
     ELSE
         a.i = 0
     END IF

END SUB
```

DOLLARS

The DOLLARS toolbox contains three functions for working with monetary amounts.

QuickBASIC provides a way for you to put commas between groups of three digits in numbers as they're printed or displayed. However, the Comma$ and DollarString$ functions have the added advantage of allowing you to manipulate the string results further before outputting the results.

The Round function is presented here as a means of rounding dollar amounts to the nearest cent, but you can also use it for scientific and engineering calculations when you want to round numbers to a given number of decimal places.

Name	Type	Description
DOLLARS.BAS		Demo module
Comma$	Func	Double-precision with commas inserted
DollarString$	Func	Dollar representation rounded with commas
Round#	Func	Rounding at specified decimal place

Demo Module: DOLLARS

```
' *****************************************
' **  Name:        DOLLARS                **
' **  Type:        Toolbox                **
' **  Module:      DOLLARS.BAS            **
' **  Language:    Microsoft QuickBASIC 4.00  **
' *****************************************
'
' USAGE:         No command line parameters
' .MAK FILE:     (none)
' PARAMETERS:    (none)
' VARIABLES:     n#          Number for demonstration of the functions

DECLARE FUNCTION Comma$ (n#)
DECLARE FUNCTION DollarString$ (amount#, length%)
DECLARE FUNCTION Round# (n#, powerOfTen%)
```

(continued)

continued

```
CLS
n# = 1234567.76543#
PRINT "Number n#:", , n#
PRINT "Comma$(n#)", , Comma$(n#)
PRINT "Comma$(Round#(n#, -2))", Comma$(Round#(n#, -2))
PRINT
PRINT "DollarString$(n#, 20)", ":"; DollarString$(n#, 20); ":"
PRINT , , " 12345678901234567890"
PRINT

PRINT "Round#(n#, -3)", Round#(n#, -3)
PRINT "Round#(n#, -2)", Round#(n#, -2)
PRINT "Round#(n#, -1)", Round#(n#, -1)
PRINT "Round#(n#, 0)", , Round#(n#, 0)
PRINT "Round#(n#, 1)", , Round#(n#, 1)
PRINT "Round#(n#, 2)", , Round#(n#, 2)
```

Function: Comma$

Returns a string representation of a given double-precision number, with commas separating groups of three digits to the left of the decimal point. The returned string is the same as that returned by the QuickBASIC STR$ function, except for the addition of the commas.

```
' **********************************************
' **   Name:        Comma$                    **
' **   Type:        Function                  **
' **   Module:      DOLLARS.BAS               **
' **   Language:    Microsoft QuickBASIC 4.00 **
' **********************************************
'
' Creates a string representing a double-precision
' number, with commas inserted every three digits.
'
' EXAMPLE OF USE:    n$ = Comma$(n#)
' PARAMETERS:        n#     Number to be formatted
' VARIABLES:         tn$    Temporary string of the number
'                    dp%    Position of the decimal point
'                    i%     Index into tn$
' MODULE LEVEL
'   DECLARATIONS:           DECLARE FUNCTION Comma$ (n#)
```

(continued)

continued

```
FUNCTION Comma$ (n#) STATIC
    tn$ = STR$(n#)
    dp% = INSTR(tn$, ".")
    IF dp% = 0 THEN
        dp% = LEN(tn$) + 1
    END IF
    IF dp% > 4 THEN
        FOR i% = dp% - 3 TO 3 STEP -3
            tn$ = LEFT$(tn$, i% - 1) + "," + MID$(tn$, i%)
        NEXT i%
    END IF
    Comma$ = LTRIM$(tn$)
END FUNCTION
```

Function: DollarString$

Returns a string representation of a dollar amount, as passed in a double-precision variable. The Round# function rounds the number to the nearest penny, and the Comma$ function separates each group of three digits to the left of the decimal point with commas. The string is then padded on the left with spaces until the desired string length is achieved, and a dollar sign is placed to the left of the spaces. Thus, you can conveniently display the dollar amounts in columns.

```
' **************************************************
' **  Name:          DollarString$                **
' **  Type:          Function                     **
' **  Module:        DOLLARS.BAS                  **
' **  Language:      Microsoft QuickBASIC 4.00    **
' **************************************************
'
' Returns a string representation of a dollar amount,
' rounded to the nearest cent, with commas separating
' groups of three digits, and with a preceding dollar sign.
'
' EXAMPLE OF USE:    d$ = DollarString$(dollars#)
' PARAMETERS:        dollars#   Amount of money
' VARIABLES:         tmp$       Temporary working string
' MODULE LEVEL
'   DECLARATIONS:    DECLARE FUNCTION Comma$ (n#)
'                    DECLARE FUNCTION DollarString$ (amount#, length%)
'                    DECLARE FUNCTION Round# (n#, place%)
```

(continued)

continued

```
FUNCTION DollarString$ (amount#, length%) STATIC
    tmp$ = SPACE$(length%) + "$" + Comma$(Round#(amount#, -2))
    DollarString$ = RIGHT$(tmp$, length%)
    tmp$ = ""
END FUNCTION
```

Function: Round#

Rounds numbers to any decimal position, as specified by the passed power of ten rounding value. For example, to round pi to the nearest integer value, you would use Round#(3.1416#, 0); to round ²/₃ of ten dollars to the nearest cent, Round#(6.6666667#, −2); and finally, to round the distance to the moon to the nearest thousand miles, Round#(238857#, 3).

```
' ****************************************
' **   Name:        Round#               **
' **   Type:        Function             **
' **   Module:      DOLLARS.BAS          **
' **   Language:    Microsoft QuickBASIC 4.00  **
' ****************************************
'
' Rounds a number at the power of 10 decimal place.
'
' EXAMPLE OF USE:  x# = Round#(n#, powerOfTen%)
' EXAMPLES:        Round#(12.3456#, -2) = 12.35#
'                  Round#(12.3456#, -1) = 12.3#
'                  Round#(12.3456#,  0) = 12#
'                  Round#(12.3456#,  1) = 10#
' PARAMETERS:      n#          Number to be rounded
'                  powerOfTen% Power of 10 for rounding the number
' VARIABLES:       pTen#       10 raised to the indicated power of 10
' MODULE LEVEL
'   DECLARATIONS:            DECLARE FUNCTION Round# (n#, powerOfTen%)
'
FUNCTION Round# (n#, powerOfTen%) STATIC
    pTen# = 10# ^ powerOfTen%
    Round# = INT(n# / pTen# + .5#) * pTen#
END FUNCTION
```

DOSCALLS

These routines use the Interrupt and InterruptX subprograms, provided as part of the QuickBASIC package, to access the operating system through software interrupts. The information returned by these functions and subprograms is extensive and useful.

The DOSCALLS demo module proceeds in this way:

The BufferedKeyInput$ function prompts you to enter up to nine characters. The appearance of the prompt and the input action from the keyboard seem very similar to the QuickBASIC INPUT statement, but there are some fundamental differences.

Next, the DOSVersion! function returns the MS-DOS version number.

The SetDrive subprogram temporarily switches the current drive, and the GetDrive$ function displays the results.

The GetMediaDescriptor subprogram returns several useful pieces of information about the current disk drive.

The Verify state is normally set using the MS-DOS VERIFY command, but with the GetVerifyState% function and the SetVerifyState subprogram, your programs can now control this setting directly.

The GetDiskFreeSpace subprogram returns five useful details about the structure of the data and free space on any disk drive in your system.

The GetCountry subprogram returns a data structure filled with details that enable you to modify your program outputs for use in other countries. Also returned is the address of the MS-DOS character translation subroutine called CaseMap, which translates certain characters for some foreign languages.

The TranslateCountry$ function uses the address returned by the GetCountry subprogram to translate a string of characters for the currently set country.

The GetDirectory$ function and SetDirectory subprogram let you determine or set the current directory-path string.

The WriteToDevice subprogram is useful for outputting strings directly to the indicated device, using the MS-DOS output handler rather than QuickBASIC's. One advantage of this approach is in being able to use the ANSI.SYS escape-code sequences to control cursor movement, screen mode, and color attributes.

Finally, the GetFileAttributes and SetFileAttributes subprograms let you determine or change the file attribute bits as desired. With these routines, it's easy to hide or unhide files and to set or clear the archive bit for use by the MS-DOS XCOPY command.

Name	Type	Description
DOSCALLS.BAS		Demo module
BufferedKeyInput$	Func	ASCII string of specified length
DOSVersion!	Func	Version number of MS-DOS returned
GetCountry	Sub	Current country setting
GetDirectory$	Func	Path to disk directory specified
GetDiskFreeSpace	Sub	Disk space format and usage for input drive
GetDrive$	Func	Current drive string
GetFileAttributes	Sub	Attribute bits for given file
GetMediaDescriptor	Sub	Drive information for system
GetVerifyState%	Func	Verify setting (state)
SetDirectory	Sub	Sets current directory
SetDrive	Sub	Sets current disk drive
SetFileAttributes	Sub	Sets the attribute bits for a given file
SetVerifyState	Sub	Sets or clears verify state (writing to file)
TranslateCountry$	Func	Translates string—current country setting
WriteToDevice	Sub	Outputs a string to a device

Demo Module: DOSCALLS

```
' *************************************************
' ** Name:         DOSCALLS                      **
' ** Type:         Toolbox                       **
' ** Module:       DOSCALLS.BAS                  **
' ** Language:     Microsoft QuickBASIC 4.00     **
' *************************************************
'
' Demonstrates several interrupt calls to MS-DOS.
'
' USAGE:         No command line parameters
' REQUIREMENTS:  MS-DOS 3.0 or later
'                MIXED.QLB/.LIB
' .MAK FILE:     (none)
' PARAMETERS:    (none)
' VARIABLES:     buffer$      String for buffered input demonstration
```

(continued)

continued

```
'            x$           Buffered input string
'            drive$       Current disk drive name
'            desc         Structure of type MediaDescriptorType
'            state%       Current status of the Verify state
'            oppositeState%   Opposite state for Verify
'            disk         Structure of type DiskFreeSpaceType
'            country      Structure of type CountryType
'            i%           Loop index for creating translation characters
'            a$           Characters to be translated
'            path$        Current directory
'            result%      Result code from call to SetDirectory
'            t$           Temporary copy of TIME$
'            attr         Structure of type FileAttributesType
'            fileName$    Name of file for determining file attributes

TYPE RegType
    ax    AS INTEGER
    bx    AS INTEGER
    cx    AS INTEGER
    dx    AS INTEGER
    bp    AS INTEGER
    si    AS INTEGER
    di    AS INTEGER
    flags AS INTEGER
END TYPE

TYPE RegTypeX
    ax    AS INTEGER
    bx    AS INTEGER
    cx    AS INTEGER
    dx    AS INTEGER
    bp    AS INTEGER
    si    AS INTEGER
    di    AS INTEGER
    flags AS INTEGER
    ds    AS INTEGER
    es    AS INTEGER
END TYPE

TYPE MediaDescriptorType
    sectorsPerAllocationUnit AS INTEGER
    bytesPerSector AS INTEGER
    FATIdentificationByte AS INTEGER
END TYPE
```

(continued)

continued

```
    TYPE DiskFreeSpaceType
        sectorsPerCluster AS INTEGER
        bytesPerSector AS INTEGER
        clustersPerDrive AS LONG
        availableClusters AS LONG
        availableBytes AS LONG
    END TYPE

    TYPE CountryType
        dateTimeFormat AS STRING * 11
        currencySymbol AS STRING * 4
        thousandsSeparator AS STRING * 1
        decimalSeparator AS STRING * 1
        dateSeparator AS STRING * 1
        timeSeparator AS STRING * 1
        currencyThenSymbol AS INTEGER
        currencySymbolSpace AS INTEGER
        currencyPlaces AS INTEGER
        hours24 AS INTEGER
        caseMapSegment AS INTEGER
        caseMapOffset AS INTEGER
        dataListSeparator AS STRING * 1
    END TYPE

    TYPE FileAttributesType
        readOnly AS INTEGER
        hidden AS INTEGER
        systemFile AS INTEGER
        archive AS INTEGER
        result AS INTEGER
    END TYPE

' Subprograms
DECLARE SUB Interrupt (intnum%, inreg AS RegType, outreg AS RegType)
DECLARE SUB InterruptX (intnum%, inreg AS RegTypeX, outreg AS RegTypeX)
DECLARE SUB SetDrive (drive$)
DECLARE SUB GetMediaDescriptor (drive$, desc AS MediaDescriptorType)
DECLARE SUB SetVerifyState (state%)
DECLARE SUB GetDiskFreeSpace (drive$, disk AS DiskFreeSpaceType)
DECLARE SUB GetCountry (country AS CountryType)
DECLARE SUB CaseMap (character%, BYVAL Segment%, BYVAL Offset%)
DECLARE SUB SetDirectory (path$, result%)
DECLARE SUB WriteToDevice (handle%, a$, result%)
DECLARE SUB GetFileAttributes (fileName$, attr AS FileAttributesType)
DECLARE SUB SetFileAttributes (fileName$, attr AS FileAttributesType)
```

(continued)

continued

```
' Functions
  DECLARE FUNCTION DOSVersion! ()
  DECLARE FUNCTION BufferedKeyInput$ (n%)
  DECLARE FUNCTION GetDrive$ ()
  DECLARE FUNCTION GetVerifyState% ()
  DECLARE FUNCTION TranslateCountry$ (a$, country AS CountryType)
  DECLARE FUNCTION GetDirectory$ (drive$)

' Try the Buffered Keyboard Input call
  CLS
  PRINT "BufferedKeyInput$:"
  PRINT "Enter a string of up to nine characters...  ";
  x$ = BufferedKeyInput$(9)
  PRINT
  PRINT "Here's the nine-character string result... ";
  PRINT CHR$(34); x$; CHR$(34)

' Get the MS-DOS version number
  PRINT
  PRINT "DosVersion!:"
  PRINT "DOS Version number is "; DOSVersion!

' Demonstrate the GetDrive and SetDrive routines
  PRINT
  PRINT "GetDrive$ and SetDrive:"
  drive$ = GetDrive$
  PRINT "The current drive is "; drive$
  PRINT "Setting the current drive to A:"
  SetDrive "A:"
  PRINT "Now the current drive is "; GetDrive$
  PRINT "Setting the current drive back to "; drive$
  SetDrive drive$
  PRINT "Now the current drive is "; GetDrive$

' Call the MS-DOS "Media Descriptor" function for the current drive
  PRINT
  PRINT "GetMediaDescriptor"
  DIM desc AS MediaDescriptorType
  GetMediaDescriptor drive$, desc
  PRINT "Drive                        "; drive$
  PRINT "Sectors per allocation unit "; desc.sectorsPerAllocationUnit
  PRINT "Bytes per sector            "; desc.bytesPerSector
  PRINT "FAT identification byte     &H"; HEX$(desc.FATIdentificationByte)
```

(continued)

continued

```
' Wait for user
  PRINT
  PRINT
  PRINT "Press any key to continue"
  DO
  LOOP UNTIL INKEY$ <> ""
  CLS

' Demonstrate the GetVerifyState and SetVerifyState routines
  PRINT
  PRINT "GetVerifyState% and SetVerifyState:"
  state% = GetVerifyState%
  PRINT "Current verify state is"; state%
  oppositeState% = 1 AND NOT state%
  SetVerifyState oppositeState%
  PRINT "Now the verify state is"; GetVerifyState%
  SetVerifyState state%
  PRINT "Now the verify state is"; GetVerifyState%

' Determine free space on the current drive
  PRINT
  PRINT "GetDiskFreeSpace:"
  DIM disk AS DiskFreeSpaceType
  GetDiskFreeSpace drive$, disk
  PRINT "Sectors per cluster      "; disk.sectorsPerCluster
  PRINT "Bytes per sector         "; disk.bytesPerSector
  PRINT "Total clusters on drive  "; disk.clustersPerDrive
  PRINT "Available clusters       "; disk.availableClusters
  PRINT "Available bytes          "; disk.availableBytes

' Wait for user
  PRINT
  PRINT
  PRINT "Press any key to continue"
  DO
  LOOP UNTIL INKEY$ <> ""
  CLS

' Get country-dependent information
  PRINT
  PRINT "GetCountry:"
  DIM country AS CountryType
  GetCountry country
  PRINT "Date and time format     "; country.dateTimeFormat
  PRINT "Currency symbol          "; country.currencySymbol
  PRINT "Thousands separator      "; country.thousandsSeparator
```

(continued)

continued

```
        PRINT "Decimal separator          "; country.decimalSeparator
        PRINT "Date separator             "; country.dateSeparator
        PRINT "Time separator             "; country.timeSeparator
        PRINT "Currency before symbol     "; country.currencyThenSymbol
        PRINT "Currency symbol space      "; country.currencySymbolSpace
        PRINT "Currency decimal places";    country.currencyPlaces
        PRINT "24-hour time               "; country.hours24
        PRINT "Case map segment           "; country.caseMapSegment
        PRINT "Case map offset            "; country.caseMapOffset
        PRINT "Data list separator        "; country.dataListSeparator

    ' Let's translate lowercase characters for the current country
        PRINT
        PRINT "TranslateCountry$:"
        FOR i% = 128 TO 175
            a$ = a$ + CHR$(i%)
        NEXT i%
        PRINT "Character codes 128 to 175, before and after translation... "
        PRINT a$
        PRINT TranslateCountry$(a$, country)

    ' Wait for user
        PRINT
        PRINT
        PRINT "Press any key to continue"
        DO
        LOOP UNTIL INKEY$ <> ""
        CLS

    ' Demonstrate the SetDirectory and GetDirectory routines
        PRINT
        PRINT "GetDirectory$ and SetDirectory:"
        path$ = GetDirectory$(drive$)
        PRINT "Current directory is "; path$
        SetDirectory GetDrive$ + "\", result%
        PRINT "Now the directory is "; GetDirectory$(drive$)
        SetDirectory path$, result%
        PRINT "Now the directory is "; GetDirectory$(drive$)

    ' Write to a file or device
        PRINT
        PRINT "WriteToDevice:"
        PRINT "Writing a 'bell' character to the CRT"
        WriteToDevice 1, CHR$(7), result%
        t$ = TIME$
```

(continued)

continued

```
    DO
    LOOP UNTIL t$ <> TIME$
    PRINT "Writing a 'bell' character to the printer"
    WriteToDevice 4, CHR$(7), result%

' Wait for user
    PRINT
    PRINT
    PRINT "Press any key to continue"
    DO
    LOOP UNTIL INKEY$ <> ""
    CLS

' Demonstrate the GetFileAttributes and SetFileAttributes routines
    PRINT
    PRINT "GetFileAttributes and SetFileAttributes:"
    DIM attr AS FileAttributesType
    fileName$ = "C:\IBMDOS.COM"
    GetFileAttributes fileName$, attr
    PRINT "File attributes for "; fileName$
    PRINT "Result of call "; attr.result
    PRINT "Read only      "; attr.readOnly
    PRINT "Hidden         "; attr.hidden
    PRINT "System         "; attr.systemFile
    PRINT "Archive        "; attr.archive
    PRINT
    attr.hidden = 0
    SetFileAttributes fileName$, attr
    GetFileAttributes fileName$, attr
    PRINT "File attributes for "; fileName$
    PRINT "Result of call "; attr.result
    PRINT "Read only      "; attr.readOnly
    PRINT "Hidden         "; attr.hidden
    PRINT "System         "; attr.systemFile
    PRINT "Archive        "; attr.archive
    PRINT
    attr.hidden = 1
    SetFileAttributes fileName$, attr
    GetFileAttributes fileName$, attr
    PRINT "File attributes for "; fileName$
    PRINT "Result of call "; attr.result
    PRINT "Read only      "; attr.readOnly
    PRINT "Hidden         "; attr.hidden
    PRINT "System         "; attr.systemFile
    PRINT "Archive        "; attr.archive
    PRINT
```

Function: BufferedKeyInput$

Calls the MS-DOS Buffered Keyboard Input routine, which is similar in concept to QuickBASIC's LINE INPUT statement but contains some useful differences.

When you call the BufferedKeyInput$ function, you pass an integer that tells the MS-DOS routine the maximum number of characters to be input. If extra characters are typed, the computer beeps, and the keystrokes are ignored. The Backspace and Left arrow keys allow editing of the input, and the screen is constantly updated to display the input buffer at the current cursor location.

The returned string is always n% characters in length, even if the user entered fewer than n% characters. If necessary, the string is padded on the right with spaces to bring the length up to n%.

```
' *************************************************
' ** Name:           BufferedKeyInput$         **
' ** Type:           Function                  **
' ** Module:         DOSCALLS.BAS              **
' ** Language:       Microsoft QuickBASIC 4.00 **
' *************************************************
'
' Calls the "Buffered Keyboard Input" MS-DOS function
' and returns the entered string of characters.
'
' EXAMPLE OF USE:    x$ = BufferedKeyInput$(n%)
' PARAMETERS:        buffer$    Buffer for keyboard input
' VARIABLES:         regX       Structure of type RegTypeX
'                    bufSize%   Length of buffer$
'                    b$         Working copy of buffer$
'                    count%     Count of characters entered
' MODULE LEVEL
'   DECLARATIONS:    TYPE RegTypeX
'                        ax    AS INTEGER
'                        bx    AS INTEGER
'                        cx    AS INTEGER
'                        dx    AS INTEGER
'                        bp    AS INTEGER
'                        si    AS INTEGER
'                        di    AS INTEGER
'                        flags AS INTEGER
```

(continued)

continued

```
'                    ds   AS INTEGER
'                    es   AS INTEGER
'               END TYPE
'
'   DECLARE SUB InterruptX (intnum%, inreg AS RegTypeX, outreg AS RegTypeX)
'   DECLARE FUNCTION BufferedKeyInput$ (n%)
'
   FUNCTION BufferedKeyInput$ (n%) STATIC
       DIM regX AS RegTypeX
       b$ = CHR$(n% + 1) + SPACE$(n% + 2)
       regX.ax = &HA00
       regX.ds = VARSEG(b$)
       regX.dx = SADD(b$)
       InterruptX &H21, regX, regX
       count% = ASC(MID$(b$, 2, 1))
       BufferedKeyInput$ = MID$(b$, 3, count%) + SPACE$(n% - count%)
   END FUNCTION
```

Function: DOSVersion!

Returns the version number of MS-DOS. Sometimes it's necessary to know the current version of MS-DOS before proceeding with certain MS-DOS functions.

```
'  **********************************************
'  **   Name:        DOSVersion!                **
'  **   Type:        Function                   **
'  **   Module:      DOSCALLS.BAS               **
'  **   Language:    Microsoft QuickBASIC 4.00  **
'  **********************************************
'
'  Returns the version number of MS-DOS.
'
'  EXAMPLE OF USE:  PRINT "MS-DOS Version number is "; DOSVersion!
'  PARAMETERS:      (none)
'  VARIABLES:       reg       Structure of type RegType
'                   major%    Integer part of the MS-DOS version number
'                   minor%    Fractional part of the MS-DOS version number
'  MODULE LEVEL
'    DECLARATIONS:  TYPE RegType
'                     ax    AS INTEGER
'                     bx    AS INTEGER
```

(continued)

continued

```
'                    cx    AS INTEGER
'                    dx    AS INTEGER
'                    bp    AS INTEGER
'                    si    AS INTEGER
'                    di    AS INTEGER
'                    flags AS INTEGER
'               END TYPE
'
'     DECLARE SUB Interrupt (intnum%, inreg AS RegType, outreg AS RegType)
'     DECLARE FUNCTION DOSVersion! ()
'
FUNCTION DOSVersion! STATIC
    DIM reg AS RegType
    reg.ax = &H3000
    Interrupt &H21, reg, reg
    major% = reg.ax MOD 256
    minor% = reg.ax \ 256
    DOSVersion! = major% + minor% / 100!
END FUNCTION
```

Subprogram: GetCountry

Returns information from MS-DOS about the current country settings. This information can be invaluable for programs slated to be marketed in more than one country. A program's data output can be modified to conform to the standards of each country. For example, the date 3-4-88 can refer to March 4th or April 3rd, depending on which part of the world you are in.

The date and time format string indicates the order of the six numeric values that make up a given date and time.

Several variables are returned to indicate the desirable way to format monetary values. These determine whether the currency symbol is before or after the monetary value, whether a space separates the two, and the number of decimal places to use.

The currency symbol is a four-character string such as "Lira". For dollars, the string contains three spaces followed by a $.

The thousands separator is a one-character string, usually a decimal point or a comma.

The decimal separator is also a one-character string, usually a decimal point or a comma.

The date separator is a one-character string such as "-" or "/".

The time separator is a one-character string such as ":".

The hours designation indicates whether a 24-hour format or an A.M. and P.M. 12-hour format is more commonly used. The CaseMap address is the segment and offset address of the MS-DOS character translation function. Refer to the TranslateCountry$ function to see how this address is used. (The CaseMap subprogram is discussed in Part III of this book.)

The data list separator is a one-character string such as ",".

```
' ***************************************************
' **   Name:       GetCountry                      **
' **   Type:       Subprogram                      **
' **   Module:     DOSCALLS.BAS                    **
' **   Language:   Microsoft QuickBASIC 4.00       **
' ***************************************************
'
' Returns country-dependent information as defined
' by MS-DOS.
'
' EXAMPLE OF USE:   GetCountry country
' PARAMETERS:       country    Structure of type CountryType
' VARIABLES:        regX       Structure of type RegTypeX
'                   c$         Buffer for data returned from interrupt
' MODULE LEVEL
'   DECLARATIONS:   TYPE RegTypeX
'                       ax    AS INTEGER
'                       bx    AS INTEGER
'                       cx    AS INTEGER
'                       dx    AS INTEGER
'                       bp    AS INTEGER
'                       si    AS INTEGER
'                       di    AS INTEGER
'                       flags AS INTEGER
'                       ds    AS INTEGER
'                       es    AS INTEGER
'                   END TYPE
'
'                   TYPE CountryType
'                       DateTimeFormat AS STRING * 11
'                       CurrencySymbol AS STRING * 4
'                       ThousandsSeparator AS STRING * 1
'                       DecimalSeparator AS STRING * 1
'                       DateSeparator AS STRING * 1
'                       TimeSeparator AS STRING * 1
```

(continued)

continued

```
'                        CurrencyThenSymbol AS INTEGER
'                        CurrencySymbolSpace AS INTEGER
'                        CurrencyPlaces AS INTEGER
'                        Hours24 AS INTEGER
'                        caseMapSegment AS INTEGER
'                        caseMapOffset AS INTEGER
'                        DataListSeparator AS STRING * 1
'                    END TYPE
'
'   DECLARE SUB InterruptX (intnum%, inreg AS RegTypeX, outreg AS RegTypeX)
'   DECLARE SUB GetCountry (country AS CountryType)
'
   SUB GetCountry (country AS CountryType)
       DIM regX AS RegTypeX
       regX.ax = &H3800
       c$ = SPACE$(32)
       regX.ds = VARSEG(c$)
       regX.dx = SADD(c$)
       InterruptX &H21, regX, regX
       SELECT CASE CVI(LEFT$(c$, 2))
       CASE 0
           country.dateTimeFormat = "h:m:s m/d/y"
       CASE 1
           country.dateTimeFormat = "h:m:s d/m/y"
       CASE 2
           country.dateTimeFormat = "y/m/d h:m:s"
       CASE ELSE
           country.dateTimeFormat = "h:m:s m/d/y"
       END SELECT
       country.currencySymbol = MID$(c$, 3, 4)
       country.thousandsSeparator = MID$(c$, 8, 1)
       country.decimalSeparator = MID$(c$, 10, 1)
       country.dateSeparator = MID$(c$, 12, 1)
       country.timeSeparator = MID$(c$, 14, 1)
       country.currencyThenSymbol = ASC(MID$(c$, 16)) AND 1
       country.currencySymbolSpace = (ASC(MID$(c$, 16)) AND 2) \ 2
       country.currencyPlaces = ASC(MID$(c$, 17))
       country.hours24 = ASC(MID$(c$, 18))
       country.caseMapSegment = CVI(MID$(c$, 21, 2))
       country.caseMapOffset = CVI(MID$(c$, 19, 2))
       country.dataListSeparator = MID$(c$, 23, 1)
   END SUB
```

Function: GetDirectory$

Returns the complete path for any drive on your system. The called MS-DOS function doesn't return the drive designation or the first slash, representing the root directory, but the GetDirectory$ function adds these parts to the returned string for you.

For the current directory of the current, default drive, pass a null string. For a specific drive, pass a string containing the letter of the drive in the first character position. For example, GetDirectory$("A:") might return *A:\QB4\SOURCE*.

```
' **************************************************
' **   Name:         GetDirectory$               **
' **   Type:         Function                    **
' **   Module:       DOSCALLS.BAS                **
' **   Language:     Microsoft QuickBASIC 4.00   **
' **************************************************
'
' Returns the name of the current directory for any drive.
'
' EXAMPLE OF USE:    path$ = GetDirectory$(drive$)
' PARAMETERS:        drive$     Drive of concern, or null string for default
'                               drive
' VARIABLES:         regX       Structure of type RegTypeX
'                    d$         Working copy of drive$
'                    p$         Buffer space for returned path
' MODULE LEVEL
'   DECLARATIONS:    TYPE RegTypeX
'                      ax    AS INTEGER
'                      bx    AS INTEGER
'                      cx    AS INTEGER
'                      dx    AS INTEGER
'                      bp    AS INTEGER
'                      si    AS INTEGER
'                      di    AS INTEGER
'                      flags AS INTEGER
'                      ds    AS INTEGER
'                      es    AS INTEGER
'                    END TYPE
'
'   DECLARE SUB InterruptX (intnum%, inreg AS RegTypeX, outreg AS RegTypeX)
'   DECLARE FUNCTION GetDirectory$ (drive$)
```

(continued)

continued

```
FUNCTION GetDirectory$ (drive$) STATIC
    DIM regX AS RegTypeX
    IF drive$ = "" THEN
        d$ = GetDrive$
    ELSE
        d$ = UCASE$(drive$)
    END IF
    drive% = ASC(d$) - 64
    regX.dx = drive%
    regX.ax = &H4700
    p$ = SPACE$(64)
    regX.ds = VARSEG(p$)
    regX.si = SADD(p$)
    InterruptX &H21, regX, regX
    p$ = LEFT$(p$, INSTR(p$, CHR$(0)) - 1)
    GetDirectory$ = LEFT$(d$, 1) + ":\" + p$
    IF regX.flags AND 1 THEN
        GetDirectory$ = ""
    END IF
END FUNCTION
```

Subprogram: GetDiskFreeSpace

Returns information about the current usage and format of a given disk drive's contents. The data structure of type DiskFreeSpaceType lists the various information returned by this subprogram. Some information, such as the sectors per cluster, bytes per sector, and total clusters information, is constant in nature, so the subprogram always returns the same value for a given drive. The available clusters and available bytes are the variable information that this subprogram returns.

Probably the most important information this subprogram returns is the total bytes available. Call this subprogram before creating a large file on a disk to prevent the program from being interrupted by a "disk full" message. This lets you prompt the user to insert a different disk or take other action before any data is lost.

```
' ****************************************************
' **   Name:          GetDiskFreeSpace              **
' **   Type:          Subprogram                    **
' **   Module:        DOSCALLS.BAS                  **
' **   Language:      Microsoft QuickBASIC 4.00     **
' ****************************************************
'
' Get information about a drive's organization, including
' total number of bytes available.
'
' EXAMPLE OF USE:    GetDiskFreeSpace drive$, disk
' PARAMETERS:        drive$     Disk drive designation
'                    disk       Structure of type DiskFreeSpaceType
' VARIABLES:         reg        Structure of type RegType
'                    drive%     Numeric drive designation
' MODULE LEVEL
'   DECLARATIONS:    TYPE RegType
'                        ax    AS INTEGER
'                        bx    AS INTEGER
'                        cx    AS INTEGER
'                        dx    AS INTEGER
'                        bp    AS INTEGER
'                        si    AS INTEGER
'                        di    AS INTEGER
'                        flags AS INTEGER
'                    END TYPE
'
'                    TYPE DiskFreeSpaceType
'                        sectorsPerCluster AS INTEGER
'                        bytesPerSector AS INTEGER
'                        clustersPerDrive AS LONG
'                        availableClusters AS LONG
'                        availableBytes AS LONG
'                    END TYPE
'
'     DECLARE SUB Interrupt (intnum%, inreg AS RegType, outreg AS RegType)
'     DECLARE SUB GetDiskFreeSpace (drive$, disk AS DiskFreeSpaceType)
'
  SUB GetDiskFreeSpace (drive$, disk AS DiskFreeSpaceType)
      DIM reg AS RegType
      IF drive$ <> "" THEN
          drive% = ASC(UCASE$(drive$)) - 64
      ELSE
          drive% = 0
      END IF
```

(continued)

continued

```
        IF drive% >= 0 THEN
            reg.dx = drive%
        ELSE
            reg.dx = 0
        END IF
        reg.ax = &H3600
        Interrupt &H21, reg, reg
        disk.sectorsPerCluster = reg.ax
        disk.bytesPerSector = reg.cx
        IF reg.dx >= 0 THEN
            disk.clustersPerDrive = reg.dx
        ELSE
            disk.clustersPerDrive = reg.dx + 65536
        END IF
        IF reg.bx >= 0 THEN
            disk.availableClusters = reg.bx
        ELSE
            disk.availableClusters = reg.bx + 65536
        END IF
        disk.availableBytes = disk.availableClusters * reg.ax * reg.cx
    END SUB
```

Function: GetDrive$

Returns a two-character string designation for the current disk drive. The first character is always an uppercase letter, and the second character is always a colon.

```
' ***********************************************
' **   Name:          GetDrive$                **
' **   Type:          Function                 **
' **   Module:        DOSCALLS.BAS             **
' **   Language:      Microsoft QuickBASIC 4.00 **
' ***********************************************
'
' Returns the current disk drive name, such as "A:".
'
' EXAMPLE OF USE:   drive$ = GetDrive$
' PARAMETERS:       (none)
' VARIABLES:        reg         Structure of type RegType
```

(continued)

continued

```
' MODULE LEVEL
'   DECLARATIONS:  TYPE RegType
'                      ax      AS INTEGER
'                      bx      AS INTEGER
'                      cx      AS INTEGER
'                      dx      AS INTEGER
'                      bp      AS INTEGER
'                      si      AS INTEGER
'                      di      AS INTEGER
'                      flags AS INTEGER
'                  END TYPE
'
'   DECLARE SUB Interrupt (intnum%, inreg AS RegType, outreg AS RegType)
'   DECLARE FUNCTION GetDrive$ ()
'
FUNCTION GetDrive$ STATIC
    DIM reg AS RegType
    reg.ax = &H1900
    Interrupt &H21, reg, reg
    GetDrive$ = CHR$((reg.ax AND &HFF) + 65) + ":"
END FUNCTION
```

Subprogram: GetFileAttributes

Returns current attribute bits for a given file. Each file has several attribute bits that serve useful purposes in MS-DOS. For example, whenever a change is made to a file, the "archive" bit is set. The MS-DOS XCOPY utility can check the setting of this bit and copy only those files that have been modified since the last XCOPY command was given for the same set of files. XCOPY clears this bit when a file is copied.

The "read only" attribute bit protects a file by preventing you from changing or deleting its contents. You can read the file, list it, or access it in any normal way, but the operating system will generate an error if you try to edit or delete it.

The "hidden" attribute bit makes a file invisible to the user. A good example of this bit's action is shown by the module-level code that demonstrates this subprogram. The hidden file IBMDOS.COM has its "hidden" bit cleared and then reset. If you leave this bit cleared, the IBMDOS.COM file will show up in your root directory whenever you give the DIR command.

The "system" attribute bit marks files such as IBMBIO.COM and IBMDOS.COM as special system files. These two files are in the root directory of all your bootable disks and are necessary for MS-DOS to be able to successfully boot from a given disk.

The variable attr.result returns a *0* if the attempt to read the file attribute bits was successful.

```
' **************************************************
' **   Name:        GetFileAttributes             **
' **   Type:        Subprogram                    **
' **   Module:      DOSCALLS.BAS                  **
' **   Language:    Microsoft QuickBASIC 4.00     **
' **************************************************
'
' Returns the file attribute settings for a file.
'
' EXAMPLE OF USE:  GetFileAttributes fileName$, attr
' PARAMETERS:      fileName$   Name of file
'                  attr        Structure of type FileAttributesType
' VARIABLES:       regX        Structure of type RegTypeX
'                  f$          Null terminated copy of fileName$
' MODULE LEVEL
'    DECLARATIONS: TYPE RegTypeX
'                      ax    AS INTEGER
'                      bx    AS INTEGER
'                      cx    AS INTEGER
'                      dx    AS INTEGER
'                      bp    AS INTEGER
'                      si    AS INTEGER
'                      di    AS INTEGER
'                      flags AS INTEGER
'                      ds    AS INTEGER
'                      es    AS INTEGER
'                  END TYPE
'
'                  TYPE FileAttributesType
'                      readOnly AS INTEGER
'                      hidden AS INTEGER
'                      systemFile AS INTEGER
'                      archive AS INTEGER
'                      result AS INTEGER
'                  END TYPE
'
'    DECLARE SUB InterruptX (intnum%, inreg AS RegTypeX, outreg AS RegTypeX)
'    DECLARE SUB GetFileAttributes (fileName$, attr AS FileAttributesType)
```

(continued)

continued

```
    SUB GetFileAttributes (fileName$, attr AS FileAttributesType) STATIC
        DIM regX AS RegTypeX
        regX.ax = &H4300
        f$ = fileName$ + CHR$(0)
        regX.ds = VARSEG(f$)
        regX.dx = SADD(f$)
        InterruptX &H21, regX, regX
        IF regX.flags AND 1 THEN
            attr.result = regX.ax
        ELSE
            attr.result = 0
        END IF
        attr.readOnly = regX.cx AND 1
        attr.hidden = (regX.cx \ 2) AND 1
        attr.systemFile = (regX.cx \ 4) AND 1
        attr.archive = (regX.cx \ 32) AND 1
    END SUB
```

Subprogram: GetMediaDescriptor

Returns media information about any disk drive currently defined by MS-DOS. For any given drive, you can determine the number of sectors per allocation unit, the number of bytes per sector, and the FAT identification byte MS-DOS uses to determine how to treat the drive. This information is returned by the MS-DOS function 21H.

The GetDiskFreeSpace subprogram returns related information.

```
' ****************************************************
' **   Name:          GetMediaDescriptor            **
' **   Type:          Subprogram                   **
' **   Module:        DOSCALLS.BAS                 **
' **   Language:      Microsoft QuickBASIC 4.00    **
' ****************************************************
'
' Calls the MS-DOS "Get Media Descriptor" function for
' the indicated drive.  Results are returned in a
' structure of type MediaDescriptorType.
'
' EXAMPLE OF USE:     GetMediaDescriptor drive$, desc
' PARAMETERS:         drive$      Drive designation, such as "A:"
'                     desc        Structure of type MediaDescriptorType
```

(continued)

continued

```
' VARIABLES:      regX       Structure of type RegTypeX
'                 drive%     Numeric drive designation
' MODULE LEVEL
'   DECLARATIONS: TYPE RegTypeX
'                     ax    AS INTEGER
'                     bx    AS INTEGER
'                     cx    AS INTEGER
'                     dx    AS INTEGER
'                     bp    AS INTEGER
'                     si    AS INTEGER
'                     di    AS INTEGER
'                     flags AS INTEGER
'                     ds    AS INTEGER
'                     es    AS INTEGER
'                 END TYPE
'
'                 TYPE MediaDescriptorType
'                     sectorsPerAllocationUnit AS INTEGER
'                     bytesPerSector AS INTEGER
'                     FATIdentificationByte AS INTEGER
'                 END TYPE
'
'   DECLARE SUB InterruptX (intnum%, inreg AS RegTypeX, outreg AS RegTypeX)
'   DECLARE SUB GetMediaDescriptor (drive$, desc AS MediaDescriptorType)
'
   SUB GetMediaDescriptor (drive$, desc AS MediaDescriptorType) STATIC
       DIM regX AS RegTypeX
       IF drive$ <> "" THEN
           drive% = ASC(UCASE$(drive$)) - 64
       ELSE
           drive% = 0
       END IF
       IF drive% >= 0 THEN
           regX.dx = drive%
       ELSE
           regX.dx = 0
       END IF
       regX.ax = &H1C00
       InterruptX &H21, regX, regX
       desc.sectorsPerAllocationUnit = regX.ax AND &HFF
       desc.bytesPerSector = regX.cx
       DEF SEG = regX.ds
       desc.FATIdentificationByte = PEEK(regX.bx)
       DEF SEG
   END SUB
```

Function: GetVerifyState%

Returns the current setting of the MS-DOS Verify flag. If Verify is on, this function returns a *1*. If Verify is off, a *0* is returned.

See the SetVerifyState subprogram to see how to set the Verify on or off as desired.

```
' **************************************************
' **   Name:          GetVerifyState%            **
' **   Type:          Function                  **
' **   Module:        DOSCALLS.BAS              **
' **   Language:      Microsoft QuickBASIC 4.00 **
' **************************************************
'
' Returns the current state of the MS-DOS "Verify After
' Write" flag.
'
' EXAMPLE OF USE:    state% = GetVerifyState%
' PARAMETERS:        (none)
' VARIABLES:         reg        Structure of type RegType
' MODULE LEVEL
'   DECLARATIONS:    TYPE RegTypeX
'                        ax    AS INTEGER
'                        bx    AS INTEGER
'                        cx    AS INTEGER
'                        dx    AS INTEGER
'                        bp    AS INTEGER
'                        si    AS INTEGER
'                        di    AS INTEGER
'                        flags AS INTEGER
'                    END TYPE
'
'       DECLARE SUB Interrupt (intnum%, inreg AS RegType, outreg AS RegType)
'       DECLARE FUNCTION GetVerifyState% ()

FUNCTION GetVerifyState% STATIC
    DIM reg AS RegType
    reg.ax = &H5400
    Interrupt &H21, reg, reg
    GetVerifyState% = reg.ax AND &HFF
END FUNCTION
```

Subprogram: SetDirectory

Sets the current directory for the default drive in the same way as the MS-DOS CHDIR command.

For example, to cause a program to change to the directory C:\TXT, use this program statement:

```
SetDirectory "C:\TXT", result%
```

The returned value of result% indicates whether the attempt to change the directory was successful. If result% is *0*, the directory change was successful.

```
' ***************************************************
' **   Name:        SetDirectory                   **
' **   Type:        Subprogram                     **
' **   Module:      DOSCALLS.BAS                   **
' **   Language:    Microsoft QuickBASIC 4.00      **
' ***************************************************
'
' Sets the current directory.
'
' EXAMPLE OF USE:   SetDirectory path$, result%
' PARAMETERS:       path$      The path to the directory
'                   result%    Returned error code, zero if successful
' VARIABLES:        regX       Structure of type RegTypeX
'                   p$         Null terminated copy of path$
' MODULE LEVEL
'    DECLARATIONS:  TYPE RegTypeX
'                      ax    AS INTEGER
'                      bx    AS INTEGER
'                      cx    AS INTEGER
'                      dx    AS INTEGER
'                      bp    AS INTEGER
'                      si    AS INTEGER
'                      di    AS INTEGER
'                      flags AS INTEGER
'                      ds    AS INTEGER
'                      es    AS INTEGER
'                   END TYPE
'
'    DECLARE SUB InterruptX (intnum%, inreg AS RegTypeX, outreg AS RegTypeX)
```

(continued)

continued

```
'    DECLARE SUB SetDirectory (path$, result%)
'
    SUB SetDirectory (path$, result%) STATIC
        DIM regX AS RegTypeX
        regX.ax = &H3B00
        p$ = path$ + CHR$(0)
        regX.ds = VARSEG(p$)
        regX.dx = SADD(p$)
        InterruptX &H21, regX, regX
        IF regX.flags AND 1 THEN
            result% = regX.ax
        ELSE
            result% = 0
        END IF
    END SUB
```

Subprogram: SetDrive

Lets a QuickBASIC program change the current disk drive. Another way of doing the same thing would be to use the SHELL statement:

```
SHELL "CD " + d$
```

However, this subprogram is much more efficient and much faster.

```
' *********************************************
' **   Name:         SetDrive                **
' **   Type:         Subprogram              **
' **   Module:       DOSCALLS.BAS            **
' **   Language:     Microsoft QuickBASIC 4.00 **
' *********************************************
'
' Calls MS-DOS to set the current drive.
'
' EXAMPLE OF USE:   SetDrive drive$
' PARAMETERS:       drive$    Drive designation, such as "A:"
' VARIABLES:        reg       Structure of type RegType
'                   drive%    Numeric value of drive
' MODULE LEVEL
'   DECLARATIONS:   TYPE RegTypeX
'                       ax    AS INTEGER
'                       bx    AS INTEGER
'                       cx    AS INTEGER
```

(continued)

continued

```
'                    dx    AS INTEGER
'                    bp    AS INTEGER
'                    si    AS INTEGER
'                    di    AS INTEGER
'                    flags AS INTEGER
'                END TYPE
'
'    DECLARE SUB Interrupt (intnum%, inreg AS RegType, outreg AS RegType)
'    DECLARE SUB SetDrive (drive$)

SUB SetDrive (drive$) STATIC
    DIM reg AS RegType
    IF drive$ <> "" THEN
        drive% = ASC(UCASE$(drive$)) - 65
    ELSE
        drive% = 0
    END IF
    IF drive% >= 0 THEN
        reg.dx = drive%
    ELSE
        reg.dx = 0
    END IF
    reg.ax = &HE00
    Interrupt &H21, reg, reg
END SUB
```

Subprogram: SetFileAttributes

Sets the file attribute bits for a file as desired. For example, to make a file invisible to the user, set the "hidden" attribute bit. To protect a file from accidentally being modified or deleted, set the "read only" attribute bit.

The GetFileAttributes subprogram describes these file attribute bits in more detail.

```
' ***************************************************
' **   Name:         SetFileAttributes             **
' **   Type:         Subprogram                    **
' **   Module:       DOSCALLS.BAS                  **
' **   Language:     Microsoft QuickBASIC 4.00     **
' ***************************************************
```

(continued)

continued

```
' Sets attribute bits for a file.
'
' EXAMPLE OF USE:  SetFileAttributes fileName$, attr
' PARAMETERS:      fileName$  Name of file
'                  attr       Structure of type FileAttributesType
' VARIABLES:       regX       Structure of type RegTypeX
'                  f$         Null terminated copy of fileName$
' MODULE LEVEL
'   DECLARATIONS:  TYPE RegTypeX
'                      ax    AS INTEGER
'                      bx    AS INTEGER
'                      cx    AS INTEGER
'                      dx    AS INTEGER
'                      bp    AS INTEGER
'                      si    AS INTEGER
'                      di    AS INTEGER
'                      flags AS INTEGER
'                      ds    AS INTEGER
'                      es    AS INTEGER
'                  END TYPE
'
'                  TYPE FileAttributesType
'                      readOnly AS INTEGER
'                      hidden AS INTEGER
'                      systemFile AS INTEGER
'                      archive AS INTEGER
'                      result AS INTEGER
'                  END TYPE
'
'   DECLARE SUB InterruptX (intnum%, inreg AS RegTypeX, outreg AS RegTypeX)
'   DECLARE SUB SetFileAttributes (fileName$, attr AS FileAttributesType)

SUB SetFileAttributes (fileName$, attr AS FileAttributesType)
    DIM regX AS RegTypeX
    regX.ax = &H4301
    IF attr.readOnly THEN
        regX.cx = 1
```

(continued)

continued

```
        ELSE
            regX.cx = 0
        END IF
        IF attr.hidden THEN
            regX.cx = regX.cx + 2
        END IF
        IF attr.systemFile THEN
            regX.cx = regX.cx + 4
        END IF
        IF attr.archive THEN
            regX.cx = regX.cx + 32
        END IF
        f$ = fileName$ + CHR$(0)
        regX.ds = VARSEG(f$)
        regX.dx = SADD(f$)
        InterruptX &H21, regX, regX
        IF regX.flags AND 1 THEN
            attr.result = regX.ax
        ELSE
            attr.result = 0
        END IF
END SUB
```

Subprogram: SetVerifyState

Sets or clears the write verify flag MS-DOS uses during disk file writing, duplicating the actions of the MS-DOS commands VERIFY ON and VERIFY OFF. If a parameter (state%) of 0 is passed to the routine, the subprogram sets the Verify state to off. If non-zero, it sets it to on.

To determine the current setting of the Verify flag, use the GetVerifyState% function.

```
' *************************************************
' **   Name:          SetVerifyState             **
' **   Type:          Subprogram                 **
' **   Module:        DOSCALLS.BAS               **
' **   Language:      Microsoft QuickBASIC 4.00  **
' *************************************************
```

(continued)

continued

```
' Sets or clears the "Verify After Write" MS-DOS flag.
'
' EXAMPLE OF USE:   SetVerifyState state%
' PARAMETERS:       -state%     If 0, resets Verify;  If non-zero,
'                               then sets Verify on
' VARIABLES:        reg         Structure of type RegType
' MODULE LEVEL
'   DECLARATIONS:   TYPE RegTypeX
'                       ax    AS INTEGER
'                       bx    AS INTEGER
'                       cx    AS INTEGER
'                       dx    AS INTEGER
'                       bp    AS INTEGER
'                       si    AS INTEGER
'                       di    AS INTEGER
'                       flags AS INTEGER
'                   END TYPE
'
'       DECLARE SUB Interrupt (intnum%, inreg AS RegType, outreg AS RegType)
'       DECLARE SUB SetVerifyState (state%)
'
    SUB SetVerifyState (state%) STATIC
        DIM reg AS RegType
        IF state% THEN
            reg.ax = &H2E01
        ELSE
            reg.ax = &H2E00
        END IF
        Interrupt &H21, reg, reg
    END SUB
```

Function: TranslateCountry$

Returns the translated version of the string passed to it, according to the current MS-DOS country setting. Only characters with byte values in the range 128 through 255 are candidates for translation.

Before calling this function, you must call the GetCountry subprogram to fill in the structure of type GetCountryType with the address of the translation routine in the operating system. This housekeeping is all taken care of automatically if you only remember to call GetCountry before calling TranslateCountry$.

The TranslateCountry$ function calls an assembly-language subprogram named CaseMap to translate each character of the passed string. CaseMap demonstrates the powerful DECLARE statement of QuickBASIC. (CaseMap is discussed in Part III of this book.) Notice that the segment% and offset% variables representing the address of the MS-DOS translation routine are passed by value rather than by address, the default.

```
' *************************************************
' **   Name:          TranslateCountry$           **
' **   Type:          Function                    **
' **   Module:        DOSCALLS.BAS                **
' **   Language:      Microsoft QuickBASIC 4.00   **
' *************************************************
'
' Returns a string of characters translated according to
' the current country setting of MS-DOS.
'
' EXAMPLE OF USE:  b$ = TranslateCountry$(a$, country)
' PARAMETERS:      a$         String to be translated
'                  country    Structure of type CountryType
' VARIABLES:       i%         Index to each character of a$
'                  c%         Byte value of each character in a$
' MODULE LEVEL
'   DECLARATIONS:  TYPE CountryType
'                    DateTimeFormat AS STRING * 11
'                    CurrencySymbol AS STRING * 4
'                    ThousandsSeparator AS STRING * 1
'                    DecimalSeparator AS STRING * 1
'                    DateSeparator AS STRING * 1
'                    TimeSeparator AS STRING * 1
'                    CurrencyThenSymbol AS INTEGER
'                    CurrencySymbolSpace AS INTEGER
'                    CurrencyPlaces AS INTEGER
'                    Hours24 AS INTEGER
'                    caseMapSegment AS INTEGER
'                    caseMapOffset AS INTEGER
'                    DataListSeparator AS STRING * 1
'                  END TYPE
'
'                  DECLARE SUB CaseMap (character%, BYVAL Segment%, BYVAL Offset%)
'                  DECLARE FUNCTION TranslateCountry$ (a$, country AS CountryType)
```

(continued)

continued

```
FUNCTION TranslateCountry$ (a$, country AS CountryType) STATIC
    FOR i% = 1 TO LEN(a$)
        c% = ASC(MID$(a$, i%))
        CaseMap c%, country.caseMapSegment, country.caseMapOffset
        MID$(a$, i%, 1) = CHR$(c%)
    NEXT i%
    TranslateCountry$ = a$
END FUNCTION
```

Subprogram: WriteToDevice

Outputs a string of bytes or characters to any device or file. QuickBASIC provides comprehensive input and output capabilities and should be used whenever possible. This routine is for those rare instances when accessing the MS-DOS output routines is of benefit. For example, the STDOUT toolbox is a good example of the use of the MS-DOS level code for output. QuickBASIC PRINT statements bypass the extended screen and keyboard control device named ANSI.SYS. Using this WriteToDevice subprogram (or the routines in the STDOUT toolbox) lets you use the ANSI.SYS driver's capabilities.

```
' *************************************************
' **   Name:          WriteToDevice              **
' **   Type:          Subprogram                 **
' **   Module:        DOSCALLS.BAS               **
' **   Language:      Microsoft QuickBASIC 4.00  **
' *************************************************
'
' Writes bytes to a file or device.
'
' EXAMPLE OF USE:   WriteToDevice handle%, a$, result%
' PARAMETERS:       handle%   File or device handle
'                   a$        String to be output
'                   result%   Error code returned from MS-DOS
' VARIABLES:        regX      Structure of type RegTypeX
' MODULE LEVEL
'   DECLARATIONS:   TYPE RegTypeX
'                       ax   AS INTEGER
'                       bx   AS INTEGER
'                       cx   AS INTEGER
'                       dx   AS INTEGER
```

(continued)

continued

```
'                   bp     AS INTEGER
'                   si     AS INTEGER
'                   di     AS INTEGER
'                   flags  AS INTEGER
'                   ds     AS INTEGER
'                   es     AS INTEGER
'               END TYPE
'
'   DECLARE SUB InterruptX (intnum%, inreg AS RegTypeX, outreg AS RegTypeX)
'   DECLARE SUB WriteToDevice (handle%, a$, result%)
'
    SUB WriteToDevice (handle%, a$, result%) STATIC
        DIM regX AS RegTypeX
        regX.ax = &H4000
        regX.cx = LEN(a$)
        regX.bx = handle%
        regX.ds = VARSEG(a$)
        regX.dx = SADD(a$)
        InterruptX &H21, regX, regX
        IF regX.flags AND 1 THEN
            result% = regX.ax
        ELSEIF regX.ax <> LEN(a$) THEN
            result% = -1
        ELSE
            result% = 0
        END IF
    END SUB
```

EDIT

The EDIT toolbox is a collection of subprograms for line and screen input of strings. The EditLine subprogram allows full input editing on a single line, and the EditBox subprogram allows user input and editing inside a rectangular area of the screen. The DrawBox, FormatTwo, and InsertCharacter subprograms enhance the capabilities of the EditBox routine and provide capabilities that can be useful in themselves.

Name	Type	Description
EDIT.BAS		Demo module
DrawBox	Sub	Creates a double-lined box on the display
EditBox	Sub	Allows editing in a boxed area of the screen
EditLine	Sub	Allows editing of string at cursor position
FormatTwo	Sub	Splits string into two strings
InsertCharacter	Sub	Inserts a character

Demo Module: EDIT

```
' *********************************************
' **   Name:        EDIT                     **
' **   Type:        Toolbox                  **
' **   Module:      EDIT.BAS                 **
' **   Language:    Microsoft QuickBASIC 4.00 **
' *********************************************
'
' USAGE:        No command line parameters
' .MAK FILE:    EDIT.BAS
'               KEYS.BAS
' PARAMETERS:   (none)
' VARIABLES:    a$        String to be edited by the user

  CONST FALSE = 0
  CONST TRUE = NOT FALSE

' Key code numbers
  CONST BACKSPACE = 8
  CONST CTRLLEFTARROW = 29440
```

(continued)

continued

```
    CONST CTRLRIGHTARROW = 29696
    CONST CTRLY = 25
    CONST CTRLQ = 17
    CONST DELETE = 21248
    CONST DOWNARROW = 20480
    CONST ENDKEY = 20224
    CONST ENTER = 13
    CONST ESCAPE = 27
    CONST HOME = 18176
    CONST INSERTKEY = 20992
    CONST LEFTARROW = 19200
    CONST RIGHTARROW = 19712
    CONST TABKEY = 9
    CONST UPARROW = 18432

' Functions
    DECLARE FUNCTION KeyCode% ()

' Subprograms
    DECLARE SUB EditLine (a$, exitCode%)
    DECLARE SUB DrawBox (row1%, col1%, row2%, col2%)
    DECLARE SUB EditBox (a$, row1%, col1%, row2%, col2%)
    DECLARE SUB FormatTwo (a$, b$, col%)
    DECLARE SUB InsertCharacter (x$(), kee$, cp%, rp%, wide%, high%)

' Demonstrate the EditLine subprogram
    a$ = " Edit this line, and then press Up arrow, Down arrow, or Enter "
    CLS
    COLOR 14, 1
    EditLine a$, exitCode%
    COLOR 7, 0
    PRINT
    PRINT
    PRINT "Result of edit ..."
    COLOR 14, 0
    PRINT a$
    COLOR 7, 0
    PRINT
    SELECT CASE exitCode%
    CASE 0
        PRINT "Enter";
    CASE -1
        PRINT "Down arrow";
```

(continued)

continued

```
        CASE 1
            PRINT "Up arrow";
        CASE ELSE
        END SELECT
        PRINT " key pressed."

' Demonstrate the EditBox subprogram
        a$ = "Now, edit text inside this box.  Press "
        a$ = a$ + "Esc to end the editing..."
        COLOR 12, 1
        DrawBox 8, 17, 19, 57
        COLOR 11, 1
        EditBox a$, 8, 17, 19, 57
        LOCATE 21, 1
        COLOR 7, 0
        PRINT "Result..."
        COLOR 14, 0
        PRINT a$
        COLOR 7, 0
```

Subprogram: DrawBox

Draws a rectangular, double-lined box on the screen. No attempt is made to save the screen contents under the box area, and no control of the character colors is provided. The DrawBox subprogram simply provides a fast, flexible way to get a rectangular area of the screen cleared and outlined using the current foreground and background color settings. Use the COLOR statement before calling this subprogram if you want to change the foreground and background colors.

The WINDOWS.BAS module provides a more comprehensive method of creating and removing windows for information and menuing tasks.

```
' *****************************************
' **   Name:         DrawBox               **
' **   Type:         Subprogram            **
' **   Module:       EDIT.BAS              **
' **   Language:     Microsoft QuickBASIC 4.00  **
' *****************************************
'
' Draws a double-lined box.
```

(continued)

continued

```
' EXAMPLE OF USE:    DrawBox row1%, col1%, row2%, col2%
' PARAMETERS:        row1%    Screen text row at upper left corner of the box
'                    col1%    Screen text column at upper left corner of the box
'                    row2%    Screen text row at lower right corner of the box
'                    col2%    Screen text column at lower right corner of the
'                             box
' VARIABLES:         wide%    Inside width of box
'                    row3%    Loop row number for creating sides of box
' MODULE LEVEL
'   DECLARATIONS:    DECLARE SUB DrawBox (row1%, col1%, row2%, col2%)
'
  SUB DrawBox (row1%, col1%, row2%, col2%) STATIC

    ' Determine inside width of box
    wide% = col2% - col1% - 1

    ' Across the top
    LOCATE row1%, col1%, 0
    PRINT CHR$(201);
    PRINT STRING$(wide%, 205);
    PRINT CHR$(187);

    ' Down the sides
    FOR row3% = row1% + 1 TO row2% - 1
        LOCATE row3%, col1%, 0
        PRINT CHR$(186);
        PRINT SPACE$(wide%);
        PRINT CHR$(186);
    NEXT row3%

    ' Across the bottom
    LOCATE row2%, col1%, 0
    PRINT CHR$(200);
    PRINT STRING$(wide%, 205);
    PRINT CHR$(188);

  END SUB
```

Subprogram: EditBox

Lets a user input and edit string characters in a rectangular area of the screen. This routine doesn't draw a box around the area on the display, but you can easily create one by calling the DrawBox subprogram before calling EditBox.

This subprogram is a simple text editor. Features include automatic wordwrap and reformatting, line insert and delete, and support of many of the same editing keys used in the QuickBASIC editing environment. The keys acted upon are Left arrow, Right arrow, Up arrow, Down arrow, Home, End, Insert, Backspace, Delete, Ctrl-Y, Ctrl-Q-Y, Ctrl-Right arrow, Ctrl-Left arrow, Enter, and Escape.

You can force a reformat of the entire rectangular area by moving the cursor to the upper left corner of the rectangular area and then pressing the Backspace key. The cursor won't move anywhere, but all text in the area will be reformatted.

To escape from the editing mode, press the Escape key. The string result of the edit is returned in a$ to the calling program. Note that linefeeds and all double spaces are removed from a$ and that a$ is trimmed of spaces from each end before being returned.

```
' *********************************************
' **   Name:          EditBox                 **
' **   Type:          Subprogram              **
' **   Module:        EDIT.BAS                **
' **   Language:      Microsoft QuickBASIC 4.00 **
' *********************************************
'
' Allows the user to edit text inside a rectangular area.
'
' EXAMPLE OF USE:   EditBox a$, row1%, col1%, row2%, col2%
' PARAMETERS:       a$      String to be edited
'                   row1%   Screen text row at upper left corner of the area
'                   col1%   Screen text column at upper left corner of the area
'                   row2%   Screen text row at lower right corner of the area
'                   col2%   Screen text column at lower right corner of the area
' VARIABLES:        r1%     Upper inside row of rectangular area
'                   r2%     Lower inside row of rectangular area
'                   c1%     Left inside column of rectangular area
'                   c2%     Right inside column of rectangular area
'                   wide%   Width of area
'                   high%   Height of area
'                   rp%     Index to current working row
'                   cp%     Index to current working column
'                   insert% Flag for insert/replace mode
'                   quit%   Flag for quitting the subprogram
'                   across% Saved current cursor column
'                   down%   Saved current cursor row
'                   x$()    Workspace string array
'                   i%      Looping index
'                   b$      Works with a$ to format a$ into x$()
```

(continued)

continued

```
'                       keyNumber%  Integer code for any key press
'                       c$   Temporary string workspace
'                       ds%  Index to double-space groupings
'                       sp%  Index to character where split of string is to occur
'                       ctrlQflag%  Indicates Ctrl-Q has been pressed
'                       kee$  Character entered from keyboard
' MODULE LEVEL
'   DECLARATIONS:   DECLARE FUNCTION KeyCode% ()
'                   DECLARE SUB EditBox (a$, row1%, col1%, row2%, col2%)
'                   DECLARE SUB FormatTwo (a$, b$, col%)
'                   DECLARE SUB InsertCharacter (x$(), kee$, cp%, rp%,
'                                                wide%, high%)
'
  SUB EditBox (a$, row1%, col1%, row2%, col2%) STATIC

    ' Set up some working variables
    r1% = row1% + 1
    r2% = row2% - 1
    c1% = col1% + 2
    c2% = col2% - 2
    wide% = c2% - c1% + 1
    high% = r2% - r1% + 1
    rp% = 1
    cp% = 1
    insert% = TRUE
    quit% = FALSE

    ' Record the current cursor location
    across% = POS(0)
    down% = CSRLIN

    ' Dimension a workspace array
    REDIM x$(1 TO high%)

    ' Format a$ into array space
    FOR i% = 1 TO high%
        FormatTwo a$, b$, wide%
        x$(i%) = a$
        a$ = b$
    NEXT i%

    ' Display the strings
    FOR i% = 1 TO high%
        LOCATE r1% + i% - 1, c1%, 0
        PRINT x$(i%);
    NEXT i%
```

(continued)

continued

```
' Process each keystroke
  DO

    ' Update the current line
    LOCATE r1% + rp% - 1, c1%, 0
    PRINT x$(rp%);

    ' Place the cursor
    IF insert% THEN
        LOCATE r1% + rp% - 1, c1% + cp% - 1, 1, 6, 7
    ELSE
        LOCATE r1% + rp% - 1, c1% + cp% - 1, 1, 1, 7
    END IF

    ' Grab next keystroke
    keyNumber% = KeyCode%

    ' Process the key
    SELECT CASE keyNumber%

      CASE INSERTKEY
          IF insert% THEN
              insert% = FALSE
          ELSE
              insert% = TRUE
          END IF

      CASE BACKSPACE

        ' Rub out character to the left
        IF cp% > 1 THEN
            x$(rp%) = x$(rp%) + " "
            b$ = LEFT$(x$(rp%), cp% - 2)
            c$ = MID$(x$(rp%), cp%)
            x$(rp%) = b$ + c$
            cp% = cp% - 1

          ' Upper left corner, so reformat the whole box
        ELSEIF rp% = 1 THEN

            ' Pull all the strings together
            a$ = ""
            FOR i% = 1 TO high%
                a$ = a$ + LTRIM$(RTRIM$(x$(i%))) + " "
            NEXT i%
```

(continued)

continued

```
        ' Remove double spaces
        ds% = INSTR(a$, "  ")
        DO WHILE ds%
            a$ = LEFT$(a$, ds% - 1) + MID$(a$, ds% + 1)
            ds% = INSTR(a$, "  ")
        LOOP

        ' Format into the array and display lines
        FOR i% = 1 TO high%
            FormatTwo a$, b$, wide%
            x$(i%) = a$
            a$ = b$
            LOCATE r1% + i% - 1, c1%, 0
            PRINT x$(i%);
        NEXT i%

    ' Concatenate to the preceding line
    ELSE

        ' Use the InsertCharacter sub to insert a space
        rp% = rp% - 1
        cp% = wide% + 1
        InsertCharacter x$(), " ", rp%, cp%, wide%, high%

        ' Remove the extra spaces introduced
        IF cp% > 2 THEN
            b$ = LEFT$(x$(rp%), cp% - 3)
            c$ = MID$(x$(rp%), cp%)
        ELSE
            b$ = ""
            c$ = MID$(x$(rp%), cp% + 1)
        END IF

        ' Pull the line pieces together
        x$(rp%) = LEFT$(b$ + c$ + SPACE$(3), wide%)

        ' Adjust the cursor position
        cp% = cp% - 1

        ' Display the lines
        FOR i% = 1 TO high%
            LOCATE r1% + i% - 1, c1%, 0
            PRINT x$(i%);
        NEXT i%
    END IF
```

(continued)

continued

```
CASE DELETE
    x$(rp%) = x$(rp%) + " "
    b$ = LEFT$(x$(rp%), cp% - 1)
    c$ = MID$(x$(rp%), cp% + 1)
    x$(rp%) = b$ + c$

CASE UPARROW
    IF rp% > 1 THEN
        rp% = rp% - 1
    END IF

CASE DOWNARROW
    IF rp% < high% THEN
        rp% = rp% + 1
    END IF

CASE LEFTARROW
    IF cp% > 1 THEN
        cp% = cp% - 1
    END IF

CASE RIGHTARROW
    IF cp% < wide% THEN
        cp% = cp% + 1
    END IF

CASE ENTER
    IF rp% < high% AND x$(high%) = SPACE$(wide%) THEN

        ' Shuffle lines down
        FOR i% = high% TO rp% + 1 STEP -1
            x$(i%) = x$(i% - 1)
        NEXT i%

        ' Split current line at cursor
        sp% = wide% - cp% + 1
        IF sp% THEN
            MID$(x$(rp%), cp%, sp%) = SPACE$(sp%)
        END IF

        ' Move to next line
        rp% = rp% + 1
        x$(rp%) = MID$(x$(rp%), cp%) + SPACE$(cp% - 1)
        cp% = 1
```

(continued)

continued

```
                ' Display the modified lines
                FOR i% = rp% - 1 TO high%
                    LOCATE r1% + i% - 1, c1%, 0
                    PRINT x$(i%);
                NEXT i%

            ELSE

                ' Nowhere to push things down
                BEEP

            END IF

        CASE HOME
            cp% = 1

        CASE ENDKEY
            cp% = wide% + 1

            ' Move back to just after last character
            IF x$(rp%) <> SPACE$(wide%) THEN
                DO UNTIL MID$(x$(rp%), cp% - 1, 1) <> " "
                    cp% = cp% - 1
                LOOP
            ELSE
                cp% = 1
            END IF

        CASE CTRLRIGHTARROW

            ' Find next space
            DO UNTIL MID$(x$(rp%), cp%, 1) = " " OR cp% = wide%
                cp% = cp% + 1
            LOOP

            ' Find first non-space character
            DO UNTIL MID$(x$(rp%), cp%, 1) <> " " OR cp% = wide%
                cp% = cp% + 1
            LOOP

        CASE CTRLLEFTARROW

            ' Find first space to the left
            DO UNTIL MID$(x$(rp%), cp%, 1) = " " OR cp% = 1
                cp% = cp% - 1
            LOOP
```

(continued)

continued

```
        ' Find first non-space character to the left
        DO UNTIL MID$(x$(rp%), cp%, 1) <> " " OR cp% = 1
            cp% = cp% - 1
        LOOP

        ' Find next space to the left
        DO UNTIL MID$(x$(rp%), cp%, 1) = " " OR cp% = 1
            cp% = cp% - 1
        LOOP

        ' Adjust cursor position to first non-space character
        IF cp% > 1 THEN
            cp% = cp% + 1
        END IF

    CASE CTRLY
        IF rp% < high% THEN
          ' Shuffle lines up, spacing out the last
          FOR i% = rp% TO high%
              IF i% < high% THEN
                  x$(i%) = x$(i% + 1)
              ELSE
                  x$(i%) = SPACE$(wide%)
              END IF
              LOCATE r1% + i% - 1, c1%, 0
              PRINT x$(i%);
          NEXT i%
        END IF

      ' Move cursor to far left
        cp% = 1

    CASE CTRLQ
        ctrlQflag% = TRUE

    CASE ESCAPE
        quit% = TRUE

    CASE IS > 255
        SOUND 999, 1

    CASE IS < 32
        SOUND 999, 1

    CASE ELSE
        kee$ = CHR$(keyNumber%)
```

(continued)

continued

```
        ' Insert mode
        IF insert% THEN
            InsertCharacter x$(), kee$, rp%, cp%, wide%, high%
            FOR i% = 1 TO high%
                LOCATE r1% + i% - 1, c1%, 0
                PRINT x$(i%);
            NEXT i%

            ' Must be overstrike mode
        ELSE
            MID$(x$(rp%), cp%, 1) = kee$
            IF cp% < wide% + 1 THEN
                cp% = cp% + 1
            ELSE
                IF rp% < high% THEN
                    LOCATE r1% + rp% - 1, c1%, 0
                    PRINT x$(rp%);
                    rp% = rp% + 1
                    cp% = 1
                END IF
            END IF
        END IF

        ' Correct for bottom right corner problem
        IF rp% > high% THEN
            cp% = wide%
            rp% = high%
        END IF

        ' Check for Ctrl-Q-Y combination (del to end of line)
        IF kee$ = "y" AND ctrlQflag% THEN
            cp% = cp% - 1
            IF cp% = 0 THEN
                cp% = wide%
                rp% = rp% - 1
            END IF
            sp% = wide% - cp% + 1
            MID$(x$(rp%), cp%, sp%) = SPACE$(sp%)
        END IF

        ' Clear out the possible Ctrl-Q signal
        ctrlQflag% = FALSE

    END SELECT

LOOP UNTIL quit%
```

(continued)

continued

```
' Concatenate the array strings to form the result
  a$ = ""
  FOR i% = 1 TO high%
      a$ = a$ + " " + LTRIM$(RTRIM$(x$(i%)))
  NEXT i%

' Remove double spaces
  ds% = INSTR(a$, "  ")
  DO WHILE ds%
      a$ = LEFT$(a$, ds% - 1) + MID$(a$, ds% + 1)
      ds% = INSTR(a$, "  ")
  LOOP

' Trim both ends of spaces
  a$ = LTRIM$(RTRIM$(a$))

' Restore original cursor position
  LOCATE down%, across%, 1

END SUB
```

Subprogram: EditLine

Allows the user to edit a single line of text. The string is displayed at the current cursor location using the current foreground and background colors. Many of the same editing keys from the QuickBASIC editing environment are supported in the expected manner. For example, pressing Ctrl-Right arrow moves the cursor to the start of the next word, and pressing Ctrl-Q-Y deletes to the end of the line. Insert and overstrike modes are both supported, and you can delete characters by pressing the Delete or Backspace key.

To exit the editing, press the Enter, Up arrow, or Down arrow key. The exitCode% value is set to *0, 1,* or *–1* respectively, allowing your calling program to determine which key terminated the editing.

```
' *********************************************
' **  Name:         EditLine                 **
' **  Type:         Subprogram               **
' **  Module:       EDIT.BAS                 **
' **  Language:     Microsoft QuickBASIC 4.00 **
' *********************************************
```

(continued)

continued

```
' Allows the user to edit a string at the current cursor position
' on the screen.  Keys acted upon are Ctrl-Y, Ctrl-Q-Y, Right arrow,
' Left arrow, Ctrl-Left arrow, Ctrl-Right arrow, Home, End,
' Insert, Escape, Backspace, and Delete.
' Pressing Enter, Up arrow, or Down arrow terminates
' the subprogram and returns exitCode% of 0, +1, or -1.
'
' EXAMPLE OF USE:  EditLine a$, exitCode%
' PARAMETERS:      a$           String to be edited
'                  exitCode%    Returned code indicating the terminating
'                               key press
' VARIABLES:       row%         Saved current cursor row
'                  col%         Saved current cursor column
'                  length%      Length of a$
'                  ptr%         Location of cursor during the editing
'                  insert%      Insert mode toggle
'                  quit%        Flag for quitting the editing
'                  original$    Saved copy of starting a$
'                  keyNumber%   Integer code for any key press
'                  ctrlQflag%   Indicates Ctrl-Q key press
'                  kee$         Character of key just pressed
'                  sp%          Length of space string
' MODULE LEVEL
'   DECLARATIONS:  DECLARE FUNCTION KeyCode% ()
'                  DECLARE SUB EditLine (a$, exitCode%)
'
   SUB EditLine (a$, exitCode%) STATIC

   ' Set up some variables
     row% = CSRLIN
     col% = POS(0)
     length% = LEN(a$)
     ptr% = 0
     insert% = TRUE
     quit% = FALSE
     original$ = a$

   ' Main processing loop
     DO

       ' Display the line
         LOCATE row%, col%, 0
         PRINT a$;
```

(continued)

continued

```
    ' Show appropriate cursor type
    IF insert% THEN
        LOCATE row%, col% + ptr%, 1, 6, 7
    ELSE
        LOCATE row%, col% + ptr%, 1, 1, 7
    END IF

    ' Get next keystroke
    keyNumber% = KeyCode%

    ' Process the key
    SELECT CASE keyNumber%

        CASE INSERTKEY
            IF insert% THEN
                insert% = FALSE
            ELSE
                insert% = TRUE
            END IF

        CASE BACKSPACE
            IF ptr% THEN
                a$ = a$ + " "
                a$ = LEFT$(a$, ptr% - 1) + MID$(a$, ptr% + 1)
                ptr% = ptr% - 1
            END IF

        CASE DELETE
            a$ = a$ + " "
            a$ = LEFT$(a$, ptr%) + MID$(a$, ptr% + 2)

        CASE UPARROW
            exitCode% = 1
            quit% = TRUE

        CASE DOWNARROW
            exitCode% = -1
            quit% = TRUE

        CASE LEFTARROW
            IF ptr% THEN
                ptr% = ptr% - 1
            END IF
```

(continued)

continued

```
CASE RIGHTARROW
    IF ptr% < length% - 1 THEN
        ptr% = ptr% + 1
    END IF

CASE ENTER
    exitCode% = 0
    quit% = TRUE

CASE HOME
    ptr% = 0

CASE ENDKEY
    ptr% = length% - 1

CASE CTRLRIGHTARROW
    DO UNTIL MID$(a$, ptr% + 1, 1) = " " OR ptr% = length% - 1
        ptr% = ptr% + 1
    LOOP
    DO UNTIL MID$(a$, ptr% + 1, 1) <> " " OR ptr% = length% - 1
        ptr% = ptr% + 1
    LOOP

CASE CTRLLEFTARROW
    DO UNTIL MID$(a$, ptr% + 1, 1) = " " OR ptr% = 0
        ptr% = ptr% - 1
    LOOP
    DO UNTIL MID$(a$, ptr% + 1, 1) <> " " OR ptr% = 0
        ptr% = ptr% - 1
    LOOP
    DO UNTIL MID$(a$, ptr% + 1, 1) = " " OR ptr% = 0
        ptr% = ptr% - 1
    LOOP
    IF ptr% THEN
        ptr% = ptr% + 1
    END IF

CASE CTRLY
    a$ = SPACE$(length%)
    ptr% = 0

CASE CTRLQ
    ctrlQflag% = TRUE
```

(continued)

continued

```
        CASE ESCAPE
            a$ = original$
            ptr% = 0
            insert% = TRUE

        CASE IS > 255
            SOUND 999, 1

        CASE IS < 32
            SOUND 999, 1

        CASE ELSE

          ' Convert key code to character string
            kee$ = CHR$(keyNumber%)

          ' Insert or overstrike
            IF insert% THEN
                a$ = LEFT$(a$, ptr%) + kee$ + MID$(a$, ptr% + 1)
                a$ = LEFT$(a$, length%)
            ELSE
                IF ptr% < length% THEN
                    MID$(a$, ptr% + 1, 1) = kee$
                END IF
            END IF

          ' Are we up against the wall?
            IF ptr% < length% THEN
                ptr% = ptr% + 1
            ELSE
                SOUND 999, 1
            END IF

          ' Special check for Ctrl-Q-Y (del to end of line)
            IF kee$ = "y" AND ctrlQflag% THEN
                IF ptr% <= length% THEN
                    sp% = length% - ptr% + 1
                    MID$(a$, ptr%, sp%) = SPACE$(sp%)
                    ptr% = ptr% - 1
                END IF
            END IF
```

(continued)

continued

```
            ' Clear out the Ctrl-Q signal
            ctrlQflag% = FALSE

        END SELECT

    LOOP UNTIL quit%
END SUB
```

Subprogram: FormatTwo

Formats text lines to a given maximum length. The value of col% is used to find a point in a$ where a$ can be split into two strings between words. The length of the returned a$ will be less than or equal to col%, and the rest of the original a$ will be returned in b$.

Notice that repeated calls to this subprogram can format an entire paragraph of text. An example of this is shown in the subprogram EditBox.

```
' *************************************************
' **    Name:          FormatTwo                  **
' **    Type:          Subprogram                 **
' **    Module:        EDIT.BAS                   **
' **    Language:      Microsoft QuickBASIC 4.00  **
' *************************************************
'
' Splits a string into two strings between words,
' and with spaces padded to the first string to bring it to
' length, col%.
'
' EXAMPLE OF USE:   FormatTwo a$, b$, col%
' PARAMETERS:       a$      String to be split
'                   b$      Returns the tail of the string
'                   col%    Maximum length of a$ after being split
' VARIABLES:        ptr%    Pointer to split point in a$
' MODULE LEVEL
'   DECLARATIONS:   DECLARE SUB FormatTwo (a$, b$, col%)
'
    SUB FormatTwo (a$, b$, col%) STATIC

        ' Be sure string is long enough
        a$ = a$ + SPACE$(col%)
```

(continued)

continued

```
    ' Look for rightmost space
    ptr% = col% + 1
    DO WHILE MID$(a$, ptr%, 1) <> " " AND ptr% > 1
        ptr% = ptr% - 1
    LOOP

    ' Do the split
    IF ptr% = 1 THEN
        b$ = MID$(a$, col% + 1)
        a$ = LEFT$(a$, col%)
    ELSE
        b$ = MID$(a$, ptr% + 1)
        a$ = LEFT$(a$, ptr% - 1)
    END IF

    ' Pad the first string with spaces to length col%
    a$ = LEFT$(a$ + SPACE$(col%), col%)

    ' Trim extra spaces from end of second string
    b$ = RTRIM$(b$)

END SUB
```

Subprogram: InsertCharacter

Inserts a character into the array of text being maintained by the Edit-Box subprogram. While in Insert mode, the EditBox subprogram calls InsertCharacter. The character insertion is simple enough, but this subprogram also handles the chore of performing automatic wordwrap and formatting.

This task of character insertion could have been performed in the EditBox subprogram, but breaking the code out into a separate subprogram makes it much easier to isolate this task from the others. One great advantage of QuickBASIC is the ability to break complex programming tasks into smaller, more manageable tasks.

```
' *************************************************
' **   Name:         InsertCharacter             **
' **   Type:         Subprogram                  **
' **   Module:       EDIT.BAS                    **
' **   Language:     Microsoft QuickBASIC 4.00   **
' *************************************************
```

(continued)

continued

```
' Handles the task of inserting a character
' for the EditBox subprogram.
'
' EXAMPLE OF USE:   InsertCharacter x$(), kee$, rp%, cp%, wide%, high%
' PARAMETERS:       x$()       Array in EditBox where character is to be
'                              inserted
'                   kee$       Character to be inserted
'                   rp%        Row location of insert
'                   cp%        Column location of insert
'                   wide%      Width of rectangular area being edited
'                   high%      Height of rectangular area being edited
' VARIABLES:        dum$       Marker character
'                   b$         String from array at insertion point
'                   c$         Right part of string at insertion point
'                   i%         Looping index
'                   ds%        Position in string of double spaces
' MODULE LEVEL
'   DECLARATIONS:   DECLARE SUB InsertCharacter (x$(), kee$, cp%, rp%,
'                                                wide%, high%)
'
  SUB InsertCharacter (x$(), kee$, rp%, cp%, wide%, high%) STATIC

    ' First, insert a dummy character as a marker
    dum$ = CHR$(255)
    b$ = LEFT$(x$(rp%), cp% - 1)
    c$ = MID$(x$(rp%), cp%)
    b$ = b$ + dum$ + c$

    ' If end of string is a space, then drop it
    IF RIGHT$(b$, 1) = " " THEN
        x$(rp%) = LEFT$(b$, wide%)

      ' Otherwise, need to adjust the lines
    ELSE

      ' If not in the last line, then tack them all together
      IF rp% < high% THEN
          FOR i% = rp% + 1 TO high%
              b$ = b$ + " " + x$(i%)
          NEXT i%
      END IF
```

(continued)

continued

```
            ' Trim both ends
            b$ = LTRIM$(RTRIM$(b$))

            ' Remove all double spaces
            ds% = INSTR(b$, "  ")
            DO WHILE ds%
                b$ = LEFT$(b$, ds% - 1) + MID$(b$, ds% + 1)
                ds% = INSTR(b$, "  ")
            LOOP

            ' Reformat the lines
            FOR i% = rp% TO high%
                FormatTwo b$, c$, wide%
                x$(i%) = b$
                b$ = c$
            NEXT i%

        END IF

    ' Find out where that dummy character is now
    FOR rp% = 1 TO high%
        cp% = INSTR(x$(rp%), dum$)
        IF cp% THEN
            EXIT FOR
        END IF
    NEXT rp%

    ' Replace the dummy character with the keystroke character
    IF cp% THEN
        MID$(x$(rp%), cp%, 1) = kee$
    END IF

    ' Increment the cursor location
    IF cp% < wide% + 1 THEN
        cp% = cp% + 1
    ELSE
        IF rp% < high% THEN
            cp% = 1
            rp% = rp% + 1
        END IF
    END IF

END SUB
```

ERROR

The ERROR toolbox contains a single subprogram that displays an error message in a box. If you have a color monitor, you can make the display quite eye-catching. In this example, the message is yellow on a red background.

Name	Type	Description
ERROR.BAS		Demo module
ErrorMessage	Sub	Error message display

Demo Module: ERROR

```
' *************************************************
' **   Name:         ERROR                       **
' **   Type:         Toolbox                     **
' **   Module:       ERROR.BAS                   **
' **   Language:     Microsoft QuickBASIC 4.00   **
' *************************************************
' USAGE:            No command line parameters
' .MAK FILE:        (none)
' PARAMETERS:       (none)
' VARIABLES:        (none)

' Subprogram
  DECLARE SUB ErrorMessage (message$)

' Demonstrate the subprogram

  ErrorMessage "This is a sample message for ErrorMessage"
```

Subprogram: ErrorMessage

Provides a convenient, noticeable way to display error messages.

QuickBASIC has a built-in mechanism for terminating a program when a serious error occurs. For example, if you try to divide by 0, the program immediately halts and displays the message *Division by zero.*

In other situations, you might want to terminate a program because of a serious error that QuickBASIC would otherwise let pass. One approach in such a situation would be to use QuickBASIC's ERROR n% statement. This works fine, but unless one of the built-in error messages happens to fit the given situation, you're stuck with the default message *Unprintable error,* which sounds ghastly.

A second approach to terminating a program in a controlled way would be to print your own descriptive error message and then follow with the SYSTEM statement. In many cases this technique is sufficient, but it's preferable to present a more polished, eye-catching display.

This subprogram lets you systematically display your own error messages in a unique error-message window, just before terminating and returning to MS-DOS. The display—in this example, a red background and bright yellow message—immediately lets you know that a serious error has been detected.

The table of color-defining constants in this subprogram can be useful in any program where you use the COLOR statement. A statement such as *COLOR YELLOW, RED* is much more descriptive than the equivalent *COLOR 23, 4*. It also makes programming easier because you don't have to remember or look up the numbers for the various colors.

```
' **************************************************
' **   Name:         ErrorMessage               **
' **   Type:         Subprogram                 **
' **   Module:       ERROR.BAS                  **
' **   Language:     Microsoft QuickBASIC 4.00  **
' **************************************************
'
' Displays an error message and then exits to the system.
'
' EXAMPLE OF USE: ErrorMessage "This is a sample message for ErrorMessage"
' PARAMETERS:     message$             String to be displayed in the error box
' VARIABLES:      lm%                  Length of message$ during processing
'                 col%                 Screen character column for left edge
'                                      of error box
' MODULE LEVEL
'   DECLARATIONS: DECLARE SUB ErrorMessage (message$)
```

(continued)

continued

```
SUB ErrorMessage (message$) STATIC

  ' Define color constants
    CONST BLACK = 0
    CONST BLUE = 1
    CONST GREEN = 2
    CONST CYAN = 3
    CONST RED = 4
    CONST MAGENTA = 5
    CONST BROWN = 6
    CONST WHITE = 7
    CONST BRIGHT = 8
    CONST BLINK = 16
    CONST YELLOW = BROWN + BRIGHT

  ' Trim off spaces on each end of message
    message$ = LTRIM$(RTRIM$(message$))

  ' Make message length an odd number
    IF LEN(message$) MOD 2 = 0 THEN
        message$ = message$ + " "
    END IF

  ' Minimum length of message is 9 characters
    DO WHILE LEN(message$) < 9
        message$ = " " + message$ + " "
    LOOP

  ' Maximum length of message is 75
    message$ = LEFT$(message$, 75)

  ' Initialization of display
    SCREEN 0
    WIDTH 80
    CLS

  ' Calculate screen locations
    lm% = LEN(message$)
    col% = 38 - lm% \ 2

  ' Create the error box
    COLOR RED + BRIGHT, RED
    LOCATE 9, col%
    PRINT CHR$(201); STRING$(lm% + 2, 205); CHR$(187)
```

(continued)

continued

```
            LOCATE 10, col%
            PRINT CHR$(186); SPACE$(lm% + 2); CHR$(186)
            LOCATE 11, col%
            PRINT CHR$(186); SPACE$(lm% + 2); CHR$(186)
            LOCATE 12, col%
            PRINT CHR$(200); STRING$(lm% + 2, 205); CHR$(188)

        ' The title
            COLOR CYAN + BRIGHT, RED
            LOCATE 10, 36
            PRINT "* ERROR *";

        ' The message$
            COLOR YELLOW, RED
            LOCATE 11, col% + 2
            PRINT message$;

        ' System will prompt for "any key"
            COLOR WHITE, BLACK
            LOCATE 22, 1
            SYSTEM

    END SUB
```

FIGETPUT

The FIGETPUT toolbox demonstrates the FileGet$ function and FilePut subprogram, routines that allow efficient binary-mode access to files up to 32767 bytes in length. Because each of these routines uses binary-file mode, an entire file can be read by one GET statement or written by one PUT statement. Any type of file containing no more than 32767 bytes can be read into or written from a QuickBASIC string variable by these routines. When reading an ASCII file, the FileGet$ function returns all lines of the file in one string. A carriage return/line feed pair of characters marks the separation of each line in the file.

These routines can be useful for file-processing utility programs, such as byte-for-byte file comparisons, text searches, and file ciphering.

To demonstrate the routines, the module-level code reads a copy of itself into a single string, converts all characters to uppercase, counts the occurrences of each letter of the alphabet, and saves the resulting string in a file named FIGETPUT.TST. For a meaningful character count save FIGETPUT.BAS in ASCII format.

Name	Type	Description
FIGETPUT.BAS		Demo module
FileGet$	Func	Returns a string with contents of file
FilePut	Sub	Writes contents of string into binary file

Demo Module: FIGETPUT

```
' *************************************************
' **   Name:        FIGETPUT                     **
' **   Type:        Toolbox                      **
' **   Module:      FIGETPUT.BAS                 **
' **   Language:    Microsoft QuickBASIC 4.00    **
' *************************************************
'
' Reads itself (FIGETPUT.BAS) into a string,
' converts characters to uppercase, counts occurrences of
' the characters "A" through "Z," and saves the
' result in a file named FIGETPUT.TST.
```

(continued)

continued

```
' USAGE:         No command line parameters
' .MAK FILE:     (none)
' PARAMETERS:    filename
' VARIABLES:     count%()    Tally array for the 26 alpha characters
'                fileName$   Name of file to be processed
'                a$          Contents of the file
'                i%          Looping index
'                c%          ASCII value of each file byte

' Functions
  DECLARE FUNCTION FileGet$ (fileName$)

' Subprograms
  DECLARE SUB FilePut (fileName$, a$)

' Dimension array of counts for each ASCII code "A" to "Z"
  DIM count%(65 TO 90)

' Read in the file (must be no greater than 32767 bytes long)
  a$ = FileGet$("FIGETPUT.BAS")

' Convert to uppercase
  a$ = UCASE$(a$)

' Count the letters
  FOR i% = 1 TO LEN(a$)
      c% = ASC(MID$(a$, i%, 1))
      IF c% >= 65 AND c% <= 90 THEN
          count%(c%) = count%(c%) + 1
      END IF
  NEXT i%

' Output the results
  CLS
  PRINT "Alphabetic character count for FIGETPUT.BAS"
  PRINT
  FOR i% = 65 TO 90
      PRINT CHR$(i%); " -"; count%(i%),
  NEXT i%

' Write out the new file
  FilePut "FIGETPUT.TST", a$

' All done
  END
```

Function: FileGet$

Uses the binary file mode to read the contents of any MS-DOS file into a string variable. The file length must be fewer than 32768 bytes to fit in one string. If you try to read a larger file, an error message is displayed, and the program halts.

```
' *************************************************
' **    Name:          FileGet$                  **
' **    Type:          Function                  **
' **    Module:        FIGETPUT.BAS              **
' **    Language:      Microsoft QuickBASIC 4.00 **
' *************************************************
'
' Returns a string containing the contents of a file.
' Maximum file length is 32767 bytes.
'
' EXAMPLE OF USE:    a$ = FileGet$(fileName$)
' PARAMETERS:        fileName$      Name of file to be accessed
' VARIABLES:         fileNumber     Next available free file number
'                    length&        Length of file
'                    a$             String for binary read of file
' MODULE LEVEL
'    DECLARATIONS:   DECLARE FUNCTION FileGet$ (fileName$)
'
   FUNCTION FileGet$ (fileName$) STATIC
      fileNumber = FREEFILE
      OPEN fileName$ FOR BINARY AS #fileNumber
      length& = LOF(fileNumber)
      IF length& <= 32767 THEN
          a$ = SPACE$(length&)
          GET #fileNumber, , a$
          FileGet$ = a$
          a$ = ""
      ELSE
          PRINT "FileGet$()... file too large"
          SYSTEM
      END IF
      CLOSE #fileNumber
   END FUNCTION
```

Subprogram: FilePut

Writes the contents of any string variable to a file using binary file mode. The biggest file that you can create in this way is 32767 bytes because that's the longest string you can build.

```
' **************************************************
' **  Name:          FilePut                      **
' **  Type:          Subprogram                   **
' **  Module:        FIGETPUT.BAS                 **
' **  Language:      Microsoft QuickBASIC 4.00    **
' **************************************************
'
' Writes contents of a$ into a binary file named fileName$.
'
' EXAMPLE OF USE:   FilePut fileName$, a$
' PARAMETERS:       fileName$ Name of file to be written
'                   a$        Bytes to be placed in the file
' VARIABLES:        fileNumber Next available free file number
' MODULE LEVEL
'   DECLARATIONS:   DECLARE SUB FilePut (fileName$, a$)
'
  SUB FilePut (fileName$, a$) STATIC

    ' Find available file number
    fileNumber = FREEFILE

    ' Truncate any previous contents
    OPEN fileName$ FOR OUTPUT AS #fileNumber
    CLOSE #fileNumber

    ' Write string to file
    OPEN fileName$ FOR BINARY AS #fileNumber
    PUT #fileNumber, , a$

    ' All done
    CLOSE #fileNumber

  END SUB
```

FILEINFO

The FILEINFO toolbox contains subprograms that obtain directory information about files. Basically, this program mimics the MS-DOS DIR command or the QuickBASIC FILES command.

As set up, this program finds normal file entries. You can change the FILEATTRIBUTE constant to access other types of files. Refer to the CONST statements that define the various file attribute bits.

The starting path$ for the search is set to the current directory, but you can change the path$ assignment to search any desired drive or directory.

Name	Type	Description
FILEINFO.BAS		Demo module
FindFirstFile	Sub	Finds first file that matches parameter
FindNextFile	Sub	Locates next file that matches parameter
GetFileData	Sub	Extracts file directory information

Demo Module: FILEINFO

```
' ***************************************************
' **    Name:         FILEINFO                     **
' **    Type:         Toolbox                      **
' **    Module:       FILEINFO.BAS                 **
' **    Language:     Microsoft QuickBASIC 4.00    **
' ***************************************************
'
' Collection of subprograms and functions for accessing
' directory information about files.
'
'   USAGE:          No command line parameters
'   REQUIREMENTS:   MIXED.QLB/.LIB
'   .MAK FILE:      (none)
'   PARAMETERS:     (none)
'   VARIABLES:      path$      Path to files for gathering directory
'                              information; wildcard characters accepted
'
'                   dta$       Disk transfer area buffer string
```

(continued)

continued

```
'                   result%    Code returned as result of directory search
'                   file       Structure of type FileDataType
'                   n%         File count

' File search attribute bits
CONST ISNORMAL = 0
CONST ISREADONLY = 1
CONST ISHIDDEN = 2
CONST ISSYSTEM = 4
CONST ISVOLUMELABEL = 8
CONST ISSUBDIRECTORY = 16
CONST ISARCHIVED = 32

' Here we'll search for normal files and subdirectories
CONST FILEATTRIBUTE = ISNORMAL + ISSUBDIRECTORY

TYPE RegTypeX
    ax   AS INTEGER
    bx   AS INTEGER
    cx   AS INTEGER
    dx   AS INTEGER
    bp   AS INTEGER
    si   AS INTEGER
    di   AS INTEGER
    flags AS INTEGER
    ds   AS INTEGER
    es   AS INTEGER
END TYPE

TYPE FileDataType
    finame    AS STRING * 12
    year      AS INTEGER
    month     AS INTEGER
    day       AS INTEGER
    hour      AS INTEGER
    minute    AS INTEGER
    second    AS INTEGER
    attribute AS INTEGER
    size      AS LONG
END TYPE

' Subprograms
DECLARE SUB INTERRUPTX (intnum%, inreg AS RegTypeX, outreg AS RegTypeX)
DECLARE SUB FindFirstFile (path$, dta$, result%)
```

(continued)

continued

```
    DECLARE SUB FindNextFile (dta$, result%)
    DECLARE SUB GetFileData (dta$, file AS FileDataType)

' Data structures
    DIM file AS FileDataType

' For demonstration purposes, list current directory
    CLS
    path$ = "*.*"

' Always start by finding the first match
    FindFirstFile path$, dta$, result%

' Check that the path$ got us off to a good start
    IF result% THEN
        PRINT "Error: FindFirstFile - found no match for path$"
        SYSTEM
    END IF

' List all the files in this directory
    DO
        IF n% MOD 19 = 0 THEN
            CLS
            PRINT TAB(4); "File"; TAB(18); "Date"; TAB(29); "Time";
            PRINT TAB(39); "Size"; TAB(48); "Attributes"
            PRINT
        END IF
        GetFileData dta$, file
        PRINT file.finame;
        PRINT USING "  ##/##/####"; file.month, file.day, file.year;
        PRINT USING "  ##:##:##"; file.hour, file.minute, file.second;
        PRINT USING "  ########"; file.size;
        PRINT USING "  &"; RIGHT$("0" + HEX$(file.attribute), 2)
        PRINT "     &H";
        PRINT USING "&"; RIGHT$("0" + HEX$(file.attribute), 2)
        n% = n% + 1
        FindNextFile dta$, result%
        IF n% MOD 19 = 0 THEN
            PRINT
            PRINT "Press any key to continue"
            DO
            LOOP WHILE INKEY$ = ""
        END IF
    LOOP UNTIL result%
    PRINT
    PRINT n%; "files found"
```

QUICKBASIC TOOLBOXES AND PROGRAMS

Subprogram: FindFirstFile

Finds the first directory entry that matches a given path$. This subprogram is called once before FindNextFile is called numerous times to find the rest of the entries.

The result of this file search is returned in the dta$ variable. Call the GetFileData subprogram to extract the information from the string.

```
' **************************************************
' **  Name:          FindFirstFile                **
' **  Type:          Subprogram                   **
' **  Module:        FILEINFO.BAS                 **
' **  Language:      Microsoft QuickBASIC 4.00    **
' **************************************************
'
' Finds first file that matches the path$.
'
' EXAMPLE OF USE:    FindFirstFile path$, dta$, result%
' PARAMETERS:        path$      Complete path, including wildcard characters if
'                               desired, for the directory search
'                    dta$       Disk transfer area buffer space
'                    result%    Returned result code for the search
' VARIABLES:         reg        Structure of type RegTypeX
'                    thePath$   Null terminated version of path$
'                    sgmt%      Current DTA address segment
'                    ofst%      Current DTA address offset
' MODULE LEVEL
'   DECLARATIONS:    File search attribute bits
'                       CONST ISNORMAL = 0
'                       CONST ISREADONLY = 1
'                       CONST ISHIDDEN = 2
'                       CONST ISSYSTEM = 4
'                       CONST ISVOLUMELABEL = 8
'                       CONST ISSUBDIRECTORY = 16
'                       CONST ISARCHIVED = 32
'
'                       CONST FILEATTRIBUTE = ISNORMAL + ISSUBDIRECTORY
'
'                    TYPE RegTypeX
'                        ax    AS INTEGER
'                        bx    AS INTEGER
'                        cx    AS INTEGER
```

(continued)

continued

```
'                     dx    AS INTEGER
'                     bp    AS INTEGER
'                     si    AS INTEGER
'                     di    AS INTEGER
'                     flags AS INTEGER
'                     ds    AS INTEGER
'                     es    AS INTEGER
'                  END TYPE
'
'  DECLARE SUB INTERRUPTX (intnum%, inreg AS RegTypeX, outreg AS RegTypeX)
'  DECLARE SUB FindFirstFile (path$, dta$, result%)
'
   SUB FindFirstFile (path$, dta$, result%) STATIC

   ' Initialization
     DIM reg AS RegTypeX

   ' The path must be a null terminated string
     thePath$ = path$ + CHR$(0)

   ' Get current DTA address
     reg.ax = &H2F00
     INTERRUPTX &H21, reg, reg
     sgmt% = reg.es
     ofst% = reg.bx

   ' Set dta address
     dta$ = SPACE$(43)
     reg.ax = &H1A00
     reg.ds = VARSEG(dta$)
     reg.dx = SADD(dta$)
     INTERRUPTX &H21, reg, reg

   ' Find first file match
     reg.ax = &H4E00
     reg.cx = FILEATTRIBUTE
     reg.ds = VARSEG(thePath$)
     reg.dx = SADD(thePath$)
     INTERRUPTX &H21, reg, reg

   ' The carry flag tells if a file was found or not
     result% = reg.flags AND 1
```

(continued)

continued

```
      ' Reset the original DTA
      reg.ax = &H1A00
      reg.ds = sgmt%
      reg.dx = ofst%
      INTERRUPTX &H21, reg, reg

END SUB
```

Subprogram: FindNextFile

Continues the search for file directory entries after the FindFirstFile subprogram was called once. This subprogram is usually called repeatedly until all files that match the original path$ are found. The value of result% is *0* until the last file is found.

The dta$ variable carries the important information about the search from call to call of this subprogram. Be careful not to alter its contents between calls to this routine. To extract details about each file's directory entry, pass dta$ to the subprogram GetFileData.

```
' *****************************************
' **   Name:         FindNextFile           **
' **   Type:         Subprogram             **
' **   Module:       FILEINFO.BAS           **
' **   Language:     Microsoft QuickBASIC 4.00  **
' *****************************************
'
' Locates next file. FindFirstFile must be called
' before this subprogram is called.
'
' EXAMPLE OF USE: FindNextFile dta$, result%
' PARAMETERS:       dta$       Previously filled-in Disk Transfer Area
'                              buffer string
'                   result%    Result code for the search
' VARIABLES:        reg        Structure of type RegTypeX
'                   thePath$   Null terminated version of path$
'                   sgmt%      Current DTA address segment
'                   ofst%      Current DTA address offset
' MODULE LEVEL
'   DECLARATIONS:   CONST ISNORMAL = 0
'                   CONST ISREADONLY = 1
```

(continued)

continued

```
'                    CONST ISHIDDEN = 2
'                    CONST ISSYSTEM = 4
'                    CONST ISVOLUMELABEL = 8
'                    CONST ISSUBDIRECTORY = 16
'                    CONST ISARCHIVED = 32
'
'                    CONST FILEATTRIBUTE = ISNORMAL + ISSUBDIRECTORY
'
'                TYPE RegTypeX
'                    ax    AS INTEGER
'                    bx    AS INTEGER
'                    cx    AS INTEGER
'                    dx    AS INTEGER
'                    bp    AS INTEGER
'                    si    AS INTEGER
'                    di    AS INTEGER
'                    flags AS INTEGER
'                    ds    AS INTEGER
'                    es    AS INTEGER
'                END TYPE
'
'   DECLARE SUB INTERRUPTX (intnum%, inreg AS RegTypeX, outreg AS RegTypeX)
'   DECLARE SUB FindNextFile (dta$, result%)
'
  SUB FindNextFile (dta$, result%) STATIC

    ' Initialization
    DIM reg AS RegTypeX

    ' Be sure dta$ was built (FindFirstFile should have been called)
    IF LEN(dta$) <> 43 THEN
        result% = 2
        EXIT SUB
    END IF

    ' Get current DTA address
    reg.ax = &H2F00
    INTERRUPTX &H21, reg, reg
    sgmt% = reg.es
    ofst% = reg.bx

    ' Set dta address
    reg.ax = &H1A00
```

(continued)

continued

```
            reg.ds = VARSEG(dta$)
            reg.dx = SADD(dta$)
            INTERRUPTX &H21, reg, reg

          ' Find next file match
            reg.ax = &H4F00
            reg.cx = FILEATTRIBUTE
            reg.ds = VARSEG(thePath$)
            reg.dx = SADD(thePath$)
            INTERRUPTX &H21, reg, reg

          ' The carry flag tells whether a file was found or not
            result% = reg.flags AND 1

          ' Reset the original DTA
            reg.ax = &H1A00
            reg.ds = sgmt%
            reg.dx = ofst%
            INTERRUPTX &H21, reg, reg

        END SUB
```

Subprogram: GetFileData

Extracts the information about a file's directory entry from the variable dta$ passed back from calls to FindFirstFile and FindNextFile. The information is returned in the data structure of type FileDataType and includes the date and time of the last file update, the filename, the file size, and the file attribute byte.

```
  ' ***************************************************
  ' **   Name:          GetFileData                  **
  ' **   Type:          Subprogram                   **
  ' **   Module:        FILEINFO.BAS                 **
  ' **   Language:      Microsoft QuickBASIC 4.00    **
  ' ***************************************************
  '
  ' Extracts the file directory information from a Disk
  ' Transfer Area (dta$) that has been filled in by a
  ' call to either FindFirstFile or FindNextFile.
  '
  ' EXAMPLE OF USE:  GetFileData dta$, file
```

(continued)

```
' PARAMETERS:    dta$         Disk Transfer Area buffer string passed back from
'                             either FindFirstFile or FindNextFile
' VARIABLES:     tim&         Time stamp of the file
'                dat&         Date stamp of the file
'                f$           Filename during extraction
' MODULE LEVEL
'   DECLARATIONS: TYPE FileDataType
'                    finame    AS STRING * 12
'                    year      AS INTEGER
'                    month     AS INTEGER
'                    day       AS INTEGER
'                    hour      AS INTEGER
'                    minute    AS INTEGER
'                    second    AS INTEGER
'                    attribute AS INTEGER
'                    size      AS LONG
'                 END TYPE
'
'                 DECLARE SUB GetFileData (dta$, file AS FileDataType)
'
   SUB GetFileData (dta$, file AS FileDataType) STATIC

       file.attribute = ASC(MID$(dta$, 22, 1))
       tim& = CVI(MID$(dta$, 23, 2))
       IF tim& < 0 THEN
           tim& = tim& + 65536
       END IF
       file.second = tim& AND &H1F
       file.minute = (tim& \ 32) AND &H3F
       file.hour = (tim& \ 2048) AND &H1F
       dat& = CVI(MID$(dta$, 25, 2))
       file.day = dat& AND &H1F
       file.month = (dat& \ 32) AND &HF
       file.year = ((dat& \ 512) AND &H1F) + 1980
       file.size = CVL(MID$(dta$, 27, 4))
       f$ = MID$(dta$, 31) + CHR$(0)
       file.finame = LEFT$(f$, INSTR(f$, CHR$(0)) - 1)

   END SUB
```

FRACTION

The FRACTION toolbox is a set of subprograms and functions for working with fractions. The fractions are handled as data structures, defined by the TYPE statement in the module-level code. This effectively allows fractions, comprising a pair of long integer numerator and denominator numbers, to be referenced as a new type of variable.

The demo module displays examples of the LeastComMul& and GreatestComDiv& functions and then prompts you to enter fraction problems involving the addition, subtraction, multiplication, or division of two fractions. Enter the problems using the format displayed on screen. The results, reduced to lowest terms, will be displayed.

Name	Type	Description
FRACTION.BAS		Demo module
Fraction2String$	Func	Converts type Fraction variable to a string
FractionAdd	Sub	Adds two fractions and reduces
FractionDiv	Sub	Divides two fractions and reduces
FractionMul	Sub	Multiplies two fractions and reduces
FractionReduce	Sub	Reduces fraction to lowest terms
FractionSub	Sub	Subtracts two fractions and reduces
GreatestComDiv&	Func	Returns greatest common divisor
LeastComMul&	Func	Returns least common multiple
SplitFractions	Sub	Parses fraction problem string
String2Fraction	Sub	Converts a string to Fraction variable

Demo Module: FRACTION

```
' *****************************************************
' **   Name:         FRACTION                        **
' **   Type:         Toolbox                         **
' **   Module:       FRACTION.BAS                    **
' **   Language:     Microsoft QuickBASIC 4.00       **
' *****************************************************
```

(continued)

continued

```
' Demonstrates a collection of functions and subprograms
' for working with fractions.
'
' USAGE:        No command line parameters
' .MAK FILE:    (none)
' PARAMETERS:   (none)
' VARIABLES:    a           Structure of type Fraction
'               b           Structure of type Fraction
'               c           Structure of type Fraction
'               f$          Input string for fraction problems
'               fa$         First fraction in string format
'               fb$         Second fraction in string format
'               operator$   Function indicator
'               fc$         Resultant fraction in string output form

' Data structure definitions
  TYPE Fraction
      Num AS LONG
      Den AS LONG
  END TYPE

' Subprograms
  DECLARE SUB FractionReduce (a AS Fraction)
  DECLARE SUB String2Fraction (f$, a AS Fraction)
  DECLARE SUB FractionAdd (a AS Fraction, b AS Fraction, c AS Fraction)
  DECLARE SUB FractionDiv (a AS Fraction, b AS Fraction, c AS Fraction)
  DECLARE SUB FractionMul (a AS Fraction, b AS Fraction, c AS Fraction)
  DECLARE SUB FractionSub (a AS Fraction, b AS Fraction, c AS Fraction)
  DECLARE SUB SplitFractions (f$, fa$, operator$, fb$)

' Functions
  DECLARE FUNCTION Fraction2String$ (a AS Fraction)
  DECLARE FUNCTION GreatestComDiv& (n1&, n2&)
  DECLARE FUNCTION LeastComMul& (n1&, n2&)

' Data structures
  DIM a AS Fraction
  DIM b AS Fraction
  DIM c AS Fraction

' Demonstrate the LeastComMul& function
  CLS
  PRINT "LeastComMul&(21&, 49&)   =", LeastComMul&(21&, 49&)
  PRINT
```

(continued)

continued

```
' Demonstrate the GreatestComDiv& function
  PRINT "GreatestComDiv&(21&, 49&) =", GreatestComDiv&(21&, 49&)
  PRINT

' Demonstrate the fraction routines
  DO
      PRINT
      PRINT "Enter a fraction problem, or simply press Enter"
      PRINT "Example: 2/3 + 4/5"
      PRINT
      LINE INPUT f$
      IF INSTR(f$, "/") = 0 THEN
          EXIT DO
      END IF
      SplitFractions f$, fa$, operator$, fb$
      String2Fraction fa$, a
      String2Fraction fb$, b
      SELECT CASE operator$
      CASE "+"
          FractionAdd a, b, c
      CASE "-"
          FractionSub a, b, c
      CASE "*"
          FractionMul a, b, c
      CASE "/"
          FractionDiv a, b, c
      CASE ELSE
          BEEP
      END SELECT
      fc$ = Fraction2String$(c)
      PRINT "Result (reduced to lowest terms) is "; fc$
  LOOP
```

Function: Fraction2String$

Returns a string representation of a fraction. The numerator and denominator values are converted to strings by the QuickBASIC STR$ function, and a slash (/) is concatenated between them to form the resultant string.

```
' ****************************************************
' ** Name:          Fraction2String$          **
' ** Type:          Function                  **
' ** Module:        FRACTION.BAS              **
' ** Language:      Microsoft QuickBASIC 4.00 **
' ****************************************************
'
' Converts a type Fraction variable to a string.
'
' EXAMPLE OF USE:   fa$ = Fraction2String$(a)
' PARAMETERS:       a             Structure of type Fraction
' VARIABLES:        (none)
' MODULE LEVEL
'   DECLARATIONS:   TYPE Fraction
'                       Num AS LONG
'                       Den AS LONG
'                   END TYPE
'
'                   DECLARE FUNCTION Fraction2String$ (a AS Fraction)
'
  FUNCTION Fraction2String$ (a AS Fraction) STATIC
      Fraction2String$ = STR$(a.Num) + "/" + STR$(a.Den)
  END FUNCTION
```

Subprogram: FractionAdd

Adds fraction a to fraction b, reduces the result to lowest terms, and returns the result in fraction c.

```
' ****************************************************
' ** Name:          FractionAdd               **
' ** Type:          Subprogram                **
' ** Module:        FRACTION.BAS              **
' ** Language:      Microsoft QuickBASIC 4.00 **
' ****************************************************
'
' Adds two fractions and reduces the result to lowest terms.
'
' EXAMPLE OF USE:   FractionAdd a, b, c
' PARAMETERS:       a             First fraction to add
'                   b             Second fraction to add
'                   c             Resulting fraction
```

(continued)

continued

```
' VARIABLES:      (none)
' MODULE LEVEL
'   DECLARATIONS: TYPE Fraction
'                     Num AS LONG
'                     Den AS LONG
'                 END TYPE
'
'    DECLARE SUB FractionReduce (a AS Fraction)
'    DECLARE SUB FractionAdd (a AS Fraction, b AS Fraction, c AS Fraction)
'    DECLARE FUNCTION GreatestComDiv& (n1&, n2&)

SUB FractionAdd (a AS Fraction, b AS Fraction, c AS Fraction)
    c.Num = a.Num * b.Den + a.Den * b.Num
    c.Den = a.Den * b.Den
    FractionReduce c
END SUB
```

Subprogram: FractionDiv

Divides fraction b into fraction a, reduces the result to lowest terms, and returns the result in fraction c.

```
' *********************************************
' **   Name:       FractionDiv                **
' **   Type:       Subprogram                 **
' **   Module:     FRACTION.BAS               **
' **   Language:   Microsoft QuickBASIC 4.00  **
' *********************************************
'
' Divides two fractions and reduces the result to
' lowest terms.
'
' EXAMPLE OF USE: FractionDiv a, b, c
' PARAMETERS:     a           First fraction
'                 b           Fraction to divide into first
'                 c           Resulting fraction
' VARIABLES:      (none)
' MODULE LEVEL
'   DECLARATIONS: TYPE Fraction
'                     Num AS LONG
'                     Den AS LONG
'                 END TYPE
```

(continued)

continued

```
'       DECLARE SUB FractionReduce (a AS Fraction)
'       DECLARE SUB FractionDiv (a AS Fraction, b AS Fraction, c AS Fraction)
'       DECLARE FUNCTION GreatestComDiv& (n1&, n2&)
'
  SUB FractionDiv (a AS Fraction, b AS Fraction, c AS Fraction)
      c.Num = a.Num * b.Den
      c.Den = a.Den * b.Num
      FractionReduce c
  END SUB
```

Subprogram: FractionMul

Multiplies fraction a times fraction b, reduces the result to lowest terms, and returns the result in fraction c.

```
' ************************************************
' **   Name:        FractionMul                  **
' **   Type:        Subprogram                   **
' **   Module:      FRACTION.BAS                 **
' **   Language:    Microsoft QuickBASIC 4.00    **
' ************************************************
'
' Multiplies two fractions and reduces the result to
' lowest terms.
'
' EXAMPLE OF USE:   FractionMul a, b, c
' PARAMETERS:       a            First fraction to multiply
'                   b            Second fraction to multiply
'                   c            Resulting fraction
' VARIABLES:        (none)
' MODULE LEVEL
'   DECLARATIONS:   TYPE Fraction
'                       Num AS LONG
'                       Den AS LONG
'                   END TYPE
'
'       DECLARE SUB FractionReduce (a AS Fraction)
'       DECLARE SUB FractionMul (a AS Fraction, b AS Fraction, c AS Fraction)
'       DECLARE FUNCTION GreatestComDiv& (n1&, n2&)
```

(continued)

continued

```
SUB FractionMul (a AS Fraction, b AS Fraction, c AS Fraction)
    c.Num = a.Num * b.Num
    c.Den = a.Den * b.Den
    FractionReduce c
END SUB
```

Subprogram: FractionReduce

Reduces a fraction to its lowest terms by dividing the numerator and denominator by their greatest common divisor.

```
' *****************************************
' ** Name:         FractionReduce         **
' ** Type:         Subprogram             **
' ** Module:       FRACTION.BAS           **
' ** Language:     Microsoft QuickBASIC 4.00 **
' *****************************************
'
' Reduces a fraction to its lowest terms.
'
' EXAMPLE OF USE:  FractionReduce a
' PARAMETERS:      a           Fraction to reduce
' VARIABLES:       d&          Greatest common divisor of the numerator and
'                              denominator
' MODULE LEVEL
'   DECLARATIONS:  TYPE Fraction
'                    Num AS LONG
'                    Den AS LONG
'                  END TYPE
'
'                  DECLARE SUB FractionReduce (a AS Fraction)
'                  DECLARE FUNCTION GreatestComDiv& (n1&, n2&)

SUB FractionReduce (a AS Fraction)
    d& = GreatestComDiv&(a.Num, a.Den)
    a.Num = a.Num / d&
    a.Den = a.Den / d&
END SUB
```

Subprogram: FractionSub

Subtracts fraction b from fraction a, reduces the result to lowest terms, and returns the result in fraction c.

```
' *************************************************
' ** Name:         FractionSub                   **
' ** Type:         Subprogram                    **
' ** Module:       FRACTION.BAS                  **
' ** Language:     Microsoft QuickBASIC 4.00     **
' *************************************************
'
' Subtracts two fractions and reduces the result to
' lowest terms.
'
' EXAMPLE OF USE:  FractionSub a, b, c
' PARAMETERS:      a           First fraction
'                  b           Fraction to subtract from the first
'                  c           Resulting fraction
' VARIABLES:       (none)
' MODULE LEVEL
'   DECLARATIONS:  TYPE Fraction
'                    Num AS LONG
'                    Den AS LONG
'                  END TYPE
'
'     DECLARE SUB FractionReduce (a AS Fraction)
'     DECLARE SUB FractionSub (a AS Fraction, b AS Fraction, c AS Fraction)
'     DECLARE FUNCTION GreatestComDiv& (n1&, n2&)

  SUB FractionSub (a AS Fraction, b AS Fraction, c AS Fraction)
    c.Num = a.Num * b.Den - a.Den * b.Num
    c.Den = a.Den * b.Den
    FractionReduce c
  END SUB
```

Function: GreatestComDiv&

Returns the greatest common divisor of two long integers.

The greatest common divisor of the numerator and denominator of a fraction is efficient for reducing the fraction to its lowest terms, as demonstrated by the FractionReduce subprogram.

```
' *************************************************
' **   Name:        GreatestComDiv&               **
' **   Type:        Function                      **
' **   Module:      FRACTION.BAS                  **
' **   Language:    Microsoft QuickBASIC 4.00     **
' *************************************************
'
' Returns the greatest common divisor of two long integers.
'
' EXAMPLE OF USE:   gcd& = GreatestComDiv& (n1&, n2&)
' PARAMETERS:       n1&        First long integer
'                   n2&        Second long integer
' VARIABLES:        ta&        Working copy of n1&
'                   tb&        Working copy of n2&
'                   tc&        Working variable
' MODULE LEVEL
'    DECLARATIONS:  DECLARE FUNCTION GreatestComDiv& (n1&, n2&)
'
   FUNCTION GreatestComDiv& (n1&, n2&)
       ta& = n1&
       tb& = n2&
       DO
           tc& = ta& MOD tb&
           ta& = tb&
           tb& = tc&
       LOOP WHILE tc&
       GreatestComDiv& = ta&
   END FUNCTION
```

Function: LeastComMul&

Returns the least common multiple of two long integers.

Although this function is not used by any other routine in the FRACTION.BAS module, it is included because of its close ties to the GreatestComDiv& function. In fact, by using the GreatestComDiv& function in the calculations, the LeastComMul& function is shortened to one program line, as shown.

```
' *************************************************
' ** Name:         LeastComMul&                  **
' ** Type:         Function                      **
' ** Module:       FRACTION.BAS                  **
' ** Language:     Microsoft QuickBASIC 4.00     **
' *************************************************
'
' Returns the least common multiple of two long integers.
'
' EXAMPLE OF USE:  lcm& = LeastComMul& (n1&, n2&)
' PARAMETERS:      n1&         First long integer
'                  n2&         Second long integer
' VARIABLES:       (none)
' MODULE LEVEL
'   DECLARATIONS:  DECLARE FUNCTION LeastComMul& (n1&, n2&)
'
  FUNCTION LeastComMul& (n1&, n2&)
      LeastComMul& = ABS(n1& * n2& / GreatestComDiv&(n1&, n2&))
  END FUNCTION
```

Subprogram: SplitFractions

Splits the input fraction problem string into two fraction strings and one operator string.

This subprogram has a special purpose in the FRACTION.BAS program. After you enter a fraction problem, this subprogram splits your input into three strings: a string representation of the first fraction, a one-character symbol representing the desired mathematical operation, and a string representation of the second fraction.

The results of this subprogram are passed to the String2Fraction subprogram before the indicated calculations are performed.

```
' ****************************************************
' **   Name:          SplitFractions                **
' **   Type:          Subprogram                    **
' **   Module:        FRACTION.BAS                  **
' **   Language:      Microsoft QuickBASIC 4.00     **
' ****************************************************
'
' Splits an input fraction problem string into
' three strings representing each of the two
' fractions and a one-character string of the
' operation given.
'
' EXAMPLE OF USE: SplitFractions f$, fa$, operator$, fb$
' PARAMETERS:      f$         Input string from the FRACTIONS demonstration
'                             program
'                  fa$        First fraction, extracted from f$
'                  operator$  Mathematical operation symbol, from f$
'                  fb$        Second fraction, extracted from f$
' VARIABLES:       i%         Looping index
'                  ndx%       Index to mathematical operation symbol
' MODULE LEVEL
'   DECLARATIONS: DECLARE SUB SplitFractions (f$, fa$, operator$, fb$)
'
    SUB SplitFractions (f$, fa$, operator$, fb$)
        fa$ = ""
        fb$ = ""
        operator$ = ""
        FOR i% = 1 TO 4
            ndx% = INSTR(f$, MID$("+-*/", i%, 1))
            IF ndx% THEN
                IF i% = 4 THEN
                    ndx% = INSTR(ndx% + 1, f$, "/")
                END IF
                fa$ = LEFT$(f$, ndx% - 1)
                fb$ = MID$(f$, ndx% + 1)
                operator$ = MID$(f$, ndx%, 1)
                EXIT FOR
            END IF
        NEXT i%
    END SUB
```

Subprogram: String2Fraction

Converts a string representation of a fraction to a data structure of type Fraction. This routine is useful for converting user input of fractional values to type Fraction variables.

This subprogram extracts numerator and denominator values from a string representation of a fraction and fills in a data structure of type Fraction with the results.

```
' **************************************************
' **   Name:         String2Fraction              **
' **   Type:         Subprogram                   **
' **   Module:       FRACTION.BAS                 **
' **   Language:     Microsoft QuickBASIC 4.00    **
' **************************************************
'
' Converts a string to a type Fraction variable.
'
' EXAMPLE OF USE: String2Fraction f$, a
' PARAMETERS:      f$         String representation of a fraction
'                  a          Structure of type Fraction
' VARIABLES:       (none)
' MODULE LEVEL
'   DECLARATIONS:  DECLARE SUB String2Fraction (f$, a AS Fraction)
'
SUB String2Fraction (f$, a AS Fraction)
    a.Num = VAL(f$)
    a.Den = VAL(MID$(f$, INSTR(f$, "/") + 1))
END SUB
```

GAMES

The GAMES toolbox is a collection of subprograms and functions that provide some common tasks for programming games with QuickBASIC. QuickBASIC is an ideal language for developing many graphics- and text-oriented games, partly because of the interactive nature of the development process, and partly because of the excellent set of graphics functions and subprograms provided by the language.

Name	Type	Description
GAMES.BAS		Demo module
Card$	Func	Returns name of card given a number from 1 through 52
Collision%	Func	Returns TRUE or FALSE collision condition
Dice%	Func	Returns total showing for throwing N dice
FillArray	Sub	Fills an integer array with a sequence of numbers defined by the bounds
Shuffle$	Func	Randomizes character bytes in a string
ShuffleArray	Sub	Randomizes integers in an array

Demo Module: GAMES

```
' ************************************************
' **   Name:         GAMES                      **
' **   Type:         Toolbox                    **
' **   Module:       GAMES.BAS                  **
' **   Language:     Microsoft QuickBASIC 4.00  **
' ************************************************
'
' USAGE:          No command line parameters
' REQUIREMENTS:   CGA
' .MAK FILE:      (none)
' PARAMETERS:     (none)
' VARIABLES:      a$              String containing the 26 letters of the
'                                 alphabet
'                 x%              Lower bound for array a%()
'                 y%              Upper bound for array a%()
```

(continued)

continued

```
'              a%()            Array of numbers to be shuffled
'              i%              Looping index
'              size%           Dimension of bouncing ball array
'              object%()       Array for GET and PUT of bouncing ball
'              backGround%()   Array for GET and PUT of background
'              dx%             X velocity of bouncing ball
'              dy%             Y velocity of bouncing ball
'              px%             X coordinate of bouncing ball
'              py%             Y coordinate of bouncing ball
'              testNumber%     One of four bounce direction tests
'              test%           Result of the Collision% test

' Constants
  CONST FALSE = 0
  CONST TRUE = NOT FALSE

' Functions
  DECLARE FUNCTION Shuffle$ (a$)
  DECLARE FUNCTION Dice% (numberOfDice%)
  DECLARE FUNCTION Card$ (cardNumber%)
  DECLARE FUNCTION Collision% (object%(), backGround%())

' Subprograms
  DECLARE SUB FillArray (a%())
  DECLARE SUB ShuffleArray (a%())

' Demonstration of the Shuffle$ function
  CLS
  RANDOMIZE TIMER
  a$ = "abcdefghijklmnopqrstuvwxyz"
  PRINT "a$           = "; a$
  PRINT "Shuffle$(a$) = "; Shuffle$(a$)
  PRINT

' Demonstration of the FillArray subprogram
  x% = -7
  y% = 12
  DIM a%(x% TO y%)
  PRINT "FillArray a%()   where DIM a%( -7 TO 12) ..."
  FillArray a%()
  FOR i% = x% TO y%
      PRINT a%(i%);
  NEXT i%
  PRINT
```

(continued)

continued

```
' Demonstration of the ShuffleArray subprogram
  PRINT
  PRINT "ShuffleArray a%() ..."
  ShuffleArray a%()
  FOR i% = x% TO y%
      PRINT a%(i%);
  NEXT i%
  PRINT

' Demonstration of the Dice% function
  PRINT
  PRINT "Dice%(2)..."
  FOR i% = 1 TO 20
      PRINT Dice%(2);
  NEXT i%
  PRINT

' Deal a hand of seven cards
  PRINT
  PRINT "Seven random cards, without replacement..."
  REDIM a%(1 TO 54)
  FillArray a%()
  ShuffleArray a%()
  FOR i% = 1 TO 7
      PRINT Card$(a%(i%))
  NEXT i%
  PRINT

' Wait for user to press a key
  PRINT
  PRINT "Press any key to continue"
  DO
  LOOP WHILE INKEY$ = ""

' Demonstration of the Collision% function
  size% = 6
  DIM object%(size%), backGround%(size%)

' Set medium resolution graphics mode
  SCREEN 1

' Create the bouncing ball
  CIRCLE (2, 2), 2, 3
  PAINT (2, 2), 3
  GET (0, 0)-(4, 4), object%
```

(continued)

continued

```
' Make solid border around screen
  LINE (14, 18)-(305, 187), 1, B
  PAINT (0, 0), 1

  PRINT " Collision% function... Press any key to quit "

' Make three obstacles
  CIRCLE (115, 78), 33, 2, , , .6
  PAINT (115, 78), 2
  CIRCLE (205, 78), 33, 2, , , .6
  PAINT (205, 78), 2
  LINE (90, 145)-(230, 155), 2, BF

' Initialize position and velocity of the object
  dx% = 1
  dy% = 1
  px% = 160
  py% = 44
  PUT (px%, py%), object%

' Move the object around the screen, avoiding collisions,
' until any key is pressed
  DO
      testNumber% = 0
      DO
          PUT (px%, py%), object%
          px% = px% + dx%
          py% = py% + dy%
          GET (px%, py%)-(px% + 4, py% + 4), backGround%
          PUT (px%, py%), object%
          test% = Collision%(object%(), backGround%())
          IF test% THEN
              testNumber% = testNumber% + 1
              PUT (px%, py%), object%
              px% = px% - dx%
              py% = py% - dy%
              SELECT CASE testNumber%
              CASE 1
                  dx% = -dx%
              CASE 2
                  dx% = -dx%
                  dy% = -dy%
```

(continued)

continued

```
                CASE 3
                    dy% = -dy%
                CASE ELSE
            END SELECT
            PUT (px%, py%), object%
        END IF
    LOOP UNTIL test% = 0
LOOP UNTIL INKEY$ <> ""

' Clean up a little
SCREEN 0
WIDTH 80
CLS
SYSTEM
```

Function: Card$

Returns the name of a card from a standard, 52-card deck, given a number from 1 through 52.

The passed number is first checked to determine the suit. Numbers from 1 through 13 indicate a Spade, 14 through 26 a Club, and so on. The face name or the number of the card is then determined using the MOD function.

If the number is less than 1 or greater than 52, this function returns *Joker*, making it convenient to deal a 54-card deck if desired.

```
' ****************************************
' ** Name:        Card$                  **
' ** Type:        Function               **
' ** Module:      GAMES.BAS              **
' ** Language:    Microsoft QuickBASIC 4.00 **
' ****************************************
'
' Returns the name of a playing card given a number
' from 1 to 52.  Any other number returns "Joker."
'
' EXAMPLE OF USE:  PRINT Card$(n%)
' PARAMETERS:      n%         Number from 1 to 52 representing a card (any
'                             other number returns a Joker)
' VARIABLES:       suit$      Name of one of the four card suits
```

(continued)

continued

```
' MODULE LEVEL
'   DECLARATIONS:  DECLARE FUNCTION Card$ (cardNumber%)
'
    FUNCTION Card$ (cardNumber%)

        SELECT CASE (cardNumber% - 1) \ 13      ' Which suit?
        CASE 0
            suit$ = " of Spades"
        CASE 1
            suit$ = " of Clubs"
        CASE 2
            suit$ = " of Hearts"
        CASE 3
            suit$ = " of Diamonds"
        CASE ELSE
            Card$ = "Joker"
            EXIT FUNCTION
        END SELECT

        SELECT CASE (cardNumber% - 1) MOD 13    ' Which card?
        CASE 0
            Card$ = "Ace" + suit$
        CASE 1 TO 9
            Card$ = MID$(STR$(cardNumber% MOD 13), 2) + suit$
        CASE 10
            Card$ = "Jack" + suit$
        CASE 11
            Card$ = "Queen" + suit$
        CASE 12
            Card$ = "King" + suit$
        END SELECT

    END FUNCTION
```

Function: Collision%

Returns −1 or 0 (TRUE or FALSE), indicating whether a collision or near collision has occurred between two graphics objects stored in integer arrays.

The graphics images are copied into the arrays by using the QuickBASIC GET statement. If you're not familiar with using the GET and PUT statements to create graphics animation, refer to your

QuickBASIC documentation. These two statements provide a powerful method for quickly moving or duplicating graphics objects on your screen.

To use the Collision function, you must pass two integer arrays of the same dimension. Normally, the background is copied into one array (using the GET statement) just before the object stored in the second is PUT on the screen at that same location. These two arrays are passed to the Collision% function, and the returned result determines whether the object overlaps (or very nearly overlaps) any pixel already on the screen.

The check for near collision of pixels proceeds as follows. The first three integers in each array are skipped, as these integers contain object-dimensioning information and don't represent any pixel. The remaining integers from each array are compared to the corresponding integers from the other. Pixels having color attribute 0 represent the background and are stored in the integer array as one or more 0 bits. If an integer is 0, then all the pixels it represents are of the background color. If an integer is non-zero, then one or more of the pixels stored in it have a non-zero color attribute. To make the collision check fast and efficient, this function simply checks for non-zero bits in any corresponding integers from the two arrays. The pixels might not actually be overlapping, but they'll be very close neighbors. If a near collision is detected, the remaining integers are not checked, and the function returns a value of TRUE. If all the integers are checked and no collisions are detected, the function returns FALSE.

The demonstration module shows one way to use the collision function to allow objects to bounce off each other. The bouncing ball moves around quickly in the "square face," bouncing off the mouth, eyes, and screen edges. Try experimenting by changing the size of the mouth or eyes or by drawing additional objects on the screen. The ball should bounce off any non-zero pixel objects.

```
' ***************************************************
' **    Name:           Collision%                  **
' **    Type:           Function                    **
' **    Module:         GAMES.BAS                   **
' **    Language:       Microsoft QuickBASIC 4.00   **
' ***************************************************
```

(continued)

continued

```
' Returns TRUE if any non-zero pixels occur in the
' same byte of video memory, as saved in the object%()
' and backGround%() arrays.  The arrays must be the
' same size.
'
' EXAMPLE OF USE:   test% = Collision%(object%(), backGround%())
' PARAMETERS:       object%()       First array, filled in with the GET
'                                   statement
'                   backGround%()   Second array, filled in with the GET
'                                   statement
' VARIABLES:        lo%             Lower bound of first array
'                   up%             Upper bound of first array
'                   lb%             Lower bound of second array
'                   ub%             Upper bound of second array
'                   i%              Index to integers in each array
' MODULE LEVEL
'   DECLARATIONS:   CONST FALSE = 0
'                   CONST TRUE = NOT FALSE
'                   DECLARE FUNCTION Collision% (object%(), backGround%())
'
   FUNCTION Collision% (object%(), backGround%()) STATIC
       lo% = LBOUND(object%)
       uo% = UBOUND(object%)
       lb% = LBOUND(backGround%)
       ub% = UBOUND(backGround%)
       IF lo% <> lb% OR uo% <> ub% THEN
           PRINT "Error: Collision - The object and background"
           PRINT "graphics arrays have different dimensions."
           SYSTEM
       END IF
       FOR i% = lo% + 2 TO uo%
           IF object%(i%) THEN
               IF backGround%(i%) THEN
                   Collision% = TRUE
                   EXIT FUNCTION
               END IF
           END IF
       NEXT i%
       Collision% = FALSE
   END FUNCTION
```

Function: Dice%

Returns a total for all dots that are showing when n% pseudorandom dice are thrown.

The QuickBASIC RND function creates the pseudorandom sequence of unpredictable numbers to simulate the dice. Unless you want the same scores to show up every time a program is run, you should randomize the QuickBASIC random number generator by using the RANDOMIZE statement.

```
' ****************************************************
' **   Name:          Dice%                         **
' **   Type:          Function                      **
' **   Module:        GAMES.BAS                     **
' **   Language:      Microsoft QuickBASIC 4.00     **
' ****************************************************
'
' Returns the total of the dots showing when any
' desired number of dice are rolled.
'
' EXAMPLE OF USE:    total% = Dice%(n%)
' PARAMETERS:        n%          Number of dice
' VARIABLES:         toss%       Loop index for throwing the n% dice
'                    total%      Total of the dots showing
' MODULE LEVEL
'   DECLARATIONS:    DECLARE FUNCTION Dice% (numberOfDice%)
'
  FUNCTION Dice% (numberOfDice%)
     IF numberOfDice% < 1 THEN
         PRINT "Error: Dice%() - Can't throw fewer than one die"
         SYSTEM
     END IF
     FOR toss% = 1 TO numberOfDice%
         total% = total% + INT(RND * 6) + 1
     NEXT toss%
     Dice% = total%
  END FUNCTION
```

Subprogram: FillArray

Fills an integer array with a sequence of numbers defined by the bounds. For example, consider these two statements:

```
DIM year%(1900 TO 1999)
FillArray year%
```

The array will be filled with year numbers from 1900 through 1999.

As a second example, consider an array dimensioned from 1 through 52. After filling this array with the numbers 1 through 52, the array contents can be shuffled efficiently with the ShuffleArray subprogram. The result is a freshly shuffled deck of 52 cards. Pulling these random "cards" sequentially from the array prevents duplication of a card.

```
' *********************************************
' **  Name:         FillArray                **
' **  Type:         Subprogram               **
' **  Module:       GAMES.BAS                **
' **  Language:     Microsoft QuickBASIC 4.00 **
' *********************************************
'
' Initializes an integer array by putting i% into
' each i%th element.
'
' EXAMPLE OF USE:  FillArray a%()
' PARAMETERS:      a%()       Array to be filled with a sequence of numbers
' VARIABLES:       i%         Looping index
' MODULE LEVEL
'   DECLARATIONS:  DECLARE SUB FillArray (a%())
'
  SUB FillArray (a%()) STATIC
      FOR i% = LBOUND(a%) TO UBOUND(a%)
          a%(i%) = i%
      NEXT i%
  END SUB
```

Function: Shuffle$

Shuffles the contents of a string by randomly swapping bytes throughout the string.

```
' **************************************************
' **   Name:          Shuffle$                    **
' **   Type:          Function                    **
' **   Module:        GAMES.BAS                   **
' **   Language:      Microsoft QuickBASIC 4.00   **
' **************************************************
'
' Randomizes the order of the character bytes in a$.
'
' EXAMPLE OF USE:    b$ = Shuffle$(a$)
' PARAMETERS:    a$          String to be shuffled
' VARIABLES:     x$          Working string space
'                lenx%       Number of bytes in the string
'                i%          Pointer to each byte
'                j%          Pointer to randomly selected byte
'                t$          Temporary byte-swapping string
' MODULE LEVEL
'    DECLARATIONS:  DECLARE FUNCTION Shuffle$ (a$)
'
  FUNCTION Shuffle$ (a$) STATIC
      x$ = a$
      lenx% = LEN(x$)
      FOR i% = 1 TO lenx%
          j% = INT(RND * lenx% + 1)
          t$ = MID$(x$, i%, 1)
          MID$(x$, i%, 1) = MID$(x$, j%, 1)
          MID$(x$, j%, 1) = t$
      NEXT i%
      Shuffle$ = x$
      x$ = ""
  END FUNCTION
```

Subprogram: ShuffleArray

Shuffles the contents of an integer array. The array dimensions are automatically determined, and each integer entry is swapped with a randomly selected second entry.

```
' **************************************************
' **  Name:         ShuffleArray                   **
' **  Type:         Subprogram                     **
' **  Module:       GAMES.BAS                      **
' **  Language:     Microsoft QuickBASIC 4.00      **
' **************************************************
'
' Randomizes the order of the integers in a%()
' by swapping contents in a pseudorandom order.
'
' EXAMPLE OF USE:  ShuffleArray a%()
' PARAMETERS:      a%()        Array to be shuffled
' VARIABLES:       lb%         Lower bound of the array
'                  ub%         Upper bound of the array
'                  range%      Number of array entries
'                  i%          Looping index
'
' MODULE LEVEL
'   DECLARATIONS:  DECLARE SUB ShuffleArray (a%())
'
  SUB ShuffleArray (a%()) STATIC
      lb% = LBOUND(a%)
      ub% = UBOUND(a%)
      range% = ub% - lb% + 1
      FOR i% = lb% TO ub%
          SWAP a%(i%), a%(INT(RND * range% + lb%))
      NEXT i%
  END SUB
```

HEX2BIN

The HEX2BIN program reads in a file containing hexadecimal notation and creates a file containing the bytes that are indicated. Characters that are not in the set of hexadecimal characters are ignored, and each byte is assumed to be indicated by a pair of hexadecimal characters.

This program converts the hexadecimal format files created by the BIN2HEX program into the object code files they represent. For example, you can create the MOUSE.OBJ file from the MOUSE.HEX file if you don't have the Microsoft Macro Assembler. (If you do have the Macro Assembler, you should create MOUSE.OBJ directly from the MOUSE.ASM listing.)

The command line for performing this conversion (assuming you've compiled HEX2BIN to an executable program to be run from the MS-DOS prompt) is:

HEX2BIN MOUSE.HEX MOUSE.OBJ

Refer to the BIN2HEX program for information about creating this and the other .HEX files.

Program Module: HEX2BIN

```
' ****************************************************
' **  Name:       HEX2BIN                           **
' **  Type:       Program                           **
' **  Module:     HEX2BIN.BAS                       **
' **  Language:   Microsoft QuickBASIC 4.00         **
' ****************************************************
'
' Reads in a hexadecimal format file and writes out a binary
' file created from the hexadecimal byte numbers.
'
' USAGE:        HEX2BIN inFileName.ext outFileName.ext
' .MAK FILE:    HEX2BIN.BAS
'               PARSE.BAS
'               STRINGS.BAS
' PARAMETERS:   inFileName.ext    Name of hexadecimal format file to be read
```

(continued)

continued

```
'                   outFileName.ext  Name of file to be created
' VARIABLES:        cmd$             Working copy of the command line
'                   inFile$          Name of input file
'                   outFile$         Name of output file
'                   h$               Pair of hexadecimal characters representing
'                                    each byte
'                   i%               Index into list of hexadecimal character pairs
'                   byte$            Buffer for binary file access

  DECLARE SUB ParseWord (a$, sep$, word$)
  DECLARE FUNCTION FilterIn$ (a$, set$)

' Get the input and output filenames from the command line
  cmd$ = COMMAND$
  ParseWord cmd$, " ,", inFile$
  ParseWord cmd$, " ,", outFile$

' Verify both filenames were given
  IF outFile$ = "" THEN
      PRINT
      PRINT "Usage: HEX2BIN inFileName.ext outFileName.ext"
      SYSTEM
  END IF

' Open the input file
  OPEN inFile$ FOR INPUT AS #1

' Truncate the output file if it already exists
  OPEN outFile$ FOR OUTPUT AS #2
  CLOSE #2

' Now open it for binary output
  OPEN outFile$ FOR BINARY AS #2 LEN = 1

' Process each line of the hexadecimal file
  DO
      LINE INPUT #1, h$
      h$ = FilterIn$(UCASE$(h$), "0123456789ABCDEF")
      FOR i% = 1 TO LEN(h$) STEP 2
          byte$ = CHR$(VAL("&H" + MID$(h$, i%, 2)))
          PUT #2, , byte$
      NEXT i%
  LOOP WHILE NOT EOF(1)

' Clean up and quit
  CLOSE
  END
```

JUSTIFY

The JUSTIFY toolbox contains the subprogram, Justify, which pads a string with spaces between words in a pseudorandom manner until the string is a desired number of characters. This sounds simple, but the process is surprisingly complicated. For example, the inserted spaces must fall randomly between words, but it's desirable to keep the density of spaces as even as possible. You wouldn't want five spaces between the first two words and two spaces between the next two words.

The demo module prints a paragraph justified to three different widths. As shown in the demo, the FormatTwo subprogram works hand in hand with the Justify subprogram to format a long string into several smaller strings. By padding the resulting shorter strings with a fixed number of spaces on the left, you're able to format paragraphs of text between arbitrary margins. Refer to .MAK FILE in the comment lines of the listing to see the other modules you must load for this program to run correctly.

Name	Type	Description
JUSTIFY.BAS		Demo module
Justify	Sub	Adjusts strings to specified widths

Demo Module: JUSTIFY

```
' *************************************************
' **   Name:        JUSTIFY                      **
' **   Type:        Toolbox                      **
' **   Module:      JUSTIFY.BAS                  **
' **   Language:    Microsoft QuickBASIC 4.00    **
' *************************************************
'
' Demonstrates the Justify subprogram.
'
' USAGE:          No command line parameters
```

(continued)

continued

```
' .MAK FILE:      JUSTIFY.BAS
'                 EDIT.BAS
'                 PARSE.BAS
'                 KEYS.BAS
' PARAMETERS:     (none)
' VARIABLES:      a$          String to be justified
'                 col%        Number of columns for each example of Justify
'                 x$          Working copy of a$
'                 y$          Working string space

DECLARE SUB Justify (a$, n%)
DECLARE SUB ParseLine (x$, sep$, a$())
DECLARE SUB FormatTwo (a$, b$, col%)

CLS
a$ = ""
a$ = a$ + "This paragraph is used to demonstrate the Justify "
a$ = a$ + "subprogram.  First, the entire paragraph is "
a$ = a$ + "placed in a single string variable.  This string "
a$ = a$ + "is then split between words into shorter strings, "
a$ = a$ + "and these shorter strings are then justified in "
a$ = a$ + "order to align both the left and right edges of "
a$ = a$ + "the text."

FOR col% = 50 TO 70 STEP 10
    x$ = a$
    DO
        FormatTwo x$, y$, col%
        IF y$ <> "" THEN
            Justify x$, col%
        END IF
        PRINT x$
        x$ = y$
    LOOP WHILE y$ <> ""
    PRINT
NEXT col%

END
```

Subprogram: Justify

Inserts spaces between words until the given string is the desired length. Spaces are not added before the first word or after the last word, resulting in a string that is left- and right-justified to the length indicated.

```
' **************************************************
' **   Name:         Justify                      **
' **   Type:         Subprogram                   **
' **   Module:       JUSTIFY.BAS                  **
' **   Language:     Microsoft QuickBASIC 4.00    **
' **************************************************
'
' Spaces words with extra spaces until line
' is n% characters long.
'
' EXAMPLE OF USE:   Justify a$, n%
' PARAMETERS:       a$         String to be justified
'                   n%         Desired string length
' VARIABLES:        ary$()     Array to store individual words from the string
'                   cnt%       Count of non-space characters
'                   i%         Looping index
'                   j%         Count of words
'                   each%      Minimum space count to insert between words
' MODULE LEVEL
'   DECLARATIONS:   DECLARE SUB Justify (a$, n%)
'                   DECLARE SUB ParseLine (x$, sep$, a$())
'                   DECLARE SUB FormatTwo (a$, b$, col%)
'
   SUB Justify (a$, n%) STATIC

     ' If string is shorter than n%, don't bother
     IF LEN(a$) < n% THEN
         EXIT SUB
     END IF

     ' Array for list of words from original string
     REDIM ary$(1 TO n%)

     ' Split line up into individual words
     ParseLine a$, " ", ary$()
```

(continued)

continued

```
' Count the words and total of non-space characters
cnt% = 0
FOR i% = n% TO 1 STEP -1
    cnt% = cnt% + LEN(ary$(i%))
    IF ary$(i%) = "" THEN
        j% = i% - 1
    END IF
NEXT i%

' If only one or zero words, there's not much we can do
IF j% < 2 THEN
    a$ = LEFT$(ary$(1) + SPACE$(n%), n%)
    EXIT SUB
END IF

' We want an extra space at the ends of sentences, questions, etc.
FOR i% = 1 TO j% - 1
    IF INSTR(".!?", RIGHT$(ary$(i%), 1)) THEN
        ary$(i%) = ary$(i%) + " "
        cnt% = cnt% + 1
    END IF
NEXT i%

' How many spaces minimum to add to each word?
each% = (n% - cnt%) \ (j% - 1)

' Tack on the minimum spaces to each word
FOR i% = 1 TO j% - 1
    ary$(i%) = ary$(i%) + SPACE$(each%)
    cnt% = cnt% + each%
NEXT i%

' Which is quicker, adding remaining spaces, or
' adding spaces to all and removing a few of them?
IF (n% - cnt%) < j% \ 2 THEN

    ' We'll add a few spaces at random
    DO UNTIL cnt% = n%
        DO
            i% = INT(RND * (j% - 1) + 2)
        LOOP UNTIL LEFT$(ary$(i%), 1) <> " "
        ary$(i%) = " " + ary$(i%)
        cnt% = cnt% + 1
    LOOP
```

(continued)

continued

```
    ELSE

        ' We'll add a space to each, and then remove some at random
        FOR i% = 2 TO j%
            ary$(i%) = " " + ary$(i%)
            cnt% = cnt% + 1
        NEXT i%

        ' Now we'll take a few away at random
        DO UNTIL cnt% = n%
            DO
                i% = INT(RND * (j% - 1) + 2)
            LOOP UNTIL LEFT$(ary$(i%), 1) = " "
            ary$(i%) = MID$(ary$(i%), 2)
            cnt% = cnt% - 1
        LOOP

    END IF

    ' Glue it all back together
    a$ = ary$(1)
    FOR i% = 2 TO j%
        a$ = a$ + ary$(i%)
    NEXT i%

END SUB
```

KEYS

The KEYS toolbox performs two enhanced keyboard input functions. It prints the unique integer number returned by the KeyCode% or InKeyCode% function for any key pressed. Run the program and press a few keys to see the numbers. To try the InKeyCode% function for one second at a time, press the Escape key followed immediately by other keys.

The QuickBASIC INKEY$ function returns a string of zero, one, or two characters, depending on whether a key was pressed and whether the key has an extended key code. The two functions presented here always return a unique integer for any key pressed, even if the key normally returns an extended key code. For example, pressing the letter "a" returns *97*, F1 returns *15104*, Alt-F1 returns *26624*, and the Home key returns *18176*. Run the program to determine other returned values.

The EDIT.BAS module uses these functions and presents a table of CONST statements that define several common editing keys. Note that most standard alphanumeric keys return the expected ASCII code number.

Name	Type	Description
KEYS.BAS		Demo module
InKeyCode%	Func	Returns unique integer for any key pressed
KeyCode%	Func	Waits and returns integer value for key

Demo Module: KEYS

```
' *************************************************
' **   Name:       KEYS                          **
' **   Type:       Toolbox                       **
' **   Module:     KEYS.BAS                      **
' **   Language:   Microsoft QuickBASIC 4.00     **
' *************************************************
```

(continued)

continued

```
' Demonstrates keyboard access functions.
' USAGE:          No command line parameters
' .MAK FILE:      (none)
' PARAMETERS:     (none)
' VARIABLES:      kee%      Unique integer returned by KeyCode% and
'                           InKeyCode%


DECLARE FUNCTION KeyCode% ()
DECLARE FUNCTION InKeyCode% ()

CLS
PRINT "Press any key to see the unique number returned by KeyCode%."
PRINT "Press Esc to see InKeyCode% results for 1 second."
PRINT "Press Esc twice in a row to quit."
PRINT

DO
    kee% = KeyCode%
    PRINT kee%
    IF kee% = 27 THEN
        t0 = TIMER
        DO
            kee% = InKeyCode%
            PRINT kee%;
            IF kee% THEN
                PRINT
            END IF
            IF kee% = 27 THEN
                quitFlag% = -1
                t0 = t0 - 1
            END IF
        LOOP UNTIL TIMER - t0 > 1
        PRINT
    END IF
LOOP UNTIL quitFlag%

END
```

Function: InKeyCode%

Immediately returns a unique integer for any key pressed or *0* if no key was pressed.

```
' *************************************************
' ** Name:          InKeyCode%                   **
' ** Type:          Function                    **
' ** Module:        KEYS.BAS                    **
' ** Language:      Microsoft QuickBASIC 4.00   **
' *************************************************
'
' Returns a unique integer for any key pressed or
' a zero if no key was pressed.
'
' EXAMPLE OF USE:   k% = InKeyCode%
' PARAMETERS:       (none)
' VARIABLES:        (none)
' MODULE LEVEL
'   DECLARATIONS:   DECLARE FUNCTION KeyCode% ()
'
  FUNCTION InKeyCode% STATIC
      InKeyCode% = CVI(INKEY$ + STRING$(2, 0))
  END FUNCTION
```

Function: KeyCode%

Waits until a key is pressed, and then returns the unique key-code integer for each key on the keyboard.

```
' *************************************************
' ** Name:          KeyCode%                     **
' ** Type:          Function                    **
' ** Module:        KEYS.BAS                    **
' ** Language:      Microsoft QuickBASIC 4.00   **
' *************************************************
'
' Returns a unique integer for any key pressed.
'
' EXAMPLE OF USE:   k% = KeyCode%
' PARAMETERS:       (none)
' VARIABLES:        (none)
```

(continued)

continued

```
' MODULE LEVEL
'   DECLARATIONS:  DECLARE FUNCTION KeyCode% ()
'
  FUNCTION KeyCode% STATIC
      DO
          k$ = INKEY$
      LOOP UNTIL k$ <> ""
      KeyCode% = CVI(k$ + CHR$(0))
  END FUNCTION
```

LOOK

The LOOK program is a utility for viewing text-file contents. The program displays ASCII text-file contents and provides limited keyboard control to allow scrolling or paging through files.

This program presents the FileRead subprogram for reading ASCII files into an array of strings and also demonstrates the VIEW PRINT statement for limiting printing and scrolling of text to only those display lines desired.

Name	Type	Description
LOOK.BAS		Program module
FileRead	Sub	Reads lines of ASCII files into an array

Program Module: LOOK

```
' *****************************************
' **   Name:         LOOK                         **
' **   Type:         Program                      **
' **   Module:       LOOK.BAS                     **
' **   Language:     Microsoft QuickBASIC 4.00    **
' *****************************************
'
' USAGE:        LOOK filename.ext
' .MAK FILE:    LOOK.BAS
'               KEYS.BAS
' PARAMETERS:   filename.ext   Name of file to view
' VARIABLES:    a$()           Array of lines from the file
'               fileName$      Name of file, from the command line
'               lineCount%     Count of lines read from the file
'               linePtr%       First file line currently on the display
'               i%             Loop index for printing 24 lines
'               quitFlag%      Indicates Escape key press
'               updateFlag%    Indicates if update of screen is necessary

' Constants
  CONST FALSE = 0
  CONST TRUE = NOT FALSE
```

(continued)

continued

```
' Key code numbers
  CONST UPARROW = 18432
  CONST DOWNARROW = 20480
  CONST PGUP = 18688
  CONST PGDN = 20736
  CONST HOME = 18176
  CONST ENDKEY = 20224
  CONST ESCAPE = 27

' Functions
  DECLARE FUNCTION KeyCode% ()

' Subprograms
  DECLARE SUB FileRead (fileName$, lineCount%, a$())

' Dimension string array
' NOTE:
' Must be dimensioned big enough to read in all lines from the file
  DIM a$(1 TO 2000)

' Get the command line parameters
  fileName$ = COMMAND$

' Read in the file
  ON ERROR GOTO FileError
  FileRead fileName$, lineCount%, a$()
  ON ERROR GOTO 0

' Prepare the screen
  SCREEN 0, 0, 0, 0
  CLS

' Set line pointer
  linePtr% = 1

' Main loop
  DO

    ' Print information bar at top
      VIEW PRINT 1 TO 1
      COLOR 0, 3
      LOCATE 1, 1
      PRINT " Line:"; LEFT$(STR$(linePtr%) + SPACE$(7), 8);
      PRINT "File: "; LEFT$(fileName$ + SPACE$(19), 19);
```

(continued)

continued

```
        PRINT "Quit: ESC"; SPACE$(3);
        PRINT "Move: "; CHR$(24); " "; CHR$(25); " PGUP PGDN HOME END ";

    ' Update the 24 lines of text
        VIEW PRINT 2 TO 25
        COLOR 7, 1
        FOR i% = 0 TO 23
            LOCATE i% + 2, 1
            PRINT LEFT$(a$(i% + linePtr%) + SPACE$(80), 80);
        NEXT i%

    ' Wait for a meaningful key to be pressed
        SELECT CASE KeyCode%
        CASE UPARROW
            IF linePtr% > 1 THEN
                linePtr% = linePtr% - 1
            END IF
        CASE DOWNARROW
            IF linePtr% < lineCount% THEN
                linePtr% = linePtr% + 1
            END IF
        CASE PGUP
            IF linePtr% > 1 THEN
                linePtr% = linePtr% - 24
                IF linePtr% < 1 THEN
                    linePtr% = 1
                END IF
            END IF
        CASE PGDN
            IF linePtr% < lineCount% - 24 THEN
                linePtr% = linePtr% + 24
                IF linePtr% > lineCount% THEN
                    linePtr% = lineCount%
                END IF
            END IF
        CASE HOME
            IF linePtr% > 1 THEN
                linePtr% = 1
            END IF
        CASE ENDKEY
            IF linePtr% < lineCount% - 24 THEN
                linePtr% = lineCount% - 24
            END IF
```

(continued)

continued

```
            CASE ESCAPE
                quitFlag% = TRUE
            CASE ELSE
                updateFlag% = FALSE
            END SELECT

    LOOP UNTIL quitFlag%

    ' Set color back to normal
    COLOR 7, 0
    END

FileError:
    PRINT
    PRINT "Usage: LOOK filename.ext"
    SYSTEM
    RESUME NEXT
```

Subprogram: FileRead

Reads all lines of a text (ASCII) file into a string array and returns the array of lines from the file and the count of the read lines.

The string array must be large enough to hold all the lines from the file. The file to read must be readable using the LINE INPUT statement.

```
' **************************************************
' **   Name:          FileRead                    **
' **   Type:          Subprogram                  **
' **   Module:        LOOK.BAS                    **
' **   Language:      Microsoft QuickBASIC 4.00   **
' **************************************************
'
' Reads lines of an ASCII file into a$().  The
' lineCount% is set to the number of lines read
' in.  If a$() wasn't dimensioned large enough,
' then lineCount% will be set to -1.
'
' EXAMPLE OF USE:   FileRead fileName$, lineCount%, a$()
' PARAMETERS:       fileName$     Name of file to be read into the array
'                   lineCount%    Returned count of lines read from the file
```

(continued)

```
'                    a$()           String array of file contents
' VARIABLES:         FileNumber%    Next available free file number
'                    i%             Index for string array
' MODULE LEVEL
'   DECLARATIONS:    DECLARE SUB FileRead (fileName$, lineCount%, a$())
'
  SUB FileRead (fileName$, lineCount%, a$()) STATIC
      FileNumber% = FREEFILE
      OPEN fileName$ FOR INPUT AS FileNumber%
      FOR i% = LBOUND(a$) TO UBOUND(a$)
          LINE INPUT #FileNumber%, a$(i%)
          lineCount% = i%
          IF EOF(FileNumber%) THEN
              EXIT FOR
          END IF
      NEXT i%
      IF NOT EOF(FileNumber%) THEN
          lineCount% = -1
      END IF
  END SUB
```

MONTH

The MONTH program demonstrates how to use the CALENDAR.BAS toolbox to perform calendar-related calculations.

When MONTH is run, a display of three one-month calendars is created. The current system date determines the second month displayed; the previous and next month are also shown.

Included with the display are instructions on how to increment or decrement the years or months. Press the lowercase *y* key to display the same three months of the previous year. Press a shifted (uppercase) *Y* to increment the year. In the same way, press *M* to increment or *m* to decrement the range of months displayed.

Program Module: MONTH

```
' ****************************************************
' **   Name:          MONTH                         **
' **   Type:          Program                       **
' **   Module:        MONTH.BAS                     **
' **   Language:      Microsoft QuickBASIC 4.00     **
' ****************************************************
'
' Creates and displays a three-month calendar.
' USAGE:          No command line parameters
' .MAK FILE:      MONTH.BAS
'                 CALENDAR.BAS
' PARAMETERS:     (none)
' VARIABLES:      year%      Year of concern
'                 month%     Month of concern
'                 quitFlag%  Indicates that program is to terminate
'                 day%       Day near middle of the month
'                 d2$        Date for second calendar month
'                 j2&        Julian day number for second calendar month
'                 d1$        Date for first calendar month
'                 j1&        Julian day number for first calendar month
'                 d3$        Date for third calendar month
'                 j3&        Julian day number for third calendar month
'                 k$         Key press character
```

(continued)

continued

```
' Constants
  CONST FALSE = 0
  CONST TRUE = NOT FALSE

' Functions
  DECLARE FUNCTION Date2Julian& (dat$)
  DECLARE FUNCTION MDY2Date$ (month%, day%, year%)
  DECLARE FUNCTION Date2Year% (dat$)
  DECLARE FUNCTION Date2Month% (dat$)
  DECLARE FUNCTION Julian2Date$ (julian&)

' Subprograms
  DECLARE SUB OneMonthCalendar (dat$, row%, col%)

' Get today's month and year
  year% = Date2Year%(DATE$)
  month% = Date2Month%(DATE$)

' Make calendars until the Esc key is pressed
  DO UNTIL quitFlag%

     ' Get Julian day number for about the middle of the month
       day% = 15
       d2$ = MDY2Date$(month%, day%, year%)
       j2& = Date2Julian&(d2$)

     ' Get last month's date
       j1& = j2& - 30
       d1$ = Julian2Date$(j1&)

     ' Get next month's date
       j3& = j2& + 30
       d3$ = Julian2Date$(j3&)

     ' Display the heading
       CLS
       LOCATE 1, 57
       PRINT "THREE-MONTH CALENDAR"
       LOCATE 2, 57
       PRINT "QuickBASIC 4.0"

     ' Create the three calendar sheets
       OneMonthCalendar d1$, 1, 1
       OneMonthCalendar d2$, 8, 25
       OneMonthCalendar d3$, 15, 49
```

(continued)

continued

```
    ' Display the instructions
        LOCATE 17, 1
        PRINT "Press <Y> to increment the year"
        LOCATE 18, 1
        PRINT "Press <y> to decrement the year"
        LOCATE 19, 1
        PRINT "Press <M> to increment the months"
        LOCATE 20, 1
        PRINT "Press <m> to decrement the months"
        LOCATE 22, 1
        PRINT "Press the Esc key to quit"

    ' Wait for a keystroke
        DO
            k$ = INKEY$
        LOOP UNTIL k$ <> ""

    ' Check for appropriate keystroke
        SELECT CASE k$
        CASE "y"
            year% = year% - 1
        CASE "Y"
            year% = year% + 1
        CASE "m"
            month% = month% - 3
        CASE "M"
            month% = month% + 3
        CASE CHR$(27)
            quitFlag% = TRUE
        CASE ELSE
        END SELECT

    ' Adjust month for proper range
        IF month% < 1 THEN
            month% = month% + 12
            year% = year% - 1
        ELSEIF month% > 12 THEN
            month% = month% - 12
            year% = year% + 1
        END IF

    LOOP

' All done
    END
```

MOUSGCRS

The MOUSGCRS program is a utility for designing graphics-mode mouse cursors.

This program lets you create new graphics-mode cursors for programs that use the Microsoft Mouse. The program's output is a QuickBASIC subprogram file that other programs can load and use. To run MOUSGCRS, your computer must have CGA graphics capability and a mouse.

This module can also be used as a toolbox for choosing any of the predefined cursors. For an example of a program using this module as a toolbox, see the OBJECT.BAS utility program.

The MOUSE.ASM subprogram must be assembled and loaded with the QuickBASIC environment for this program to run correctly. See the MOUSE.ASM subprogram in Part III of this book for more information on loading this routine.

Two masks are displayed while this program is running. The memory-resident mouse driver uses the screen mask to define areas of the cursor where the background pixels are to be left alone (0s) or blanked out (1s) before the cursor mask is displayed. Often, the screen-mask pixels define an area of the same shape but slightly larger than the cursor mask, creating an outline around the cursor when it's located on a pure white background.

To edit a cursor, click with either the left or right mouse button on any of the small squares that make up the two masks. The left button sets pixel locations on, and the right button sets them off. To change the hot spot to a new location, press both mouse buttons simultaneously.

When you're ready to try out your cursor creation, click on the "Try new cursor" box. A solid white area at the right side of the screen lets you view your new cursor against a white background.

Click on the "Try standard cursors" box to select one of the predefined cursors. Each time you click on this box, the cursor changes to the next available predefined cursor type, allowing you to preview them all.

When you click on the "Create cursor subroutine" box, the currently defined cursor masks are written to a QuickBASIC subprogram source file named GCURSOR.BAS. This file can be loaded by or merged with any program in which you want to use the new cursor. To create more than one cursor, be sure to rename the GCURSOR.BAS file after creating each cursor subprogram.

Program Module: MOUSGCRS

```
' *********************************************
' ** Name:         MOUSGCRS                  **
' ** Type:         Program                   **
' ** Module:       MOUSGCRS.BAS              **
' ** Language:     Microsoft QuickBASIC 4.00 **
' *********************************************
'
' Program for the interactive design of graphics-
' mode mouse cursor subroutines.
'
' USAGE:         No command line parameters
' REQUIREMENTS:  CGA
'                MIXED.QLB/.LIB
'                Mouse
' .MAK FILE:     MOUSGCRS.BAS
'                BITS.BAS
'                MOUSSUBS.BAS
' PARAMETERS:    (none)
' VARIABLES:     curs$()       Array of binary cursor string data
'                defaultMask$  Pattern mask for the default cursor
'                xdef%         Default hot spot X value
'                ydef%         Default hot spot Y value
'                mask$         Pattern mask for a cursor
'                xHot%         Hot spot X value
'                yHot%         Hot spot Y value
'                maskChr%      Index into the pattern mask
'                maskPtr%      Index to the background or foreground mask
'                              pattern
'                y%            Cursor bit pointer, vertical
'                x%            Cursor bit pointer, horizontal
'                xbox%         X location on screen for cursor bit box
```

(continued)

continued

'	ybox%	Y location on screen for cursor bit box
'	xh%	Screen X location for hot spot
'	yh%	Screen Y location for hot spot
'	click$	DRAW string for creating the click boxes
'	quitFlag%	Indication that user wants to quit
'	t$	Copy of TIME$
'	toggle%	Once per second toggle for hot spot visibility
'	pxl%	Pixel value at the hot spot
'	leftButton%	Current state of the left mouse button
'	rightButton%	Current state of the right mouse button
'	resetBox%	Indicates cursor is in the "Try standard
'		cursors" box
'	tryBox%	Indicates cursor is in the "Try new cursor"
'		box
'	subBox%	Indicates cursor is in the "Create cursor
'		subroutine" box
'	quitBox%	Indicates cursor is in the "Quit" box
'	xold%	X location of just-modified pixel box
'	yold%	Y location of just-modified pixel box
'	ix%	X bit pointer for pixel change
'	iy%	Y bit pointer for pixel change
'	q$	Double-quote character

```
' Define constants
  CONST FALSE = 0
  CONST TRUE = NOT FALSE

' Subprograms
  DECLARE SUB Cursdflt (mask$, xHot%, yHot%)
  DECLARE SUB Curschek (mask$, xHot%, yHot%)
  DECLARE SUB Curshand (mask$, xHot%, yHot%)
  DECLARE SUB Curshour (mask$, xHot%, yHot%)
  DECLARE SUB Cursjet (mask$, xHot%, yHot%)
  DECLARE SUB Cursleft (mask$, xHot%, yHot%)
  DECLARE SUB Cursplus (mask$, xHot%, yHot%)
  DECLARE SUB Cursup (mask$, xHot%, yHot%)
  DECLARE SUB Cursx (mask$, xHot%, yHot%)
  DECLARE SUB MouseShow ()
  DECLARE SUB MouseNow (lbutton%, rbutton%, xMouse%, yMouse%)
  DECLARE SUB MouseHide ()
  DECLARE SUB MouseMaskTranslate (mask$, xHot%, yHot%, cursor$)
  DECLARE SUB MouseSetGcursor (cursor$)
```

(continued)

continued

```
' Arrays
  DIM curs$(0 TO 8)

' Initialization
  SCREEN 2
  CLS

' Create set of cursors
  Cursdflt defaultMask$, xdef%, ydef%
  MouseMaskTranslate defaultMask$, xdef%, ydef%, curs$(0)

  Curschek mask$, xHot%, yHot%
  MouseMaskTranslate mask$, xHot%, yHot%, curs$(1)

  Curshand mask$, xHot%, yHot%
  MouseMaskTranslate mask$, xHot%, yHot%, curs$(2)

  Curshour mask$, xHot%, yHot%
  MouseMaskTranslate mask$, xHot%, yHot%, curs$(3)

  Cursjet mask$, xHot%, yHot%
  MouseMaskTranslate mask$, xHot%, yHot%, curs$(4)

  Cursleft mask$, xHot%, yHot%
  MouseMaskTranslate mask$, xHot%, yHot%, curs$(5)

  Cursplus mask$, xHot%, yHot%
  MouseMaskTranslate mask$, xHot%, yHot%, curs$(6)

  Cursup mask$, xHot%, yHot%
  MouseMaskTranslate mask$, xHot%, yHot%, curs$(7)

  Cursx mask$, xHot%, yHot%
  MouseMaskTranslate mask$, xHot%, yHot%, curs$(8)

' Set the default cursor
  MouseSetGcursor curs$(0)

' Make the default cursor the starting point for editing
  mask$ = defaultMask$
  xHot% = xdef%
  yHot% = ydef%
```

(continued)

continued

```
' Place titles above pixel boxes
  LOCATE 2, 22, 0
  PRINT "Screen mask";
  LOCATE 2, 50, 0
  PRINT "Cursor mask";

' Outline the pixel boxes, filling the "ones" using the Mask$
  maskChr% = 0
  FOR maskPtr% = 0 TO 1
      FOR y% = 1 TO 16
          FOR x% = 1 TO 16
              xbox% = x% * 12 + maskPtr% * 222 + 107
              ybox% = y% * 9 + 10
              maskChr% = maskChr% + 1
              LINE (xbox%, ybox%)-(xbox% + 12, ybox% + 9), 1, B
              IF MID$(mask$, maskChr%, 1) = "1" THEN
                  LINE (xbox% + 3, ybox% + 2)-(xbox% + 9, ybox% + 7), 1, BF
              END IF
              IF maskPtr% = 0 THEN
                  IF x% = xHot% + 1 AND y% = yHot% + 1 THEN
                      xh% = xbox%
                      yh% = ybox%
                  END IF
              END IF
          NEXT x%
      NEXT y%
  NEXT maskPtr%

' Instruction text at bottom of display
  LOCATE 23, 1
  PRINT TAB(16); "Left button        Right button        Both buttons"
  PRINT TAB(16); "to set pixel       to clear pixel      for hot spot";

' Print menu items
  LOCATE 3, 2, 0
  PRINT "Try";
  LOCATE 4, 2, 0
  PRINT "standard";
  LOCATE 5, 2, 0
  PRINT "cursors";
  LOCATE 9, 2, 0
  PRINT "Try new";
  LOCATE 10, 2, 0
  PRINT "cursor";
```

(continued)

continued

```
    LOCATE 14, 2, 0
    PRINT "Create"
    LOCATE 15, 2, 0
    PRINT "cursor";
    LOCATE 16, 2, 0
    PRINT "subroutine";
    LOCATE 16, 74, 0
    PRINT "Quit";

' Make click box draw string
    click$ = "R20D10L20U10BF5BR1F3E6"

' Draw the click boxes
    DRAW "BM20,45" + click$
    DRAW "BM20,85" + click$
    DRAW "BM20,132" + click$
    DRAW "BM592,132" + click$

' Make a white cursor testing area
    LOCATE 5, 71
    PRINT "Cursor";
    LOCATE 6, 71
    PRINT "viewing";
    LOCATE 7, 71
    PRINT "area";
    LINE (560, 60)-(610, 100), 1, BF

' Turn on the mouse
    MouseShow

' Main processing loop control
    DO
        GOSUB MainLoop
    LOOP UNTIL quitFlag%

' Exit the loop and end program because Quitflag% has been set
    CLS
    SYSTEM


' Main processing loop
MainLoop:
```

(continued)

continued

```
' Toggle the hot spot once per second
  IF t$ <> TIME$ THEN
      t$ = TIME$
      IF toggle% = 1 THEN
          toggle% = 0
      ELSE
          toggle% = 1
      END IF
      pxl% = POINT(xh% + 3, yh% + 2) XOR toggle%
      LINE (xh% + 5, yh% + 3)-(xh% + 7, yh% + 6), pxl%, BF
      pxl% = POINT(xh% + 3 + 222, yh% + 2) XOR toggle%
      LINE (xh% + 5 + 222, yh% + 3)-(xh% + 7 + 222, yh% + 6), pxl%, BF
  END IF

' What is the mouse location and button state right now?
  MouseNow leftButton%, rightButton%, x%, y%

' Are both buttons being pressed right now?
  IF leftButton% AND rightButton% THEN
      GOSUB WhichBox
      IF xbox% THEN
          GOSUB SetHotSpot
      END IF
  END IF

' Are we traversing the "Try standard cursors" click box?
  IF x% > 20 AND x% < 40 AND y% > 45 AND y% < 55 THEN
      IF resetBox% = 0 THEN
          MouseHide
          resetBox% = 1
          LINE (17, 43)-(43, 57), 1, B
          MouseShow
      END IF
  ELSE
      IF resetBox% = 1 THEN
          MouseHide
          resetBox% = 0
          LINE (17, 43)-(43, 57), 0, B
          MouseShow
      END IF
  END IF
```

(continued)

continued

```
' Are we traversing the "Try new cursor" click box?
IF x% > 20 AND x% < 40 AND y% > 85 AND y% < 95 THEN
    IF tryBox% = 0 THEN
        MouseHide
        tryBox% = 1
        LINE (17, 83)-(43, 97), 1, B
        MouseShow
    END IF
ELSE
    IF tryBox% = 1 THEN
        MouseHide
        tryBox% = 0
        LINE (17, 83)-(43, 97), 0, B
        MouseShow
    END IF
END IF

' Are we traversing the "Create cursor subroutine" click box?
IF x% > 20 AND x% < 40 AND y% > 132 AND y% < 142 THEN
    IF subBox% = 0 THEN
        MouseHide
        subBox% = 1
        LINE (17, 130)-(43, 144), 1, B
        MouseShow
    END IF
ELSE
    IF subBox% = 1 THEN
        MouseHide
        subBox% = 0
        LINE (17, 130)-(43, 144), 0, B
        MouseShow
    END IF
END IF

' Are we traversing the "Quit" click box?
IF x% > 592 AND x% < 612 AND y% > 132 AND y% < 142 THEN
    IF quitBox% = 0 THEN
        MouseHide
        quitBox% = 1
        LINE (589, 130)-(615, 144), 1, B
        MouseShow
    END IF
```

(continued)

continued

```
        ELSE
            IF quitBox% = 1 THEN
                MouseHide
                quitBox% = 0
                LINE (589, 130)-(615, 144), 0, B
                MouseShow
            END IF
        END IF

    ' If just one button or the other is pressed, then check further
        IF leftButton% XOR rightButton% THEN
            GOSUB ButtonWasPressed
        ELSE
            xold% = 0
            yold% = 0
        END IF

    ' End of main loop
        RETURN

    ' Is the mouse currently pointing at a pixel box?
WhichBox:
        IF x% > 320 THEN
            maskPtr% = 1
            x% = x% - 222
        ELSE
            maskPtr% = 0
        END IF
        ix% = (x% - 107) \ 12
        iy% = (y% - 10) \ 9
        xbox% = 0
        ybox% = 0
        IF ix% >= 1 AND ix% <= 16 THEN
            IF iy% >= 1 AND iy% <= 16 THEN
                xbox% = ix% * 12 + maskPtr% * 222 + 107
                ybox% = iy% * 9 + 10
            END IF
        END IF
        RETURN
```

(continued)

continued

```
    ' Move the hot spot to the current pixel box
SetHotSpot:
    IF (xbox% <> xh% AND xbox% - 222 <> xh%) OR ybox% <> yh% THEN
        MouseHide
        pxl% = POINT(xh% + 3, yh% + 2)
        LINE (xh% + 5, yh% + 3)-(xh% + 7, yh% + 6), pxl%, BF
        pxl% = POINT(xh% + 3 + 222, yh% + 2)
        LINE (xh% + 5 + 222, yh% + 3)-(xh% + 7 + 222, yh% + 6), pxl%, BF
        MouseShow
        IF xbox% > 320 THEN
            xh% = xbox% - 222
        ELSE
            xh% = xbox%
        END IF
        yh% = ybox%
    END IF
    RETURN

    ' Process the button press depending on mouse location
ButtonWasPressed:
    IF quitBox% THEN
        GOSUB DoQuitBox
    ELSEIF resetBox% THEN
        GOSUB DoResetCursor
    ELSEIF tryBox% THEN
        GOSUB DoSetNewCursor
    ELSEIF subBox% THEN
        GOSUB DoSetNewCursor
        GOSUB DoCreateSub
    ELSE
        GOSUB DoPixelControl
    END IF
    RETURN

    ' Button was pressed while mouse was in the "Quit" box
DoQuitBox:
    MouseHide
    quitFlag% = TRUE
    RETURN
```

(continued)

continued

```
    ' Button was pressed while mouse was in the "Try new cursor" box
DoSetNewCursor:
    MouseHide
    maskChr% = 0
    FOR maskPtr% = 0 TO 1
        FOR y% = 1 TO 16
            FOR x% = 1 TO 16
                xbox% = x% * 12 + maskPtr% * 222 + 107
                ybox% = y% * 9 + 10
                maskChr% = maskChr% + 1
                IF POINT(xbox% + 3, ybox% + 2) THEN
                    MID$(mask$, maskChr%, 1) = "1"
                ELSE
                    MID$(mask$, maskChr%, 1) = "0"
                END IF
                IF xbox% = xh% AND ybox% = yh% THEN
                    xHot% = x% - 1
                    yHot% = y% - 1
                END IF
            NEXT x%
        NEXT y%
    NEXT maskPtr%
    MouseMaskTranslate mask$, xHot%, yHot%, cursor$
    MouseSetGcursor cursor$
    MouseShow
    RETURN

    ' Button was pressed while mouse was in the "Try standard cursors" box
DoResetCursor:
    MouseHide
    cursorIndex% = (cursorIndex% + 1) MOD 9
    MouseSetGcursor curs$(cursorIndex%)
    MouseShow
    DO
        MouseNow leftButton%, rightButton%, xMouse%, yMouse%
    LOOP UNTIL leftButton% = 0 AND rightButton% = 0
    RETURN

    ' Button was pressed while mouse was in the "Create cursor subroutine" box
DoCreateSub:
    q$ = CHR$(34)
    OPEN "GCURSOR.BAS" FOR OUTPUT AS #1
```

(continued)

continued

```
    PRINT #1, "    ' ************************************************"
    PRINT #1, "    ' **  Name:          Gcursor                    **"
    PRINT #1, "    ' **  Type:          Subprogram                 **"
    PRINT #1, "    ' **  Module:        GCURSOR.BAS                **"
    PRINT #1, "    ' **  Language:      Microsoft QuickBASIC 4.00  **"
    PRINT #1, "    ' ************************************************"
    PRINT #1, "    '"
    PRINT #1, "    SUB Gcursor (mask$, xHot%, yHot%) STATIC"
    PRINT #1, ""
    PRINT #1, "        mask$ = "; q$; q$
    FOR i% = 0 TO 31
        PRINT #1, "        mask$ = mask$ + ";
        PRINT #1, q$; MID$(mask$, 16 * i% + 1, 16); q$
        IF i% = 15 THEN
            PRINT #1, ""
        END IF
    NEXT i%
    PRINT #1, ""
    PRINT #1, "        xHot% ="; STR$(xHot%)
    PRINT #1, "        yHot% ="; STR$(yHot%)
    PRINT #1, ""
    PRINT #1, "    END SUB"
    RETURN

' Set or clear pixel box if mouse is on one
DoPixelControl:
    GOSUB WhichBox
    IF xbox% THEN
        IF xold% <> xbox% OR yold% <> ybox% THEN
            xold% = xbox%
            yold% = ybox%
            MouseHide
            IF leftButton% THEN
                LINE (xbox% + 3, ybox% + 2)-(xbox% + 9, ybox% + 7), 1, BF
            ELSE
                LINE (xbox% + 3, ybox% + 2)-(xbox% + 9, ybox% + 7), 0, BF
            END IF
            MouseShow
        END IF
    END IF
    RETURN
```

MOUSSUBS

The MOUSSUBS toolbox presents a collection of subprograms for accessing and using your mouse. Your computer must have CGA graphics capability and a mouse for this program to be useful. If you have a mouse but are limited to monochrome text modes, see the MOUSTCRS.BAS module.

The assembly-language subroutine named MOUSE.ASM must be assembled and linked with these routines or included in the user library loaded with QuickBASIC. See the MOUSE.ASM subprogram description in Part III of this book for more information on doing this.

To use these subprograms in your own programs, load this module (along with the MOUSE.ASM routine), and be sure to declare the subprograms used by your main program module. For examples of programs that use this module as a toolbox, see the OBJECT.BAS, MOUSGCRS.BAS, MOUSTCRS.BAS, and WINDOWS.BAS program modules.

Each subprogram that creates cursors defines a graphics-mode mouse cursor by filling in the pattern mask string and hot spot location variables. After this subprogram is called, call MouseMaskTranslate to translate the variables to a binary format string, which should then be passed to the MouseSetGcursor subprogram to quickly set the indicated cursor.

You might find it helpful to follow the program listing as the interactive demonstration progresses.

Name	Type	Description
MOUSSUBS.BAS		Demo module
Curschek	Sub	Check mark mouse cursor
Cursdflt	Sub	Arrow mouse cursor pointing up and left
Curshand	Sub	Pointing hand mouse cursor
Curshour	Sub	Hourglass mouse cursor
Cursjet	Sub	Jet-shaped mouse cursor
Cursleft	Sub	Left arrow mouse cursor
Cursplus	Sub	Plus sign mouse cursor
Cursup	Sub	Up arrow mouse cursor

(continued)

continued

Name	Type	Description
Cursx	Sub	X-mark mouse cursor
MouseHide	Sub	Turns off mouse visibility
MouseInches	Sub	Sets mouse-to-cursor motion ratio
MouseInstall	Sub	Checks mouse availability; resets mouse parameters
MouseLightPen	Sub	Mouse emulation of a lightpen
MouseMaskTranslate	Sub	Translates pattern/hot spot to binary
MouseMickey	Sub	Returns motion increments since last call
MouseNow	Sub	Current state/location of the mouse
MousePressLeft	Sub	Location of mouse—left button press
MousePressRight	Sub	Location of mouse—right button press
MousePut	Sub	Moves cursor to the given position
MouseRange	Sub	Limits mouse cursor motion to rectangle
MouseReleaseLeft	Sub	Location of mouse—left button release
MouseReleaseRight	Sub	Location of mouse—right button release
MouseSetGcursor	Sub	Sets graphics-mode mouse cursor
MouseShow	Sub	Activates and displays mouse cursor
MouseSoftCursor	Sub	Sets text-mode attributes (mouse cursor)
MouseWarp	Sub	Sets mouse double-speed threshold

Demo Module: MOUSSUBS

```
' ****************************************************
' **   Name:         MOUSSUBS                       **
' **   Type:         Toolbox                        **
' **   Module:       MOUSSUBS.BAS                   **
' **   Language:     Microsoft QuickBASIC 4.00      **
' ****************************************************
'
' Collection of subprograms for using the Microsoft Mouse.
'
' Note:         The assembly-language subroutine named MOUSE.ASM
'               must be assembled and linked with these routines
'               or included in the user library loaded with
'               QuickBASIC.
' USAGE:        No command line parameters
' REQUIREMENTS: CGA
'               MIXED.QLB/.LIB
'               Mouse
```

(continued)

continued

```
' .MAK FILE:    MOUSSUBS.BAS
'               BITS.BAS
' PARAMETERS:   (none)
' VARIABLES:    i%              Looping index
'               mask$           Pattern mask for each graphics mouse cursor
'               xHot%           X hot spot location
'               yHot%           Y hot spot location
'               curs$           Binary bit pattern for defining mouse cursor
'               j%              Test for left mouse button press and release
'               leftButton%     State of left mouse button
'               rightButton%    State of right mouse button
'               xMouse%         X location of mouse
'               yMouse%         Y location of mouse
'               mflag%          Indicates mouse is available
'               horizontal%     Horizontal mouse mickies
'               vertical%       Vertical mouse mickies
'               xpLeft%         X location of last left button press
'               ypLeft%         Y location of last left button press
'               xrLeft%         X location of last left button release
'               yrLeft%         Y location of last left button release
'               xpRight%        X location of last right button press
'               ypRight%        Y location of last right button press
'               xrRight%        X location of last right button release
'               yrRight%        Y location of last right button release
'               t0              Timer value
'
' Functions
  DECLARE FUNCTION BinStr2Bin% (b$)

' Subprograms
  DECLARE SUB Mouse (m1%, m2%, m3%, m4%)
  DECLARE SUB MouseRange (x1%, y1%, x2%, y2%)
  DECLARE SUB MousePut (xMouse%, yMouse%)
  DECLARE SUB MouseHide ()
  DECLARE SUB MouseInches (horizontal%, vertical%)
  DECLARE SUB MouseInstall (mflag%)
  DECLARE SUB MouseMickey (horizontal%, vertical%)
  DECLARE SUB MousePressLeft (leftCount%, xMouse%, yMouse%)
  DECLARE SUB MousePressRight (rightCount%, xMouse%, yMouse%)
  DECLARE SUB MouseReleaseLeft (leftCount%, xMouse%, yMouse%)
  DECLARE SUB MouseReleaseRight (rightCount%, xMouse%, yMouse%)
  DECLARE SUB MouseWarp (threshold%)
  DECLARE SUB Cursdflt (mask$, xHot%, yHot%)
  DECLARE SUB Curschek (mask$, xHot%, yHot%)
  DECLARE SUB Curshand (mask$, xHot%, yHot%)
  DECLARE SUB Curshour (mask$, xHot%, yHot%)
```

(continued)

continued

```
    DECLARE SUB Cursjet (mask$, xHot%, yHot%)
    DECLARE SUB Cursleft (mask$, xHot%, yHot%)
    DECLARE SUB Cursplus (mask$, xHot%, yHot%)
    DECLARE SUB Cursup (mask$, xHot%, yHot%)
    DECLARE SUB Cursx (mask$, xHot%, yHot%)
    DECLARE SUB MouseMaskTranslate (mask$, xHot%, yHot%, cursor$)
    DECLARE SUB MouseNow (leftButton%, rightButton%, xMouse%, yMouse%)
    DECLARE SUB MouseSetGcursor (cursor$)
    DECLARE SUB MouseShow ()

' Check for mouse
SCREEN 2
CLS
MouseInstall mflag%
PRINT "MouseInstall ... "; mflag%

' Demonstrate the available graphics-mode cursors
PRINT
PRINT "Click left mouse button to see the graphics-mode cursors..."
MouseShow

FOR i% = 1 TO 9
    SELECT CASE i%
    CASE 1
        Curschek mask$, xHot%, yHot%
    CASE 2
        Curshand mask$, xHot%, yHot%
    CASE 3
        Curshour mask$, xHot%, yHot%
    CASE 4
        Cursjet mask$, xHot%, yHot%
    CASE 5
        Cursleft mask$, xHot%, yHot%
    CASE 6
        Cursplus mask$, xHot%, yHot%
    CASE 7
        Cursup mask$, xHot%, yHot%
    CASE 8
        Cursx mask$, xHot%, yHot%
    CASE ELSE
        Cursdflt mask$, xHot%, yHot%
    END SELECT
    MouseMaskTranslate mask$, xHot%, yHot%, curs$
    FOR j% = -1 TO 0
```

(continued)

continued

```
            DO
                MouseNow leftButton%, rightButton%, xMouse%, yMouse%
            LOOP UNTIL leftButton% = j%
        NEXT j%
        MouseSetGcursor curs$
    NEXT i%

' Mouse hide and show
    PRINT "MouseHide ... (Press any key to continue)"
    MouseHide
    DO
    LOOP UNTIL INKEY$ <> ""
    PRINT "MouseShow ... (Press any key to continue)"
    MouseShow
    DO
    LOOP UNTIL INKEY$ <> ""

' Mouse inches per screen
    MouseHide
    PRINT
    PRINT "Setting MouseWarp to 9999 to prevent doubling of speed."
    MouseWarp 9999
    PRINT
    PRINT "Setting MouseInches to 8 by 11. (8 inches of mouse motion"
    PRINT "across desk to move across screen, and 11 inches vertical"
    PRINT "mouse motion from top to bottom of screen) ..."
    PRINT
    PRINT "Press any key to continue"
    MouseInches 8, 11
    MouseShow
    DO
    LOOP UNTIL INKEY$ <> ""

' Resetting the mouse
    MouseHide
    PRINT
    PRINT "Resetting the mouse"
    MouseInstall mflag%

' Show realtime mouse data
    CLS
    PRINT "Instantaneous mouse information (Press any key to continue)"
    MouseShow
```

(continued)

continued

```
    DO
        MouseMickey horizontal%, vertical%
        MouseNow leftButton%, rightButton%, xMouse%, yMouse%
        MousePressLeft leftCount%, xpLeft%, ypLeft%
        MouseReleaseLeft leftCount%, xrLeft%, yrLeft%
        MousePressRight rightCount%, xpRight%, ypRight%
        MouseReleaseRight rightCount%, xrRight%, yrRight%
        LOCATE 3, 1
        PRINT "Mickies       ";
        PRINT USING "######, ######"; horizontal%, vertical%
        PRINT "Position      ";
        PRINT USING "######, ######"; xMouse%, yMouse%
        PRINT
        PRINT "Buttons       ";
        PRINT USING "######, ######"; leftButton%, rightButton%
        PRINT
        PRINT "Left Press    ";
        PRINT USING "######, ######"; xpLeft%, ypLeft%
        PRINT "Left Release  ";
        PRINT USING "######, ######"; xrLeft%, yrLeft%
        PRINT
        PRINT "Right Press   ";
        PRINT USING "######, ######"; xpRight%, ypRight%
        PRINT "Right Release ";
        PRINT USING "######, ######"; xrRight%, yrRight%
    LOOP UNTIL INKEY$ <> ""

' Mouse placement
    CLS
    MouseHide
    PRINT "MousePut..."
    MouseShow
    FOR i% = 1 TO 20
        xMouse% = RND * 639
        yMouse% = RND * 199
        MousePut xMouse%, yMouse%
        t0 = TIMER
        DO
        LOOP UNTIL TIMER - t0 > .2
    NEXT i%

' Range limiting
    CLS
    MouseHide
    PRINT "Range limited to a rectangular area ..."
```

(continued)

continued

```
    PRINT "Press any key to continue"
    MouseShow
    MouseRange 200, 50, 400, 100
    DO
    LOOP UNTIL INKEY$ <> ""

'   All done
    SCREEN 0
    CLS
```

Subprogram: Curschek

Creates a graphics mouse cursor; fills in the pattern mask and hot spot values for defining a check mark cursor.

```
' **************************************************
' **   Name:          Curschek                     **
' **   Type:          Subprogram                   **
' **   Module:        MOUSSUBS.BAS                 **
' **   Language:      Microsoft QuickBASIC 4.00    **
' **************************************************
'
' Defines a graphics-mode mouse cursor (check mark).
'
' EXAMPLE OF USE:   Curschek mask$, xHot%, yHot%
' PARAMETERS:       mask$      Pattern mask for creating cursor
'                   xHot%      X location for cursor hot spot
'                   yHot%      Y location for cursor hot spot
' VARIABLES:        (none)
' MODULE LEVEL
'    DECLARATIONS:  DECLARE SUB Curschek (mask$, xHot%, yHot%)
'
    SUB Curschek (mask$, xHot%, yHot%) STATIC

        mask$ = ""
        mask$ = mask$ + "1111111111110000"
        mask$ = mask$ + "1111111111100000"
        mask$ = mask$ + "1111111111000000"
        mask$ = mask$ + "1111111110000001"
        mask$ = mask$ + "1111111100000011"
        mask$ = mask$ + "0000011000000111"
        mask$ = mask$ + "0000000000001111"
```

(continued)

continued

```
        mask$ = mask$ + "0000000000011111"
        mask$ = mask$ + "1100000000111111"
        mask$ = mask$ + "1111000001111111"
        mask$ = mask$ + "1111111111111111"
        mask$ = mask$ + "1111111111111111"
        mask$ = mask$ + "1111111111111111"
        mask$ = mask$ + "1111111111111111"
        mask$ = mask$ + "1111111111111111"
        mask$ = mask$ + "1111111111111111"

        mask$ = mask$ + "0000000000000000"
        mask$ = mask$ + "0000000000000110"
        mask$ = mask$ + "0000000000001100"
        mask$ = mask$ + "0000000000011000"
        mask$ = mask$ + "0000000000110000"
        mask$ = mask$ + "0000000001100000"
        mask$ = mask$ + "0111000011000000"
        mask$ = mask$ + "0001110110000000"
        mask$ = mask$ + "0000011100000000"
        mask$ = mask$ + "0000000000000000"
        mask$ = mask$ + "0000000000000000"
        mask$ = mask$ + "0000000000000000"
        mask$ = mask$ + "0000000000000000"
        mask$ = mask$ + "0000000000000000"
        mask$ = mask$ + "0000000000000000"

        xHot% = 6
        yHot% = 7

    END SUB
```

Subprogram: Cursdflt

Creates a graphics mouse cursor; fills in the pattern mask and hot spot values for defining the default cursor (an arrow pointing up and left).

```
' ***********************************************
' **  Name:         Cursdflt                   **
' **  Type:         Subprogram                 **
' **  Module:       MOUSSUBS.BAS               **
' **  Language:     Microsoft QuickBASIC 4.00  **
' ***********************************************
```

(continued)

continued

```
' Defines a default graphics-mode mouse cursor (arrow pointing up and left).
'
' EXAMPLE OF USE:  Cursdflt mask$, xHot%, yHot%
' PARAMETERS:      mask$     Pattern mask for creating cursor
'                  xHot%     X location for cursor hot spot
'                  yHot%     Y location for cursor hot spot
' VARIABLES:       (none)
' MODULE LEVEL
'   DECLARATION:   DECLARE SUB Cursdflt (mask$, xHot%, yHot%)
'
   SUB Cursdflt (mask$, xHot%, yHot%) STATIC

      mask$ = ""
      mask$ = mask$ + "1111111111111111"
      mask$ = mask$ + "1001111111111111"
      mask$ = mask$ + "1000111111111111"
      mask$ = mask$ + "1000011111111111"
      mask$ = mask$ + "1000001111111111"
      mask$ = mask$ + "1000000111111111"
      mask$ = mask$ + "1000000011111111"
      mask$ = mask$ + "1000000001111111"
      mask$ = mask$ + "1000000000111111"
      mask$ = mask$ + "1000000000011111"
      mask$ = mask$ + "1000000000001111"
      mask$ = mask$ + "1000000000000111"
      mask$ = mask$ + "1000100001111111"
      mask$ = mask$ + "1001100001111111"
      mask$ = mask$ + "1111110000111111"
      mask$ = mask$ + "1111110000111111"

      mask$ = mask$ + "0000000000000000"
      mask$ = mask$ + "0000000000000000"
      mask$ = mask$ + "0010000000000000"
      mask$ = mask$ + "0011000000000000"
      mask$ = mask$ + "0011100000000000"
      mask$ = mask$ + "0011110000000000"
      mask$ = mask$ + "0011111000000000"
      mask$ = mask$ + "0011111100000000"
      mask$ = mask$ + "0011111110000000"
      mask$ = mask$ + "0011111111000000"
      mask$ = mask$ + "0011111111100000"
      mask$ = mask$ + "0011111000000000"
      mask$ = mask$ + "0010001100000000"
```

(continued)

continued

```
        mask$ = mask$ + "0000001100000000"
        mask$ = mask$ + "0000000110000000"
        mask$ = mask$ + "0000000110000000"

        xHot% = 1
        yHot% = 1

    END SUB
```

Subprogram: Curshand

Creates a graphics mouse cursor; fills in the pattern mask and hot spot values for defining a pointing hand cursor.

```
' ****************************************************
' **    Name:          Curshand                     **
' **    Type:          Subprogram                   **
' **    Module:        MOUSSUBS.BAS                 **
' **    Language:      Microsoft QuickBASIC 4.00    **
' ****************************************************
'
' Defines a graphics-mode mouse cursor (pointing hand).
'
' EXAMPLE OF USE:   Curshand mask$, xHot%, yHot%
' PARAMETERS:       mask$       Pattern mask for creating cursor
'                   xHot%       X location for cursor hot spot
'                   yHot%       Y location for cursor hot spot
' VARIABLES:        (none)
' MODULE LEVEL
'   DECLARATIONS:   DECLARE SUB Curshand (mask$, xHot%, yHot%)
'
    SUB Curshand (mask$, xHot%, yHot%) STATIC

        mask$ = ""
        mask$ = mask$ + "1110000111111111"
        mask$ = mask$ + "1110000111111111"
        mask$ = mask$ + "1110000111111111"
        mask$ = mask$ + "1110000111111111"
        mask$ = mask$ + "1110000111111111"
        mask$ = mask$ + "1110000000000000"
        mask$ = mask$ + "1110000000000000"
        mask$ = mask$ + "1110000000000000"
        mask$ = mask$ + "0000000000000000"
```

(continued)

continued

```
        mask$ = mask$ + "0000000000000000"
        mask$ = mask$ + "0000000000000000"
        mask$ = mask$ + "0000000000000000"
        mask$ = mask$ + "0000000000000000"
        mask$ = mask$ + "0000000000000000"
        mask$ = mask$ + "0000000000000000"
        mask$ = mask$ + "0000000000000000"

        mask$ = mask$ + "0001111000000000"
        mask$ = mask$ + "0001001000000000"
        mask$ = mask$ + "0001001000000000"
        mask$ = mask$ + "0001001000000000"
        mask$ = mask$ + "0001001000000000"
        mask$ = mask$ + "0001001111111111"
        mask$ = mask$ + "0001001001001001"
        mask$ = mask$ + "0001001001001001"
        mask$ = mask$ + "1111001001001001"
        mask$ = mask$ + "1001000000000001"
        mask$ = mask$ + "1001000000000001"
        mask$ = mask$ + "1001000000000001"
        mask$ = mask$ + "1000000000000001"
        mask$ = mask$ + "1000000000000001"
        mask$ = mask$ + "1000000000000001"
        mask$ = mask$ + "1111111111111111"

        xHot% = 5
        yHot% = 0

END SUB
```

Subprogram: Curshour

Creates a graphics mouse cursor; fills in the pattern mask and hot spot values for defining an hourglass cursor.

```
' *****************************************************
' **   Name:          Curshour                       **
' **   Type:          Subprogram                     **
' **   Module:        MOUSSUBS.BAS                   **
' **   Language:      Microsoft QuickBASIC 4.00      **
' *****************************************************
```

(continued)

continued

```
' Defines a graphics-mode mouse cursor (hourglass).
'
' EXAMPLE OF USE:   Curshour mask$, xHot%, yHot%
' PARAMETERS:       mask$      Pattern mask for creating cursor
'                   xHot%      X location for cursor hot spot
'                   yHot%      Y location for cursor hot spot
' VARIABLES:        (none)
' MODULE LEVEL
'   DECLARATIONS:   DECLARE SUB Curshour (mask$, xHot%, yHot%)
'
    SUB Curshour (mask$, xHot%, yHot%) STATIC

    mask$ = ""
    mask$ = mask$ + "0000000000000000"
    mask$ = mask$ + "0000000000000000"
    mask$ = mask$ + "0000000000000000"
    mask$ = mask$ + "1000000000000001"
    mask$ = mask$ + "1100000000000011"
    mask$ = mask$ + "1110000000000111"
    mask$ = mask$ + "1111000000001111"
    mask$ = mask$ + "1110000000000111"
    mask$ = mask$ + "1100000000000011"
    mask$ = mask$ + "1000000000000001"
    mask$ = mask$ + "0000000000000000"
    mask$ = mask$ + "0000000000000000"
    mask$ = mask$ + "0000000000000000"
    mask$ = mask$ + "0000000000000000"
    mask$ = mask$ + "0000000000000000"
    mask$ = mask$ + "0000000000000000"

    mask$ = mask$ + "0000000000000000"
    mask$ = mask$ + "0111111111111110"
    mask$ = mask$ + "0110000000000110"
    mask$ = mask$ + "0011000000001100"
    mask$ = mask$ + "0001100000011000"
    mask$ = mask$ + "0000110000110000"
    mask$ = mask$ + "0000011001100000"
    mask$ = mask$ + "0000001111000000"
    mask$ = mask$ + "0000011001100000"
    mask$ = mask$ + "0000110000110000"
    mask$ = mask$ + "0001100110011000"
    mask$ = mask$ + "0011001111001100"
```

(continued)

continued

```
        mask$ = mask$ + "0110011111100110"
        mask$ = mask$ + "0111111111111110"
        mask$ = mask$ + "0000000000000000"
        mask$ = mask$ + "0000000000000000"

        xHot% = 7
        yHot% = 7

    END SUB
```

Subprogram: Cursjet

Creates a graphics mouse cursor; fills in the pattern mask and hot spot values for defining a jet aircraft cursor.

```
' ***************************************************
' **   Name:           Cursjet                     **
' **   Type:           Subprogram                  **
' **   Module:         MOUSSUBS.BAS                **
' **   Language:       Microsoft QuickBASIC 4.00   **
' ***************************************************
'
' Defines a graphics-mode mouse cursor (jet aircraft).
'
' EXAMPLE OF USE:   Cursjet mask$, xHot%, yHot%
' PARAMETERS:       mask$       Pattern mask for creating cursor
'                   xHot%       X location for cursor hot spot
'                   yHot%       Y location for cursor hot spot
' VARIABLES:        (none)
' MODULE LEVEL
'   DECLARATIONS:   DECLARE SUB Cursjet (mask$, xHot%, yHot%)
'
    SUB Cursjet (mask$, xHot%, yHot%) STATIC

        mask$ = ""
        mask$ = mask$ + "1111111111111111"
        mask$ = mask$ + "1111111011111111"
        mask$ = mask$ + "1111110001111111"
        mask$ = mask$ + "1111100000111111"
        mask$ = mask$ + "1111100000111111"
        mask$ = mask$ + "1111100000111111"
        mask$ = mask$ + "1111000000011111"
```

(continued)

continued

```
        mask$ = mask$ + "1110000000001111"
        mask$ = mask$ + "1100000000000111"
        mask$ = mask$ + "1000000000000011"
        mask$ = mask$ + "1000000000000011"
        mask$ = mask$ + "1111100000111111"
        mask$ = mask$ + "1111100000111111"
        mask$ = mask$ + "1111000000011111"
        mask$ = mask$ + "1110000000001111"
        mask$ = mask$ + "1111111111111111"

        mask$ = mask$ + "0000000000000000"
        mask$ = mask$ + "0000000000000000"
        mask$ = mask$ + "0000000100000000"
        mask$ = mask$ + "0000001110000000"
        mask$ = mask$ + "0000001110000000"
        mask$ = mask$ + "0000001110000000"
        mask$ = mask$ + "0000011111000000"
        mask$ = mask$ + "0000111111100000"
        mask$ = mask$ + "0001111111110000"
        mask$ = mask$ + "0011111111111000"
        mask$ = mask$ + "0110001110001100"
        mask$ = mask$ + "0000001110000000"
        mask$ = mask$ + "0000001110000000"
        mask$ = mask$ + "0000011111000000"
        mask$ = mask$ + "0000110001100000"
        mask$ = mask$ + "0000000000000000"

        xHot% = 7
        yHot% = 1

    END SUB
```

Subprogram: Cursleft

Creates a graphics mouse cursor; fills in the pattern mask and hot spot values for defining a left arrow cursor.

```
' *************************************************
' **   Name:       Cursleft                      **
' **   Type:       Subprogram                    **
' **   Module:     MOUSSUBS.BAS                  **
' **   Language:   Microsoft QuickBASIC 4.00     **
' *************************************************
```

(continued)

continued

```
' Defines a graphics-mode mouse cursor (left arrow).
'
' EXAMPLE OF USE:  Cursleft mask$, xHot%, yHot%
' PARAMETERS:      mask$      Pattern mask for creating cursor
'                  xHot%      X location for cursor hot spot
'                  yHot%      Y location for cursor hot spot
' VARIABLES:       (none)
' MODULE LEVEL
'   DECLARATIONS:    DECLARE SUB Cursleft (mask$, xHot%, yHot%)
'
  SUB Cursleft (mask$, xHot%, yHot%) STATIC

     mask$ = ""
     mask$ = mask$ + "1111111000011111"
     mask$ = mask$ + "1111000000011111"
     mask$ = mask$ + "0000000000000000"
     mask$ = mask$ + "0000000000000000"
     mask$ = mask$ + "0000000000000000"
     mask$ = mask$ + "1111000000011111"
     mask$ = mask$ + "1111111000011111"
     mask$ = mask$ + "1111111111111111"
     mask$ = mask$ + "1111111111111111"
     mask$ = mask$ + "1111111111111111"
     mask$ = mask$ + "1111111111111111"
     mask$ = mask$ + "1111111111111111"
     mask$ = mask$ + "1111111111111111"
     mask$ = mask$ + "1111111111111111"
     mask$ = mask$ + "1111111111111111"
     mask$ = mask$ + "1111111111111111"

     mask$ = mask$ + "0000000000000000"
     mask$ = mask$ + "0000000011000000"
     mask$ = mask$ + "0000011111000000"
     mask$ = mask$ + "0111111111111110"
     mask$ = mask$ + "0000011111000000"
     mask$ = mask$ + "0000000011000000"
     mask$ = mask$ + "0000000000000000"
     mask$ = mask$ + "0000000000000000"
     mask$ = mask$ + "0000000000000000"
     mask$ = mask$ + "0000000000000000"
     mask$ = mask$ + "0000000000000000"
     mask$ = mask$ + "0000000000000000"
     mask$ = mask$ + "0000000000000000"
```

(continued)

continued

```
        mask$ = mask$ + "0000000000000000"
        mask$ = mask$ + "0000000000000000"
        mask$ = mask$ + "0000000000000000"

        xHot% = 0
        yHot% = 3

    END SUB
```

Subprogram: Cursplus

Creates a graphics mouse cursor; fills in the pattern mask and hot spot values for defining a plus sign cursor.

```
' **************************************************
' **   Name:           Cursplus                   **
' **   Type:           Subprogram                 **
' **   Module:         MOUSSUBS.BAS               **
' **   Language:       Microsoft QuickBASIC 4.00  **
' **************************************************
'
' Defines a graphics-mode mouse cursor (plus sign).
'
' EXAMPLE OF USE:   Cursplus mask$, xHot%, yHot%
' PARAMETERS:       mask$      Pattern mask for creating cursor
'                   xHot%      X location for cursor hot spot
'                   yHot%      Y location for cursor hot spot
' VARIABLES:        (none)
' MODULE LEVEL
'   DECLARATIONS:   DECLARE SUB Cursplus (mask$, xHot%, yHot%)
'
    SUB Cursplus (mask$, xHot%, yHot%) STATIC

        mask$ = ""
        mask$ = mask$ + "1111110000111111"
        mask$ = mask$ + "1111110000111111"
        mask$ = mask$ + "1111110000111111"
        mask$ = mask$ + "0000000000000000"
        mask$ = mask$ + "0000000000000000"
        mask$ = mask$ + "0000000000000000"
        mask$ = mask$ + "1111110000111111"
        mask$ = mask$ + "1111110000111111"
        mask$ = mask$ + "1111110000111111"
```

(continued)

continued

```
        mask$ = mask$ + "1111111111111111"
        mask$ = mask$ + "1111111111111111"
        mask$ = mask$ + "1111111111111111"
        mask$ = mask$ + "1111111111111111"
        mask$ = mask$ + "1111111111111111"
        mask$ = mask$ + "1111111111111111"
        mask$ = mask$ + "1111111111111111"

        mask$ = mask$ + "0000000000000000"
        mask$ = mask$ + "0000000110000000"
        mask$ = mask$ + "0000000110000000"
        mask$ = mask$ + "0000000110000000"
        mask$ = mask$ + "0111111111111110"
        mask$ = mask$ + "0000000110000000"
        mask$ = mask$ + "0000000110000000"
        mask$ = mask$ + "0000000110000000"
        mask$ = mask$ + "0000000000000000"
        mask$ = mask$ + "0000000000000000"
        mask$ = mask$ + "0000000000000000"
        mask$ = mask$ + "0000000000000000"
        mask$ = mask$ + "0000000000000000"
        mask$ = mask$ + "0000000000000000"
        mask$ = mask$ + "0000000000000000"
        mask$ = mask$ + "0000000000000000"

        xHot% = 7
        yHot% = 4

END SUB
```

Subprogram: Cursup

Creates a graphics mouse cursor; fills in the pattern mask and hot spot values for defining an up arrow cursor.

```
' ***************************************************
' **   Name:       Cursup                          **
' **   Type:       Subprogram                      **
' **   Module:     MOUSSUBS.BAS                    **
' **   Language:   Microsoft QuickBASIC 4.00       **
' ***************************************************
```

(continued)

continued

```
' Defines a graphics-mode mouse cursor (up arrow).
'
' EXAMPLE OF USE:   Cursup mask$, xHot%, yHot%
' PARAMETERS:       mask$      Pattern mask for creating cursor
'                   xHot%      X location for cursor hot spot
'                   yHot%      Y location for cursor hot spot
' VARIABLES:        (none)
' MODULE LEVEL
'   DECLARATIONS:   DECLARE SUB Cursup (mask$, xHot%, yHot%)
'
  SUB Cursup (mask$, xHot%, yHot%) STATIC

    mask$ = ""
    mask$ = mask$ + "1111100111111111"
    mask$ = mask$ + "1111000011111111"
    mask$ = mask$ + "1110000001111111"
    mask$ = mask$ + "1110000001111111"
    mask$ = mask$ + "1100000000111111"
    mask$ = mask$ + "1100000000111111"
    mask$ = mask$ + "1000000000011111"
    mask$ = mask$ + "1000000000011111"
    mask$ = mask$ + "0000000000001111"
    mask$ = mask$ + "0000000000001111"
    mask$ = mask$ + "1111000011111111"
    mask$ = mask$ + "1111000011111111"
    mask$ = mask$ + "1111000011111111"
    mask$ = mask$ + "1111000011111111"
    mask$ = mask$ + "1111000011111111"
    mask$ = mask$ + "1111000011111111"

    mask$ = mask$ + "0000000000000000"
    mask$ = mask$ + "0000011000000000"
    mask$ = mask$ + "0000111100000000"
    mask$ = mask$ + "0000111100000000"
    mask$ = mask$ + "0001111110000000"
    mask$ = mask$ + "0001111110000000"
    mask$ = mask$ + "0011111111000000"
    mask$ = mask$ + "0011111111000000"
    mask$ = mask$ + "0111111111100000"
    mask$ = mask$ + "0000011000000000"
    mask$ = mask$ + "0000011000000000"
    mask$ = mask$ + "0000011000000000"
```

(continued)

continued

```
        mask$ = mask$ + "0000011000000000"
        mask$ = mask$ + "0000011000000000"
        mask$ = mask$ + "0000011000000000"
        mask$ = mask$ + "0000000000000000"

        xHot% = 5
        yHot% = 0

    END SUB
```

Subprogram: Cursx

Creates a graphics mouse cursor; fills in the pattern mask and hot spot values for defining an X-mark cursor.

```
' ****************************************************
' **   Name:          Cursx                         **
' **   Type:          Subprogram                    **
' **   Module:        MOUSSUBS.BAS                  **
' **   Language:      Microsoft QuickBASIC 4.00     **
' ****************************************************
'
' Defines a graphics-mode mouse cursor (X mark).
'
' EXAMPLE OF USE:  Cursx mask$, xHot%, yHot%
' PARAMETERS:      mask$      Pattern mask for creating cursor
'                  xHot%      X location for cursor hot spot
'                  yHot%      Y location for cursor hot spot
' VARIABLES:       (none)
' MODULE LEVEL
'   DECLARATIONS:  DECLARE SUB Cursx (mask$, xHot%, yHot%)
'
    SUB Cursx (mask$, xHot%, yHot%) STATIC

        mask$ = ""
        mask$ = mask$ + "0000011111100000"
        mask$ = mask$ + "0000000110000000"
        mask$ = mask$ + "0000000000000000"
        mask$ = mask$ + "1100000000000011"
        mask$ = mask$ + "1111000000001111"
        mask$ = mask$ + "1100000000000011"
        mask$ = mask$ + "0000000000000000"
```

(continued)

continued

```
    mask$ = mask$ + "0000000110000000"
    mask$ = mask$ + "0000001111000000"
    mask$ = mask$ + "1111111111111111"
    mask$ = mask$ + "1111111111111111"
    mask$ = mask$ + "1111111111111111"
    mask$ = mask$ + "1111111111111111"
    mask$ = mask$ + "1111111111111111"
    mask$ = mask$ + "1111111111111111"
    mask$ = mask$ + "1111111111111111"

    mask$ = mask$ + "0000000000000000"
    mask$ = mask$ + "0111000000001110"
    mask$ = mask$ + "0001110000111000"
    mask$ = mask$ + "0000110001100000"
    mask$ = mask$ + "0000001111000000"
    mask$ = mask$ + "0000110001100000"
    mask$ = mask$ + "0001110000111000"
    mask$ = mask$ + "0111000000001110"
    mask$ = mask$ + "0000000000000000"
    mask$ = mask$ + "0000000000000000"
    mask$ = mask$ + "0000000000000000"
    mask$ = mask$ + "0000000000000000"
    mask$ = mask$ + "0000000000000000"
    mask$ = mask$ + "0000000000000000"
    mask$ = mask$ + "0000000000000000"
    mask$ = mask$ + "0000000000000000"

    xHot% = 7
    yHot% = 4

END SUB
```

Subprogram: MouseHide

Deactivates the mouse cursor, making it invisible and inaccessible. Use the MouseShow subprogram to reactivate the cursor.

```
' *****************************************
' ** Name:         MouseHide              **
' ** Type:         Subprogram             **
' ** Module:       MOUSSUBS.BAS           **
' ** Language:     Microsoft QuickBASIC 4.00 **
' *****************************************
'
' Hides the mouse cursor.
'
' EXAMPLE OF USE:  MouseHide
'
' PARAMETERS:      (none)
' VARIABLES:       (none)
' MODULE LEVEL
'   DECLARATIONS:  DECLARE SUB Mouse (m1%, m2%, m3%, m4%)
'                  DECLARE SUB MouseHide ()
'
  SUB MouseHide STATIC
      Mouse 2, 0, 0, 0
  END SUB
```

Subprogram: MouseInches

Sets the ratio of mouse motion to cursor motion. The horizontal% and vertical% parameters indicate the number of inches of desktop motion that your mouse must move to move the mouse cursor from one edge of the screen to the other. Note that the vertical and horizontal values are independent of each other.

Before calling this subprogram, set the double-speed threshold to a large value by calling the MouseWarp subprogram. This prevents fast mouse motion from doubling the cursor velocity, keeping the motion ratios constant.

```
' ***************************************************
' **   Name:        MouseInches                    **
' **   Type:        Subprogram                     **
' **   Module:      MOUSSUBS.BAS                   **
' **   Language:    Microsoft QuickBASIC 4.00      **
' ***************************************************
'
' Sets mouse motion ratio in inches per screen.
'
' EXAMPLE OF USE:    MouseInches horizontal%, vertical%
' PARAMETERS:        horizontal%    Inches of horizontal mouse motion per
'                                   screen width
'                    vertical%      Inches of vertical% mouse motion per
'                                   screen height
' VARIABLES:         h%             Calculated value to pass to mouse driver
'                    v%             Calculated value to pass to mouse driver
' MODULE LEVEL
'   DECLARATIONS:    DECLARE SUB Mouse (m1%, m2%, m3%, m4%)
'                    DECLARE SUB MouseInches (horizontal%, vertical%)
'
SUB MouseInches (horizontal%, vertical%) STATIC
    IF horizontal% > 100 THEN
        horizontal% = 100
    END IF
    IF vertical% > 100 THEN
        vertical% = 100
    END IF
    h% = horizontal% * 5 \ 2
    v% = vertical% * 8
    Mouse 15, 0, h%, v%
END SUB
```

Subprogram: MouseInstall

Checks the memory-resident mouse driver to determine whether a mouse is available. The value of mflag% is returned as *0* if no mouse is available and as *-1* if one is.

This subprogram also initializes the mouse driver to the default state. The original cursor is set, and the mouse velocity, threshold, and other parameters are all set to their original states.

Normally, this subprogram is called immediately when a program is run.

```
' *****************************************************
' **   Name:          MouseInstall                    **
' **   Type:          Subprogram                      **
' **   Module:        MOUSSUBS.BAS                    **
' **   Language:      Microsoft QuickBASIC 4.00       **
' *****************************************************
'
' Determines whether mouse is available and resets all mouse parameters.
'
' EXAMPLE OF USE:  MouseInstall mflag%
' PARAMETERS:      mflag%      Returned indication of mouse availability
' VARIABLES:       (none)
' MODULE LEVEL
'   DECLARATIONS:  DECLARE SUB Mouse (m1%, m2%, m3%, m4%)
'                  DECLARE SUB MouseInstall (mflag%)
'
  SUB MouseInstall (mflag%) STATIC
      mflag% = 0
      Mouse mflag%, 0, 0, 0
  END SUB
```

Subprogram: MouseLightPen

Activates or deactivates lightpen emulation by the mouse.

The QuickBASIC PEN function provides ten unique functions for accessing information on the lightpen, depending on the parameter you pass to it. This complete set of lightpen functions can be emulated using the mouse rather than the lightpen. To activate lightpen emulation, call MouseLightPen with a non-zero parameter. To deactivate lightpen emulation, use a zero parameter.

```
' *****************************************************
' **   Name:          MouseLightPen                   **
' **   Type:          Subprogram                      **
' **   Module:        MOUSSUBS.BAS                    **
' **   Language:      Microsoft QuickBASIC 4.00       **
' *****************************************************
```

(continued)

continued

```
' Activates and deactivates lightpen emulation mode.
'
' EXAMPLE OF USE:  MouseLightPen switch%
' PARAMETERS:      switch%    non-zero to activate lightpen emulation,
'                             zero to deactivate
' VARIABLES:       (none)
' MODULE LEVEL
'   DECLARATIONS:  DECLARE SUB Mouse (m1%, m2%, m3%, m4%)
'                  DECLARE SUB MouseLightPen (switch%)
'
SUB MouseLightPen (switch%) STATIC
    IF switch% THEN
        Mouse 13, 0, 0, 0
    ELSE
        Mouse 14, 0, 0, 0
    END IF
END SUB
```

Subprogram: MouseMaskTranslate

Translates the pattern mask and hot spot values for a given graphics-mode mouse cursor to a binary format string suitable for passing to the memory-resident mouse driver for setting the cursor.

This translation process is relatively time-consuming and should normally only be performed once, when a program first starts up. To save multiple cursors for quick switching between cursor types, save only the cursor$ result from this subprogram. The call to MouseSetCursor, using this binary format cursor$, is very fast.

```
' *****************************************************
' **  Name:       MouseMaskTranslate              **
' **  Type:       Subprogram                      **
' **  Module:     MOUSSUBS.BAS                    **
' **  Language:   Microsoft QuickBASIC 4.00       **
' *****************************************************
'
' Translates mouse graphics cursor Mask$ to Cursor$.
'
' EXAMPLE OF USE:  MouseMaskTranslate mask$, xHot%, yHot%, cursor$
```

(continued)

continued

```
' PARAMETERS:        mask$       Pattern mask that defines a mouse
'                                graphics-mode cursor
'                    xHot%       X location of the hot spot
'                    yHot%       Y location of the hot spot
'                    cursor$     The returned binary buffer string
'                                for the cursor
' VARIABLES:         i%          Looping index
'                    b%          Integer formed from string bit representations
' MODULE LEVEL
'   DECLARATIONS:  DECLARE SUB MouseMaskTranslate (mask$, xHot%, yHot%,
'                              cursor$)
'
    SUB MouseMaskTranslate (mask$, xHot%, yHot%, cursor$) STATIC
        cursor$ = CHR$(xHot%) + CHR$(yHot%) + STRING$(64, 0)
        IF LEN(mask$) = 512 THEN
            FOR i% = 1 TO 32
                b% = BinStr2Bin%(MID$(mask$, i% * 16 - 15, 16))
                MID$(cursor$, i% + i% + 1, 2) = MKI$(b%)
            NEXT i%
        END IF
    END SUB
```

Subprogram: MouseMickey

Returns the mouse "mickies," or relative motion counts, since the last call to this routine. If the mouse has not been moved since the last call, zeros are returned.

```
' ***********************************************
' **  Name:         MouseMickey                **
' **  Type:         Subprogram                 **
' **  Module:       MOUSSUBS.BAS               **
' **  Language:     Microsoft QuickBASIC 4.00  **
' ***********************************************
'
' Reads mouse mickey counts.
'
' EXAMPLE OF USE:  MouseMickey horizontal%, vertical%
' PARAMETERS:      horizontal%   Horizontal motion mickey counts
'                  vertical%     Vertical motion mickey counts
' VARIABLES:       (none)
```

(continued)

continued

```
' MODULE LEVEL
'   DECLARATIONS:   DECLARE SUB Mouse (m1%, m2%, m3%, m4%)
'                   DECLARE SUB MouseMickey (horizontal, vertical%)
'
  SUB MouseMickey (horizontal%, vertical%) STATIC
      Mouse 11, 0, horizontal%, vertical%
  END SUB
```

Subprogram: MouseNow

Returns the state of the mouse buttons and the mouse location. This subprogram is one of the most useful routines presented. Four parameters are passed back: the states of the two mouse buttons and the horizontal and vertical location of the mouse.

The horizontal position is scaled according to the current video mode. In most cases, the X position at the right edge of the screen is 639, no matter what the screen pixel range is. Check the returned values for the mode you want to use.

```
' ****************************************************
' **   Name:          MouseNow                      **
' **   Type:          Subprogram                    **
' **   Module:        MOUSSUBS.BAS                  **
' **   Language:      Microsoft QuickBASIC 4.00     **
' ****************************************************
'
' Returns the state of the mouse.
'
' EXAMPLE OF USE:  MouseNow leftButton%, rightButton%, xMouse%, yMouse%
' PARAMETERS:      leftButton%     Indicates left mouse button state
'                  rightButton%    Indicates right mouse button state
'                  xMouse%         X location of mouse
'                  yMouse%         Y location of mouse
' VARIABLES:       m2%             Mouse driver parameter containing button
'                                  press information
' MODULE LEVEL
'   DECLARATIONS:  DECLARE SUB Mouse (m1%, m2%, m3%, m4%)
'                  DECLARE SUB MouseNow (leftButton%, rightButton%,
'                                        xMouse%, yMouse%)
'
  SUB MouseNow (leftButton%, rightButton%, xMouse%, yMouse%) STATIC
      Mouse 3, m2%, xMouse%, yMouse%
      leftButton% = ((m2% AND 1) <> 0)
      rightButton% = ((m2% AND 2) <> 0)
  END SUB
```

Subprogram: MousePressLeft

Returns the position of the mouse at the time the left button was last pressed. Also returned is the number of left button presses since the last call to this subprogram.

```
' ***************************************************
' **   Name:         MousePressLeft                **
' **   Type:         Subprogram                    **
' **   Module:       MOUSSUBS.BAS                  **
' **   Language:     Microsoft QuickBASIC 4.00     **
' ***************************************************
'
' Returns the mouse state at last press of left button.
'
' EXAMPLE OF USE:  MousePressLeft leftCount%, xMouse%, yMouse%
' PARAMETERS:      leftCount%   Number of times the left button has been
'                               pressed since the last call to this
'                               subprogram
'                  xMouse%      X location of the mouse at the last press
'                               of the left button
'                  yMouse%      Y location of the mouse at the last press
'                               of the left button
' VARIABLES:       m1%          Parameter for call to mouse driver
' MODULE LEVEL
'   DECLARATIONS:  DECLARE SUB Mouse (m1%, m2%, m3%, m4%)
'                  DECLARE SUB MousePressLeft (leftCount%, xMouse%, yMouse%)
'
  SUB MousePressLeft (leftCount%, xMouse%, yMouse%) STATIC
      m1% = 5
      leftCount% = 0
      Mouse m1%, leftCount%, xMouse%, yMouse%
  END SUB
```

Subprogram: MousePressRight

Returns the position of the mouse at the time the right button was last pressed. Also returned is the number of right button presses since the last call to this subprogram.

```
' **************************************************
' **   Name:          MousePressRight            **
' **   Type:          Subprogram                 **
' **   Module:        MOUSSUBS.BAS               **
' **   Language:      Microsoft QuickBASIC 4.00  **
' **************************************************
'
' Returns the mouse state at last press of right button.
'
  SUB MousePressRight (rightCount%, xMouse%, yMouse%) STATIC
      m1% = 5
      rightCount% = 1
      Mouse m1%, rightCount%, xMouse%, yMouse%
  END SUB
```

Subprogram: MousePut

Allows you to move the mouse to any desired location.

```
' **************************************************
' **   Name:          MousePut                   **
' **   Type:          Subprogram                 **
' **   Module:        MOUSSUBS.BAS               **
' **   Language:      Microsoft QuickBASIC 4.00  **
' **************************************************
'
' Sets the mouse position.
'
' EXAMPLE OF USE:   MousePut xMouse%, yMouse%
' PARAMETERS:       xMouse%    Horizontal location to place cursor
'                   yMouse%    Vertical location to place cursor
' VARIABLES:        (none)
' MODULE LEVEL
'   DECLARATIONS:   DECLARE SUB Mouse (m1%, m2%, m3%, m4%)
'                   DECLARE SUB MousePut (xMouse%, yMouse%)
'
  SUB MousePut (xMouse%, yMouse%) STATIC
      Mouse 4, 0, xMouse%, yMouse%
  END SUB
```

Subprogram: MouseRange

Sets a rectangular area of the screen to which the mouse cursor will be limited. The mouse cursor will stay in the bounds defined, no matter which way the mouse is moved.

```
' *************************************************
' **   Name:         MouseRange                  **
' **   Type:         Subprogram                  **
' **   Module:       MOUSSUBS.BAS                **
' **   Language:     Microsoft QuickBASIC 4.00   **
' *************************************************
'
' Sets mouse range of motion.
'
' EXAMPLE OF USE:   MouseRange x1%, y1%, x2%, y2%
' PARAMETERS:       x1%        Upper left corner X coordinate
'                   y1%        Upper left corner Y coordinate
'                   x2%        Lower right corner X coordinate
'                   y2%        Lower right corner Y coordinate
' VARIABLES:        (none)
' MODULE LEVEL
'   DECLARATIONS:   DECLARE SUB Mouse (m1%, m2%, m3%, m4%)
'                   DECLARE SUB MouseRange (x1%, y1%, x2%, y2%)

  SUB MouseRange (x1%, y1%, x2%, y2%) STATIC
      Mouse 7, 0, x1%, x2%
      Mouse 8, 0, y1%, y2%
  END SUB
```

Subprogram: MouseReleaseLeft

Returns the position of the mouse at the time the left button was last released. Also returned is the number of left button releases since the last call to this subprogram.

```
' *************************************************
' **   Name:         MouseReleaseLeft            **
' **   Type:         Subprogram                  **
' **   Module:       MOUSSUBS.BAS                **
' **   Language:     Microsoft QuickBASIC 4.00   **
' *************************************************
```

(continued)

continued

```
' Returns the mouse state at last release of left button.
'
' EXAMPLE OF USE:   MouseReleaseLeft leftCount%, xMouse%, yMouse%
' PARAMETERS:       leftCount%   Number of times the left button has been
'                                released since the last call to this
'                                subprogram
'                   xMouse%      X location of the mouse at the last
'                                release of the left button
'                   yMouse%      Y location of the mouse at the last
'                                release of the left button
' VARIABLES:        m1%          Parameter for call to mouse driver
' MODULE LEVEL
'   DECLARATIONS:   DECLARE SUB Mouse (m1%, m2%, m3%, m4%)
'                   DECLARE SUB MouseReleaseLeft (leftCount%, xMouse%,
'                                                  yMouse%)

  SUB MouseReleaseLeft (leftCount%, xMouse%, yMouse%) STATIC
      m1% = 6
      leftCount% = 0
      Mouse m1%, leftCount%, xMouse%, yMouse%
  END SUB
```

Subprogram: MouseReleaseRight

Returns the position of the mouse at the time the right button was last released. Also returned is the number of right button releases since the last call to this subprogram.

```
' *********************************************
' ** Name:       MouseReleaseRight           **
' ** Type:       Subprogram                  **
' ** Module:     MOUSSUBS.BAS                **
' ** Language:   Microsoft QuickBASIC 4.00   **
' *********************************************
'
' Returns the mouse state at last release of right button.
'
' EXAMPLE OF USE:   MouseReleaseRight rightCount%, xMouse%, yMouse%
' PARAMETERS:       rightCount%  Number of times the right button has been
'                                released since the last call to this
'                                subprogram
'                   xMouse%      X location of the mouse at the last
'                                release of the right button
'                   yMouse%      Y location of the mouse at the last
'                                release of the right button
```

(continued)

continued

```
' VARIABLES:      m1%              Parameter for call to mouse driver
' MODULE LEVEL
'   DECLARATIONS: DECLARE SUB Mouse (m1%, m2%, m3%, m4%)
'                 DECLARE SUB MouseReleaseRight (rightCount%, xMouse%,
'                                                              yMouse%)
'
  SUB MouseReleaseRight (rightCount%, xMouse%, yMouse%) STATIC
     m1% = 6
     rightCount% = 1
     Mouse m1%, rightCount%, xMouse%, yMouse%
  END SUB
```

Subprogram: MouseSetGcursor

Sets the mouse cursor using the binary-format cursor string created by an earlier call to the subprogram MouseMaskTranslate.

To quickly switch among a selection of mouse cursors, keep the binary-format cursor strings available, and call this subprogram to change cursors.

```
' *************************************************
' ** Name:        MouseSetGcursor              **
' ** Type:        Subprogram                   **
' ** Module:      MOUSSUBS.BAS                 **
' ** Language:    Microsoft QuickBASIC 4.00    **
' *************************************************
'
' Sets mouse graphics cursor using cursor$.
'
' EXAMPLE OF USE:  MouseSetGcursor cursor$
' PARAMETERS:      cursor$   Binary format cursor string
' VARIABLES:       xHot%     X hot spot location
'                  yHot%     Y hot spot location
' MODULE LEVEL
'   DECLARATIONS: DECLARE SUB Mouse (m1%, m2%, m3%, m4%)
'                 DECLARE SUB MouseSetGcursor (cursor$)
'
  SUB MouseSetGcursor (cursor$) STATIC
     xHot% = ASC(LEFT$(cursor$, 1))
     yHot% = ASC(MID$(cursor$, 2, 1))
     Mouse 9, xHot%, yHot%, SADD(cursor$) + 2
  END SUB
```

Subprogram: MouseShow

Activates the mouse cursor, making it visible and movable by the mouse. To turn the cursor off, use the MouseHide subprogram.

When you are updating the screen, such as when printing text in a graphics mode, it's a good idea to hide the mouse just before printing and then show it after the printing is done. This helps prevent glitches or blank spots from appearing due to overlapping and unsynchronized pixel mapping between your program and the mouse driver.

```
' ***************************************************
' **   Name:          MouseShow                    **
' **   Type:          Subprogram                   **
' **   Module:        MOUSSUBS.BAS                 **
' **   Language:      Microsoft QuickBASIC 4.00    **
' ***************************************************
'
' Shows the mouse cursor.
'
' EXAMPLE OF USE:  MouseShow
' PARAMETERS:      (none)
' VARIABLES:       (none)
' MODULE LEVEL
'   DECLARATIONS:  DECLARE SUB Mouse (m1%, m2%, m3%, m4%)
'                  DECLARE SUB MouseShow ()
'
  SUB MouseShow STATIC
      Mouse 1, 0, 0, 0
  END SUB
```

Subprogram: MouseSoftCursor

Sets the software mouse cursor for text mode. This cursor changes the attributes of screen characters (foreground/background color, intensity, or underscoring) when the display adapter is in text mode. The easiest way to get a feel for how these masks work is by running the MOUSTCRS.BAS program.

```
' *****************************************************
' **   Name:         MouseSoftCursor              **
' **   Type:         Subprogram                   **
' **   Module:       MOUSSUBS.BAS                 **
' **   Language:     Microsoft QuickBASIC 4.00    **
' *****************************************************
'
' Sets text-mode software cursor.
'
' EXAMPLE OF USE:  MouseSoftCursor screenMask%, cursorMask%
' PARAMETERS:      screenMask%    Integer bit pattern for the screen mask
'                  cursorMask%    Integer bit pattern for the cursor mask
' VARIABLES:       (none)
' MODULE LEVEL
'   DECLARATIONS:  DECLARE SUB MouseSoftCursor (screenMaks%, cursorMask%)
'                  DECLARE SUB Mouse (m1%, m2%, m3%, m4%)
'
  SUB MouseSoftCursor (screenMask%, cursorMask%) STATIC
      Mouse 10, 0, screenMask%, cursorMask%
  END SUB
```

Subprogram: MouseWarp

Sets the double-speed threshold for the mouse in units of mickies per second. The default setting is 64 mickies per second.

Whenever the mouse is moved at a rate greater than the threshold value, the cursor motion is doubled. This helps zip the cursor across the screen during quick moves but allows slower, more accurate motion at slower speeds.

To use the MouseInches subprogram to approximate the action of an absolute-motion pointing device, set the threshold to a large, unreachable value. For example, MouseWarp 9999 effectively turns off the threshold checking.

```
' *****************************************************
' **   Name:         MouseWarp                    **
' **   Type:         Subprogram                   **
' **   Module:       MOUSSUBS.BAS                 **
' **   Language:     Microsoft QuickBASIC 4.00    **
' *****************************************************
```

(continued)

continued

```
' Sets double-speed threshold.
'
' EXAMPLE OF USE:    MouseWarp threshold%
' PARAMETERS:        threshold%    Mickies per second rate of threshold
' VARIABLES:         (none)
' MODULE LEVEL
'   DECLARATIONS:    DECLARE SUB Mouse (m1%, m2%, m3%, m4%)
'                    DECLARE SUB MouseWarp (threshold%)
'
  SUB MouseWarp (threshold%) STATIC
      Mouse 19, 0, 0, threshold%
  END SUB
```

MOUSTCRS

The MOUSTCRS program lets you experiment with the screen and cursor masks that define the action of the software mouse cursor in text modes.

Run the program and move the mouse cursor to any of the mask bits displayed near the bottom of the screen. Click with the left mouse button on any bit to toggle that bit, and move the cursor around the screen to see how the cursor's appearance is affected.

To set any screen and cursor mask combination in your own programs, record the hexadecimal numbers for the two masks, and pass these two numbers to the MouseSoftCursor subprogram in the MOUSSUBS.BAS toolbox.

Program Module: MOUSTCRS

```
' **************************************************
' **   Name:          MOUSTCRS                    **
' **   Type:          Program                     **
' **   Module:        MOUSTCRS.BAS                **
' **   Language:      Microsoft QuickBASIC 4.00   **
' **************************************************
'
' USAGE:          No command line parameters
' REQUIREMENTS:   MIXED.QLB/.LIB
'                 Mouse
' .MAK FILE:      MOUSTCRS.BAS
'                 MOUSSUBS.BAS
'                 BITS.BAS
'                 ATTRIB.BAS
' PARAMETERS:     (none)
' VARIABLES:      screenMask%    Integer bit mask for screen mask
'                 cursorMask%    Integer bit mask for cursor mask
'                 leftCount%     Count of left mouse button presses
'                 xm%            Mouse X position at last left button press
'                 ym%            Mouse Y position at last left button press
'                 row%           Code for which screen bit row was selected
'                 bit%           Bit pattern determined by screen column
'                                click on
```

(continued)

continued

```
'                   screenMask$    String of 0s and 1s for bit pattern display
'                   cursorMask$    String of 0s and 1s for bit pattern display
'                   i%             Looping index
'                   Shex$          Hexadecimal representation of the screen mask
'                   Chex$          Hexadecimal representation of the cursor mask

' Define constants
  CONST FALSE = 0
  CONST TRUE = NOT FALSE

' Functions
  DECLARE FUNCTION Bin2BinStr$ (b%)

' Subprograms
  DECLARE SUB Attrib ()
  DECLARE SUB MouseHide ()
  DECLARE SUB MouseInstall (mouseFlag%)
  DECLARE SUB MousePressLeft (leftCount%, xMouse%, yMouse%)
  DECLARE SUB MouseShow ()
  DECLARE SUB MouseSoftCursor (screenMask%, cursorMask%)

' Is the mouse out there?
  MouseInstall mouseFlag%
  IF mouseFlag% = 0 THEN
      PRINT "Mouse does not appear to be installed.  Check"
      PRINT "your mouse documentation for proper installation."
      PRINT
      SYSTEM
  END IF

' Put all attributes on the screen
  Attrib

' Set masks to initial state
  screenMask% = &H77FF
  cursorMask% = &H7700

' Create the outlined boxes
  COLOR 14, 0
  PRINT "             +---+--------+---+--------+----------+--------+"
  PRINT "             | b | bckgd  | i | foregd |   char   |   =    |"
  PRINT "             +---+--------+---+--------+----------+--------+"
  PRINT "| screen mask | 0 |  111   | 0 |  111   | 11111111 | &H77FF |"
  PRINT "| cursor mask | 0 |  111   | 0 |  111   | 00000000 | &H7700 |"
  PRINT "             +---+--------+---+--------+----------+--------+"
```

(continued)

continued

```
' Print the instructions
COLOR 11, 0
PRINT "Click the mouse on any of the mask bits shown.  Then, try the"
PRINT "new cursor by moving across the attribute fields above.";

' Special indication for quitting
COLOR 15, 0
LOCATE 17, 1, 0
PRINT "Click here";
LOCATE 18, 1, 0
PRINT "to Quit - ";
COLOR 10, 0
PRINT "X";

' Put mask bits into boxes on screen
GOSUB PrintScreenMask
GOSUB PrintCursorMask

' Activate the mouse
MouseShow

' Do the main processing loop until the quit flag is set
DO
     GOSUB MainLoop
LOOP UNTIL quitFlag%

' All done
MouseHide
CLS
SYSTEM

' Main processing loop
MainLoop:

' Where was mouse when left button was last pressed?
MousePressLeft leftCount%, xm%, ym%

' Was it on one of the two important rows of the screen?
SELECT CASE ym%
CASE 152
    row% = 1
CASE 160
    row% = 2
```

(continued)

continued

```
    CASE ELSE
        row% = 0
    END SELECT

' Was it on an important column?
    SELECT CASE xm%
    CASE 80
        IF ym% = 136 THEN
            quitFlag% = TRUE
        END IF
    CASE 160
        bit% = &H8000
    CASE 200
        bit% = &H4000
    CASE 208
        bit% = &H2000
    CASE 216
        bit% = &H1000
    CASE 256
        bit% = &H800
    CASE 296
        bit% = &H400
    CASE 304
        bit% = &H200
    CASE 312
        bit% = &H100
    CASE 360
        bit% = &H80
    CASE 368
        bit% = &H40
    CASE 376
        bit% = &H20
    CASE 384
        bit% = &H10
    CASE 392
        bit% = &H8
    CASE 400
        bit% = &H4
    CASE 408
        bit% = &H2
    CASE 416
        bit% = &H1
    CASE ELSE
        bit% = 0
    END SELECT
```

(continued)

continued

```
    ' Modify the masks and update the cursor
    IF leftCount% THEN
        SELECT CASE row%
        CASE 1
            screenMask% = screenMask% XOR bit%
        CASE 2
            cursorMask% = cursorMask% XOR bit%
        CASE ELSE
        END SELECT
        MouseSoftCursor screenMask%, cursorMask%
        GOSUB PrintScreenMask
        GOSUB PrintCursorMask
    END IF

    ' End of main processing loop
    RETURN

    ' Put screen mask bits on the screen
PrintScreenMask:
    COLOR 12, 0
    screenMask$ = ""
    screenMask$ = Bin2BinStr$(screenMask%)
    MouseHide
    FOR i% = 0 TO 15
        SELECT CASE i%
        CASE 0 TO 7
            LOCATE 20, 53 - i%, 0
            PRINT MID$(screenMask$, 16 - i%, 1);
        CASE 8 TO 10
            LOCATE 20, 48 - i%, 0
            PRINT MID$(screenMask$, 16 - i%, 1);
        CASE 11
            LOCATE 20, 44 - i%, 0
            PRINT MID$(screenMask$, 16 - i%, 1);
        CASE 12 TO 14
            LOCATE 20, 40 - i%, 0
            PRINT MID$(screenMask$, 16 - i%, 1);
        CASE 15
            LOCATE 20, 36 - i%, 0
            PRINT MID$(screenMask$, 16 - i%, 1);
        CASE ELSE
        END SELECT
```

(continued)

continued

```
    NEXT i%
    shex$ = "&H" + RIGHT$("000" + HEX$(screenMask%), 4)
    LOCATE 20, 57, 0
    COLOR 10, 0
    PRINT shex$;
    MouseShow
    RETURN

' Put cursor mask bits on the screen
PrintCursorMask:
    COLOR 12, 0
    cursorMask$ = ""
    cursorMask$ = Bin2BinStr$(cursorMask%)
    MouseHide
    FOR i% = 0 TO 15
        SELECT CASE i%
        CASE 0 TO 7
            LOCATE 21, 53 - i%, 0
            PRINT MID$(cursorMask$, 16 - i%, 1);
        CASE 8 TO 10
            LOCATE 21, 48 - i%, 0
            PRINT MID$(cursorMask$, 16 - i%, 1);
        CASE 11
            LOCATE 21, 44 - i%, 0
            PRINT MID$(cursorMask$, 16 - i%, 1);
        CASE 12 TO 14
            LOCATE 21, 40 - i%, 0
            PRINT MID$(cursorMask$, 16 - i%, 1);
        CASE 15
            LOCATE 21, 36 - i%, 0
            PRINT MID$(cursorMask$, 16 - i%, 1);
        CASE ELSE
        END SELECT
    NEXT i%
    chex$ = "&H" + RIGHT$("000" + HEX$(cursorMask%), 4)
    LOCATE 21, 57, 0
    COLOR 10, 0
    PRINT chex$;
    MouseShow
    RETURN
```

OBJECT

The OBJECT program lets you interactively create subprograms that produce graphics objects for your programs.

When a QuickBASIC program uses the GET and PUT statements for graphics animation purposes, you'll often notice the objects being created on the screen as the program first starts up. The normal procedure is to create the graphics objects using the LINE and DRAW statements and then to save the objects in integer arrays using the GET statement. The creation of the objects the first time is relatively slow, compared with the very fast PUT statement.

The OBJECT program lets you create these objects interactively and "off-line" until you're satisfied with their appearance. Then, this program automatically writes a subprogram source file that, when loaded or merged with your main program, quickly creates the integer arrays by simply reading the appropriate integers into the arrays.

The best way to get a feel for this program is to give it a try. Run it, and follow the directions. You can edit a DRAW string, try it to see what the new object looks like, and then re-edit the string until you like the results. When you select the "Save" option, the program automatically determines the smallest integer array that will hold the object you've created and writes a source code subprogram file that creates and fills an integer array with the bit pattern for your object. Later on, you can load this source code file and re-edit the object to make other changes.

To use the new object source code in your own program, merge the file into the program where you want to use the object. The program should run through the statements once, but you can use PUT statements repeatedly to animate or duplicate the image.

Name	Type	Description
OBJECT.BAS		Program module
SaveObject	Sub	Creates graphics "PUT" file source code

Program Module: OBJECT

```
' ****************************************************
' **    Name:          OBJECT                       **
' **    Type:          Program                      **
' **    Module:        OBJECT.BAS                   **
' **    Language:      Microsoft QuickBASIC 4.00    **
' ****************************************************
'
' Allows interactive graphics object creation.
' Dumps code for another program to be able to create
' the graphics object "PUT array" directly.
'
' USAGE:            No command line parameters
' REQUIREMENTS:     CGA
' .MAK FILE:        OBJECT.BAS
'                   KEYS.BAS
'                   EDIT.BAS
' PARAMETERS:       (none)
' VARIABLES:        quitFlag%       Indicates user is ready to quit
'                   modeFlag%       Indicates a valid graphics mode was selected
'                   mode%           Graphics mode
'                   xMax%           Maximum screen X coordinate
'                   yMax%           Maximum screen Y coordinate
'                   fileName$       Name of object creation subprogram file
'                   exitCode%       Return code from EditLine subprogram
'                   t$              Temporary work string while reading file
'                                   contents
'                   a$              The DRAW string
'                   editFlag%       Indicates an edit of the string is desired
'                   drawErrorFlag%  Indicates an error occurred during the DRAW
'                   keyNumber%      Integer key code returned by KeyCode%
'                                   function
'                   okayFlag%       Shared flag for determining array dimensions

' Logical constants
  CONST FALSE = 0
  CONST TRUE = NOT FALSE

' Key code constants
  CONST SKEYLC = 115
  CONST SKEYUC = SKEYLC - 32
  CONST QKEYLC = 113
  CONST QKEYUC = QKEYLC - 32
  CONST ESC = 27
```

(continued)

continued

```
' Color constants
  CONST BLACK = 0
  CONST BLUE = 1
  CONST GREEN = 2
  CONST CYAN = 3
  CONST RED = 4
  CONST MAGENTA = 5
  CONST BROWN = 6
  CONST WHITE = 7
  CONST BRIGHT = 8
  CONST BLINK = 16
  CONST YELLOW = BROWN + BRIGHT

' Functions
  DECLARE FUNCTION KeyCode% ()

' Subprograms
  DECLARE SUB DrawBox (row1%, col1%, row2%, col2%)
  DECLARE SUB EditBox (a$, row1%, col1%, row2%, col2%)
  DECLARE SUB EditLine (a$, exitCode%)
  DECLARE SUB SaveObject (mode%, xMax%, yMax%, fileName$, a$)

' Initialization
  SCREEN 0
  CLS
  quitFlag% = FALSE

' Title
  PRINT "OBJECT - Interactive graphics object editor"
  PRINT
  PRINT

' Display screen mode table
  PRINT "Adapter        SCREEN modes allowed"
  PRINT "----------     --------------------"
  PRINT "Monochrome     (none)"
  PRINT "Hercules       3"
  PRINT "CGA            1,2"
  PRINT "EGA            1,2,7,8,9"
  PRINT "MCGA           1,2,11,13"
  PRINT "VGA            1,2,7,8,9,10,11,12,13"
  PRINT
```

(continued)

continued

```
' Ask user for the graphics screen mode
  DO
      PRINT "Enter a SCREEN mode number, ";
      INPUT "based on your graphics adapter "; mode%
      modeFlag% = TRUE
      SELECT CASE mode%
      CASE 1, 7, 13
          xMax% = 319
          yMax% = 199
      CASE 2, 8
          xMax% = 639
          yMax% = 199
      CASE 9, 10
          xMax% = 639
          yMax% = 349
      CASE 11, 12
          xMax% = 639
          yMax% = 479
      CASE 3
          xMax% = 719
          yMax% = 347
      CASE ELSE
          modeFlag% = FALSE
      END SELECT
  LOOP UNTIL modeFlag% = TRUE

' Ask user for the filename
  fileName$ = "IMAGEARY.BAS" + SPACE$(20)
  SCREEN 0
  WIDTH 80
  CLS
  COLOR WHITE, BLACK
  PRINT "Name of the file where source code will be written:"
  PRINT
  PRINT "Edit the default filename IMAGEARY.BAS ";
  PRINT "if desired, and then press Enter..."
  PRINT
  PRINT SPACE$(12);
  COLOR YELLOW, BLUE
  EditLine fileName$, exitCode%
  COLOR WHITE, BLACK

' Try to read in previous contents of the file
  ON ERROR GOTO FileError
```

(continued)

continued

```
    OPEN fileName$ FOR INPUT AS #1
    ON ERROR GOTO 0
    DO UNTIL EOF(1)
        LINE INPUT #1, t$
        IF INSTR(t$, "(DRAW$)") THEN
            t$ = MID$(t$, INSTR(t$, CHR$(34)) + 1)
            t$ = LEFT$(t$, INSTR(t$, CHR$(34)) - 1)
            a$ = a$ + t$
        END IF
    LOOP
    CLOSE #1

' Main loop
    DO

        ' Prepare for DRAW string editing by the user
        SCREEN 0
        WIDTH 80
        CLS
        editFlag% = FALSE

        ' Display useful information
        PRINT "OBJECT - Screen mode"; mode%
        PRINT
        PRINT "Edit the DRAW string workspace; then press"
        PRINT "the Esc key to try out your creation..."
        PRINT
        PRINT , "               Cn       Color"
        PRINT , " H   U   E     Mx,y     Move absolute"
        PRINT , "   \ | /       M+|-x,y  Move relative"
        PRINT , " L -   - R     An       Angle (1=90,2=180...)"
        PRINT , "   / | \       TAn      Turn angle (-360 to 360)"
        PRINT , " G   D   F     Sn       Scale factor"
        PRINT , "               Pc,b     Paint (color, border)"
    PRINT "(These commands are described in detail in the ";
    PRINT "Microsoft QuickBASIC Language Reference)"

        ' Input DRAW string via EditBox subprogram
        COLOR GREEN + BRIGHT, BLUE
        DrawBox 15, 1, 24, 80
        COLOR YELLOW, BLUE
        EditBox a$, 15, 1, 24, 80
```

(continued)

continued

```
    ' Try out the DRAW string
      SCREEN mode%
      drawErrorFlag% = FALSE
      ON ERROR GOTO DrawError
      DRAW a$
      ON ERROR GOTO 0

    ' Give user idea of what to do
      LOCATE 1, 1
      PRINT "<S>ave, <Esc> to edit, or <Q>uit"

    ' Get next valid keystroke
      DO UNTIL editFlag% OR drawErrorFlag% OR quitFlag%

        ' Grab key code
          keyNumber% = KeyCode%

        ' Process the keystroke
          SELECT CASE keyNumber%

            CASE ESC
                editFlag% = TRUE

            CASE QKEYLC, QKEYUC
                quitFlag% = TRUE

            CASE SKEYLC, SKEYUC
                SaveObject mode%, xMax%, yMax%, fileName$, a$

            CASE ELSE
          END SELECT

      LOOP

  LOOP UNTIL quitFlag%

' All done
  CLS
  SCREEN 0
  WIDTH 80
  END
```

(continued)

continued

```
FileError:
  ' Create the new file
    OPEN fileName$ FOR OUTPUT AS #1
    CLOSE #1
    OPEN fileName$ FOR INPUT AS #1
    RESUME NEXT

DrawError:
    drawErrorFlag% = TRUE
    SCREEN 0
    CLS
    PRINT "Your DRAW string caused an error"
    PRINT
    PRINT "Press any key to continue"
    DO
    LOOP UNTIL INKEY$ <> ""
    RESUME NEXT

ArrayError:
    okayFlag% = FALSE
    RESUME NEXT
```

Subprogram: SaveObject

Creates a source code subprogram module file for the OBJECT program.

This subprogram performs the tricky task of finding the boundaries of the graphics object, dimensioning an integer array of exactly the right size, getting the object from the screen and into the array, and writing a source code subprogram file that will recreate the array when merged into a different program.

```
' ************************************************
' **   Name:         SaveObject                 **
' **   Type:         Subprogram                 **
' **   Module:       OBJECT.BAS                 **
' **   Language:     Microsoft QuickBASIC 4.00  **
' ************************************************
'
' Creates source code file for creating graphics mode
' objects for efficient "PUT" graphics.
```

continued

```
' EXAMPLE OF USE:   SaveObject mode%, xMax%, yMax%, fileName$, a$
' PARAMETERS:       mode%       Graphics mode
'                   xMax%       Maximum X screen coordinate for given
'                               graphics mode
'                   yMax%       Maximum Y screen coordinate for given
'                               graphics mode
'                   fileName$   Name of source code file to edit and/or
'                               create
'                   a$          The DRAW string that creates the object
'                               initially
' VARIABLES:        okayFlag%   Shared flag used to determine array size
'                   size%       Array sizing
'                   edge%       Array for efficiently finding edges of object
'                   stepSize%   Scanning step for search for object edges
'                   yTop%       Y coordinate at top edge of object
'                   yBot%       Y coordinate at bottom edge of object
'                   y1%         Starting edge search Y coordinate
'                   y2%         Ending edge search Y coordinate
'                   i%          Looping index
'                   xLeft%      X coordinate at left edge of object
'                   xRight%     X coordinate at right edge of object
'                   x1%         Starting edge search X coordinate
'                   x2%         Ending edge search X coordinate
'                   object%()   Array to hold GET object from screen
'                   objName$    Name of object, derived from filename
'                   ndx%        Index to any special characters in objName$
'                   ary$        Name of array, derived from filename
'                   d$          Works string for building lines for file
' MODULE LEVEL
'   DECLARATIONS: DECLARE FUNCTION SaveObject (mode%, xMax%, yMax%,
'                                              fileName$, a$)
'
   SUB SaveObject (mode%, xMax%, yMax%, fileName$, a$) STATIC

     ' Shared error trap variable
       SHARED okayFlag%

     ' Select the right array size for the mode
       SELECT CASE mode%
         CASE 1, 2
           size% = 93
         CASE 7, 8
           size% = 367
         CASE 9
           size% = 667
```

(continued)

continued

```
        CASE 10
            size% = 334
        CASE 11
            size% = 233
        CASE 12
            size% = 927
        CASE 13
            size% = 161
        CASE ELSE
        END SELECT

' Build the array space
    DIM edge%(size%)

' Scan to find top and bottom edges of the object
    stepSize% = 32
    yTop% = yMax%
    yBot% = 0
    y1% = 17
    y2% = yMax%
    DO
        FOR y% = y1% TO y2% STEP stepSize%
            IF y% < yTop% OR y% > yBot% THEN
                GET (0, y%)-(xMax%, y%), edge%
                LINE (0, y%)-(xMax%, y%)
                FOR i% = 2 TO size%
                    IF edge%(i%) THEN
                        IF y% < yTop% THEN
                            yTop% = y%
                        END IF
                        IF y% > yBot% THEN
                            yBot% = y%
                        END IF
                        i% = size%
                    END IF
                NEXT i%
                PUT (0, y%), edge%, PSET
            END IF
        NEXT y%
        IF yTop% <= yBot% THEN
            y1% = yTop% - stepSize% * 2
            y2% = yBot% + stepSize% * 2
            IF y1% < 17 THEN
                y1% = 17
            END IF
```

(continued)

continued

```
                IF y2% > yMax% THEN
                    y2% = yMax%
                END IF
            END IF
        stepSize% = stepSize% \ 2
    LOOP UNTIL stepSize% = 0

' Scan to find left and right edges of the object
    stepSize% = 32
    xLeft% = xMax%
    xRight% = 0
    x1% = 0
    x2% = xMax%
    DO
        FOR x% = x1% TO x2% STEP stepSize%
            IF x% < xLeft% OR x% > xRight% THEN
                GET (x%, yTop%)-(x%, yBot%), edge%
                LINE (x%, yTop%)-(x%, yBot%)
                FOR i% = 2 TO size%
                    IF edge%(i%) THEN
                        IF x% < xLeft% THEN
                            xLeft% = x%
                        END IF
                        IF x% > xRight% THEN
                            xRight% = x%
                        END IF
                        i% = size%
                    END IF
                NEXT i%
                PUT (x%, yTop%), edge%, PSET
            END IF
        NEXT x%
        IF xLeft% <= xRight% THEN
            x1% = xLeft% - stepSize% * 2
            x2% = xRight% + stepSize% * 2
            IF x1% < 0 THEN
                x1% = 0
            END IF
            IF x2% > xMax% THEN
                x2% = xMax%
            END IF
        END IF
        stepSize% = stepSize% \ 2
    LOOP UNTIL stepSize% = 0
```

(continued)

continued

```
' Draw border around the object
  LINE (xLeft% - 1, yTop% - 1)-(xRight% + 1, yBot% + 1), , B

' Build the right size integer array
  stepSize% = 256
  size% = 3
  DO
      DO
          IF size% < 3 THEN
              size% = 3
          END IF
          REDIM object%(size%)
          okayFlag% = TRUE
          ON ERROR GOTO ArrayError
          GET (xLeft%, yTop%)-(xRight%, yBot%), object%
          ON ERROR GOTO 0
          IF okayFlag% = FALSE THEN
              size% = size% + stepSize%
          ELSE
              IF stepSize% > 1 THEN
                  size% = size% - stepSize%
              END IF
          END IF
      LOOP UNTIL okayFlag%
      stepSize% = stepSize% \ 2
  LOOP UNTIL stepSize% = 0

' Make the name of the object
  objName$ = LTRIM$(RTRIM$(fileName$)) + "."
  ndx% = INSTR(objName$, "\")
  DO WHILE ndx%
      objName$ = MID$(objName$, ndx% + 1)
      ndx% = INSTR(objName$, "\")
  LOOP
  ndx% = INSTR(objName$, ":")
  DO WHILE ndx%
      objName$ = MID$(objName$, ndx% + 1)
      ndx% = INSTR(objName$, ":")
  LOOP
  ndx% = INSTR(objName$, ".")
  objName$ = LCASE$(LEFT$(objName$, ndx% - 1))
  IF objName$ = "" THEN
      objName$ = "xxxxxx"
  END IF
```

(continued)

continued

```
' Make array name
ary$ = objName$ + "%("

' Open the file for the new source lines
OPEN fileName$ FOR OUTPUT AS #1

' Print the lines
PRINT #1, " "
PRINT #1, " ' " + objName$
FOR i% = 1 TO LEN(a$) STEP 50
    PRINT #1, "    ' (DRAW$) "; CHR$(34);
    PRINT #1, MID$(a$, i%, 50); CHR$(34)
NEXT i%
PRINT #1, "    DIM " + ary$; "0 TO";
PRINT #1, STR$(size%) + ")"
PRINT #1, "    FOR i% = 0 TO"; size%
PRINT #1, "        READ h$"
PRINT #1, "        " + ary$ + "i%) = VAL(";
PRINT #1, CHR$(34) + "&H" + CHR$(34);
PRINT #1, " + h$)"
PRINT #1, "    NEXT i%"
FOR i% = 0 TO size%
    IF d$ = "" THEN
        d$ = "    DATA "
    ELSE
        d$ = d$ + ","
    END IF
    d$ = d$ + HEX$(object%(i%))
    IF LEN(d$) > 60 OR i% = size% THEN
        PRINT #1, d$
        d$ = ""
    END IF
NEXT i%
PRINT #1, " "

' Close the file
CLOSE

' Erase the border around the object
LINE (xLeft% - 1, yTop% - 1)-(xRight% + 1, yBot% + 1), 0, B

END SUB
```

PARSE

The PARSE toolbox demonstrates the ParseLine and ParseWord subprograms. A sample string of text (x$) is parsed by each of these subprograms, and the results are displayed for review.

The purpose of these subprograms is to split a string into substrings, where each substring is delineated by any of a given set of characters that you define. For example, a string can be parsed into individual words by splitting the string wherever spaces or commas occur.

A common use for these subprograms would be the processing of a list of commands passed to a QuickBASIC program from the MS-DOS command line, available in the special variable COMMAND$. The HEX2BIN, BIN2HEX, and QBFMT programs use the PARSE toolbox in this way.

Name	Type	Description
PARSE.BAS		Demo module
ParseLine	Sub	Breaks a string into individual words
ParseWord	Sub	Parses and removes first word from string

Demo Module: PARSE ✓

```
' **************************************************
' **  Name:         PARSE                         **
' **  Type:         Toolbox                       **
' **  Module:       PARSE.BAS                     **
' **  Language:     Microsoft QuickBASIC 4.00     **
' **************************************************
'
' USAGE:          No command line parameters
' .MAK FILE:      (none)
' PARAMETERS:     (none)
```

(continued)

continued

```
' VARIABLES:      a$()      Array of words parsed from x$
'                 x$        String to be parsed
'                 sep$      Characters defining word separation
'                 word$     Each word from the string
'                 n%        Index to each word in array

  DECLARE SUB ParseLine (x$, sep$, a$())
  DECLARE SUB ParseWord (a$, sep$, word$)

' Initialization
  CLS
  DIM a$(1 TO 99)

' Demonstrate ParseWord
  x$ = "This is a test line. A,B,C, etc."
  sep$ = " ,"
  PRINT "x$:", x$
  PRINT "sep$:", CHR$(34); sep$; CHR$(34)
  ParseWord x$, sep$, word$
  PRINT "ParseWord x$, sep$, word$"
  PRINT "x$:", x$
  PRINT "word$:", word$

' Demonstrate ParseLine
  PRINT
  x$ = "This is a test line. A,B,C, etc."
  sep$ = " ,"
  PRINT "x$:", x$
  PRINT "sep$:", CHR$(34); sep$; CHR$(34)
  ParseLine x$, sep$, a$()
  PRINT "ParseLine x$, sep$, a$()"
  PRINT "a$()..."
  DO
      n% = n% + 1
      PRINT n%, a$(n%)
  LOOP UNTIL a$(n% + 1) = ""

' All done
  END
```

Subprogram: ParseLine

Parses a string into individual words, returning the list of words in a string array. You can list any characters in sep$ to define the division between words, but the most commonly used characters are space, comma, and tab. The string array will contain a null string after the last word parsed from the string.

```
' **************************************************
' **  Name:         ParseLine                     **
' **  Type:         Subprogram                    **
' **  Module:       PARSE.BAS                     **
' **  Language:     Microsoft QuickBASIC 4.00     **
' **************************************************
'
' Breaks a string into an array of words, as defined
' by any characters listed in sep$.
'
' EXAMPLE OF USE:   ParseLine x$, sep$, a$()
' PARAMETERS:       x$       String to be parsed
'                   sep$     List of characters defined as word separators
'                   a$()     Returned array of words
' VARIABLES:        t$       Temporary work string
'                   i%       Index to array entries
' MODULE LEVEL
'   DECLARATIONS:   DECLARE SUB ParseLine (x$, sep$, a$())
'
    SUB ParseLine (x$, sep$, a$()) STATIC
        t$ = x$
        FOR i% = LBOUND(a$) TO UBOUND(a$)
            ParseWord t$, sep$, a$(i%)
            IF a$(i%) = "" THEN
                EXIT FOR
            END IF
        NEXT i%
        t$ = ""
    END SUB
```

Subprogram: ParseWord

Extracts the first word from the front of a string, returning the word and the original string minus the leading word. You can call this routine repeatedly to parse out each word, one at a time. You set the characters that separate words in sep$. For example, to parse words separated by either spaces or commas, set as follows:

```
sep$ = " ,"
```

```
' ***************************************************
' **   Name:          ParseWord                    **
' **   Type:          Subprogram                   **
' **   Module:        PARSE.BAS                    **
' **   Language:      Microsoft QuickBASIC 4.00    **
' ***************************************************
'
' Breaks off the first word in a$, as delimited by
' any characters listed in sep$.
'
' EXAMPLE OF USE:   ParseWord a$, sep$, word$
' PARAMETERS:       a$        String to be parsed
'                   sep$      List of characters defined as word separators
'                   word$     Returned first word parsed from a$
' VARIABLES:        lena%     Length of a$
'                   i%        Looping index
'                   j%        Looping index
'                   k%        Looping index
' MODULE LEVEL
'   DECLARATIONS:   DECLARE SUB ParseWord (a$, sep$, word$)
'
  SUB ParseWord (a$, sep$, word$) STATIC
      word$ = ""
      lena% = LEN(a$)
      IF a$ = "" THEN
          EXIT SUB
      END IF
      FOR i% = 1 TO lena%
          IF INSTR(sep$, MID$(a$, i%, 1)) = 0 THEN
              EXIT FOR
          END IF
```

(continued)

continued

```
        NEXT i%
        FOR j% = i% TO lena%
            IF INSTR(sep$, MID$(a$, j%, 1)) THEN
                EXIT FOR
            END IF
        NEXT j%
        FOR k% = j% TO lena%
            IF INSTR(sep$, MID$(a$, k%, 1)) = 0 THEN
                EXIT FOR
            END IF
        NEXT k%
        IF i% > lena% THEN
            a$ = ""
            EXIT SUB
        END IF
        IF j% > lena% THEN
            word$ = MID$(a$, i%)
            a$ = ""
            EXIT SUB
        END IF
        word$ = MID$(a$, i%, j% - i%)
        IF k% > lena% THEN
            a$ = ""
        ELSE
            a$ = MID$(a$, k%)
        END IF
END SUB
```

PROBSTAT

The PROBSTAT toolbox is a collection of functions for probability and statistics calculations.

Name	Type	Description
PROBSTAT.BAS		Demo module
ArithmeticMean#	Func	Arithmetic mean of an array of numbers
Combinations#	Func	Combinations of n items, r at a time
Factorial#	Func	Factorial of a number
GeometricMean#	Func	Geometric mean of an array of numbers
HarmonicMean#	Func	Harmonic mean of an array of numbers
Permutations#	Func	Permutations of n items, r at a time
QuadraticMean#	Func	Quadratic mean of an array of numbers

Demo Module: PROBSTAT

```
' ****************************************************
' **   Name:        PROBSTAT                        **
' **   Type:        Toolbox                         **
' **   Module:      PROBSTAT.BAS                    **
' **   Language:    Microsoft QuickBASIC 4.00       **
' ****************************************************
'
' Demonstrates several probability- and statistics-
' related mathematical functions.
'
' USAGE:         No command line parameters
' .MAK FILE:     (none)
' PARAMETERS:    (none)
' VARIABLES:     a#()    Array of numbers to be processed
'                i%      Index into array
'                n&      Number of items for combinations and permutations
'                r&      Quantity for combinations and permutations
```

(continued)

continued

```
      DECLARE FUNCTION Combinations# (n&, r&)
      DECLARE FUNCTION Factorial# (n&)
      DECLARE FUNCTION Permutations# (n&, r&)
      DECLARE FUNCTION GeometricMean# (a#())
      DECLARE FUNCTION HarmonicMean# (a#())
      DECLARE FUNCTION ArithmeticMean# (a#())
      DECLARE FUNCTION QuadraticMean# (a#())

    ' Demonstrations
      CLS
      PRINT "PROBSTAT"
      PRINT
      PRINT "Array of numbers..."
      DIM a#(-3 TO 6)
      FOR i% = -3 TO 6
          READ a#(i%)
          PRINT a#(i%),
      NEXT i%
      PRINT
      DATA 1.2,3.4,5.6,7.8,9.1,2.3,4.5,6.7,8.9,1.2

      PRINT
      PRINT "Arithmetic mean = "; ArithmeticMean#(a#())
      PRINT "Geometric mean  = "; GeometricMean#(a#())
      PRINT "Harmonic mean   = "; HarmonicMean#(a#())
      PRINT "Quadratic mean  = "; QuadraticMean#(a#())
      PRINT

      n& = 17
      r& = 5
      PRINT "Combinations of"; n&; "objects taken";
      PRINT r&; "at a time = "; Combinations#(n&, r&)

      PRINT "Permutations of"; n&; "objects taken";
      PRINT r&; "at a time = "; Permutations#(n&, r&)

      PRINT
      PRINT "Factorial of 17 = "; Factorial#(17&)

    ' All done
      END
```

Function: ArithmeticMean#

Returns the arithmetic mean of an array of double-precision numbers.

```
' ****************************************************
' **   Name:          ArithmeticMean#              **
' **   Type:          Function                     **
' **   Module:        PROBSTAT.BAS                 **
' **   Language:      Microsoft QuickBASIC 4.00    **
' ****************************************************
'
' Returns the arithmetic mean of an array of numbers.
'
' EXAMPLE OF USE:   ArithmeticMean# a#()
' PARAMETERS:       a#()       Array of double-precision numbers to be
'                              processed
' VARIABLES:        n%         Count of array entries
'                   sum#       Sum of the array entries
'                   i%         Looping index
' MODULE LEVEL
'   DECLARATIONS:   DECLARE FUNCTION ArithmeticMean# (a#())
'
  FUNCTION ArithmeticMean# (a#()) STATIC
      n% = 0
      sum# = 0
      FOR i% = LBOUND(a#) TO UBOUND(a#)
          n% = n% + 1
          sum# = sum# + a#(i%)
      NEXT i%
      ArithmeticMean# = sum# / n%
  END FUNCTION
```

Function: Combinations#

Calculates the number of combinations of n& items taken r& at a time. This function returns a double-precision result to allow for larger answers.

```
' ****************************************************
' **   Name:          Combinations#                **
' **   Type:          Function                     **
' **   Module:        PROBSTAT.BAS                 **
' **   Language:      Microsoft QuickBASIC 4.00    **
' ****************************************************
'
' Returns the number of combinations of n& items
' taken r& at a time.
```

(continued)

continued

```
' EXAMPLE OF USE:   c# = Combinations#(n&, r&)
' PARAMETERS:       n&          Number of items
'                   r&          Taken r& at a time
' VARIABLES:        result#     Working result variable
'                   j&          Working copy of r&
'                   k&          Difference between n& and r&
'                   h&          Values from r& through n&
'                   i&          Values from 1 through j&
' MODULE LEVEL
'   DECLARATIONS:   DECLARE FUNCTION Combinations# (n&, r&)
'
  FUNCTION Combinations# (n&, r&) STATIC
      result# = 1
      j& = r&
      k& = n& - r&
      h& = n&
      IF j& > k& THEN
          SWAP j&, k&
      END IF
      FOR i& = 1 TO j&
          result# = (result# * h&) / i&
          h& = h& - 1
      NEXT i&
      Combinations# = result#
  END FUNCTION
```

Function: Factorial#

Returns the factorial of a long integer. The returned value is double-precision, allowing for larger arguments. This is a recursive function. If the argument n& is greater than 1, n& is multiplied by the result of finding the factorial of n& − 1. The result is that this function will call itself n& times.

Notice that the STATIC keyword is missing from the end of the FUNCTION statement because recursive functions must not be defined as STATIC.

```
' ***************************************************
' **  Name:       Factorial#                      **
' **  Type:       Function                        **
' **  Module:     PROBSTAT.BAS                    **
' **  Language:   Microsoft QuickBASIC 4.00       **
' ***************************************************
```

(continued)

continued

```
' Returns the factorial of n& (recursive).
'
' EXAMPLE OF USE:   f# = Factorial#(n&)
' PARAMETERS:       n&           Number to be evaluated
' VARIABLES:        (none)
' MODULE LEVEL
'   DECLARATIONS:   DECLARE FUNCTION Factorial# (n&)
'
  FUNCTION Factorial# (n&)
     IF n& > 1 THEN
         Factorial# = n& * Factorial#(n& - 1)
     ELSE
         Factorial# = 1
     END IF
  END FUNCTION
```

Function: GeometricMean#

Returns the geometric mean of an array of double-precision numbers.

```
' **********************************************
' ** Name:        GeometricMean#                **
' ** Type:        Function                      **
' ** Module:      PROBSTAT.BAS                  **
' ** Language:    Microsoft QuickBASIC 4.00     **
' **********************************************
'
' Returns the geometric mean of an array of numbers.
'
' EXAMPLE OF USE:   gm# = GeometricMean#(a#())
' PARAMETERS:       a#()         Array of numbers to be processed
' VARIABLES:        n%           Count of numbers
'                   product#     Product of all the numbers
'                   i%           Index to array entries
' MODULE LEVEL
'   DECLARATIONS:   DECLARE FUNCTION GeometricMean# (a#())
'
  FUNCTION GeometricMean# (a#()) STATIC
     n% = 0
     product# = 1
     FOR i% = LBOUND(a#) TO UBOUND(a#)
         n% = n% + 1
         product# = product# * a#(i%)
     NEXT i%
     GeometricMean# = product# ^ (1 / n%)
  END FUNCTION
```

Function: HarmonicMean#

Returns the harmonic mean of an array of double-precision numbers.

```
' ****************************************************
' ** Name:          HarmonicMean#                   **
' ** Type:          Function                        **
' ** Module:        PROBSTAT.BAS                    **
' ** Language:      Microsoft QuickBASIC 4.00       **
' ****************************************************
'
' Returns the harmonic mean of an array of numbers.
'
' EXAMPLE OF USE:   hm# = HarmonicMean#(a#())
' PARAMETERS:       a#()       Array of numbers to be processed
' VARIABLES:        n%         Number of array entries
'                   sum#       Sum of the reciprocal of each number
'                   i%         Index to each array entry
' MODULE LEVEL
'   DECLARATIONS:   DECLARE FUNCTION HarmonicMean# (a#())

  FUNCTION HarmonicMean# (a#()) STATIC
      n% = 0
      sum# = 0
      FOR i% = LBOUND(a#) TO UBOUND(a#)
          n% = n% + 1
          sum# = sum# + 1# / a#(i%)
      NEXT i%
      HarmonicMean# = n% / sum#
  END FUNCTION
```

Function: Permutations#

Returns the number of permutations of n& items taken r& at a time.

```
' ****************************************************
' ** Name:          Permutations#                   **
' ** Type:          Function                        **
' ** Module:        PROBSTAT.BAS                    **
' ** Language:      Microsoft QuickBASIC 4.00       **
' ****************************************************
'
' Returns the permutations of n& items taken r& at a time.
```

(continued)

continued

```
' EXAMPLE OF USE:  perm# = Permutations#(n&, r&)
' PARAMETERS:      n&          Number of items
'                  r&          Taken r& at a time
' VARIABLES:       p#          Working variable for permutations
'                  i&          Loop index
' MODULE LEVEL
'   DECLARATIONS:  DECLARE FUNCTION Permutations# (n&, r&)
'
  FUNCTION Permutations# (n&, r&) STATIC
      p# = 1
      FOR i& = n& - r& + 1 TO n&
          p# = p# * i&
      NEXT i&
      Permutations# = p#
  END FUNCTION
```

Function: QuadraticMean#

Returns the quadratic mean of an array of double-precision numbers.

```
' ***********************************************
' **  Name:        QuadraticMean#              **
' **  Type:        Function                    **
' **  Module:      PROBSTAT.BAS                **
' **  Language:    Microsoft QuickBASIC 4.00   **
' ***********************************************
'
' Returns the quadratic mean of an array of numbers.
'
' EXAMPLE OF USE:  qm# = QuadraticMean#(a#())
' PARAMETERS:      a#()        Array of numbers to be processed
' VARIABLES:       n%          Count of array entries
'                  sum#        Sum of the square of each number
' MODULE LEVEL
'   DECLARATIONS:  DECLARE FUNCTION QuadraticMean# (a#())
'
  FUNCTION QuadraticMean# (a#()) STATIC
      n% = 0
      sum# = 0
      FOR i% = LBOUND(a#) TO UBOUND(a#)
          n% = n% + 1
          sum# = sum# + a#(i%) ^ 2
      NEXT i%
      QuadraticMean# = SQR(sum# / n%)
  END FUNCTION
```

QBFMT

The QBFMT program reformats QuickBASIC modules by indenting the lines according to the structure of the statements. For example, all lines found between matching DO and LOOP statements are indented four character columns more than the DO and LOOP statements. Of course, nested structures are indented even farther.

One advantage of processing a file with this program is that improperly matched statements are detected. Improper matching can happen if, for example, you forget to type an *END IF* statement to match an *IF*. A special comment line is placed in the file at the point where each error is detected.

This utility program was an immense help throughout the creation of this book. Each module was formatted with this program, resulting in a consistent structure, style, and general appearance to the listings.

Notice that QuickBASIC programs to be processed by the QBFMT program must be saved in text format and have the extension .BAS.

Name	Type	Description
QBFMT.BAS		Program module
Indent	Sub	Performs line indention
SetCode	Sub	Determines indention code by keyword
SplitUp	Sub	Splits line into major components

Program Module: QBFMT

```
' *************************************************
' **   Name:         QBFMT                       **
' **   Type:         Program                     **
' **   Module:       QBFMT.BAS                   **
' **   Language:     Microsoft QuickBASIC 4.00   **
' *************************************************
'
' Reformats a QuickBASIC program by indenting
' lines according to the structure of the statements.  The
' default amount is 4 spaces if no indention parameter
' is given on the command line.
```

(continued)

continued

```
' USAGE:   QBFMT filename [indention]
'          Command$ = filename [indention]
' .MAK FILE:    QBFMT.BAS
'               PARSE.BAS
'               STRINGS.BAS
' PARAMETERS:   filename(.BAS)   Name of QuickBASIC module to be formatted;
'                                the module must be saved in "Text" format
' VARIABLES:    md$              Working copy of COMMAND$ contents
'               fileName$        Name of QuickBASIC module to be formatted
'               dpoint%          Position of the decimal point character
'                                in cmd$
'               ndent$           Part of cmd$ dealing with optional
'                                indention amount
'               indention%       Number of character columns per
'                                indention level
'               progline$        Each line of the file being processed
'               indentLevel%     Keeps track of current indention amount
'               nest$            Message placed in file if faulty structure
'                                detected

  DECLARE FUNCTION LtrimSet$ (a$, set$)
  DECLARE FUNCTION RtrimSet$ (a$, set$)
  DECLARE SUB Indent (a$, indention%, indentLevel%)
  DECLARE SUB ParseWord (a$, sep$, word$)
  DECLARE SUB SetCode (a$, keyWord$, code%)
  DECLARE SUB SplitUp (a$, comment$, keyWord$)

' Decipher the user command line
  cmd$ = COMMAND$
  IF cmd$ = "" THEN
      PRINT
      PRINT "Usage:  QBFMT filename(.BAS) [indention]"
      SYSTEM
  ELSE
      ParseWord cmd$, " ,", fileName$
      dpoint% = INSTR(fileName$, ".")
      IF dpoint% THEN
          fileName$ = LEFT$(fileName$, dpoint% - 1)
      END IF
      ParseWord cmd$, " ,", ndent$
      indention% = VAL(ndent$)
      IF indention% < 1 THEN
          indention% = 4
      END IF
  END IF
```

(continued)

continued

```
    ' Try to open the indicated files
    PRINT
    ON ERROR GOTO ErrorTrapOne
    OPEN fileName$ + ".BAS" FOR INPUT AS #1
    OPEN fileName$ + ".@$@" FOR OUTPUT AS #2
    ON ERROR GOTO 0

    ' Process each line of the file
    DO
        LINE INPUT #1, progLine$
        Indent progLine$, indention%, indentLevel%
        PRINT progLine$
        PRINT #2, progLine$
        IF indentLevel% < 0 OR (EOF(1) AND indentLevel% <> 0) THEN
            SOUND 555, 5
            SOUND 333, 9
            nest$ = "'<<<<<<<<<<<<<<<<<<<< Nesting error detected!"
            PRINT nest$
            PRINT #2, nest$
            indentLevel% = 0
        END IF
    LOOP UNTIL EOF(1)

    ' Close all files
    CLOSE

    ' Delete any old .BAK file
    ON ERROR GOTO ErrorTrapTwo
    KILL fileName$ + ".BAK"
    ON ERROR GOTO 0

    ' Rename the files
    NAME fileName$ + ".BAS" AS fileName$ + ".BAK"
    NAME fileName$ + ".@$@" AS fileName$ + ".BAS"

    ' We're done
    END

    '----------- Error trapping routines

ErrorTrapOne:
    PRINT "Error while opening files"
    SYSTEM

ErrorTrapTwo:
    RESUME NEXT
```

Subprogram: Indent

Performs the task of indenting each line of a program for the QBFMT program. The indention amount is determined by the first word of each line, and spaces are added to the front end of each line accordingly.

```
' *************************************************
' **   Name:           Indent                    **
' **   Type:           Subprogram                **
' **   Module:         QBFMT.BAS                 **
' **   Language:       Microsoft QuickBASIC 4.00 **
' *************************************************
'
' Determines the indention for each line.
'
' EXAMPLE OF USE:   Indent a$, indention%, indentLevel%
' PARAMETERS:       a$              Program line to be indented
'                   indention%      Spaces to add for each indention level
'                   indentLevel%    Level of indention
' VARIABLES:        comment$        Part of program line that represents a
'                                   REMARK
'                   keyWord$        First word of the program line
'                   code%           Indention control code determined by
'                                   keyWord$
' MODULE LEVEL
'   DECLARATIONS:   DECLARE SUB Indent (a$, indention%, indentLevel%)
'
SUB Indent (a$, indention%, indentLevel%) STATIC

    ' Break line into manageable parts
    SplitUp a$, comment$, keyWord$

    IF keyWord$ <> "" THEN

        ' Set indention code according to type of keyword
        SetCode a$, keyWord$, code%

        ' Build a string of spaces for the indicated indention
        SELECT CASE code%
        CASE -2
            a$ = SPACE$(indention% * indentLevel%) + a$
        CASE -1
            a$ = SPACE$(indention% * indentLevel%) + a$
            indentLevel% = indentLevel% - 1
```

(continued)

continued

```
            CASE 0
                a$ = SPACE$(indention% * (indentLevel% + 1)) + a$
            CASE 1
                indentLevel% = indentLevel% + 1
                a$ = SPACE$(indention% * indentLevel%) + a$
            CASE ELSE
            END SELECT
        ELSE
            a$ = SPACE$(indention% * indentLevel% + 2)
        END IF

    ' Round out the position of trailing comments
        IF comment$ <> "" THEN
            IF a$ <> SPACE$(LEN(a$)) AND a$ <> "" THEN
                a$ = a$ + SPACE$(16 - (LEN(a$) MOD 16))
            END IF
        END IF

    ' Tack the comment back onto the end of the line
        a$ = a$ + comment$

END SUB
```

Subprogram: SetCode

Determines the indention code for the QBFMT program based on the first word of each program line. For example, if the first word of a program line is *FOR*, a code number is returned that signals the QBFMT program to indent the following lines one more level. When *NEXT* is encountered, the indention level decreases by one.

```
' ************************************************
' **  Name:       SetCode                       **
' **  Type:       Subprogram                    **
' **  Module:     QBFMT.BAS                     **
' **  Language:   Microsoft QuickBASIC 4.00     **
' ************************************************
'
' Determines a code number for the type of indention
' implied by the various types of keywords that begin
' each line of QuickBASIC programs.
```

(continued)

continued

```
' EXAMPLE OF USE:   SetCode a$, keyWord$, code%
' PARAMETERS:       a$         Program line to indent
'                   keyWord$   First word of the program line
'                   code%      Returned code indicating the action to be taken
' VARIABLES:        (none)
' MODULE LEVEL
'   DECLARATIONS:   DECLARE SUB SetCode (a$, keyWord$, code%)
'
  SUB SetCode (a$, keyWord$, code%) STATIC
      SELECT CASE keyWord$
      CASE "DEF"
          IF INSTR(a$, "=") THEN
              code% = 0
          ELSE
              IF INSTR(a$, " SEG") = 0 THEN
                  code% = 1
              END IF
          END IF
      CASE "ELSE"
          code% = -2
      CASE "ELSEIF"
          code% = -2
      CASE "CASE"
          code% = -2
      CASE "END"
          IF a$ <> "END" THEN
              code% = -1
          ELSE
              code% = 0
          END IF
      CASE "FOR"
          code% = 1
      CASE "DO"
          code% = 1
      CASE "SELECT"
          code% = 1
      CASE "IF"
          IF RIGHT$(a$, 4) = "THEN" THEN
              code% = 1
          ELSE
              code% = 0
          END IF
      CASE "NEXT"
          code% = -1
```

(continued)

continued

```
            CASE "LOOP"
                code% = -1
            CASE "SUB"
                code% = 1
            CASE "FUNCTION"
                code% = 1
            CASE "TYPE"
                code% = 1
            CASE "WHILE"
                code% = 1
            CASE "WEND"
                code% = -1
            CASE ELSE
                code% = 0
        END SELECT
END SUB
```

Subprogram: SplitUp

Breaks each program line into its major components for the QBFMT program. Leading spaces and tabs are removed, and the first word and any REMARK part are returned. Later, after the line is indented the proper amount, the parts of the line are patched back together and output to the program listing file.

```
' ****************************************************
' **   Name:          SplitUp                       **
' **   Type:          Subprogram                    **
' **   Module:        QBFMT.BAS                     **
' **   Language:      Microsoft QuickBASIC 4.00     **
' ****************************************************
'
' Splits the line into statement, comment, and keyword.
'
' EXAMPLE OF USE:   SplitUp a$, comment$, keyWord$
' PARAMETERS:       a$          Program line to be split up
'                   comment$    Part of line following "REM" or "'"
'                   keyWord$    First word of program line
' VARIABLES:        set$        Characters to be trimmed, space and tab
'                   strFlag%    Indication of a quoted string
'                   k%          Index to start of REMARK
'                   i%          Looping index
```

(continued)

continued

```
'                       m%              Pointer to REMARK
'                       sptr%           Pointer to first space following the
'                                       first word in a$
' MODULE LEVEL
'    DECLARATIONS:   DECLARE SUB SplitUp (a$, comment$, keyWord$)
'
  SUB SplitUp (a$, comment$, keyWord$) STATIC
      set$ = " " + CHR$(9)
      strFlag% = 0
      k% = 0
      FOR i% = LEN(a$) TO 1 STEP -1
          IF MID$(a$, i%, 1) = CHR$(34) THEN
              IF strFlag% = 0 THEN
                  strFlag% = 1
              ELSE
                  strFlag% = 0
              END IF
          END IF
          IF MID$(a$, i%, 1) = "'" OR MID$(a$, i%, 3) = "REM" THEN
              IF strFlag% = 0 THEN
                  k% = i%
              END IF
          END IF
      NEXT i%
      IF k% > 0 THEN
          m% = 0
          FOR j% = k% - 1 TO 1 STEP -1
              IF INSTR(set$, MID$(a$, j%, 1)) = 0 THEN
                  IF m% = 0 THEN m% = j%
              END IF
          NEXT j%
          IF m% THEN
              comment$ = MID$(a$, m% + 1)
              a$ = LEFT$(a$, m%)
          ELSE
              comment$ = a$
              a$ = ""
          END IF
      ELSE
          comment$ = ""
      END IF
      a$ = LtrimSet$(a$, set$)
      a$ = RtrimSet$(a$, set$)
```

(continued)

continued

```
        comment$ = LtrimSet$(comment$, set$)
        comment$ = RtrimSet$(comment$, set$)
        sptr% = INSTR(a$, " ")
        IF sptr% THEN
            keyWord$ = UCASE$(LEFT$(a$, sptr% - 1))
        ELSE
            keyWord$ = UCASE$(a$)
        END IF
    END SUB
```

QBTREE

> The QBTREE program performs a recursive directory search and then displays all file entries indented for each level of subdirectory encountered. If a command line parameter is given, the search starts at the indicated path. If no command line parameter is given, the search begins with the current directory.

Name	Type	Description
QBTREE.BAS		Program module
FileTreeSearch	Sub	Recursive directory search routine

Program Module: QBTREE

```
' *************************************************
' **   Name:         QBTREE                      **
' **   Type:         Program                     **
' **   Module:       QBTREE.BAS                  **
' **   Language:     Microsoft QuickBASIC 4.00   **
' *************************************************
'
' This program creates a list of directories and
' subdirectories, and all files in them.  If no
' command line path is given, the search
' begins with the current directory.
'
' USAGE:         QBTREE [path]
' REQUIREMENTS:  MIXED.QLB/.LIB
' .MAK FILE:     QBTREE.BAS
'                FILEINFO.BAS
' PARAMETERS:    path       Path for starting directory search
' VARIABLES:     path$      Path string, from the command line, or set
'                           to "*.*"
'
'                indent%    Indention amount for printing

      TYPE RegTypeX
         ax    AS INTEGER
         bx    AS INTEGER
```

(continued)

continued

```
        cx    AS INTEGER
        dx    AS INTEGER
        bp    AS INTEGER
        si    AS INTEGER
        di    AS INTEGER
        flags AS INTEGER
        ds    AS INTEGER
        es    AS INTEGER
    END TYPE

    TYPE FileDataType
        finame    AS STRING * 12
        year      AS INTEGER
        month     AS INTEGER
        day       AS INTEGER
        hour      AS INTEGER
        minute    AS INTEGER
        second    AS INTEGER
        attribute AS INTEGER
        size      AS LONG
    END TYPE

' Subprograms
    DECLARE SUB Interruptx (intnum%, inreg AS RegTypeX, outreg AS RegTypeX)
    DECLARE SUB FindFirstFile (path$, dta$, result%)
    DECLARE SUB FindNextFile (dta$, result%)
    DECLARE SUB GetFileData (dta$, file AS FileDataType)
    DECLARE SUB FileTreeSearch (path$, indent%)

' Create structure for deciphering the DTA file search results
    DIM file AS FileDataType

' Get the command line path for starting the file search
    path$ = COMMAND$

' If no path was given, then use "*.*" to search the current directory
    IF path$ = "" THEN
        path$ = "*.*"
    END IF
' If only a drive was given, then add "*.*"
    IF LEN(path$) = 2 AND RIGHT$(path$, 1) = ":" THEN
        path$ = path$ + "*.*"
    END IF
```

(continued)

continued

```
' Adjust the given path if necessary
  IF INSTR(path$, "*") = 0 AND INSTR(path$, "?") = 0 THEN
      FindFirstFile path$, dta$, result%
      IF result% = 0 OR RIGHT$(path$, 1) = "\" THEN
          IF RIGHT$(path$, 1) <> "\" THEN
              path$ = path$ + "\"
          END IF
          path$ = path$ + "*.*"
      END IF
  END IF

' Start with a clean slate
  CLS

' Call the recursive search subprogram
  FileTreeSearch path$, indent%

' That's all there is to it
  END
```

Subprogram: FileTreeSearch

Performs a recursive search for filenames in directories. Whenever a subdirectory is encountered, the subprogram builds a modified search path string (by adding the subdirectory name to the end of the current search path) and calls itself again. In this way, all files in all subdirectories are located, starting with the initial search path given.

The filenames are printed with an indention amount that is a function of the level of recursion. This means that each subdirectory entry is indented four spaces more than its parent directory.

```
' ***********************************************
' **   Name:         FileTreeSearch            **
' **   Type:         Subprogram                **
' **   Module:       QBTREE.BAS                **
' **   Language:     Microsoft QuickBASIC 4.00 **
' ***********************************************
'
' Directory searching and listing subprogram for
' the QBTREE program.  (recursive)
```

(continued)

continued

```
' EXAMPLE OF USE:   FileTreeSearch path$, indent%
' PARAMETERS:       path$      Path for search of files
'                   indent%    Level of indention, function of recursion
'                              level
' VARIABLES:        file       Structure of type FileDataType
'                   path$      Path for search of files
'                   dta$       Disk Transfer Area buffer string
'                   result%    Returned result code from FindFirstFile or
'                              FindNextFile
'                   newPath$   Path with added subdirectory for recursive
'                              search
' MODULE LEVEL
'   DECLARATIONS: TYPE FileDataType
'                   finame     AS STRING * 12
'                   year       AS INTEGER
'                   month      AS INTEGER
'                   day        AS INTEGER
'                   hour       AS INTEGER
'                   minute     AS INTEGER
'                   second     AS INTEGER
'                   attribute  AS INTEGER
'                   size       AS LONG
'                 END TYPE
'
'                 DECLARE SUB FindFirstFile (path$, dta$, result%)
'                 DECLARE SUB FindNextFile (dta$, result%)
'                 DECLARE SUB GetFileData (dta$, file AS FileDataType)
'                 DECLARE SUB FileTreeSearch (path$, indent%)
'
   SUB FileTreeSearch (path$, indent%)

     ' Create structure for deciphering the DTA file search results
       DIM file AS FileDataType

     ' Find the first file given the current search path
       FindFirstFile path$, dta$, result%

     ' Search through the directory for all files
       DO UNTIL result%

         ' Unpack the Disk Transfer Area for file information
           GetFileData dta$, file
```

(continued)

continued

```
    ' Skip the "." and ".." files
      IF LEFT$(file.finame, 1) <> "." THEN

        ' Print the filename, indented to show tree structure
          PRINT SPACE$(indent% * 4); file.finame;

        ' Print any other desired file information here
          PRINT TAB(50); file.size;
          PRINT TAB(58); file.attribute

        ' If we found a directory, then recursively search through it
          IF file.attribute AND &H10 THEN

            ' Modify path$ to add this new directory to the search path
              newPath$ = path$
              IF INSTR(newPath$, "\") = 0 THEN
                  newPath$ = "\" + newPath$
              END IF
              DO WHILE RIGHT$(newPath$, 1) <> "\"
                  newPath$ = LEFT$(newPath$, LEN(newPath$) - 1)
              LOOP
              newPath$ = newPath$ + file.finame + "\*.*"

            ' Example of recursion here
              FileTreeSearch newPath$, indent% + 1

          END IF

      END IF

    ' Try to find the next file in this directory
      FindNextFile dta$, result%

  LOOP

END SUB
```

QCAL

The QCAL program provides scientific calculator functions from the MS-DOS command line. This program is a modified and expanded version of MINICAL.BAS, presented earlier in this book. The original version's goal was to demonstrate the methods used to create a small, modular program. The functionality of the program wasn't the important issue. Here, the program has been enhanced, and several new functions and capabilities make this program more useful as a utility. Run the program by typing *QCAL HELP*, *QCAL ?*, or *QCAL*, and a list of the available functions will be displayed. In addition to the original five functions, several new trigonometric, hyperbolic, and logarithmic functions have been added.

You might want to review the original MINICAL program, which is on pages 5 through 18. You'll find an explanation of how the numeric values are placed on the stack and how the functions operate on those values.

Because of the modular, structured organization of QuickBASIC programs, you can easily modify this program to include other functions. To add a new function, modify the Process and QcalHelp subprograms where applicable, and follow the same pattern of stack and variable manipulations exhibited by the other routines when writing your own.

Name	Type	Description
QCAL.BAS		Program module
DisplayStack	Sub	Displays final results of the program
NextParameter$	Func	Extracts number or command from COMMAND$
Process	Sub	Controls action for command line parameters
QcalHelp	Sub	Provides a "Help" display for program

Program Module: QCAL

```
' ****************************************************
' **   Name:         QCAL                           **
' **   Type:         Program                        **
' **   Module:       QCAL.BAS                       **
' **   Language:     Microsoft QuickBASIC 4.00      **
' ****************************************************
'
' USAGE:           QCAL [number] [function] [...]
' .MAK FILE:       QCAL.BAS
'                  QCALMATH.BAS
' PARAMETERS:      [number]      Numbers to be placed on the stack
'                  [function]    Operations to be performed on the stack
'                                contents
' VARIABLES:       cmd$          Working copy of COMMAND$
'                  stack#()      Array representing the numeric stack
'                  ptr%          Index into the stack
'                  parm$         Each number of command extracted from cmd$

' Constants
CONST PI = 3.141592653589793#

' Functions
DECLARE FUNCTION AbsoluteX# (x#)
DECLARE FUNCTION Add# (y#, x#)
DECLARE FUNCTION ArcCosine# (x#)
DECLARE FUNCTION ArcHypCosine# (x#)
DECLARE FUNCTION ArcHypSine# (x#)
DECLARE FUNCTION ArcHypTangent# (x#)
DECLARE FUNCTION ArcSine# (x#)
DECLARE FUNCTION ArcTangent# (x#)
DECLARE FUNCTION Ceil# (x#)
DECLARE FUNCTION ChangeSign# (x#)
DECLARE FUNCTION Cosine# (x#)
DECLARE FUNCTION Divide# (y#, x#)
DECLARE FUNCTION Exponential# (x#)
DECLARE FUNCTION FractionalPart# (x#)
DECLARE FUNCTION HypCosine# (x#)
DECLARE FUNCTION HypSine# (x#)
DECLARE FUNCTION HypTangent# (x#)
DECLARE FUNCTION IntegerPart# (x#)
DECLARE FUNCTION LogBase10# (x#)
DECLARE FUNCTION LogBaseN# (y#, x#)
DECLARE FUNCTION LogE# (x#)
DECLARE FUNCTION Modulus# (y#, x#)
```

(continued)

continued

```
    DECLARE FUNCTION Multiply# (y#, x#)
    DECLARE FUNCTION NextParameter$ (cmd$)
    DECLARE FUNCTION OneOverX# (x#)
    DECLARE FUNCTION Sign# (x#)
    DECLARE FUNCTION Sine# (x#)
    DECLARE FUNCTION SquareRoot# (x#)
    DECLARE FUNCTION Subtract# (y#, x#)
    DECLARE FUNCTION Tangent# (x#)
    DECLARE FUNCTION Xsquared# (x#)
    DECLARE FUNCTION YRaisedToX# (y#, x#)

' Subprograms
    DECLARE SUB QcalHelp ()
    DECLARE SUB Process (parm$, stack#(), ptr%)
    DECLARE SUB DisplayStack (stack#(), ptr%)
    DECLARE SUB SwapXY (stack#(), ptr%)

' Get the command line
    cmd$ = COMMAND$

' First check if user is asking for help
    IF cmd$ = "" OR cmd$ = "HELP" OR cmd$ = "?" THEN
        QcalHelp
        SYSTEM
    END IF

' Create a pseudo stack
    DIM stack#(1 TO 20)
    ptr% = 0

' Process each part of the command line
    DO UNTIL cmd$ = ""
        parm$ = NextParameter$(cmd$)
        Process parm$, stack#(), ptr%
        IF ptr% < 1 THEN
            PRINT "Not enough stack values"
            SYSTEM
        END IF
    LOOP

' Display results
    DisplayStack stack#(), ptr%

' All done
    END
```

QUICKBASIC TOOLBOXES AND PROGRAMS

Subprogram: DisplayStack

Displays the final results of the QCAL program. When the QCAL program is finished, one or more numeric values are left on the stack, representing the final values of the calculations. If the stack has a single value remaining on it, this number is displayed with the label *Result*.... If, however, two or more values are left on the stack after QCAL has acted on all functions, the values are displayed with the label *Stack* ..., indicating to the user that more than a single result was left on the stack.

```
' *************************************************
' **   Name:         DisplayStack                **
' **   Type:         Subprogram                  **
' **   Module:       QCAL.BAS                    **
' **   Language:     Microsoft QuickBASIC 4.00   **
' *************************************************
'
' Displays the value(s) left on the stack when QCAL
' is finished processing the command line.
'
' EXAMPLE OF USE:   DisplayStack stack#(), ptr%
' PARAMETERS:       stack#()    Array of numbers representing the stack
'                   ptr%        Index into the stack
' VARIABLES:        i%          Looping index
' MODULE LEVEL
'   DECLARATIONS:   DECLARE SUB DisplayStack (stack#(), ptr%)
'
    SUB DisplayStack (stack#(), ptr%) STATIC
        PRINT
        IF ptr% > 1 THEN
            PRINT "Stack ... ",
        ELSE
            PRINT "Result... ",
        END IF
        FOR i% = 1 TO ptr%
            PRINT stack#(i%),
        NEXT i%
        PRINT
    END SUB
```

Function: NextParameter$

Returns the first group of nonspace characters found at the left of the passed string. The passed string is then trimmed of these characters, along with any extra spaces.

The PARSE.BAS module contains alternative routines that perform the same function in a slightly different way. Take a look at the ParseWord and ParseLine routines found there. The NextParameter$ subprogram demonstrates how the code from a module can be copied and modified for a specific purpose, with any extra code removed. This results in a smaller program but has the disadvantage that any future changes to the PARSE.BAS module will probably not show up here in the QCAL.BAS module.

```
' ***************************************************
' **   Name:         NextParameter$              **
' **   Type:         Function                    **
' **   Module:       QCAL.BAS                    **
' **   Language:     Microsoft QuickBASIC 4.00   **
' ***************************************************
'
' Extracts parameters from the front of the
' command line.  Parameters are groups of any
' characters separated by spaces.
'
' EXAMPLE OF USE:   parm$ = NextParameter$(cmd$)
' PARAMETERS:       cmd$        The working copy of COMMAND$
' VARIABLES:        parm$       Each number or command from cmd$
' MODULE LEVEL
'   DECLARATIONS:   DECLARE FUNCTION NextParameter$ (cmd$)
'
    FUNCTION NextParameter$ (cmd$) STATIC
        parm$ = ""
        DO WHILE LEFT$(cmd$, 1) <> " " AND cmd$ <> ""
            parm$ = parm$ + LEFT$(cmd$, 1)
            cmd$ = MID$(cmd$, 2)
        LOOP
        DO WHILE LEFT$(cmd$, 1) = " " AND cmd$ <> ""
            cmd$ = MID$(cmd$, 2)
        LOOP
        NextParameter$ = parm$
    END FUNCTION
```

Subprogram: Process

Acts upon each command line parameter. If the parameter is a valid function, the function is called, and the stack is adjusted appropriately. If the parameter isn't a recognizable function, it is assumed to be a numeric quantity. The VAL function converts the parameter to its numeric equivalent, and the result is pushed on the stack, ready for the next operation.

This subprogram demonstrates a fairly long CASE statement. The same logic could be developed using IF THEN, ELSE IF, ELSE, and END IF statements, but the CASE statement is ideal for making selections from a large number of choices in this way.

```
' *****************************************************
' **   Name:         Process                         **
' **   Type:         Subprogram                      **
' **   Module:       QCAL.BAS                        **
' **   Language:     Microsoft QuickBASIC 4.00       **
' *****************************************************
'
' Processes each command parameter for the QCAL
' program.
'
' EXAMPLE OF USE:   Process parm$, stack#(), ptr%
' PARAMETERS:       parm$      The command line parameter to be processed
'                   stack#()   Array of numbers representing the stack
'                   ptr%       Index pointing to last stack entry
' VARIABLES:        (none)
' MODULE LEVEL
'   DECLARATIONS:   DECLARE SUB Process (parm$, stack#(), ptr%)
'
SUB Process (parm$, stack#(), ptr%) STATIC
    SELECT CASE parm$
    CASE "+"
        ptr% = ptr% - 1
        IF ptr% > 0 THEN
            stack#(ptr%) = Add#(stack#(ptr%), stack#(ptr% + 1))
        END IF
    CASE "-"
        ptr% = ptr% - 1
        IF ptr% > 0 THEN
            stack#(ptr%) = Subtract#(stack#(ptr%), stack#(ptr% + 1))
        END IF
```

(continued)

continued

```
CASE "*"
    ptr% = ptr% - 1
    IF ptr% > 0 THEN
        stack#(ptr%) = Multiply#(stack#(ptr%), stack#(ptr% + 1))
    END IF
CASE "/"
    ptr% = ptr% - 1
    IF ptr% > 0 THEN
        stack#(ptr%) = Divide#(stack#(ptr%), stack#(ptr% + 1))
    END IF
CASE "CHS"
    IF ptr% > 0 THEN
        stack#(ptr%) = ChangeSign#(stack#(ptr%))
    END IF
CASE "ABS"
    IF ptr% > 0 THEN
        stack#(ptr%) = AbsoluteX#(stack#(ptr%))
    END IF
CASE "SGN"
    IF ptr% > 0 THEN
        stack#(ptr%) = Sign#(stack#(ptr%))
    END IF
CASE "INT"
    IF ptr% > 0 THEN
        stack#(ptr%) = IntegerPart#(stack#(ptr%))
    END IF
CASE "MOD"
    ptr% = ptr% - 1
    IF ptr% > 0 THEN
        stack#(ptr%) = Modulus#(stack#(ptr%), stack#(ptr% + 1))
    END IF
CASE "FRC"
    IF ptr% > 0 THEN
        stack#(ptr%) = FractionalPart#(stack#(ptr%))
    END IF
CASE "1/X"
    IF ptr% > 0 THEN
        stack#(ptr%) = OneOverX#(stack#(ptr%))
    END IF
CASE "SQR"
    IF ptr% > 0 THEN
        stack#(ptr%) = SquareRoot#(stack#(ptr%))
    END IF
```

(continued)

continued

```
            CASE "X2"
                IF ptr% > 0 THEN
                    stack#(ptr%) = Xsquared#(stack#(ptr%))
                END IF
            CASE "SIN"
                IF ptr% > 0 THEN
                    stack#(ptr%) = Sine#(stack#(ptr%))
                END IF
            CASE "COS"
                IF ptr% > 0 THEN
                    stack#(ptr%) = Cosine#(stack#(ptr%))
                END IF
            CASE "TAN"
                IF ptr% > 0 THEN
                    stack#(ptr%) = Tangent#(stack#(ptr%))
                END IF
            CASE "ASN"
                IF ptr% > 0 THEN
                    stack#(ptr%) = ArcSine#(stack#(ptr%))
                END IF
            CASE "ACS"
                IF ptr% > 0 THEN
                    stack#(ptr%) = ArcCosine#(stack#(ptr%))
                END IF
            CASE "ATN"
                IF ptr% > 0 THEN
                    stack#(ptr%) = ArcTangent#(stack#(ptr%))
                END IF
            CASE "HSN"
                IF ptr% > 0 THEN
                    stack#(ptr%) = HypSine#(stack#(ptr%))
                END IF
            CASE "HCS"
                IF ptr% > 0 THEN
                    stack#(ptr%) = HypCosine#(stack#(ptr%))
                END IF
            CASE "HTN"
                IF ptr% > 0 THEN
                    stack#(ptr%) = HypTangent#(stack#(ptr%))
                END IF
            CASE "AHS"
                IF ptr% > 0 THEN
                    stack#(ptr%) = ArcHypSine#(stack#(ptr%))
                END IF
```

(continued)

continued

```
        CASE "AHC"
            IF ptr% > 0 THEN
                stack#(ptr%) = ArcHypCosine#(stack#(ptr%))
            END IF
        CASE "AHT"
            IF ptr% > 0 THEN
                stack#(ptr%) = ArcHypTangent#(stack#(ptr%))
            END IF
        CASE "LOG"
            IF ptr% > 0 THEN
                stack#(ptr%) = LogE#(stack#(ptr%))
            END IF
        CASE "LOG10"
            IF ptr% > 0 THEN
                stack#(ptr%) = LogBase10#(stack#(ptr%))
            END IF
        CASE "LOGN"
            ptr% = ptr% - 1
            IF ptr% > 0 THEN
                stack#(ptr%) = LogBaseN#(stack#(ptr%), stack#(ptr% + 1))
            END IF
        CASE "EXP"
            IF ptr% > 0 THEN
                stack#(ptr%) = Exponential#(stack#(ptr%))
            END IF
        CASE "CEIL"
            IF ptr% > 0 THEN
                stack#(ptr%) = Ceil#(stack#(ptr%))
            END IF
        CASE "Y^X"
            ptr% = ptr% - 1
            IF ptr% > 0 THEN
                stack#(ptr%) = YRaisedToX#(stack#(ptr%), stack#(ptr% + 1))
            END IF
        CASE "PI"
            ptr% = ptr% + 1
            stack#(ptr%) = PI
        CASE "SWAP"
            SwapXY stack#(), ptr%
        CASE "DUP"
            IF ptr% > 0 THEN
                stack#(ptr% + 1) = stack#(ptr%)
                ptr% = ptr% + 1
            END IF
        CASE ELSE
            ptr% = ptr% + 1
            stack#(ptr%) = VAL(parm$)
    END SELECT
END SUB
```

QUICKBASIC TOOLBOXES AND PROGRAMS

Subprogram: QcalHelp

Provides a Help display for the QCAL program.

One feature that sets good software apart from mediocre software is the ability to provide on-line help for the user. Nothing is more frustrating than a program that terminates suddenly, without any explanation of the problem or suggestion for solving it.

The QcalHelp subprogram demonstrates one approach to helping the user with a program. Entering any of the following command lines will cause the QCAL program to call QcalHelp:

```
QCAL HELP
QCAL ?
QCAL
```

```
' **************************************************
' **   Name:          QcalHelp                    **
' **   Type:          Subprogram                  **
' **   Module:        QCAL.BAS                    **
' **   Language:      Microsoft QuickBASIC 4.00   **
' **************************************************
'
' Displays a help screen when QCAL is run with no
' parameters or with a parameter of ? or HELP.
'
' EXAMPLE OF USE:  QcalHelp
' PARAMETERS:      (none)
' VARIABLES:       (none)
' MODULE LEVEL
'   DECLARATIONS:  DECLARE SUB QcalHelp ()
'
SUB QcalHelp STATIC
    PRINT
    PRINT "Usage:   QCAL [number] [function] [...] <Enter>"
    PRINT
    PRINT "Numbers are placed on an RPN stack, and functions operate"
    PRINT "on the stacked quantities.  When the program is finished,"
    PRINT "whatever is left on the stack is displayed."
    PRINT
    PRINT "List of available functions..."
    PRINT
```

(continued)

continued

```
        PRINT "Two numbers:     + - * /"
        PRINT "One number:      CHS ABS SGN INT MOD FRC CHS 1/X SQR X2 CEIL"
        PRINT "Trigonometric:   SIN COS TAN ASN ACS ATN"
        PRINT "Hyperbolic:      HSN HCS HTN AHS AHC AHT"
        PRINT "Logarithmic:     LOG LOG10 LOGN EXP Y^X"
        PRINT "Constants:       PI"
        PRINT "Stack:           SWAP DUP"
    END SUB
```

QCALMATH

QCALMATH is a toolbox of scientific functions for the QCAL program. Several functions included in QCALMATH are similar to functions provided by QuickBASIC. You could shorten QCALMATH by deleting these functions here and coding the QuickBASIC routines directly in the Process subprogram, located in the QCAL.BAS module. However, there's something to be said for keeping the functions as shown here: QCALMATH checks for additional error conditions and generates clear messages if errors exist. For example, although the SquareRoot# function duplicates a QuickBASIC function, SquareRoot# checks for values less than 0 before trying to find the square root and prints a clear message if such an attempt is made.

It's easy to add your own functions to the QCAL program. Simply create the function in the same format and style as shown in this module. You'll also need to modify the Process subprogram in the QCAL module to let the program call the new function. For the final touch, be sure to add the new function to the list displayed by the QcalHelp subprogram.

QCALMATH is the only toolbox in this book that doesn't have any module-level code to demonstrate the subprograms and functions. The QCAL program loads this toolbox and provides the demonstration code.

Name	Type	Description
QCALMATH.BAS		Toolbox
AbsoluteX#	Func	Absolute value of a number
Add#	Func	Sum of two numbers
ArcCosine#	Func	Arc cosine function of a number
ArcHypCosine#	Func	Inverse hyperbolic cosine of a number
ArcHypSine#	Func	Inverse hyperbolic sine of a number
ArcHypTangent#	Func	Inverse hyperbolic tangent of a number
ArcSine#	Func	Inverse sine of a number
ArcTangent#	Func	Inverse tangent of a number
Ceil#	Func	Smallest whole number greater than a number

(continued)

continued

Name	Type	Description
ChangeSign#	Func	Reverses sign of a number
Cosine#	Func	Cosine of a number
Divide#	Func	Result of dividing two numbers
Dup	Sub	Duplicates top entry on the stack
Exponential#	Func	Exponential function of a number
FractionalPart#	Func	Fractional part of a number
HypCosine#	Func	Hyperbolic cosine of a number
HypSine#	Func	Hyperbolic sine of a number
HypTangent#	Func	Hyperbolic tangent of a number
IntegerPart#	Func	Integer part of a number
LogBase10#	Func	Log base 10 of a number
LogBaseN#	Func	Log base *N* of a number
LogE#	Func	Natural logarithm of a number
Modulus#	Func	Remainder of the division of two numbers
Multiply#	Func	Product of two numbers
OneOverX#	Func	Result of dividing 1 by a number
Sign#	Func	Sign of a number
Sine#	Func	Sine of a number
SquareRoot#	Func	Square root of a number
Subtract#	Func	Difference between two numbers
SwapXY	Sub	Swaps top two entries on the stack
Tangent#	Func	Tangent of a number
Xsquared#	Func	Square of a number
YRaisedToX#	Func	Number raised to the power of a second

Toolbox: QCALMATH

```
' *************************************************
' **    Name:         QCALMATH                   **
' **    Type:         Toolbox                    **
' **    Module:       QCALMATH.BAS               **
' **    Language:     Microsoft QuickBASIC 4.00  **
' *************************************************
'
' Collection of math functions and subprograms for
' the QCAL program.
```

(continued)

continued

```
' USAGE:           (loaded by the QCAL program)
'.MAK FILE:        (none)
' PARAMETERS:      (none)
' VARIABLES:       (none)
' Constants
  CONST PI = 3.141592653589793#
  CONST L10 = 2.302585092994046#

' Functions
  DECLARE FUNCTION AbsoluteX# (x#)
  DECLARE FUNCTION Add# (y#, x#)
  DECLARE FUNCTION ArcCosine# (x#)
  DECLARE FUNCTION ArcHypCosine# (x#)
  DECLARE FUNCTION ArcHypSine# (x#)
  DECLARE FUNCTION ArcHypTangent# (x#)
  DECLARE FUNCTION ArcSine# (x#)
  DECLARE FUNCTION ArcTangent# (x#)
  DECLARE FUNCTION Ceil# (x#)
  DECLARE FUNCTION ChangeSign# (x#)
  DECLARE FUNCTION Cosine# (x#)
  DECLARE FUNCTION Divide# (y#, x#)
  DECLARE FUNCTION Exponential# (x#)
  DECLARE FUNCTION FractionalPart# (x#)
  DECLARE FUNCTION HypCosine# (x#)
  DECLARE FUNCTION HypSine# (x#)
  DECLARE FUNCTION HypTangent# (x#)
  DECLARE FUNCTION IntegerPart# (x#)
  DECLARE FUNCTION LogBase10# (x#)
  DECLARE FUNCTION LogBaseN# (y#, x#)
  DECLARE FUNCTION LogE# (x#)
  DECLARE FUNCTION Modulus# (y#, x#)
  DECLARE FUNCTION Multiply# (y#, x#)
  DECLARE FUNCTION OneOverX# (x#)
  DECLARE FUNCTION Sign# (x#)
  DECLARE FUNCTION Sine# (x#)
  DECLARE FUNCTION SquareRoot# (x#)
  DECLARE FUNCTION Subtract# (y#, x#)
  DECLARE FUNCTION Tangent# (x#)
  DECLARE FUNCTION Xsquared# (x#)
  DECLARE FUNCTION YRaisedToX# (y#, x#)
```

Function: AbsoluteX#

Returns the absolute value of the passed value. The absolute value of a number is that number's positive value.

```
' ****************************************************
' **   Name:          AbsoluteX#                     **
' **   Type:          Function                       **
' **   Module:        QCALMATH.BAS                   **
' **   Language:      Microsoft QuickBASIC 4.00      **
' ****************************************************
'
' EXAMPLE OF USE:   y# = AbsoluteX#(x#)
' PARAMETERS:       x#            Double-precision value to be evaluated
' VARIABLES:        (none)
' MODULE LEVEL
'   DECLARATIONS:   DECLARE FUNCTION AbsoluteX# (x#)
'
  FUNCTION AbsoluteX# (x#) STATIC
      AbsoluteX# = ABS(x#)
  END FUNCTION
```

Function: Add#

Returns the sum of two double-precision numbers.

```
' ****************************************************
' **   Name:          Add#                           **
' **   Type:          Function                       **
' **   Module:        QCALMATH.BAS                   **
' **   Language:      Microsoft QuickBASIC 4.00      **
' ****************************************************
'
' EXAMPLE OF USE:   z# = Add#(y#, x#)
' PARAMETERS:       y#            First number
'                   x#            Second number
' VARIABLES:        (none)
' MODULE LEVEL
'   DECLARATIONS:   DECLARE FUNCTION Add# (y#, x#)
'
  FUNCTION Add# (y#, x#) STATIC
      Add# = y# + x#
  END FUNCTION
```

Function: ArcCosine#

Returns the arc cosine of a number; the returned angle is expressed in radians. If the number passed is less than 1, an error message is displayed, and the program terminates.

```
' **************************************************
' **   Name:          ArcCosine#                  **
' **   Type:          Function                    **
' **   Module:        QCALMATH.BAS                **
' **   Language:      Microsoft QuickBASIC 4.00   **
' **************************************************
'
' EXAMPLE OF USE:    y# = ArcCosine#(x#)
' PARAMETERS:        x#           Number to be evaluated
' VARIABLES:         (none)
' MODULE LEVEL
'   DECLARATIONS:    DECLARE FUNCTION ArcCosine# (x#)
'
  FUNCTION ArcCosine# (x#) STATIC
      x2# = x# * x#
      IF x2# < 1# THEN
          ArcCosine# = PI / 2# - ATN(x# / SQR(1# - x# * x#))
      ELSE
          PRINT "Error: ACS(x#) where x# < 1"
          SYSTEM
      END IF
  END FUNCTION
```

Function: ArcHypCosine#

Returns the inverse hyperbolic cosine of a number. If the number passed is less than or equal to 1, an error message is displayed, and the program terminates.

```
' **************************************************
' **   Name:          ArcHypCosine#               **
' **   Type:          Function                    **
' **   Module:        QCALMATH.BAS                **
' **   Language:      Microsoft QuickBASIC 4.00   **
' **************************************************
```

(continued)

continued

```
' EXAMPLE OF USE:   y# = ArcHypCosine#(x#)
' PARAMETERS:       x#         Number to be evaluated
' VARIABLES:        (none)
' MODULE LEVEL
'   DECLARATIONS:   DECLARE FUNCTION ArcHypCosine# (x#)
'
  FUNCTION ArcHypCosine# (x#) STATIC
      IF ABS(x#) > 1# THEN
          ArcHypCosine# = LOG(x# + SQR(x# * x# - 1#))
      ELSE
          PRINT "Error: AHS(x#) where -1 <= x# <= +1"
          SYSTEM
      END IF
  END FUNCTION
```

Function: ArcHypSine#

Returns the inverse hyperbolic sine of a number.

```
' ****************************************************
' **  Name:          ArcHypSine#                    **
' **  Type:          Function                       **
' **  Module:        QCALMATH.BAS                   **
' **  Language:      Microsoft QuickBASIC 4.00      **
' ****************************************************
'
' EXAMPLE OF USE:   y# = ArcHypSine#(x#)
' PARAMETERS:       x#         Number to be evaluated
' VARIABLES:        (none)
' MODULE LEVEL
'   DECLARATIONS:   DECLARE FUNCTION AryHypSine# (x#)
'
  FUNCTION ArcHypSine# (x#) STATIC
      ArcHypSine# = LOG(x# + SQR(1# + x# * x#))
  END FUNCTION
```

Function: ArcHypTangent#

Returns the inverse hyperbolic tangent of a number. If the number passed is less than -1 or greater than 1, an error message is displayed, and the program terminates.

```
' ***********************************************
' **   Name:          ArcHypTangent#             **
' **   Type:          Function                   **
' **   Module:        QCALMATH.BAS               **
' **   Language:      Microsoft QuickBASIC 4.00  **
' ***********************************************
'
' EXAMPLE OF USE:   y# = ArcHypTangent#(x#)
' PARAMETERS:       x#           Number to be evaluated
' VARIABLES:        (none)
' MODULE LEVEL
'   DECLARATIONS:   DECLARE FUNCTION ArcHypTangent# (x#)
'
  FUNCTION ArcHypTangent# (x#) STATIC
      IF ABS(x#) < 1 THEN
          ArcHypTangent# = LOG((1# + x#) / (1# - x#)) / 2#
      ELSE
          PRINT "Error: AHT(x#) where x# <= -1 or x# >= +1"
          SYSTEM
      END IF
  END FUNCTION
```

Function: ArcSine#

Returns the inverse sine of a number. If the number passed is greater than or equal to 1, the function displays an error message, and the program terminates.

```
' ***********************************************
' **   Name:          ArcSine#                   **
' **   Type:          Function                   **
' **   Module:        QCALMATH.BAS               **
' **   Language:      Microsoft QuickBASIC 4.00  **
' ***********************************************
```

(continued)

continued

```
' EXAMPLE OF USE:   y# = ArcSine#(x#)
' PARAMETERS:       x#          Number to be evaluated
' VARIABLES:        (none)
' MODULE LEVEL
'   DECLARATIONS:   DECLARE FUNCTION ArcSine# (x#)
'
  FUNCTION ArcSine# (x#) STATIC
      x2# = x# * x#
      IF x2# < 1# THEN
          ArcSine# = ATN(x# / SQR(1# - x# * x#))
      ELSE
          PRINT "Error: ASN(x#) where x# >= 1"
          SYSTEM
      END IF
  END FUNCTION
```

Function: ArcTangent#

Returns the inverse tangent of a number.

```
' ************************************************
' **   Name:        ArcTangent#                 **
' **   Type:        Function                    **
' **   Module:      QCALMATH.BAS                **
' **   Language:    Microsoft QuickBASIC 4.00   **
' ************************************************
'
' EXAMPLE OF USE:   y# = ArcTangent#(x#)
' PARAMETERS:       x#          Number to be evaluated
' VARIABLES:        (none)
' MODULE LEVEL
'   DECLARATIONS:   DECLARE FUNCTION ArcTangent# (x#)
'
  FUNCTION ArcTangent# (x#) STATIC
      ArcTangent# = ATN(x#)
  END FUNCTION
```

Function: Ceil#

Returns the smallest whole number that is greater than a number. For example, Ceil#(3.14) returns *4*, Ceil#(−3.14) returns *−3*, and Ceil#(17) returns *17*.

```
' ***************************************************
' **   Name:         Ceil#                         **
' **   Type:         Function                      **
' **   Module:       QCALMATH.BAS                  **
' **   Language:     Microsoft QuickBASIC 4.00     **
' ***************************************************
'
' EXAMPLE OF USE:   y# = Ceil#(x#)
' PARAMETERS:       x#          Number to be evaluated
' VARIABLES:        (none)
' MODULE LEVEL
'   DECLARATIONS:   DECLARE FUNCTION Ceil# (x#)
'
  FUNCTION Ceil# (x#) STATIC
      Ceil# = -INT(-x#)
  END FUNCTION
```

Function: ChangeSign#

Returns a number with its sign changed. This function could easily be deleted from QCAL by changing the Process subprogram so that it directly performs negation in the CASE statement in which the CHS command is acted upon. I decided to provide a consistent interface between the functions in the QCALMATH module and the Process subprogram, however, making it easier to add, delete, or modify functions as desired.

```
' ***************************************************
' **   Name:         ChangeSign#                   **
' **   Type:         Function                      **
' **   Module:       QCALMATH.BAS                  **
' **   Language:     Microsoft QuickBASIC 4.00     **
' ***************************************************
'
' EXAMPLE OF USE:   y# = ChangeSign#(x#)
' PARAMETERS:       x#          Number to be evaluated
' VARIABLES:        (none)
```

(continued)

continued

```
' MODULE LEVEL
'   DECLARATIONS:  DECLARE FUNCTION ChangeSign# (x#)
'
  FUNCTION ChangeSign# (x#) STATIC
      ChangeSign# = -x#
  END FUNCTION
```

Function: Cosine#

Returns the cosine of an angle.

```
' *****************************************************
' **  Name:          Cosine#                         **
' **  Type:          Function                        **
' **  Module:        QCALMATH.BAS                    **
' **  Language:      Microsoft QuickBASIC 4.00       **
' *****************************************************
'
' EXAMPLE OF USE:   y# = Cosine#(x#)
' PARAMETERS:       x#           Angle to be evaluated
' VARIABLES:        (none)
' MODULE LEVEL
'   DECLARATIONS:  DECLARE FUNCTION Cosine# (x#)
'
  FUNCTION Cosine# (x#) STATIC
      Cosine# = COS(x#)
  END FUNCTION
```

Function: Divide#

Returns the result of dividing two numbers. If a division by 0 is attempted, the function displays an error message, and the program terminates.

```
' *****************************************************
' **  Name:          Divide#                         **
' **  Type:          Function                        **
' **  Module:        QCALMATH.BAS                    **
' **  Language:      Microsoft QuickBASIC 4.00       **
' *****************************************************
```

(continued)

continued

```
' EXAMPLE OF USE:   y# = Divide#(y#, x#)
' PARAMETERS:       y#           Number to be processed
'                   x#           Number to be processed
' VARIABLES:        (none)
' MODULE LEVEL
'   DECLARATIONS:   DECLARE FUNCTION Divide# (y#, x#)
'
  FUNCTION Divide# (y#, x#) STATIC
      IF x# <> 0 THEN
          Divide# = y# / x#
      ELSE
          PRINT "Error: Division by zero"
          SYSTEM
      END IF
  END FUNCTION
```

Subprogram: Dup

Duplicates the top entry on the stack for the QCAL program.

```
' **************************************************
' **   Name:         Dup                          **
' **   Type:         Subprogram                   **
' **   Module:       QCALMATH.BAS                 **
' **   Language:     Microsoft QuickBASIC 4.00    **
' **************************************************
'
' EXAMPLE OF USE:  Dup stack#(), ptr%
' PARAMETERS:      stack#()   Numeric stack
'                  ptr%       Index to last entry on stack
' VARIABLES:       (none)
' MODULE LEVEL
'   DECLARATIONS:  DECLARE SUB Dup (Stack#(), ptr%)
'
  SUB Dup (stack#(), ptr%) STATIC
      IF ptr% THEN
          ptr% = ptr% + 1
          stack#(ptr%) = stack#(ptr% - 1)
      END IF
  END SUB
```

Function: Exponential#

Returns the exponential function of a number.

```
' ****************************************************
' ** Name:          Exponential#                    **
' ** Type:          Function                        **
' ** Module:        QCALMATH.BAS                    **
' ** Language:      Microsoft QuickBASIC 4.00       **
' ****************************************************
'
' EXAMPLE OF USE:   y# = Exponential#(x#)
' PARAMETERS:       x#          Number to be processed
' VARIABLES:        (none)
' MODULE LEVEL
'   DECLARATIONS:   DECLARE FUNCTION Exponential# (x#)
'
  FUNCTION Exponential# (x#) STATIC
      Exponential# = EXP(x#)
  END FUNCTION
```

Function: FractionalPart#

Returns the fractional part of a number. For example, the fractional part of 3.14 is .14, of −3.14 is −.14, and of 17 is 0.

```
' ****************************************************
' ** Name:          FractionalPart#                 **
' ** Type:          Function                        **
' ** Module:        QCALMATH.BAS                    **
' ** Language:      Microsoft QuickBASIC 4.00       **
' ****************************************************
'
' EXAMPLE OF USE:   y# = FractionalPart#(x#)
' PARAMETERS:       x#          Number to be processed
' VARIABLES:        (none)
' MODULE LEVEL
'   DECLARATIONS:   DECLARE FUNCTION FractionalPart# (x#)
'
  FUNCTION FractionalPart# (x#) STATIC
      IF x# >= 0 THEN
          FractionalPart# = x# - INT(x#)
      ELSE
          FractionalPart# = x# - INT(x#) - 1#
      END IF
  END FUNCTION
```

Function: HypCosine#

Returns the hyperbolic cosine of a number.

```
' *****************************************************
' **   Name:           HypCosine#                    **
' **   Type:           Function                      **
' **   Module:         QCALMATH.BAS                  **
' **   Language:       Microsoft QuickBASIC 4.00     **
' *****************************************************
'
' EXAMPLE OF USE:   y# = HypCosine#(x#)
' PARAMETERS:       x#           Number to be processed
' VARIABLES:        (none)
' MODULE LEVEL
'   DECLARATIONS:   DECLARE FUNCTION HypCosine# (x#)
'
 FUNCTION HypCosine# (x#) STATIC
     HypCosine# = (EXP(x#) + EXP(-x#)) / 2#
 END FUNCTION
```

Function: HypSine#

Returns the hyperbolic sine of a number.

```
' *****************************************************
' **   Name:           HypSine#                      **
' **   Type:           Function                      **
' **   Module:         QCALMATH.BAS                  **
' **   Language:       Microsoft QuickBASIC 4.00     **
' *****************************************************
'
' EXAMPLE OF USE:   y# = HypSine#(x#)
' PARAMETERS:       x#           Number to be processed
' VARIABLES:        (none)
' MODULE LEVEL
'   DECLARATIONS:   DECLARE FUNCTION HypSine# (x#)
'
 FUNCTION HypSine# (x#) STATIC
     HypSine# = (EXP(x#) - EXP(-x#)) / 2#
 END FUNCTION
```

Function: HypTangent#

Returns the hyperbolic tangent of a number.

```
' ****************************************************
' **   Name:         HypTangent#                    **
' **   Type:         Function                       **
' **   Module:       QCALMATH.BAS                   **
' **   Language:     Microsoft QuickBASIC 4.00      **
' ****************************************************
'
' EXAMPLE OF USE:   y# = HypTangent#(x#)
' PARAMETERS:       x#          Number to be processed
' VARIABLES:        (none)
' MODULE LEVEL
'   DECLARATIONS:   DECLARE FUNCTION HypTangent# (x#)

  FUNCTION HypTangent# (x#) STATIC
      HypTangent# = (EXP(x#) - EXP(-x#)) / (EXP(x#) + EXP(-x#))
  END FUNCTION
```

Function: IntegerPart#

Returns the integer part of a number. For example, the integer part of 3.14 is 3, of −3.14 is −4, and of 17 is 17.

```
' ****************************************************
' **   Name:         IntegerPart#                   **
' **   Type:         Function                       **
' **   Module:       QCALMATH.BAS                   **
' **   Language:     Microsoft QuickBASIC 4.00      **
' ****************************************************
'
' EXAMPLE OF USE:   y# = IntegerPart#(x#)
' PARAMETERS:       x#          Number to be processed
' VARIABLES:        (none)
' MODULE LEVEL
'   DECLARATIONS:   DECLARE FUNCTION IntegerPart# (x#)

  FUNCTION IntegerPart# (x#) STATIC
      IntegerPart# = INT(x#)
  END FUNCTION
```

Function: LogBase10#

Returns the logarithm, base 10, of a number. If the number is not greater than 0, the function displays an error message, and the program terminates.

Look in the listing at the constant L10, defined in the module-level code of QCALMATH. This constant is the double-precision natural logarithm of 10. The constant can be replaced with LOG(10), its mathematic equivalent, but using a constant makes the program faster and the compiled program shorter.

```
' ****************************************************
' **   Name:         LogBase10#                     **
' **   Type:         Function                       **
' **   Module:       QCALMATH.BAS                   **
' **   Language:     Microsoft QuickBASIC 4.00      **
' ****************************************************
'
' EXAMPLE OF USE:   y# = Log10#(x#)
' PARAMETERS:       x#            Number to be processed
' VARIABLES:        (none)
' MODULE LEVEL
'   DECLARATIONS:   DECLARE FUNCTION LogBase10# (x#)
'
  FUNCTION LogBase10# (x#) STATIC
      IF x# > 0 THEN
          LogBase10# = LOG(x#) / L10
      ELSE
          PRINT "Error: LOG10(x#) where x# <= 0"
          SYSTEM
      END IF
  END FUNCTION
```

Function: LogBaseN#

Returns the logarithm, base *N*, of a number. This function checks for several possible error conditions. The number to be processed must be greater than 0, and the base for finding the logarithm must be greater than 0 and must not be exactly 1. If one of these checks fails, a message is displayed, and the program terminates.

```
' ****************************************************
' **   Name:        LogBaseN#                       **
' **   Type:        Function                        **
' **   Module:      QCALMATH.BAS                    **
' **   Language:    Microsoft QuickBASIC 4.00       **
' ****************************************************
'
' EXAMPLE OF USE:  y# = LogBaseN#(y#, x#)
' PARAMETERS:      y#          Number to be processed
'                  x#          The base for finding the logarithm
' VARIABLES:       (none)
' MODULE LEVEL
'   DECLARATIONS:  DECLARE FUNCTION LogBaseN# (y#, x#)
'
    FUNCTION LogBaseN# (y#, x#) STATIC
       IF x# <= 0 THEN
           PRINT "Error: LOGN(y#, x#) where x# <= 0"
           SYSTEM
       ELSEIF x# = 1# THEN
           PRINT "Error: LOGN(y#, x#) where x# = 1"
           SYSTEM
       ELSEIF y# <= 0 THEN
           PRINT "Error: LOGN(y#, x#) where y# is <= 0"
           SYSTEM
       ELSE
           LogBaseN# = LOG(y#) / LOG(x#)
       END IF
    END FUNCTION
```

Function: LogE#

Returns the natural logarithm of a number. The QuickBASIC function LOG() is used to calculate the logarithm, but this function first checks that the number is greater than 0. If the number is equal to or less than 0, an error message is displayed, and the program terminates.

```
' ****************************************************
' **   Name:          LogE#                          **
' **   Type:          Function                       **
' **   Module:        QCALMATH.BAS                   **
' **   Language:      Microsoft QuickBASIC 4.00      **
' ****************************************************
'
' EXAMPLE OF USE:   y# = LogE#(x#)
' PARAMETERS:       x#           Number to be processed
' VARIABLES:        (none)
' MODULE LEVEL
'   DECLARATIONS:   DECLARE FUNCTION LogE# (x#)
'
  FUNCTION LogE# (x#) STATIC
     IF x# > 0 THEN
        LogE# = LOG(x#)
     ELSE
        PRINT "Error: LOGE(x#) where x# <= 0"
        SYSTEM
     END IF
  END FUNCTION
```

Function: Modulus#

Returns the remainder of the division of two numbers. If a division by 0 is attempted, the function displays an error message, and the program terminates. The function is valid for non-integer quantities.

```
' ****************************************************
' **   Name:          Modulus#                       **
' **   Type:          Function                       **
' **   Module:        QCALMATH.BAS                   **
' **   Language:      Microsoft QuickBASIC 4.00      **
' ****************************************************
```

(continued)

continued

```
' EXAMPLE OF USE:   y# = Modulus#(y#, x#)
' PARAMETERS:       y#            Number to be divided
'                   x#            Number for dividing by
' VARIABLES:        (none)
' MODULE LEVEL
'   DECLARATIONS:   DECLARE FUNCTION Modulus# (y#, x#)
'
  FUNCTION Modulus# (y#, x#) STATIC
      IF x# <> 0 THEN
          Modulus# = y# - INT(y# / x#) * x#
      ELSE
          PRINT "Error: MOD(y#, x#) where x# = 0"
          SYSTEM
      END IF
  END FUNCTION
```

Function: Multiply#

Returns the product of two numbers.

```
' *************************************************
' ** Name:          Multiply#                    **
' ** Type:          Function                     **
' ** Module:        QCALMATH.BAS                 **
' ** Language:      Microsoft QuickBASIC 4.00    **
' *************************************************
'
' EXAMPLE OF USE:   y# = Multiply#(y#, x#)
' PARAMETERS:       y#            First number to be processed
'                   x#            Second number to be processed
' VARIABLES:        (none)
' MODULE LEVEL
'   DECLARATIONS:   DECLARE FUNCTION Multiply# (y#, x#)
'
  FUNCTION Multiply# (y#, x#) STATIC
      Multiply# = y# * x#
  END FUNCTION
```

Function: OneOverX#

Returns the result of dividing 1 by a number. If a division by 0 is attempted, the function displays an error message, and the program terminates.

```
' *****************************************************
' **   Name:          OneOverX#                      **
' **   Type:          Function                       **
' **   Module:        QCALMATH.BAS                   **
' **   Language:      Microsoft QuickBASIC 4.00      **
' *****************************************************
'
' EXAMPLE OF USE:    y# = OneOverX#(x#)
' PARAMETERS:        x#           Number to be processed
' VARIABLES:         (none)
' MODULE LEVEL
'   DECLARATIONS:    DECLARE FUNCTION OneOverX# (x#)
'
  FUNCTION OneOverX# (x#) STATIC
      IF x# <> 0 THEN
          OneOverX# = 1# / x#
      ELSE
          PRINT "Error: 1/x where x = 0"
          SYSTEM
      END IF
  END FUNCTION
```

Function: Sign#

Returns *−1* for all negative numbers, *1* for positive numbers, and *0* for zero.

```
' *****************************************************
' **   Name:          Sign#                          **
' **   Type:          Function                       **
' **   Module:        QCALMATH.BAS                   **
' **   Language:      Microsoft QuickBASIC 4.00      **
' *****************************************************
```

(continued)

continued

```
' EXAMPLE OF USE:   y# = Sign#(x#)
' PARAMETERS:       x#            Number to be processed
' VARIABLES:        (none)
' MODULE LEVEL
'   DECLARATIONS:   DECLARE FUNCTION Sign# (x#)
'
  FUNCTION Sign# (x#) STATIC
      Sign# = SGN(x#)
  END FUNCTION
```

Function: Sine#

Returns the sine of an angle; assumes the angle is expressed in radians.

```
' *********************************************
' ** Name:         Sine#                     **
' ** Type:         Function                  **
' ** Module:       QCALMATH.BAS              **
' ** Language:     Microsoft QuickBASIC 4.00 **
' *********************************************
'
' EXAMPLE OF USE:   y# = Sine#(x#)
' PARAMETERS:       x#            Angle, expressed in radians
' VARIABLES:        (none)
' MODULE LEVEL
'   DECLARATIONS:   DECLARE FUNCTION Sine# (x#)
'
  FUNCTION Sine# (x#) STATIC
      Sine# = SIN(x#)
  END FUNCTION
```

Function: SquareRoot#

Returns the square root of a number. Before the QuickBASIC SQR function is used to actually find the square root, the number is checked to be sure it isn't negative. If it is, an error message is displayed, and the program terminates.

```
' ****************************************************
' **   Name:          SquareRoot#                    **
' **   Type:          Function                       **
' **   Module:        QCALMATH.BAS                   **
' **   Language:      Microsoft QuickBASIC 4.00      **
' ****************************************************
'
' EXAMPLE OF USE:    y# = SquareRoot#(x#)
' PARAMETERS:        x#          Number to be processed
' VARIABLES:         (none)
' MODULE LEVEL
'   DECLARATIONS:    DECLARE FUNCTION SquareRoot# (x#)
'
  FUNCTION SquareRoot# (x#) STATIC
      IF x# >= 0 THEN
          SquareRoot# = SQR(x#)
      ELSE
          PRINT "Error: SQR(x#) where x# < 0"
          SYSTEM
      END IF
  END FUNCTION
```

Function: Subtract#

Returns the difference of two numbers.

```
' ****************************************************
' **   Name:          Subtract#                      **
' **   Type:          Function                       **
' **   Module:        QCALMATH.BAS                   **
' **   Language:      Microsoft QuickBASIC 4.00      **
' ****************************************************
'
' EXAMPLE OF USE:    y# = Subtract#(y#, x#)
' PARAMETERS:        y#          Number to be processed
'                    x#          Number to be processed
' VARIABLES:         (none)
' MODULE LEVEL
'   DECLARATIONS:    DECLARE FUNCTION Subtract# (y#, x#)
'
  FUNCTION Subtract# (y#, x#) STATIC
      Subtract# = y# - x#
  END FUNCTION
```

Subprogram: SwapXY

Swaps the top two entries on the stack.

```
' ****************************************************
' **   Name:          SwapXY                         **
' **   Type:          Subprogram                     **
' **   Module:        QCALMATH.BAS                   **
' **   Language:      Microsoft QuickBASIC 4.00      **
' ****************************************************
'
' EXAMPLE OF USE:   SwapXY stack#(), ptr%
' PARAMETERS:       stack#()    Numeric stack
'                   ptr%        Pointer to top of stack
' VARIABLES:        (none)
' MODULE LEVEL
'   DECLARATIONS:   DECLARE SUB SwapXY (stack#(), ptr%)
'
  SUB SwapXY (stack#(), ptr%) STATIC
      IF ptr% > 1 THEN
          SWAP stack#(ptr%), stack#(ptr% - 1)
      END IF
  END SUB
```

Function: Tangent#

Returns the tangent of an angle; assumes the angle is in radians.

```
' ****************************************************
' **   Name:          Tangent#                       **
' **   Type:          Function                       **
' **   Module:        QCALMATH.BAS                   **
' **   Language:      Microsoft QuickBASIC 4.00      **
' ****************************************************
'
' EXAMPLE OF USE:   y# = Tangent#(x#)
' PARAMETERS:       x#          Angle, expressed in radians
' VARIABLES:        (none)
' MODULE LEVEL
'   DECLARATIONS:   DECLARE FUNCTION Tangent# (x#)
'
  FUNCTION Tangent# (x#) STATIC
      Tangent# = TAN(x#)
  END FUNCTION
```

Function: Xsquared#

Returns the square of a number.

```
' *****************************************************
' **    Name:         Xsquared#                      **
' **    Type:         Function                       **
' **    Module:       QCALMATH.BAS                   **
' **    Language:     Microsoft QuickBASIC 4.00      **
' *****************************************************
'
' EXAMPLE OF USE:   y# = Xsquared#(x#)
' PARAMETERS:       x#           Number to be processed
' VARIABLES:        (none)
' MODULE LEVEL
'   DECLARATIONS:   DECLARE FUNCTION Xsquared# (x#)
'
  FUNCTION Xsquared# (x#) STATIC
      Xsquared# = x# * x#
  END FUNCTION
```

Function: YRaisedToX#

Returns a number raised to the power of a second number.

```
' *****************************************************
' **    Name:         YRaisedToX#                    **
' **    Type:         Function                       **
' **    Module:       QCALMATH.BAS                   **
' **    Language:     Microsoft QuickBASIC 4.00      **
' *****************************************************
'
' EXAMPLE OF USE:   z# = YRaisedToX#(y#, x#)
' PARAMETERS:       y#           Number to be raised to a power
'                   x#           Power to raise the other number to
' VARIABLES:        (none)
' MODULE LEVEL
'   DECLARATIONS:   DECLARE FUNCTION YRaisedToX# (y#, x#)
'
  FUNCTION YRaisedToX# (y#, x#) STATIC
      YRaisedToX# = y# ^ x#
  END FUNCTION
```

RANDOMS

The RANDOMS toolbox provides a collection of random number generators.

At the heart of these routines are two techniques, which are described in *The Art of Computer Programming*, Vol. 2, *Seminumerical Algorithms*, by Donald Knuth and which are combined to form the method in the Rand& function. The Rand& function returns pseudorandom integers in the range 0 through 999999999. No multiplication or division is used, the algorithm is easily translated to any language that supports 32-bit integers, and all digits in the returned numbers are equally random. A table-shuffling technique further increases the randomness of the sequence.

Several other functions use the random long integers returned by the Rand& function to create other random number distributions. For example, the RandReal!(x!, y!) function returns random real numbers in the range x! through y!. One common example of this function, RandReal!(0!, 1!), returns a pseudorandom, single-precision, floating-point value in the range 0 through 1.

The RandShuffle subprogram and the RandInteger% function are used by CIPHER to generate a repeatable but secure sequence of random byte values in the range 0 through 255. See the CIPHER program for more information on using this file-ciphering technique.

Name	Type	Description
RANDOMS.BAS		Demo module
Rand&	Func	Long integers
RandExponential!	Func	Real value with exponential distribution from mean
RandFrac!	Func	Single-precision positive value < 1.0
RandInteger%	Func	Integers within desired range
RandNormal!	Func	Single-precision value from mean and standard deviation
RandReal!	Func	Single-precision value in desired range
RandShuffle	Sub	Initializes random number generator

Demo Module: RANDOMS

```
' **************************************************
' **   Name:         RANDOMS                      **
' **   Type:         Toolbox                      **
' **   Module:       RANDOMS.BAS                  **
' **   Language:     Microsoft QuickBASIC 4.00    **
' **************************************************
' USAGE:          No command line parameters
' .MAK FILE:      (none)
' PARAMETERS:     (none)
' VARIABLES:      i%       Loop index for generating pseudorandom numbers

  DECLARE FUNCTION Rand& ()
  DECLARE FUNCTION RandExponential! (mean!)
  DECLARE FUNCTION RandFrac! ()
  DECLARE FUNCTION RandInteger% (a%, b%)
  DECLARE FUNCTION RandNormal! (mean!, stddev!)
  DECLARE FUNCTION RandReal! (x!, y!)

  DECLARE SUB RandShuffle (key$)

' Array of long integers for generating all randoms
  DIM SHARED r&(1 TO 100)

' Clear the screen
  CLS

' Shuffle the random number generator, creating a
' unique sequence for every possible second
  RandShuffle DATE$ + TIME$

  PRINT "Rand&"
  FOR i% = 1 TO 5
      PRINT Rand&,
  NEXT i%
  PRINT

  PRINT "RandInteger%(0, 9)"
  FOR i% = 1 TO 5
      PRINT RandInteger%(0, 9),
  NEXT i%
  PRINT
```

(continued)

continued

```
PRINT "RandReal!(-10!, 10!)"
FOR i% = 1 TO 5
    PRINT RandReal!(-10!, 10!),
NEXT i%
PRINT

PRINT "RandExponential!(100!)"
FOR i% = 1 TO 5
    PRINT RandExponential!(100!),
NEXT i%
PRINT

PRINT "RandNormal!(100!, 10!)"
FOR i% = 1 TO 5
    PRINT RandNormal!(100!, 10!),
NEXT i%
PRINT

PRINT "RandFrac!"
FOR i% = 1 TO 5
    PRINT RandFrac!,
NEXT i%
PRINT
```

Function: Rand&

Returns a pseudorandom long integer in the range 0 through 999999999, inclusive. Using the Rand& function provides you several advantages: It is fast because a minimal number of mathematical manipulations are performed; the sequence length is long, much greater than 2^55; and all digits in the returned random integer are equally random.

The array of long integers, r&(1 TO 100), is shared by this function and the RandShuffle subprogram. This array contains a table of 55 random integers, a table of 42 values for shuffling the order of the random numbers upon output, two index pointers into the first 55 values, and the last generated random integer.

You must call the RandShuffle subprogram once before you use the Rand& function. This initializes the tables and presets the two index numbers used to access table entries. If you don't call RandShuffle first, the Rand& function stops, you receive a *Subscript out of range* error message, and the program halts.

Here's how Rand& works. The index numbers stored in r&(98) and r&(99) are always in the range 1 through 55 and are used to access two numbers stored in the first 55 entries of r&(). The first of these values is subtracted from the second, and if the result is less than zero, 1000000000 is added to bring the result somewhere into the range 0 through 999999999. This result replaces the number at the first location accessed. Finally, the two index numbers are decremented by 1, adjusted if necessary so that they remain in the range 1 through 55, and stored back in r&(98) and r&(99) for the next call to this routine.

This table subtraction algorithm results in a good-quality random long integer, but an additional technique is used within Rand& to generate a significantly more random sequence of numbers. The generated number is used to point to one of the 42 entries in the locations r&(56) through r&(97). The previously generated number stored at that location is extracted, saved in r&(100), and replaced with the number just generated. Finally, the value saved in r&(100) is returned as the result. This randomly shuffles the order of the output values and effectively obliterates any subtle patterns that the sequence might have.

```
' *******************************************
' ** Name:          Rand&                    **
' ** Type:          Function                 **
' ** Module:        RANDOMS.BAS              **
' ** Language:      Microsoft QuickBASIC 4.00 **
' *******************************************
'
' Returns a pseudorandom long integer in the range
' 0 through 999999999.
'
' EXAMPLE OF USE:   n& = Rand&
' PARAMETERS:       (none)
' VARIABLES:        i%       First index into random number table
'                   j%       Second index into random number table
'                   t&       Working variable
' MODULE LEVEL
'   DECLARATIONS:   DECLARE FUNCTION Rand& ()
'                   DIM SHARED r&(1 TO 100)
```

(continued)

continued

```
FUNCTION Rand& STATIC

    ' Get the pointers into the table
    i% = r&(98)
    j% = r&(99)

    ' Subtract the two table values
    t& = r&(i%) - r&(j%)

    ' Adjust result if less than zero
    IF t& < 0 THEN
        t& = t& + 1000000000
    END IF

    ' Replace table entry with new random number
    r&(i%) = t&

    ' Decrement first index, keeping in range 1 through 55
    IF i% > 1 THEN
        r&(98) = i% - 1
    ELSE
        r&(98) = 55
    END IF

    ' Decrement second index, keeping in range 1 through 55
    IF j% > 1 THEN
        r&(99) = j% - 1
    ELSE
        r&(99) = 55
    END IF

    ' Use last random number to index into shuffle table
    i% = r&(100) MOD 42 + 56

    ' Grab random from table as current random number
    r&(100) = r&(i%)

    ' Put new calculated random into table
    r&(i%) = t&

    ' Return the random number grabbed from the table
    Rand& = r&(100)

END FUNCTION
```

QUICKBASIC TOOLBOXES AND PROGRAMS

Function: RandExponential!

Returns a pseudorandom real value with an exponential distribution, which is defined by the passed value of the mean.

Be sure to call the RandShuffle subprogram before using this function.

```
' *****************************************
' **   Name:          RandExponential!         **
' **   Type:          Function                 **
' **   Module:        RANDOMS.BAS              **
' **   Language:      Microsoft QuickBASIC 4.00 **
' *****************************************
'
' Returns an exponentially distributed pseudorandom,
' single-precision number given the mean of the
' distribution.
'
' EXAMPLE OF USE:    x! = RandExponential!(mean!)
' PARAMETERS:        mean!    The mean of the exponential distribution
' VARIABLES:         (none)
' MODULE LEVEL
'   DECLARATIONS:    DECLARE FUNCTION RandExponential! (mean!)

 FUNCTION RandExponential! (mean!) STATIC
     RandExponential! = -mean! * LOG(RandFrac!)
 END FUNCTION
```

Function: RandFrac!

Returns a pseudorandom real value in the range 0 through 1. This function is similar to the QuickBASIC function RND, but has a much longer sequence and a more random distribution.

Be sure to call the RandShuffle subprogram before using this function.

```
' *****************************************
' **   Name:          RandFrac!                **
' **   Type:          Function                 **
' **   Module:        RANDOMS.BAS              **
' **   Language:      Microsoft QuickBASIC 4.00 **
' *****************************************
```

(continued)

continued

```
' Returns a pseudorandom, single-precision number
' in the range 0 through 1.
'
' EXAMPLE OF USE:   x! = RandFrac!
' PARAMETERS:       (none)
' VARIABLES:        (none)
' MODULE LEVEL
'   DECLARATIONS:   DECLARE FUNCTION RandFrac! ()
'
  FUNCTION RandFrac! STATIC
      RandFrac! = Rand& / 1E+09
  END FUNCTION
```

Function: RandInteger%

Returns a pseudorandom integer in the range a% through b%, inclusive. For example, RandInteger%(0, 9) returns a random digit from 0 through 9.

The passed value of a% must be less than b%; if it is not, this function generates incorrect random numbers. These parameters must be in the legal range of 16-bit signed integers, not less than −32768 nor greater than 32767.

Be sure to call the RandShuffle subprogram before using this function.

```
' *************************************************
' **  Name:          RandInteger%                **
' **  Type:          Function                    **
' **  Module:        RANDOMS.BAS                 **
' **  Language:      Microsoft QuickBASIC 4.00   **
' *************************************************
'
' Returns a pseudorandom integer in the range
' a% to b% inclusive.
'
' EXAMPLE OF USE:   n% = RandInteger%(a%, b%)
' PARAMETERS:       a%   Minimum value for returned integer
'                   b%   Maximum value for returned integer
' VARIABLES:        (none)
```

(continued)

continued

```
' MODULE LEVEL
'   DECLARATIONS:  DECLARE FUNCTION RandInteger% (a%, b%)
'
  FUNCTION RandInteger% (a%, b%) STATIC
      RandInteger% = a% + (Rand& MOD (b% - a% + 1))
  END FUNCTION
```

Function: RandNormal!

Returns pseudorandom real values with a normal distribution, which is defined by the passed mean and standard deviation.

Be sure to call the RandShuffle subprogram before using this function.

```
' *************************************************
' **  Name:          RandNormal!                  **
' **  Type:          Function                     **
' **  Module:        RANDOMS.BAS                  **
' **  Language:      Microsoft QuickBASIC 4.00    **
' *************************************************
'
' Returns a normally distributed single-precision,
' pseudorandom number given the mean and standard deviation.
'
' EXAMPLE OF USE:   x! = RandNormal!(mean!, stddev!)
' PARAMETERS:       mean!    Mean of the distribution of returned
'                            values
'                   stddev!  Standard deviation of the distribution
' VARIABLES:        u1!      Pseudorandom positive real value
'                            less than 1
'                   u2!      Pseudorandom positive real value
'                            less than 1
'                   x!       Working value
' MODULE LEVEL
'   DECLARATIONS:  DECLARE FUNCTION RandNormal! (mean!, stddev!)
'
  FUNCTION RandNormal! (mean!, stddev!) STATIC
      u1! = RandFrac!
      u2! = RandFrac!
      x! = SQR(-2! * LOG(u1!)) * COS(6.283185 * u2)
      RandNormal! = mean! + stddev! * x!
  END FUNCTION
```

Function: RandReal!

Returns a pseudorandom real value in the range x! through y! For example, RandReal!(−10!, 10!) returns a floating-point, single-precision value in the range −10 through +10.

Be sure to call the RandShuffle subprogram before using this function.

```
' **************************************************
' **   Name:          RandReal!                   **
' **   Type:          Function                    **
' **   Module:        RANDOMS.BAS                 **
' **   Language:      Microsoft QuickBASIC 4.00   **
' **************************************************
'
' Returns a pseudorandom, single-precision real
' number in the range x! to y!.
' EXAMPLE OF USE:    z! = RandReal!(x!, y!)
' PARAMETERS:        x!    Minimum for returned value
'                    y!    Maximum for returned value
' VARIABLES:         (none)
' MODULE LEVEL
'   DECLARATIONS:    DECLARE FUNCTION RandReal! (x!, y!)
'
  FUNCTION RandReal! (x!, y!) STATIC
      RandReal! = x! + (y! - x!) * (Rand& / 1E+09)
  END FUNCTION
```

Subprogram: RandShuffle

Initializes the sequence of random numbers that the Rand& function returns. The r&() array contains all the values necessary for the Rand& function. This subprogram initializes all values in r&() based on the characters passed in key$. Refer to the Rand& function for a description of the contents of the shared array r&().

The passed string key$ is first modified to a length of 97 characters. Notice that an arbitrary string (in this subprogram, *Abra Ca Da Bra*) is concatenated to the front end of key$. Any string can be used, but at least one character must have an odd byte number. This guarantees that at least one initial table entry will be odd, a necessity of this random-number-generation algorithm.

Each character of the new key string (k$) is used to generate a pseudorandom long integer to be entered in the first 97 entries of r&(). To "warm up" the sequence, 997 iterations of the Rand& algorithm, slightly modified, are performed on the table.

Finally, starting values for the index values necessary for the Rand& function are stored in r&(98) and r&(99), and an initial value for the last generated number is stored in r&(100).

All the other random number generators in this toolbox call the Rand& function, which generates an error and quits if RandShuffle isn't run first to initialize r&(). Therefore, you must be sure to call RandShuffle once during a program run before calling any of these functions.

To generate the same sequence every time the program is run, pass the same key$ each time. To generate a unique sequence each time, pass a unique string. For example, to generate a unique sequence for every clock tick of your computer's existence, you could enter *RandShuffle(DATE$ + TIME$ + STR$(TIMER))*.

The key$ can be any reasonable length, but only the first 83 characters are used to seed the generator. Because there are 256 possible characters for each of the 83, there are 256^83 possible unique sequences. It's safe to say you'll never run out!

```
' ***************************************************
' **  Name:           RandShuffle                  **
' **  Type:           Subprogram                   **
' **  Module:         RANDOMS.BAS                  **
' **  Language:       Microsoft QuickBASIC 4.00    **
' ***************************************************
'
' Creates original table of pseudorandom long integers
' for use by the function Rand&.  The contents of key$
' are used to seed the table.
'
' EXAMPLE OF USE:   RandShuffle(key$)
' PARAMETERS:       key$              String used to seed the generator
'                   r&(1 TO 100) (shared)  Array of long integers for
'                                     generating pseudorandom numbers
' VARIABLES:        k$                Modified key string
'                   i%                Index into k$, index into table
'                   j%                Index into table
'                   k%                Loop count for warming up generator
```

(continued)

continued

```
' MODULE LEVEL
'   DECLARATIONS:   DECLARE SUB RandShuffle (key$)
'
    SUB RandShuffle (key$) STATIC

        ' Form 97-character string, with key$ as part of it
        k$ = LEFT$("Abra Ca Da Bra" + key$ + SPACE$(83), 97)

        ' Use each character to seed table
        FOR i% = 1 TO 97
            r&(i%) = ASC(MID$(k$, i%, 1)) * 8171717 + i% * 997&
        NEXT i%

        ' Preserve string space
        k$ = ""

        ' Initialize pointers into table
        i% = 97
        j% = 12

        ' Randomize the table to get it warmed up
        FOR k% = 1 TO 997

            ' Subtract entries pointed to by i% and j%
            r&(i%) = r&(i%) - r&(j%)

            ' Adjust result if less than zero
            IF r&(i%) < 0 THEN
                r&(i%) = r&(i%) + 1000000000
            END IF

            ' Decrement first index, keeping in range of 1 through 97
            IF i% > 1 THEN
                i% = i% - 1
            ELSE
                i% = 97
            END IF

            ' Decrement second index, keeping in range of 1 through 97
            IF j% > 1 THEN
                j% = j% - 1
            ELSE
                j% = 97
            END IF
```

(continued)

continued

```
        NEXT k%

    ' Initialize pointers for use by Rand& function
        r&(98) = 55
        r&(99) = 24

    ' Initialize pointer for shuffle table lookup by Rand& function
        r&(100) = 77

END SUB
```

STDOUT

The STDOUT toolbox is a collection of subprograms for outputting characters through the MS-DOS standard output channel rather than through the QuickBASIC PRINT statement.

QuickBASIC bypasses the ANSI.SYS driver. However, some nice features are built into this driver, and this toolbox lets you access them from QuickBASIC. For example, the AssignKey subprogram lets you redefine keys on the keyboard to any character or string of characters you want.

Be sure you load the ANSI.SYS driver before trying this program. Several of the escape code sequences create meaningless output if the ANSI.SYS driver is not resident. In most cases, a statement similar to the following in your CONFIG.SYS file will load the ANSI.SYS driver at boot-up time:

```
DEVICE = \DOS\ANSI.SYS
```

When you run the STDOUT demo module, pay close attention to the prompts that appear. In one case you are prompted to press the "a" and "b" keys, immediately before the program exits to MS-DOS via the SHELL statement. Be sure you press "a" and then "b" to prevent the program from getting lost.

Name	Type	Description
STDOUT.BAS		Demo module
AssignKey	Sub	Reassigns a string to a key
Attribute	Sub	Sets screen color (ANSI driver definition)
ClearLine	Sub	Clears current line from cursor to end of line
ClearScreen	Sub	Clears screen
CrLf	Sub	Sends carriage return and line feed
CursorDown	Sub	Moves cursor down specified number of lines
CursorHome	Sub	Moves cursor to upper left corner of screen

(continued)

continued

Name	Type	Description
CursorLeft	Sub	Moves cursor left specified number of spaces
CursorPosition	Sub	Moves cursor to specified row and column
CursorRight	Sub	Moves cursor right specified number of spaces
CursorUp	Sub	Moves cursor up specified number of lines
StdOut	Sub	Sends a string to standard output channel

Demo Module: STDOUT

```
' *************************************************
' **   Name:          STDOUT                     **
' **   Type:          Toolbox                    **
' **   Module:        STDOUT.BAS                 **
' **   Language:      Microsoft QuickBASIC 4.00  **
' *************************************************
'
' USAGE:           No command line parameters
' REQUIREMENTS:    MIXED.QLB/.LIB
'                  ANSI.SYS
' .MAK FILE:       (none)
' PARAMETERS:      (none)
' VARIABLES:       t0         Timer variable
'                  bell$      ASCII character 7 (bell)

' Attribute definitions
  CONST NORMAL = 0
  CONST BRIGHT = 1
  CONST UNDERSCORE = 4
  CONST BLINK = 5
  CONST REVERSE = 7
  CONST INVISIBLE = 8
  CONST BLACKFOREGROUND = 30
  CONST REDFOREGROUND = 31
  CONST GREENFOREGROUND = 32
  CONST YELLOWFOREGROUND = 33
  CONST BLUEFOREGROUND = 34
```

(continued)

continued

```
    CONST MAGENTAFOREGROUND = 35
    CONST CYANFOREGROUND = 36
    CONST WHITEFOREGROUND = 37
    CONST BLACKBACKGROUND = 40
    CONST REDBACKGROUND = 41
    CONST GREENBACKGROUND = 42
    CONST YELLOWBACKGROUND = 43
    CONST BLUEBACKGROUND = 44
    CONST MAGENTABACKGROUND = 45
    CONST CYANBACKGROUND = 46
    CONST WHITEBACKGROUND = 47

    TYPE RegTypeX
        ax    AS INTEGER
        bx    AS INTEGER
        cx    AS INTEGER
        dx    AS INTEGER
        Bp    AS INTEGER
        si    AS INTEGER
        di    AS INTEGER
        flags AS INTEGER
        ds    AS INTEGER
        es    AS INTEGER
    END TYPE

' Subprograms
    DECLARE SUB InterruptX (intnum%, inreg AS RegTypeX, outreg AS RegTypeX)
    DECLARE SUB ClearLine ()
    DECLARE SUB ClearScreen ()
    DECLARE SUB StdOut (a$)
    DECLARE SUB CrLf ()
    DECLARE SUB CursorPosition (row%, col%)
    DECLARE SUB CursorDown (n%)
    DECLARE SUB CursorLeft (n%)
    DECLARE SUB CursorRight (n%)
    DECLARE SUB CursorUp (n%)
    DECLARE SUB AssignKey (keyCode%, assign$)
    DECLARE SUB Attribute (attr%)

' Demonstrate the ClearLine and ClearScreen routines
    CLS
    PRINT "This will be erased quickly, in two steps..."
    t0 = TIMER
```

(continued)

continued

```
    DO
    LOOP UNTIL TIMER - t0 > 2
    LOCATE 1, 27
    ClearLine
    t0 = TIMER
    DO
    LOOP UNTIL TIMER - t0 > 2
    LOCATE 15, 1
    ClearScreen

' Demonstrate the StdOut routine
    bell$ = CHR$(7)
    StdOut "Sending a 'Bell' to StdOut" + bell$
    CrLf

' Set cursor position
    CursorPosition 3, 20
    StdOut "* CursorPosition 3, 20"
    CrLf

' Move the cursor around the screen
    StdOut "Cursor movements..."
    CrLf
    CursorDown 1
    StdOut "Down 1"
    CursorRight 12
    StdOut "Right 12"
    CursorDown 2
    StdOut "Down 2"
    CursorLeft 99
    StdOut "Left 99"
    CrLf

' Character attributes
    CrLf
    Attribute YELLOWFOREGROUND
    Attribute BRIGHT
    Attribute BLUEBACKGROUND
    StdOut "Bright yellow on blue"
    CrLf
    Attribute NORMAL
    StdOut "Back to normal attributes"
    CrLf
```

(continued)

continued

```
' Key reassignment
AssignKey 97, "REM The 'a' and 'b' keys have been redefined" + CHR$(13)
AssignKey 98, "EXIT" + CHR$(13)
CursorDown 1
Attribute BRIGHT
Attribute YELLOWFOREGROUND
StdOut "NOTE:"
CrLf
StdOut "Press the 'a' key and then the 'b' key ... "
CrLf
StdOut "The program will then continue ........ "
Attribute NORMAL
CrLf
SHELL
AssignKey 97, ""
AssignKey 98, ""
```

Subprogram: AssignKey

Assigns a string to any key on the keyboard. The first parameter is the key code number returned by the ASC(INKEY$) statement for a given key press. The second parameter is a string of characters assigned to the indicated key. The string can be a maximum of 63 characters in length. If the string is null, the original key definition is returned to the key.

One complication arises if the key normally returns an extended key code. Recall that such keys return *CHR$(0)*, followed by a second character that identifies the key. The AssignKey subprogram recognizes negative key numbers as extended key codes. Pass the negative of the second byte of an extended key code to indicate the key.

```
' ****************************************************
' **   Name:          AssignKey                     **
' **   Type:          Subprogram                    **
' **   Module:        STDOUT.BAS                    **
' **   Language:      Microsoft QuickBASIC 4.00     **
' ****************************************************
'
' Assigns a string to any key using ANSI.SYS driver.
'
' EXAMPLE OF USE:   AssignKey keyCode%, assign$
' PARAMETERS:       keyCode%   ASCII number for key to be reassigned
'                   assign$    String to assign to key
```

(continued)

continued

```
' VARIABLES:        k$         Command string for ANSI.SYS driver
'                   i%         Index to each character of assign$
' MODULE LEVEL
'   DECLARATIONS:   DECLARE SUB AssignKey (keyCode%, assign$)
'
  SUB AssignKey (keyCode%, assign$) STATIC
      IF keyCode% <= 0 THEN
          k$ = "[0;"
      ELSE
          k$ = "["
      END IF
      k$ = k$ + MID$(STR$(keyCode%), 2)
      IF assign$ <> "" THEN
          FOR i% = 1 TO LEN(assign$)
              k$ = k$ + ";" + MID$(STR$(ASC(MID$(assign$, i%))), 2)
          NEXT i%
      END IF
      StdOut CHR$(27) + k$ + "p"
  END SUB
```

Subprogram: Attribute

Sets screen color attributes as defined by the ANSI.SYS driver.

```
' ***************************************************
' **  Name:       Attribute                        **
' **  Type:       Subprogram                       **
' **  Module:     STDOUT.BAS                       **
' **  Language:   Microsoft QuickBASIC 4.00        **
' ***************************************************
'
' Sets the foreground, background, and other color
' attributes.
'
' EXAMPLE OF USE:  Attribute attr%
' PARAMETERS:      attr%     Number for attribute to be set
' VARIABLES:       (none)
' MODULE LEVEL
'   DECLARATIONS:  DECLARE SUB StdOut (a$)
'                  DECLARE SUB Attribute (attr%)

  SUB Attribute (attr%) STATIC
      StdOut CHR$(27) + "[" + MID$(STR$(attr%), 2) + "m"
  END SUB
```

Subprogram: ClearLine

Sends to standard output the ANSI.SYS escape-code sequence that erases the current line from the cursor to the end of the line. The current cursor position is maintained.

```
' ***************************************************
' **   Name:          ClearLine                    **
' **   Type:          Subprogram                   **
' **   Module:        STDOUT.BAS                   **
' **   Language:      Microsoft QuickBASIC 4.00    **
' ***************************************************
'
' Clears the display line from the current cursor
' position to the end of the line.
'
' EXAMPLE OF USE:   ClearLine
' PARAMETERS:       (none)
' VARIABLES:        (none)
' MODULE LEVEL
'   DECLARATIONS:   DECLARE SUB ClearLine ()
'                   DECLARE SUB StdOut (a$)
'
  SUB ClearLine STATIC
      StdOut CHR$(27) + "[K"
  END SUB
```

Subprogram: ClearScreen

Sends to standard output the ANSI.SYS escape-code sequence that clears the screen; positions the cursor at the top left of the screen.

```
' ***************************************************
' **   Name:          ClearScreen                  **
' **   Type:          Subprogram                   **
' **   Module:        STDOUT.BAS                   **
' **   Language:      Microsoft QuickBASIC 4.00    **
' ***************************************************
'
' Clears the screen and moves the cursor to the
' home position.
```

(continued)

continued

```
' EXAMPLE OF USE:   ClearScreen
' PARAMETERS:       (none)
' VARIABLES:        (none)
' MODULE LEVEL
'   DECLARATIONS:   DECLARE SUB ClearScreen ()
'                   DECLARE SUB StdOut (a$)
'
  SUB ClearScreen STATIC
    StdOut CHR$(27) + "[2J"
  END SUB
```

Subprogram: CrLf

Sends carriage return and line feed to a standard output.

```
' ***************************************************
' **   Name:         CrLf                          **
' **   Type:         Subprogram                    **
' **   Module:       STDOUT.BAS                    **
' **   Language:     Microsoft QuickBASIC 4.00     **
' ***************************************************
'
' Sends line feed and carriage return characters
' to standard output.
'
' EXAMPLE OF USE:   CrLf
' PARAMETERS:       (none)
' VARIABLES:        (none)
' MODULE LEVEL
'   DECLARATIONS:   DECLARE SUB StdOut (a$)
'                   DECLARE SUB CrLf ()
'
  SUB CrLf STATIC
    StdOut CHR$(13) + CHR$(10)
  END SUB
```

Subprogram: CursorDown

Sends to standard output the ANSI.SYS escape-code sequence that moves the cursor down the screen n% lines. The cursor stays in the same column and stops at the bottom line of the screen.

```
' ****************************************************
' **   Name:         CursorDown                     **
' **   Type:         Subprogram                     **
' **   Module:       STDOUT.BAS                     **
' **   Language:     Microsoft QuickBASIC 4.00      **
' ****************************************************
'
' Moves the cursor n% lines down the screen.
'
' EXAMPLE OF USE:    CursorDown n%
' PARAMETERS:        n%          Number of lines to move the cursor down
' VARIABLES:         (none)
' MODULE LEVEL
'   DECLARATIONS:    DECLARE SUB StdOut (a$)
'                    DECLARE SUB CursorDown (n%)
'
  SUB CursorDown (n%) STATIC
      StdOut CHR$(27) + "[" + MID$(STR$(n%), 2) + "B"
  END SUB
```

Subprogram: CursorHome

Sends to standard output the ANSI.SYS escape-code sequence that moves the cursor to the home position; does not erase the display.

```
' ****************************************************
' **   Name:         CursorHome                     **
' **   Type:         Subprogram                     **
' **   Module:       STDOUT.BAS                     **
' **   Language:     Microsoft QuickBASIC 4.00      **
' ****************************************************
'
' Moves the cursor to the top left of the
' screen.
'
' EXAMPLE OF USE:    CursorHome
```

(continued)

QUICKBASIC TOOLBOXES AND PROGRAMS

continued

```
' PARAMETERS:      (none)
' VARIABLES:       (none)
' MODULE LEVEL
'   DECLARATIONS:  _DECLARE SUB CursorHome
'
  SUB CursorHome STATIC
      StdOut CHR$(27) + "[H"
  END SUB
```

Subprogram: CursorLeft

Sends to standard output the ANSI.SYS escape-code sequence that moves the cursor to the left n% columns. The cursor stays in the same row and stops at the left column of the screen.

```
' *************************************************
' **  Name:         CursorLeft                   **
' **  Type:         Subprogram                   **
' **  Module:       STDOUT.BAS                   **
' **  Language:     Microsoft QuickBASIC 4.00    **
' *************************************************
'
' Moves the cursor n% columns left on the screen.
'
' EXAMPLE OF USE:  CursorLeft n%
' PARAMETERS:      n%       Number of columns to move the cursor left
' VARIABLES:       (none)
' MODULE LEVEL
'   DECLARATIONS:  DECLARE SUB CursorLeft (n%)
'
  SUB CursorLeft (n%) STATIC
      StdOut CHR$(27) + "[" + MID$(STR$(n%), 2) + "D"
  END SUB
```

Subprogram: CursorPosition

Sends to standard output the ANSI.SYS escape-code sequence that moves the cursor to a given row and column.

```
' *****************************************************
' **   Name:         CursorPosition             **
' **   Type:         Subprogram                 **
' **   Module:       STDOUT.BAS                 **
' **   Language:     Microsoft QuickBASIC 4.00  **
' *****************************************************
'
' Moves the cursor to the indicated row and column.
'
' EXAMPLE OF USE:   CursorPosition row%, col%
' PARAMETERS:       row%       Row to move the cursor to
'                   col%       Column to move the cursor to
' VARIABLES:        row$       String representation of row%
'                   col$       String representation of col%
' MODULE LEVEL
'   DECLARATIONS:   DECLARE SUB CursorPosition (row%, col%)

SUB CursorPosition (row%, col%) STATIC
    row$ = MID$(STR$(row%), 2)
    col$ = MID$(STR$(col%), 2)
    StdOut CHR$(27) + "[" + row$ + ";" + col$ + "H"
END SUB
```

Subprogram: CursorRight

Sends to standard output the ANSI.SYS escape-code sequence that moves the cursor to the right n% columns. The cursor stays in the same row and stops at the right column of the screen.

```
' *****************************************************
' **   Name:         CursorRight                **
' **   Type:         Subprogram                 **
' **   Module:       STDOUT.BAS                 **
' **   Language:     Microsoft QuickBASIC 4.00  **
' *****************************************************
```

(continued)

continued

```
' Moves the cursor n% columns right on the screen.
'
' EXAMPLE OF USE:   CursorRight n%
' PARAMETERS:       n%        Number of columns to move the cursor right
' VARIABLES:        (none)
' MODULE LEVEL
'   DECLARATIONS:   DECLARE SUB CursorRight (n%)
'
  SUB CursorRight (n%) STATIC
      StdOut CHR$(27) + "[" + MID$(STR$(n%), 2) + "C"
  END SUB
```

Subprogram: CursorUp

Sends to standard output the ANSI.SYS escape-code sequence that moves the cursor up the screen n% lines. The cursor stays in the same column and stops at the top line of the screen.

```
' ***************************************************
' **   Name:         CursorUp                      **
' **   Type:         Subprogram                    **
' **   Module:       STDOUT.BAS                    **
' **   Language:     Microsoft QuickBASIC 4.00     **
' ***************************************************
'
' Moves the cursor n% lines up the screen.
'
' EXAMPLE OF USE:   CursorUp n%
' PARAMETERS:       n%        Number of lines to move the cursor up
' VARIABLES:        (none)
' MODULE LEVEL
'   DECLARATIONS:   DECLARE SUB CursorUp (n%)
'
  SUB CursorUp (n%) STATIC
      StdOut CHR$(27) + "[" + MID$(STR$(n%), 2) + "A"
  END SUB
```

Subprogram: StdOut

Sends a string of bytes to the standard output device. The string is output through the MS-DOS function for string output, bypassing the QuickBASIC PRINT statement.

```
' **************************************************
' **   Name:          StdOut                      **
' **   Type:          Subprogram                  **
' **   Module:        STDOUT.BAS                  **
' **   Language:      Microsoft QuickBASIC 4.00   **
' **************************************************
'
' Writes string to the MS-DOS standard output.
'
' EXAMPLE OF USE:   StdOut a$
' PARAMETERS:       a$           String to be output
' VARIABLES:        regX         Structure of type RegTypeX
' MODULE LEVEL
'   DECLARATIONS:   DECLARE SUB InterruptX (intnum%, inreg AS RegTypeX,
'                                           outreg AS RegTypeX)
'                   DECLARE SUB StdOut (a$)
'
  SUB StdOut (a$) STATIC
      DIM regX AS RegTypeX
      regX.ax = &H4000
      regX.cx = LEN(a$)
      regX.bx = 1
      regX.ds = VARSEG(a$)
      regX.dx = SADD(a$)
      InterruptX &H21, regX, regX
      IF regX.flags AND 1 THEN
          PRINT "Error while calling StdOut:"; regX.ax
          SYSTEM
      END IF
  END SUB
```

STRINGS

The STRINGS toolbox provides several common (and not so common) string-manipulation functions and subprograms.

Name	Type	Description
STRINGS.BAS		Demo module
Ascii2Ebcdic$	Func	Converts string from ASCII to EBCDIC
BestMatch$	Func	Returns best match to input string
BuildAEStrings	Sub	Builds ASCII and EBCDIC character translation tables
Center$	Func	Centers string by padding with spaces
Detab$	Func	Replaces tab characters with spaces
Ebcdic2Ascii$	Func	Converts a string from EBCDIC to ASCII
Entab$	Func	Replaces spaces with tab characters
FilterIn$	Func	Retains only specified characters in string
FilterOut$	Func	Deletes specified characters from string
Lpad$	Func	Returns left-justified input string
LtrimSet$	Func	Deletes specified characters from left
Ord%	Func	Returns byte number for ANSI mnemonic
Repeat$	Func	Combines multiple copies into one string
Replace$	Func	Replaces specified characters in string
Reverse$	Func	Reverses order of characters in a string
ReverseCase$	Func	Reverses case for each character in a string
Rpad$	Func	Returns right-justified input string
RtrimSet$	Func	Deletes specified characters from right
Translate$	Func	Exchanges characters in string from table

Demo Module: STRINGS

```
' **************************************************
' **  Name:         STRINGS                       **
' **  Type:         Toolbox                       **
' **  Module:       STRINGS.BAS                   **
' **  Language:     Microsoft QuickBASIC 4.00     **
' **************************************************
' USAGE:          No command line parameters
' .MAK FILE:      (none)
' PARAMETERS:     (none)
' VARIABLES:      a$      Working string for demonstrations
'                 b$      Working string for demonstrations
'                 c$      Working string for demonstrations
'                 x$      Working string for demonstrations
'                 y$      Working string for demonstrations
'                 set$    Set of characters that define word separations

  DECLARE FUNCTION Ascii2Ebcdic$ (a$)
  DECLARE FUNCTION BestMatch$ (a$, x$, y$)
  DECLARE FUNCTION Center$ (a$, n%)
  DECLARE FUNCTION Detab$ (a$, tabs%)
  DECLARE FUNCTION Ebcdic2Ascii$ (e$)
  DECLARE FUNCTION Entab$ (a$, tabs%)
  DECLARE FUNCTION FilterIn$ (a$, set$)
  DECLARE FUNCTION FilterOut$ (a$, set$)
  DECLARE FUNCTION Lpad$ (a$, n%)
  DECLARE FUNCTION LtrimSet$ (a$, set$)
  DECLARE FUNCTION Ord% (a$)
  DECLARE FUNCTION Repeat$ (a$, n%)
  DECLARE FUNCTION Replace$ (a$, find$, substitute$)
  DECLARE FUNCTION Reverse$ (a$)
  DECLARE FUNCTION ReverseCase$ (a$)
  DECLARE FUNCTION Rpad$ (a$, n%)
  DECLARE FUNCTION RtrimSet$ (a$, set$)
  DECLARE FUNCTION Translate$ (a$, f$, t$)

' Subprograms
  DECLARE SUB BuildAEStrings ()

' Quick demonstrations
  CLS
  a$ = "This is a test"
  PRINT "a$", , a$
  PRINT "ReverseCase$(a$)", ReverseCase$(a$)
```

(continued)

continued

```
    PRINT "Reverse$(a$)", , Reverse$(a$)
    PRINT "Repeat$(a$, 3)", Repeat$(a$, 3)
    PRINT

    set$ = "T this"
    PRINT "set$", , set$
    PRINT "LtrimSet$(a$, set$)", LtrimSet$(a$, set$)
    PRINT "RtrimSet$(a$, set$)", RtrimSet$(a$, set$)
    PRINT "FilterOut$(a$, set$)", FilterOut$(a$, set$)
    PRINT "FilterIn$(a$, set$)", FilterIn$(a$, set$)
    PRINT

    a$ = "elephant"
    x$ = "alpha"
    y$ = "omega"
    PRINT "a$", , a$
    PRINT "x$", , x$
    PRINT "y$", , y$
    PRINT "BestMatch$(a$, x$, y$)", BestMatch$(a$, x$, y$)
    PRINT

    PRINT "Press any key to continue"
    DO
    LOOP UNTIL INKEY$ <> ""

    CLS
    a$ = "BEL"
    PRINT "a$", , a$
    PRINT "Ord%(a$)", , Ord%(a$)
    PRINT

    a$ = "This is a test"
    find$ = "s"
    substitute$ = "<s>"
    PRINT "a$", , , a$
    PRINT "find$", , , find$
    PRINT "substitute$", , , substitute$
    PRINT "Replace$(a$, find$, substitute$)", Replace$(a$, find$, substitute$)
    PRINT

    PRINT "a$", , a$
    PRINT "Lpad$(a$, 40)", , ":"; Lpad$(a$, 40); ":"
    PRINT "Rpad$(a$, 40)", , ":"; Rpad$(a$, 40); ":"
    PRINT "Center$(a$, 40)", ":"; Center$(a$, 40); ":"
    PRINT
```

(continued)

continued

```
a$ = "a$ character" + STRING$(2, 9) + "count" + CHR$(9) + "is"
PRINT a$; LEN(a$)
PRINT "a$ = Detab$(a$, 8)"
a$ = Detab$(a$, 8)
PRINT a$; LEN(a$)
PRINT "a$ = Entab$(a$, 8)"
a$ = Entab$(a$, 8)
PRINT a$; LEN(a$)
PRINT

PRINT "Press any key to continue"
DO
LOOP UNTIL INKEY$ <> ""

CLS
a$ = "You know this test string has vowels."
x$ = "aeiou"
y$ = "eioua"
PRINT "a$", , a$
PRINT "x$", , x$
PRINT "y$", , y$
PRINT "Translate$(a$, x$, y$)", Translate$(a$, x$, y$)
PRINT

a$ = "This is a test."
b$ = Ascii2Ebcdic$(a$)
c$ = Ebcdic2Ascii$(b$)
PRINT "a$", , a$
PRINT "b$ = Ascii2Ebcdic$(a$)", b$
PRINT "c$ = Ebcdic2Ascii$(b$)", c$
PRINT

END
```

Function: Ascii2Ebcdic$

Converts a string of ASCII characters to EBCDIC equivalents.

Almost all computers use the ASCII character set to define which byte represents which character. This standard makes it possible for computers, printers, plotters, and other equipment to communicate effectively. However, IBM's larger computers have long used the EBCDIC character set, an alternative way for computers and peripherals to communicate. If files are to be transferred to or from an IBM mainframe, it's necessary to translate character bytes between the two methods. This function, along with its counterpart Ebcdic2Ascii$, translates strings of characters between the ASCII character set and the EBCDIC character set.

These functions and the BuildAEStrings subprogram share a pair of string variables, ascii$ and ebcdic$. The SHARED statement lets these two strings be accessed by each of these three routines while remaining invisible and unalterable to all other parts of a program.

The BuildAEStrings subprogram is called only once, to build both the ascii$ and ebcdic$ translation strings the first time that the Ascii2Ebcdic$ or Ebcdic2Ascii$ function is called. All subsequent calls to these functions use these strings immediately, as the contents of the strings are preserved between calls.

Refer to the BuildAEStrings subprogram for more information about how these two strings are built. Refer to the Translate$ function for more information about the character-by-character translation.

```
' ***************************************************
' **   Name:           Ascii2Ebcdic$               **
' **   Type:           Function                    **
' **   Module:         STRINGS.BAS                 **
' **   Language:       Microsoft QuickBASIC 4.00   **
' ***************************************************
'
' Returns a$ with each character translated from ASCII to EBCDIC.
'
' EXAMPLE OF USE:  e$ = Ascii2Ebcdic$(a$)
' PARAMETERS:      a$         String of ASCII characters to be
'                             converted
' VARIABLES:       ebcdic$    Table of translation characters
'                  ascii$     Table of translation characters
' MODULE LEVEL
'   DECLARATIONS:  DECLARE FUNCTION Ascii2Ebcdic$ (a$)
'
  FUNCTION Ascii2Ebcdic$ (a$) STATIC
      SHARED ebcdic$, ascii$
      IF ebcdic$ = "" THEN
          BuildAEStrings
      END IF
      Ascii2Ebcdic$ = Translate$(a$, ascii$, ebcdic$)
  END FUNCTION
```

Function: BestMatch$

Compares two strings with a third and returns the string that most closely matches the third.

Everybody's talking "artificial intelligence" these days. Programs capable of making decisions based on "fuzzy" facts are already being used for voice analysis, pattern matching, and other similar tasks. This function provides a way to make an educated guess as to the best pattern match when comparing two strings.

The method of comparison used here scans substrings of the target string and checks for occurrences of these substrings in each of the other two strings. A score is kept for the number of substring matches found for each string. The score is weighted heavier for longer substring matches. For example, finding an occurrence of the substring "ABC" is worth 6 points, while finding separate occurrences of "E," "F," and "G" is worth a total of only 3 points.

When all substrings of the target string have been checked, the points are compared for each test string. The highest score wins, and that string is returned as the result.

```
' *************************************************
' **   Name:         BestMatch$                    **
' **   Type:         Function                      **
' **   Module:       STRINGS.BAS                   **
' **   Language:     Microsoft QuickBASIC 4.00     **
' *************************************************
'
' Returns either x$ or y$, whichever is a best match to a$.
'
' EXAMPLE OF USE:    b$ = BestMatch$(a$, x$, y$)
' PARAMETERS:    a$          The string to be matched
'                x$          The first string to compare with a$
'                y$          The second string to compare with a$
' VARIABLES:     ua$         Uppercase working copy of a$
'                ux$         Uppercase working copy of x$
'                uy$         Uppercase working copy of y$
'                lena%       Length of a$
'                i%          Length of substrings of ua$
'                j%          Index into ua$
'                t$          Substrings of ua$
'                xscore%     Accumulated score for substring matches
'                            found in ux$
```

(continued)

continued

```
'                  yscore%     Accumulated score for substring matches
'                              found in uy$
' MODULE LEVEL
'   DECLARATIONS:  DECLARE FUNCTION BestMatch$ (a$, x$, y$)
'
  FUNCTION BestMatch$ (a$, x$, y$) STATIC
      ua$ = UCASE$(a$)
      ux$ = UCASE$(x$)
      uy$ = UCASE$(y$)
      lena% = LEN(ua$)
      FOR i% = 1 TO lena%
          FOR j% = 1 TO lena% - i% + 1
              t$ = MID$(ua$, j%, i%)
              IF INSTR(ux$, t$) THEN
                  xscore% = xscore% + i% + i%
              END IF
              IF INSTR(uy$, t$) THEN
                  yscore% = yscore% + i% + i%
              END IF
          NEXT j%
      NEXT i%
      IF xscore% > yscore% THEN
          BestMatch$ = x$
      ELSE
          BestMatch$ = y$
      END IF
  END FUNCTION
```

Subprogram: BuildAEStrings

Initializes the ASCII-EBCDIC translation table strings. This subprogram is called once per program run, by either the Ascii2Ebcdic$ or Ebcdic2Ascii$ function, when one is called first. Each function checks to see whether the shared strings, ascii$ and ebcdic$, are filled in or whether they are still null (empty) strings. If they are null, this subprogram is called to fill them in before they are used as character translation tables.

The method used to fill in the strings can easily create strings containing any binary bytes. First, ebcdic$ is created as a string of hexadecimal characters, each pair of which represents a single byte. At this point, ebcdic$ is twice the desired length. The processing loop near the end of the function converts each pair of hexadecimal characters to the byte it represents and replaces the hexadecimal characters with these bytes. After all hexadecimal character pairs are converted, the first half of ebcdic$ contains the desired string of bytes. The second half of ebcdic$ is deleted.

The string variable ascii$ is filled in with binary byte values 0 through 127. This string is built to be passed to the Translate$ function, which requires a string table for both lookup as well as replacement.

```
' **************************************************
' **    Name:         BuildAEStrings               **
' **    Type:         Subprogram                   **
' **    Module:       STRINGS.BAS                  **
' **    Language:     Microsoft QuickBASIC 4.00    **
' **************************************************
'
' Called by the Ascii2Ebcdic$ and Ebcdic2Ascii$
' functions to build the translation strings.
' This subprogram is called only once.
'
' EXAMPLE OF USE:   Called automatically by either the Ascii2Ebcdic$ or
'                   Ebcdic2Ascii$ function
' PARAMETERS:       ascii$      Shared by Ascii2Ebcdic$, Ebcdic2Ascii$, and
'                               BuildAEStrings
'                   ebcdic$     Shared by Ascii2Ebcdic$, Ebcdic2Ascii$, and
'                               BuildAEStrings
' VARIABLES:        i%          Index into strings
'                   byte%       Binary value of character byte
' MODULE LEVEL
'   DECLARATIONS:   DECLARE SUB BuildAEStrings ()
'
    SUB BuildAEStrings STATIC
        SHARED ebcdic$, ascii$
        ascii$ = SPACE$(128)
        ebcdic$ = ebcdic$ + "00010203372D2E2F1605250B0C0D0E0F"
        ebcdic$ = ebcdic$ + "101112133C3D322618193F271C1D1E1F"
        ebcdic$ = ebcdic$ + "404F7F7B5B6C507D4D5D5C4E6B604B61"
        ebcdic$ = ebcdic$ + "F0F1F2F3F4F5F6F7F8F97A5E4C7E6E6F"
        ebcdic$ = ebcdic$ + "7CC1C2C3C4C5C6C7C8C9D1D2D3D4D5D6"
        ebcdic$ = ebcdic$ + "D7D8D9E2E3E4E5E6E7E8E94AE05A5F6D"
        ebcdic$ = ebcdic$ + "798182838485868788899192939495 96"
        ebcdic$ = ebcdic$ + "979899A2A3A4A5A6A7A8A9C06AD0A107"
        FOR i% = 0 TO 127
            MID$(ascii$, i% + 1, 1) = CHR$(i%)
            byte% = VAL("&H" + MID$(ebcdic$, i% + i% + 1, 2))
            MID$(ebcdic$, i% + 1, 1) = CHR$(byte%)
        NEXT i%
        ebcdic$ = LEFT$(ebcdic$, 128)
    END SUB
```

Function: Center$

Returns a string of length n% by padding a$ with spaces on both ends.

The original string is centered in the new string. If n% is less than the length of a$ (after any spaces are stripped from the ends), the string is returned with no spaces tacked on and with a length greater than n%.

One obvious use for this function is centering titles and labels on a printed or displayed page.

```
' ****************************************************
' **   Name:           Center$                     **
' **   Type:           Function                    **
' **   Module:         STRINGS.BAS                 **
' **   Language:       Microsoft QuickBASIC 4.00   **
' ****************************************************
'
' Pads a$ with spaces on both ends until text is
' centered and the string length is n%.
'
' EXAMPLE OF USE:    b$ = Center$(a$, n%)
' PARAMETERS:        a$         String of characters to be padded with spaces
'                    n%         Desired length of resulting string
' VARIABLES:         pad%       Number of spaces to pad at ends of string
' MODULE LEVEL
'   DECLARATIONS:    DECLARE FUNCTION Center$ (a$, n%)
'
FUNCTION Center$ (a$, n%) STATIC
    a$ = LTRIM$(RTRIM$(a$))
    pad% = n% - LEN(a$)
    IF pad% > 0 THEN
        Center$ = SPACE$(pad% \ 2) + a$ + SPACE$(pad% - pad% \ 2)
    ELSE
        Center$ = a$
    END IF
END FUNCTION
```

Function: Detab$

Replaces tab characters with the appropriate number of spaces.

Tab characters are useful for forcing text alignment into predictable columns and for conserving space in text files. If you then need to exchange the tab characters for the equivalent number of spaces, this function lets you do so.

Your computer display and (probably) your printer use a tab spacing constant of 8. For this reason, the most common value passed to this function for tabs% is 8. Spaces are inserted in a$ in place of tab characters to align the following characters into columns that are multiples of 8. Displaying or printing the string before and after it's processed by this function should result in exactly the same output.

Also see Entab$, which performs exactly the opposite function.

```
' **************************************************
' **  Name            Detab$                      **
' **  Type:           Function                    **
' **  Module:         STRINGS.BAS                 **
' **  Language:       Microsoft QuickBASIC 4.00   **
' **************************************************
'
' Replaces all tab characters with spaces, using
' tabs% to determine proper alignment.
'
' EXAMPLE OF USE:   b$ = Detab$(a$, tabs%)
' PARAMETERS:       a$          String with possible tab characters
'                   tabs%       Tab spacing
' VARIABLES:        t$          Working copy of a$
'                   tb$         Tab character
'                   tp%         Pointer to position in t$ of a tab character
'                   sp$         Spaces to replace a given tab character
' MODULE LEVEL
'   DECLARATIONS:   DECLARE FUNCTION Detab$ (a$, tabs%)
'
  FUNCTION Detab$ (a$, tabs%) STATIC
      t$ = a$
      tb$ = CHR$(9)
      DO
          tp% = INSTR(t$, tb$)
          IF tp% THEN
              Sp$ = SPACE$(tabs% - ((tp% - 1) MOD tabs%))
              t$ = LEFT$(t$, tp% - 1) + Sp$ + MID$(t$, tp% + 1)
          END IF
      LOOP UNTIL tp% = 0
      Detab$ = t$
      t$ = ""
  END FUNCTION
```

Function: Ebcdic2Ascii$

Converts a string of EBCDIC characters to ASCII equivalents. This function performs the exact opposite of the Ascii2Ebcdic$ function. Refer to the Ascii2Ebcdic$ function for more information.

```
' ****************************************************
' ** Name:          Ebcdic2Ascii$                   **
' ** Type:          Function                        **
' ** Module:        STRINGS.BAS                     **
' ** Language:      Microsoft QuickBASIC 4.00       **
' ****************************************************
'
' Returns a$ with each character translated from
' EBCDIC to ASCII.
'
' EXAMPLE OF USE:    b$ = Ebcdic2Ascii$(a$)
' PARAMETERS:        a$           String of EBCDIC characters to be converted
' VARIABLES:         ebcdic$      Table of translation characters
'                    ascii$       Table of translation characters
' MODULE LEVEL
'   DECLARATIONS:    DECLARE FUNCTION Ebcdic2Ascii$ (e$)
'
FUNCTION Ebcdic2Ascii$ (e$) STATIC
    SHARED ebcdic$, ascii$
    IF ebcdic$ = "" THEN
        BuildAEStrings
    END IF
    Ebcdic2Ascii$ = Translate$(e$, ebcdic$, ascii$)
END FUNCTION
```

Function: Entab$

Replaces spaces with tab characters wherever possible, providing a way to compress the size of a text file.

For the opposite function, replacing tabs with appropriate numbers of spaces, see Detab$.

```
' ****************************************************
' ** Name:          Entab$                          **
' ** Type:          Function                        **
' ** Module:        STRINGS.BAS                     **
' ** Language:      Microsoft QuickBASIC 4.00       **
' ****************************************************
```

(continued)

continued

```
' Replaces groups of spaces, where possible, with
' tab characters, keeping the alignment indicated
' by the value of tabs%.
'
' EXAMPLE OF USE:   b$ = Entab$(a$, tabs%)
' PARAMETERS:       a$              String with possible tab characters
'                   tabs%           Tab spacing
' VARIABLES:        t$              Working copy of a$
'                   tb$             Tab character
'                   i%              Index into t$
'                   k%              Count of spaces being replaced
'                   j%              Index into t$
' MODULE LEVEL
'   DECLARATIONS:   DECLARE FUNCTION Entab$ (a$, tabs%)
'
    FUNCTION Entab$ (a$, tabs%) STATIC
        t$ = a$
        tb$ = CHR$(9)
        FOR i% = (LEN(t$) \ tabs%) * tabs% + 1 TO tabs% STEP -tabs%
            IF MID$(t$, i% - 1, 1) = " " THEN
                k% = 0
                FOR j% = 1 TO tabs%
                    IF MID$(t$, i% - j%, 1) <> " " THEN
                        k% = i% - j%
                        EXIT FOR
                    END IF
                NEXT j%
                IF k% = 0 THEN
                    k% = i% - tabs% - 1
                END IF
                t$ = LEFT$(t$, k%) + tb$ + MID$(t$, i%)
            END IF
        NEXT i%
        Entab$ = t$
        t$ = ""
    END FUNCTION
```

Function: FilterIn$

Filters a string, character by character, and removes any characters that are not in the designated set. FilterIn$("EXAMPLE", "AEIOU"), for example, returns the string *EAE*, because all characters, except uppercase vowels, are removed from EXAMPLE.

To filter a string by removing characters listed in set$ (as opposed to removing all characters not in set$), see the FilterOut$ function.

```
' ****************************************************
' ** Name:           FilterIn$                       **
' ** Type:           Function                        **
' ** Module:         STRINGS.BAS                     **
' ** Language:       Microsoft QuickBASIC 4.00       **
' ****************************************************
'
' Returns a$ with all occurrences of any characters
' that are not in set$ deleted.
'
' EXAMPLE OF USE:    b$ = FilterIn$(a$, set$)
' PARAMETERS:        a$          String to be processed
'                    set$        Set of characters to be retained
' VARIABLES:         i%          Index into a$
'                    j%          Count of characters retained
'                    lena%       Length of a$
'                    t$          Working string space
'                    c$          Each character of a$
' MODULE LEVEL
'   DECLARATIONS:  DECLARE FUNCTION FilterIn$ (a$, set$)
'
    FUNCTION FilterIn$ (a$, set$) STATIC
        i% = 1
        j% = 0
        lena% = LEN(a$)
        t$ = a$
        DO UNTIL i% > lena%
            c$ = MID$(a$, i%, 1)
            IF INSTR(set$, c$) THEN
                j% = j% + 1
                MID$(t$, j%, 1) = c$
            END IF
            i% = i% + 1
        LOOP
        FilterIn$ = LEFT$(t$, j%)
        t$ = ""
    END FUNCTION
```

Function: FilterOut$

Filters a string, character by character, and removes any characters that are listed in the designated set. FilterOut$("EXAMPLE", "AEIOU"), for example, returns the string *XMPL*, because all uppercase vowels are removed from EXAMPLE.

To filter a string by removing characters not listed in set$ (as opposed to removing all characters found in set$), see the FilterIn$ function.

```
' ****************************************************
' **   Name:           FilterOut$                    **
' **   Type:           Function                      **
' **   Module:         STRINGS.BAS                   **
' **   Language:       Microsoft QuickBASIC 4.00     **
' ****************************************************
'
' Returns a$ with all occurrences of any characters
' from set$ deleted.
'
' EXAMPLE OF USE:   b$ = FilterOut$(a$, set$)
' PARAMETERS:       a$          String to be processed
'                   set$        Set of characters to be retained
' VARIABLES:        i%          Index into a$
'                   j%          Count of characters retained
'                   lena%       Length of a$
'                   t$          Working string space
'                   c$          Each character of a$
' MODULE LEVEL
'   DECLARATIONS:   DECLARE FUNCTION FilterOut$ (a$, set$)
'
    FUNCTION FilterOut$ (a$, set$) STATIC
        i% = 1
        j% = 0
        lena% = LEN(a$)
        t$ = a$
        DO UNTIL i% > lena%
            c$ = MID$(a$, i%, 1)
            IF INSTR(set$, c$) = 0 THEN
                j% = j% + 1
                MID$(t$, j%, 1) = c$
            END IF
            i% = i% + 1
        LOOP
        FilterOut$ = LEFT$(t$, j%)
        t$ = ""
    END FUNCTION
```

Function: Lpad$

Returns a left-justified string of n% characters by shifting a$ to the left and adding space characters on the right.

This function actually does an amazing amount of work for only one program line. First, the string passed as parameter a$ has all spaces removed from its left, the final goal being to left justify the string.

The desired string length is n%. To guarantee that you have at least n% characters to work with, n% space characters are added to the right of the string. Most likely, the string is now longer than desired. So, the LEFT$ function returns the first n% characters from the string, finishing the desired processing of a$ and assigning the result to Lpad$, the name of the function.

See Rpad$ for a similar function.

```
' *************************************************
' **   Name:         Lpad$                       **
' **   Type:         Function                    **
' **   Module:       STRINGS.BAS                 **
' **   Language:     Microsoft QuickBASIC 4.00   **
' *************************************************
'
' Returns a string of length n%, with a$ left justified
' and padded on the right with spaces.
'
' EXAMPLE OF USE:   b$ = Lpad$(a$, n%)
' PARAMETERS:       a$          String to be left justified and padded
'                   n%          Length of string result
' VARIABLES:        (none)
' MODULE LEVEL
'   DECLARATIONS:   DECLARE FUNCTION Lpad$ (a$, n%)
'
FUNCTION Lpad$ (a$, n%) STATIC
    Lpad$ = LEFT$(LTRIM$(a$) + SPACE$(n%), n%)
END FUNCTION
```

Function: LtrimSet$

Trims characters in set$ from the left of a$ until a character is found that is not in set$.

The QuickBASIC LTRIM$() function removes space characters from the end of a string. This function goes a step further and lets you remove any of several characters from the left of a string. For example, LtrimSet$("EXAMPLE", "AXE") returns *MPLE*.

One use for this function is to remove tabs and spaces from the left of a string.

See RtrimSet$ for a similar function.

```
' *****************************************************
' ** Name:          LtrimSet$                        **
' ** Type:          Function                         **
' ** Module:        STRINGS.BAS                      **
' ** Language:      Microsoft QuickBASIC 4.00        **
' *****************************************************
'
' Trims occurrences of any characters in set$
' from the left of a$.
'
' EXAMPLE OF USE:   b$ = LtrimSet$(a$, set$)
' PARAMETERS:       a$              String to be trimmed
'                   set$            Set of characters to be trimmed
' VARIABLES:        i%              Index into a$
' MODULE LEVEL
'   DECLARATIONS:   DECLARE FUNCTION LtrimSet$ (a$, set$)
'
  FUNCTION LtrimSet$ (a$, set$) STATIC
     IF a$ <> "" THEN
        FOR i% = 1 TO LEN(a$)
           IF INSTR(set$, MID$(a$, i%, 1)) = 0 THEN
              LtrimSet$ = MID$(a$, i%)
              EXIT FUNCTION
           END IF
        NEXT i%
     END IF
     LtrimSet$ = ""
  END FUNCTION
```

Function: Ord%

Returns the byte number defined by ANSI standard mnemonics.

This function interprets ANSI standard mnemonics for control characters and returns the numeric value of the byte the mnemonics represent (the ordinal of the mnemonic). Ord%("BEL"), for example, returns 7, the byte number for the bell character. (Recall that PRINT CHR$(7) causes your computer to beep.)

Other common control-character mnemonics include CR (carriage return), LF (line feed), FF (form feed), and NUL (the zero byte value). Many others are available, however, including mnemonics for the lowercase alphabetic characters.

```
' *************************************************
' **   Name:          Ord%                       **
' **   Type:          Function                   **
' **   Module:        STRINGS.BAS                **
' **   Language:      Microsoft QuickBASIC 4.00  **
' *************************************************
'
' Similar to ASC() function; returns
' numeric byte values for the ANSI standard
' mnemonics for control characters.
'
' EXAMPLE OF USE:  byte% = Ord%(a$)
' PARAMETERS:      a$           ANSI standard character mnemonic string
' VARIABLES:       (none)
' MODULE LEVEL
'   DECLARATIONS:  DECLARE FUNCTION Ord% (a$)
'
FUNCTION Ord% (a$) STATIC
    SELECT CASE UCASE$(a$)
    CASE "NUL"              'Null
        Ord% = 0
    CASE "SOH"              'Start of heading
        Ord% = 1
    CASE "STX"              'Start of text
        Ord% = 2
    CASE "ETX"              'End of text
        Ord% = 3
    CASE "EOT"              'End of transmission
        Ord% = 4
    CASE "ENQ"              'Enquiry
        Ord% = 5
    CASE "ACK"              'Acknowledge
        Ord% = 6
    CASE "BEL"              'Bell
        Ord% = 7
    CASE "BS"               'Backspace
        Ord% = 8
    CASE "HT"               'Horizontal tab
        Ord% = 9
```

(continued)

continued

```
        CASE "LF"                 'Line feed
            Ord% = 10
        CASE "VT"                 'Vertical tab
            Ord% = 11
        CASE "FF"                 'Form feed
            Ord% = 12
        CASE "CR"                 'Carriage return
            Ord% = 13
        CASE "SO"                 'Shift out
            Ord% = 14
        CASE "SI"                 'Shift in
            Ord% = 15
        CASE "DLE"                'Data link escape
            Ord% = 16
        CASE "DC1"                'Device control 1
            Ord% = 17
        CASE "DC2"                'Device control 2
            Ord% = 18
        CASE "DC3"                'Device control 3
            Ord% = 19
        CASE "DC4"                'Device control 4
            Ord% = 20
        CASE "NAK"                'Negative acknowledge
            Ord% = 21
        CASE "SYN"                'Synchronous idle
            Ord% = 22
        CASE "ETB"                'End of transmission block
            Ord% = 23
        CASE "CAN"                'Cancel
            Ord% = 24
        CASE "EM"                 'End of medium
            Ord% = 25
        CASE "SUB"                'Substitute
            Ord% = 26
        CASE "ESC"                'Escape
            Ord% = 27
        CASE "FS"                 'File separator
            Ord% = 28
        CASE "GS"                 'Group separator
            Ord% = 29
        CASE "RS"                 'Record separator
            Ord% = 30
        CASE "US"                 'Unit separator
            Ord% = 31
        CASE "SP"                 'Space
            Ord% = 32
```

(continued)

continued

```
        CASE "UND"              'Underline
            Ord% = 95
        CASE "GRA"              'Grave accent
            Ord% = 96
        CASE "LCA"              'Lowercase a
            Ord% = 97
        CASE "LCB"              'Lowercase b
            Ord% = 98
        CASE "LCC"              'Lowercase c
            Ord% = 99
        CASE "LCD"              'Lowercase d
            Ord% = 100
        CASE "LCE"              'Lowercase e
            Ord% = 101
        CASE "LCF"              'Lowercase f
            Ord% = 102
        CASE "LCG"              'Lowercase g
            Ord% = 103
        CASE "LCH"              'Lowercase h
            Ord% = 104
        CASE "LCI"              'Lowercase i
            Ord% = 105
        CASE "LCJ"              'Lowercase j
            Ord% = 106
        CASE "LCK"              'Lowercase k
            Ord% = 107
        CASE "LCL"              'Lowercase l
            Ord% = 108
        CASE "LCM"              'Lowercase m
            Ord% = 109
        CASE "LCN"              'Lowercase n
            Ord% = 110
        CASE "LCO"              'Lowercase o
            Ord% = 111
        CASE "LCP"              'Lowercase p
            Ord% = 112
        CASE "LCQ"              'Lowercase q
            Ord% = 113
        CASE "LCR"              'Lowercase r
            Ord% = 114
        CASE "LCS"              'Lowercase s
            Ord% = 115
        CASE "LCT"              'Lowercase t
            Ord% = 116
```

(continued)

continued

```
        CASE "LCU"              'Lowercase u
            Ord% = 117
        CASE "LCV"              'Lowercase v
            Ord% = 118
        CASE "LCW"              'Lowercase w
            Ord% = 119
        CASE "LCX"              'Lowercase x
            Ord% = 120
        CASE "LCY"              'Lowercase y
            Ord% = 121
        CASE "LCZ"              'Lowercase z
            Ord% = 122
        CASE "LBR"              'Left brace
            Ord% = 123
        CASE "VLN"              'Vertical line
            Ord% = 124
        CASE "RBR"              'Right brace
            Ord% = 125
        CASE "TIL"              'Tilde
            Ord% = 126
        CASE "DEL"              'Delete
            Ord% = 127
        CASE ELSE               'Not ANSI Standard ORD mnemonic
            Ord% = -1
    END SELECT
END FUNCTION
```

Function: Repeat$

Returns the string result of concatenating n% copies of a$. If the length of the result is less than 0 or greater than 32767, an error message is displayed, and the program terminates.

To create a string of 80 spaces, you can use the QuickBASIC function SPACE$(80). To create a string of 80 equal signs, you can use STRING$(80, "="). But how can you create an 80-character string made up of 40 repetitions of "+-"? The Repeat$ function lets you do so. Repeat$("+-", 40) would do the trick.

At first glance, this function looks like more code than is needed. Consider the short function on the following page that returns the same result.

```
FUNCTION SlowRepeat$ (a$, n%) STATIC
    x$ = ""
    FOR i% = 1 to n%
        x$ = x$ + a$
    NEXT i%
    SlowRepeat$ = x$
END FUNCTION
```

In tests of operating speed, this shorter function often ran about 10 times slower than did the Repeat$ function! The difference is in how the string space is handled.

SlowRepeat$ performs much string-manipulation overhead for each n% repetition of a$. In particular, the statement $x\$ = x\$ + a\$$ creates working copies of x$ and a$ in the string workspace for each iteration. As x$ becomes larger, this shuffling of strings begins to bog down the function, even though QuickBASIC performs these functions efficiently.

The Repeat$ function avoids much of this string-manipulation overhead by assigning string results to the MID$ of a large string (t$) that was created only once. First, t$ is created as a string of spaces long enough to hold all n% copies of a$. Each copy of a$ is then assigned to the appropriate substring location in t$ by use of the MID$ statement.

This technique can often be used to speed up other string manipulations. The difference in speed is often insignificant, except in cases where a large number of string operations are performed.

```
' ****************************************************
' **   Name:         Repeat$                        **
' **   Type:         Function                       **
' **   Module:       STRINGS.BAS                    **
' **   Language:     Microsoft QuickBASIC 4.00      **
' ****************************************************
'
' Returns a string formed by concatenating n%
' copies of a$ together.
'
' EXAMPLE OF USE:    b$ = Repeat$(a$, n%)
' PARAMETERS:        a$           String to be repeated
'                    n%           Number of copies of a$ to concatenate
' VARIABLES:         lena%        Length of a$
'                    lent&        Length of result
'                    t$           Work space for building result
'                    ndx%         Index into t$
```

(continued)

continued

```
' MODULE LEVEL
'   DECLARATIONS:  DECLARE FUNCTION Repeat$ (a$, n%)
'
  FUNCTION Repeat$ (a$, n%) STATIC
      lena% = LEN(a$)
      lent& = n% * lena%
      IF lent& < 0 OR lent& > 32767 THEN
          PRINT "ERROR: Repeat$ - Negative repetition, or result too long"
          SYSTEM
      ELSEIF lent& = 0 THEN
          Repeat$ = ""
      ELSE
          t$ = SPACE$(lent&)
          ndx% = 1
          DO
              MID$(t$, ndx%, lena%) = a$
              ndx% = ndx% + lena%
          LOOP UNTIL ndx% > lent&
          Repeat$ = t$
          t$ = ""
      END IF
  END FUNCTION
```

Function: Replace$

Replaces all occurrences of find$ in a$ with substitute$.

One common function provided by text editors and word processors is the ability to globally replace occurrences of character strings with other character strings. This function performs such a global replacement in a single string. By using this function repeatedly, you can globally edit entire files of strings.

For example, Replace$ ("This is a test", "i", "ii") returns the string *Thiis iis a test*.

```
' *************************************************
' **   Name:        Replace$                     **
' **   Type:        Function                     **
' **   Module:      STRINGS.BAS                  **
' **   Language:    Microsoft QuickBASIC 4.00    **
' *************************************************
```

(continued)

continued

```
' Replaces all occurrences of find$ in a$ with substitute$.
'
' EXAMPLE OF USE:    b$ = Replace$(a$, find$, substitute$)
' PARAMETERS:        _a$             String to make substring replacements in
'                    find$           Substring to be searched for
'                    substitutes$    String for replacing the found
'                                    substrings
' VARIABLES:         t$              Working copy of a$
'                    lenf%           Length of find$
'                    lens%           Length of substitute$
'                    i%              Index into a$, pointing at substrings
' MODULE LEVEL
'   DECLARATIONS:  DECLARE FUNCTION Replace$ (a$, find$, substitute$)
'
FUNCTION Replace$ (a$, find$, substitute$) STATIC
    t$ = a$
    lenf% = LEN(find$)
    lens% = LEN(substitute$)
    i% = 1
    DO
        i% = INSTR(i%, t$, find$)
        IF i% = 0 THEN
            EXIT DO
        END IF
        t$ = LEFT$(t$, i% - 1) + substitute$ + MID$(t$, i% + lenf%)
        i% = i% + lens%
    LOOP
    Replace$ = t$
    t$ = ""
END FUNCTION
```

Function: Reverse$

Quickly reverses the order of all characters in a string. For example, Reverse$("QuickBASIC") returns *CISABkciuQ*.

```
' *********************************************
' **  Name:        Reverse$                  **
' **  Type:        Function                  **
' **  Module:      STRINGS.BAS               **
' **  Language:    Microsoft QuickBASIC 4.00 **
' *********************************************
```

(continued)

continued

```
' Reverses the order of all characters in a$.
'
' EXAMPLE OF USE:   b$ = Reverse$(a$)
' PARAMETERS:       a$          String to be processed
' VARIABLES:        n%          Length of the string
'                   r$          Working string space
'                   i%          Index into the string
' MODULE LEVEL
'   DECLARATIONS:   DECLARE FUNCTION Reverse$ (a$)
'
    FUNCTION Reverse$ (a$) STATIC
        n% = LEN(a$)
        r$ = a$
        FOR i% = 1 TO n%
            MID$(r$, i%, 1) = MID$(a$, n% - i% + 1, 1)
        NEXT i%
        Reverse$ = r$
        r$ = ""
    END FUNCTION
```

Function: ReverseCase$

Changes the case of all alphabetical characters in a passed string. Nonalphabetic characters are left undisturbed.

Some text editors can change the case of characters from the current cursor location to the end of the line. This function was designed with that concept in mind. ReverseCase$("Testing 1,2,3"), for example, returns *tESTING 1,2,3*.

```
' ****************************************************
' **   Name:          ReverseCase$                  **
' **   Type:          Function                      **
' **   Module:        STRINGS.BAS                   **
' **   Language:      Microsoft QuickBASIC 4.00     **
' ****************************************************
'
' Changes all lowercase characters to uppercase
' and all uppercase characters to lowercase.
'
' EXAMPLE OF USE:   b$ = ReverseCase$(a$)
' PARAMETERS:       a$          String to be processed
```

(continued)

continued

```
' VARIABLES:       r$          Working copy of a$
'                  i%          Index into r$
'                  t$          Character from middle of a$
' MODULE LEVEL
'   DECLARATIONS:  DECLARE FUNCTION ReverseCase$ (a$)
'
  FUNCTION ReverseCase$ (a$) STATIC
      r$ = a$
      FOR i% = 1 TO LEN(a$)
          t$ = MID$(a$, i%, 1)
          IF LCASE$(t$) <> t$ THEN
              MID$(r$, i%, 1) = LCASE$(t$)
          ELSE
              MID$(r$, i%, 1) = UCASE$(t$)
          END IF
      NEXT i%
      ReverseCase$ = r$
      r$ = ""
  END FUNCTION
```

Function: Rpad$

Returns a right-justified string of n% characters by shifting a$ to the right as far as possible and adding space characters on the left.

See Lpad$ for a similar function.

```
' **************************************************
' **   Name:        Rpad$                         **
' **   Type:        Function                      **
' **   Module:      STRINGS.BAS                   **
' **   Language:    Microsoft QuickBASIC 4.00     **
' **************************************************
'
' Returns string of length n%, with a$ right justified
' and padded on the left with spaces.
'
' EXAMPLE OF USE:   b$ = Rpad$(a$, n%)
' PARAMETERS:       a$          String to be right justified and padded
'                   n%          Length of string result
' VARIABLES:        (none)
' MODULE LEVEL
'   DECLARATIONS:   DECLARE FUNCTION Rpad$ (a$, n%)
'
  FUNCTION Rpad$ (a$, n%) STATIC
      Rpad$ = RIGHT$(SPACE$(n%) + RTRIM$(a$), n%)
  END FUNCTION
```

Function: RtrimSet$

Trims characters in set$ from the right of a$ until a character is found that is not in set$.

The QuickBASIC RTRIM$() function removes space characters from the right of a string. This function goes a step further and lets you remove any of several characters from the right of a string. For example, RtrimSet$("EXAMPLE", "LEAVE") returns *EXAMP*.

One use for this function is to remove tabs and spaces from the right of a string.

See LtrimSet$ for a similar function.

```
' ***********************************************
' **    Name:          RtrimSet$                **
' **    Type:          Function                 **
' **    Module:        STRINGS.BAS              **
' **    Language:      Microsoft QuickBASIC 4.00 **
' ***********************************************
'
' Trims occurrences of any characters in set$
' from the right of a$.
'
' EXAMPLE OF USE:   b$ = RtrimSet$(a$, set$)
' PARAMETERS:       a$          String to be trimmed
'                   set$        Set of characters to be trimmed
' VARIABLES:        i%          Index into a$
' MODULE LEVEL
'   DECLARATIONS:   DECLARE FUNCTION RtrimSet$ (a$, set$)
'
FUNCTION RtrimSet$ (a$, set$) STATIC
    IF a$ <> "" THEN
        FOR i% = LEN(a$) TO 1 STEP -1
            IF INSTR(set$, MID$(a$, i%, 1)) = 0 THEN
                RtrimSet$ = LEFT$(a$, i%)
                EXIT FUNCTION
            END IF
        NEXT i%
    END IF
    RtrimSet$ = ""
END FUNCTION
```

Function: Translate$

Performs a table-lookup translation of the characters in a$. Each character in a$ is searched for in f$. If found, the character is replaced by the character located in the same position in t$. Take a look at a simple example to help clarify the explanation.

Translate$("EXAMPLE", "ABCDE", "vwxyz") returns *zXvMPLz*. The first character of "EXAMPLE" is found in the fifth character position of "ABCDE," so it is replaced with the fifth character of "vwxyz." (The "E" is replaced with a "z.") Then each remaining character in "EXAMPLE" is searched for and replaced in the same way.

The Ascii2Ebcdic$ and Ebcdic2Ascii$ functions call this function to translate characters from one standard set to the other.

```
' *************************************************
' **   Name:         Translate$                  **
' **   Type:         Function                    **
' **   Module:       STRINGS.BAS                 **
' **   Language:     Microsoft QuickBASIC 4.00   **
' *************************************************
'
' Returns a$ with each character translated from
' f$ to t$.  If a character from a$ is found in f$,
' it is replaced with the character located
' in the same position in t$.
'
' EXAMPLE OF USE:    b$ = Translate$ (a$, f$, t$)
' PARAMETERS:        a$         String to be translated
'                    f$         Table of lookup characters
'                    t$         Table of replacement characters
' VARIABLES:         ta$        Working copy of a$
'                    lena%      Length of a$
'                    lenf%      Length of f$
'                    lent%      Length of t$
'                    i%         Index into ta$
'                    ptr%       Pointer into f$
' MODULE LEVEL
'   DECLARATIONS:    DECLARE FUNCTION Translate$ (a$, f$, t$)
```

(continued)

continued

```
FUNCTION Translate$ (a$, f$, t$) STATIC
    ta$ = a$
    lena% = LEN(ta$)
    lenf% = LEN(f$)
    lent% = LEN(t$)
    IF lena% > 0 AND lenf% > 0 AND lent% > 0 THEN
        FOR i% = 1 TO lena%
            ptr% = INSTR(f$, MID$(ta$, i%, 1))
            IF ptr% THEN
                MID$(ta$, i%, 1) = MID$(t$, ptr%, 1)
            END IF
        NEXT i%
    END IF
    Translate$ = ta$
    ta$ = ""
END FUNCTION
```

TRIANGLE

The TRIANGLE toolbox is a collection of analytical geometry functions and subprograms for calculating parts of triangles.

The demonstration module-level code of this toolbox provides a useful triangle calculator utility.

Run the program, and enter the known sides and/or angles of a triangle when prompted. If it's possible to calculate the remaining sides and angles, the program does so and then displays the results.

Name	Type	Description
TRIANGLE.BAS		Demo module
Deg2Rad#	Func	Converts degree angular units to radians
Rad2Deg#	Func	Converts radian angular units to degrees
Triangle	Sub	Calculates sides and angles of triangle
TriangleArea#	Func	Calculates area of triangle from 3 sides

Demo Module: TRIANGLE

```
' *********************************************
' **   Name:       TRIANGLE                  **
' **   Type:       Toolbox                   **
' **   Module:     TRIANGLE.BAS              **
' **   Language:   Microsoft QuickBASIC 4.00 **
' *********************************************
'
' USAGE:         No command line parameters
' REQUIREMENTS:  CGA
' .MAK FILE:     TRIANGLE.BAS
'                QCALMATH.BAS
' PARAMETERS:    (none)
' VARIABLES:     sA$         User input of side a
'                sB$         User input of side b
'                sC$         User input of side c
'                aA$         User input of angle A
'                aB$         User input of angle B
'                aC$         User input of angle C
```

(continued)

continued

```
'                       sA#         Side A
'                       sB#         Side B
'                       sC#         Side C
'                       aA#         Angle A
'                       aB#         Angle B
'                       aC#         Angle C

' Functions
  DECLARE FUNCTION Deg2Rad# (deg#)
  DECLARE FUNCTION Rad2Deg# (rad#)
  DECLARE FUNCTION ArcCosine# (x#)
  DECLARE FUNCTION ArcSine# (x#)
  DECLARE FUNCTION TriangleArea# (sA#, sB#, sC#)

' Subprograms
  DECLARE SUB Triangle (sA#, sB#, sC#, aA#, aB#, aC#)

' Initialization
  SCREEN 2
  CLS
  PRINT "TRIANGLE"

' Draw a representative triangle
  WINDOW (0, 0)-(1, 1)
  LINE (.3,/.7)-(.8, .7)
  LINE -(.4, 1)
  LINE -(.3, .7)

' Label the triangle sides
  LOCATE 4, 26
  PRINT "a"
  LOCATE 3, 48
  PRINT "b"
  LOCATE 9, 42
  PRINT "c"

' Label the triangle angles
  LOCATE 7, 55
  PRINT "A"
  LOCATE 7, 28
  PRINT "B"
  LOCATE 2, 33
  PRINT "C"
```

(continued)

continued

```
' Ask user for the known data
  LOCATE 12, 1
  PRINT "Enter known sides and angles (deg),"
  PRINT "and press Enter for unknowns..."
  LOCATE 16, 1
  LINE INPUT "Side  a   "; sA$
  LINE INPUT "Side  b   "; sB$
  LINE INPUT "Side  c   "; sC$
  PRINT
  LINE INPUT "Angle A   "; aA$
  LINE INPUT "Angle B   "; aB$
  LINE INPUT "Angle C   "; aC$
  PRINT

' Convert to numeric values
  sA# = VAL(sA$)
  sB# = VAL(sB$)
  sC# = VAL(sC$)
  aA# = Deg2Rad#(VAL(aA$))
  aB# = Deg2Rad#(VAL(aB$))
  aC# = Deg2Rad#(VAL(aC$))

' Solve for the unknowns
  Triangle sA#, sB#, sC#, aA#, aB#, aC#

' Output the results
  LOCATE 16, 1
  PRINT "Side  a   "; sA#
  PRINT "Side  b   "; sB#
  PRINT "Side  c   "; sC#
  PRINT
  PRINT "Angle A   "; Rad2Deg#(aA#); "Deg"
  PRINT "Angle B   "; Rad2Deg#(aB#); "Deg"
  PRINT "Angle C   "; Rad2Deg#(aC#); "Deg"
  LOCATE 20, 40
  PRINT "Area = "; TriangleArea#(sA#, sB#, sC#)

' All done
  LOCATE 24, 1
  PRINT "Press any key to continue";
  DO
  LOOP WHILE INKEY = ""
  SCREEN 0
  END
```

Function: Deg2Rad#

Converts degrees to radians.

```
' **************************************************
' **   Name:          Deg2Rad#                    **
' **   Type:          Function                    **
' **   Module:        TRIANGLE.BAS                **
' **   Language:      Microsoft QuickBASIC 4.00   **
' **************************************************
'
' Converts degree angular units to radians.
'
' EXAMPLE OF USE:   r# = Deg2Rad#(deg#)
' PARAMETERS:       deg#        Degrees
' VARIABLES:        (none)
' MODULE LEVEL
'   DECLARATIONS:   DECLARE FUNCTION Deg2Rad# (deg#)
'
  FUNCTION Deg2Rad# (deg#) STATIC
      Deg2Rad# = deg# / 57.29577951308232#
  END FUNCTION
```

Function: Rad2Deg#

Converts radians to degrees.

```
' **************************************************
' **   Name:          Rad2Deg#                    **
' **   Type:          Function                    **
' **   Module:        TRIANGLE.BAS                **
' **   Language:      Microsoft QuickBASIC 4.00   **
' **************************************************
'
' Converts radian angular units to degrees.
'
' EXAMPLE OF USE:   d# = Rad2Deg#(rad#)
' PARAMETERS:       rad#        Radians
' VARIABLES:        (none)
' MODULE LEVEL
'   DECLARATIONS:   DECLARE FUNCTION Rad2Deg# (rad#)
'
  FUNCTION Rad2Deg# (rad#) STATIC
      Rad2Deg# = rad# * 57.29577951308232#
  END FUNCTION
```

Subprogram: Triangle

Calculates sides and angles of a triangle if enough sides and/or angles are given to be able to deduce the rest. Any combination of sides and angles can be given, although illegal combinations will produce unpredictable results.

Double-precision numbers are used throughout this subprogram to maintain high accuracy. Change all the pound signs to exclamation points if you prefer to work with single-precision numbers.

```
' *********************************************
' **  Name:         Triangle                 **
' **  Type:         Subprogram               **
' **  Module:       TRIANGLE.BAS             **
' **  Language:     Microsoft QuickBASIC 4.00 **
' *********************************************
'
' Calculates all sides and angles of a triangle,
' assuming enough sides and angles are given.
'
' EXAMPLE OF USE:  Triangle sA#, sB#, sC#, aA#, aB#, aC#
' PARAMETERS:      sA#        Side A
'                  sB#        Side B
'                  sC#        Side C
'                  aA#        Angle A
'                  aB#        Angle B
'                  aC#        Angle C
' VARIABLES:       i%         Looping index
' MODULE LEVEL
'   DECLARATIONS:  DECLARE SUB Triangle (sA#, sB#, sC#, aA#, aB#, aC#)
'
  SUB Triangle (sA#, sB#, sC#, aA#, aB#, aC#) STATIC

    FOR i% = 1 TO 18

      IF aA# = 0# THEN
        IF sA# <> 0# AND sB# <> 0# AND sC# <> 0# THEN
          t# = sB# * sB# + sC# * sC# - sA# * sA#
          aA# = ArcCosine#(t# / 2# / sB# / sC#)
        END IF
      END IF
```

(continued)

continued

```
        IF aB# = 0# THEN
            IF sA# <> 0# AND sB# <> 0# AND aA# <> 0# THEN
                aB# = ArcSine#(sB# * SIN(aA#) / sA#)
            END IF
        END IF

        IF aC# = 0# THEN
            IF aA# <> 0# AND aB# <> 0# THEN
                aC# = 3.141592653589793# - aA# - aB#
            END IF
        END IF

        IF sB# = 0# THEN
            IF sA# <> 0# AND aB# <> 0# AND aA# <> 0# THEN
                sB# = sA# * SIN(aB#) / SIN(aA#)
            END IF
        END IF

        IF sC# = 0# THEN
            IF sA# <> 0# AND sB# <> 0# AND aC# <> 0# THEN
                t# = sA# * sA# + sB# * sB#
                sC# = SQR(t# - 2# * sA# * sB# * COS(aC#))
            END IF
        END IF

        IF i% MOD 2 THEN
            SWAP sB#, sC#
            SWAP aB#, aC#
        ELSE
            SWAP sA#, sB#
            SWAP aA#, aB#
        END IF

    NEXT i%

END SUB
```

QUICKBASIC TOOLBOXES AND PROGRAMS

Function: TriangleArea#

Calculates the area of a triangle given the three sides of the triangle.

```
' *****************************************************
' **   Name:           TriangleArea#                **
' **   Type:           Function                     **
' **   Module:         TRIANGLE.BAS                 **
' **   Language:       Microsoft QuickBASIC 4.00    **
' *****************************************************
'
' Returns the area of a triangle given the three sides.
'
' EXAMPLE OF USE:  TriangleArea# sA#, sB#, sC#
' PARAMETERS:      sA#           Side A
'                  sB#           Side B
'                  sC#           Side C
' VARIABLES:       s#            Sum of the three sides of the triangle
'                                divided by two
'                  t1#           Temporary variable
'                  t2#           Temporary variable
'                  t3#           Temporary variable
' MODULE LEVEL
'   DECLARATIONS:  DECLARE FUNCTION TriangleArea# (sA#, sB#, sC#)
'
  FUNCTION TriangleArea# (sA#, sB#, sC#) STATIC
      s# = (sA# + sB# + sC#) / 2#
      t1# = s# - sA#
      t2# = s# - sB#
      t3# = s# - sC#
      TriangleArea# = SQR(s# * t1# * t2# * t3#)
  END FUNCTION
```

WINDOWS

The WINDOWS demo module demonstrates the windows subprograms. One lets you create several types of windows for displaying information and menu selections. A second subprogram removes the most recently created window.

The WindowsType data structure completely defines the action and appearance of the windows that you can create. Although the list of variables in this structure is fairly long, you have the advantage of complete control over the windows.

Set the action code to 0, 1, or 2. An action code of 0 indicates a return to the calling program immediately after the window is created, leaving the window on the screen. You could use this type of window for simply displaying information.

An action code of 1 creates the window and then waits for the user to press any key before continuing. The code for the key pressed is returned to the calling program, making it possible to use a type 1 window to ask yes-or-no, multiple choice, or other questions.

An action code of 2 creates the most sophisticated type of window. In this case, a menu window is created, providing several methods for the user to select from among the available menu choices. One line of the menu window is highlighted to indicate the currently selected choice. You can use the up and down arrow keys or the mouse to move this highlight to the desired line. Clicking with the mouse or pressing the Enter key selects the currently highlighted line. You can also press the key for the first unique character of a line, which immediately selects that line. The Windows subprogram then returns the line number for a type 2 action code menu.

The edgeLine variable in the WindowsType data structure should also be set to 0, 1, or 2. This parameter tells the Windows subprogram to draw a border around the window with 0-, 1-, or 2-line graphics characters.

You can select and control the foreground and background colors for each part of a window individually. The color definition constants used in the demonstration program can be very useful for setting these parameters.

The row and column variables define the placement of the upper left corner of the window. The Windows subprogram automatically sizes the window for both the number of lines and the length of the longest line. Be sure to place the window where it won't hit the edges of the screen.

The title string appears in the center of the top border of the window, and the prompt string appears in the center of the bottom border of the display. If these strings are null, nothing is displayed in the window borders.

The PCOPY statement copies screen pages for saving and restoring the background information under the windows. This technique results in very quick window appearance and disappearance without using complicated assembly-language routines. In 40-column SCREEN mode 0, you can display up to seven windows at once, one for each available screen page. Depending on the graphics adapter you have, other video modes let you display two to four windows simultaneously.

Name	Type	Description
WINDOWS.BAS		Demo module
Windows	Sub	Creates a pop-up window
WindowsPop	Sub	Removes last displayed window

Demo Module: WINDOWS

```
' **********************************************
' **  Name:         WINDOWS                   **
' **  Type:         Toolbox                   **
' **  Module:       WINDOWS.BAS               **
' **  Language:     Microsoft QuickBASIC 4.00 **
' **********************************************
' USAGE:          No command line parameters
' REQUIREMENTS:   MIXED.QLB/.LIB
'                 Mouse (optional)
' .MAK FILE:      WINDOWS.BAS
'                 BITS.BAS
'                 BIOSCALL.BAS
'                 MOUSSUBS.BAS
'                 KEYS.BAS
' PARAMETERS:     (none)
' VARIABLES:      w1      Structure of type WindowsType
'                 w2      Structure of type WindowsType
'                 w3      Structure of type WindowsType
```

(continued)

continued

```
'                   w1Text$()   Strings to display in first window
'                   w2Text$()   Strings to display in second window
'                   w3Text$()   Strings to display in third window
'                   w1Title$    Title string for first window
'                   w1Prompt$   Prompt string for first window
'                   w2Title$    Title string for second window
'                   w2Prompt$   Prompt string for second window
'                   w3Title$    Title string for third window
'                   arrow$      String showing up and down arrows
'                   entSymbol$  String showing the Enter key symbol
'                   w3Prompt$   Prompt string for third window
'                   i%          Looping index
'                   t0          Timer value

' Define color constants
 CONST BLACK = 0
 CONST BLUE = 1
 CONST GREEN = 2
 CONST CYAN = 3
 CONST RED = 4
 CONST MAGENTA = 5
 CONST BROWN = 6
 CONST WHITE = 7
 CONST BRIGHT = 8
 CONST BLINK = 16
 CONST YELLOW = BROWN + BRIGHT

 TYPE WindowsType
     action       AS INTEGER
     edgeLine     AS INTEGER
     row          AS INTEGER
     col          AS INTEGER
     fgdEdge      AS INTEGER
     bgdEdge      AS INTEGER
     fgdBody      AS INTEGER
     bgdBody      AS INTEGER
     fgdHighlight AS INTEGER
     bgdHighlight AS INTEGER
     fgdTitle     AS INTEGER
     bgdTitle     AS INTEGER
     fgdPrompt    AS INTEGER
     bgdPrompt    AS INTEGER
     returnCode   AS INTEGER
 END TYPE
```

(continued)

QUICKBASIC TOOLBOXES AND PROGRAMS

continued

```
' Functions
  DECLARE FUNCTION InKeyCode% ()

' Subprograms
  DECLARE SUB Windows (w AS WindowsType, wText$(), wTitle$, wPrompt$)
  DECLARE SUB WindowsPop ()
  DECLARE SUB VideoState (mode%, columns%, page%)
  DECLARE SUB Mouse (m1%, m2%, m3%, m4%)
  DECLARE SUB MouseMickey (horizontal%, vertical%)
  DECLARE SUB MouseNow (leftButton%, rightButton%, xMouse%, yMouse%)

' Data structures
  DIM w1 AS WindowsType
  DIM w2 AS WindowsType
  DIM w3 AS WindowsType

' Arrays
  DIM w1Text$(1 TO 5)
  DIM w2Text$(1 TO 3)
  DIM w3Text$(1 TO 9)

' Define first window
  w1.action = 0
  w1.edgeLine = 1
  w1.row = 2
  w1.col = 3
  w1.fgdEdge = YELLOW
  w1.bgdEdge = BLUE
  w1.fgdBody = BRIGHT + WHITE
  w1.bgdBody = BLUE
  w1.fgdHighlight = 0
  w1.bgdHighlight = 0
  w1.fgdTitle = YELLOW
  w1.bgdTitle = BLUE
  w1.fgdPrompt = YELLOW
  w1.bgdPrompt = BLUE
  w1Title$ = " First Window "
  w1Text$(1) = "This window demonstrates how information"
  w1Text$(2) = "can be displayed without requesting any"
  w1Text$(3) = "response from the user.  The action code"
  w1Text$(4) = "is 0, causing an immediate return to the"
  w1Text$(5) = "program after the window is displayed."
  w1Prompt$ = ""
```

(continued)

continued

```
' Define second window
  w2.action = 1
  w2.edgeLine = 2
  w2.row = 10
  w2.col = 12
  w2.fgdEdge = CYAN + BRIGHT
  w2.bgdEdge = BLACK
  w2.fgdBody = YELLOW
  w2.bgdBody = BLACK
  w2.fgdHighlight = 0
  w2.bgdHighlight = 0
  w2.fgdTitle = CYAN + BRIGHT
  w2.bgdTitle = BLUE
  w2.fgdPrompt = CYAN + BRIGHT
  w2.bgdPrompt = BLUE
  w2Title$ = " Second window, action code is 1 "
  w2Text$(1) = "This window waits for the user to press"
  w2Text$(2) = "any key before continuing.  The key code"
  w2Text$(3) = "is passed back to the calling program."
  w2Prompt$ = " Press any key to continue. "

' Define third window
  w3.action = 2
  w3.edgeLine = 2
  w3.row = 7
  w3.col = 15
  w3.fgdEdge = YELLOW
  w3.bgdEdge = WHITE
  w3.fgdBody = BLACK
  w3.bgdBody = WHITE
  w3.fgdHighlight = WHITE + BRIGHT
  w3.bgdHighlight = BLACK
  w3.fgdTitle = YELLOW
  w3.bgdTitle = WHITE
  w3.fgdPrompt = YELLOW
  w3.bgdPrompt = WHITE
  w3Title$ = " Third window, action is 2 (menu selection) "
  arrows$ = CHR$(24) + " " + CHR$(25) + " "
  entSymbol$ = CHR$(17) + CHR$(196) + CHR$(217)
  w3Prompt$ = " <Character> " + arrows$ + entSymbol$ + " or use mouse "
  w3Text$(1) = "1. This is the first line in the window."
  w3Text$(2) = "2. This is the second."
  w3Text$(3) = "3. This is the third line."
  w3Text$(4) = "4. The fourth."
  w3Text$(5) = "5. The fifth."
  w3Text$(6) = "A. You can press <A> or <a> to select this line."
```

(continued)

continued

```
    w3Text$(7) = "B. You can press <1> to <5> for one of the first 5 lines."
    w3Text$(8) = "C. Try moving the cursor up or down and pressing Enter."
    w3Text$(9) = "D. Also, try the mouse. Click with left button."

' Initialize the display
    SCREEN 0, , 0, 0
    WIDTH 80
    CLS
    FOR i% = 1 TO 20
        PRINT STRING$(80, 178)
    NEXT i%
    LOCATE 6, 24
    PRINT " * Windows toolbox demonstration * "

' Wait for any key to be pressed
    LOCATE 22, 1
    PRINT "Press any key to continue"
    DO
    LOOP UNTIL INKEY$ <> ""

' Clear the "press any key" prompt
    LOCATE 22, 1
    PRINT SPACE$(25)

' Create the three windows
    Windows w1, w1Text$(), w1Title$, w1Prompt$
    Windows w2, w2Text$(), w2Title$, w2Prompt$
    Windows w3, w3Text$(), w3Title$, w3Prompt$

' Display the result codes, and erase each window
    FOR i% = 1 TO 4
        LOCATE 21, 1
        COLOR WHITE, BLACK
        PRINT "The three return codes...";
        PRINT w1.returnCode; w2.returnCode; w3.returnCode
        COLOR YELLOW
        PRINT "Every five seconds another window will disappear..."
        COLOR WHITE, BLACK
        t0 = TIMER
        DO
        LOOP UNTIL TIMER - t0 > 5
        WindowsPop
    NEXT i%

' All done
    CLS
    END
```

Subprogram: Windows

Creates a pop-up window for displaying string data or menu selections. The data structure of type WindowsType defines the action, colors, borders, and other attributes of the windows. If you provide invalid parameters, you receive an appropriate error message, and the program terminates.

```
' *************************************************
' ** Name:        Windows                       **
' ** Type:        Subprogram                    **
' ** Module:      WINDOWS.BAS                   **
' ** Language:    Microsoft QuickBASIC 4.00     **
' *************************************************
'
' Displays a rectangular window for information display
' or menu selection.
'
' EXAMPLE OF USE:  Windows w1, wText$(), wTitle$, wPrompt$
' PARAMETERS:      w1            Structure of type WindowsType
'                  wTest$()      Array of strings to be displayed
'                  wTitle$       Title string
'                  wPrompt$      Prompt string
' VARIABLES:       mode%         Current video mode
'                  columns%      Current number of character columns
'                  page%         Current video page
'                  cursorRow%    Saved cursor row position
'                  cursorCol%    Saved cursor column position
'                  newpage%      Next video page
'                  lbText%       Lower boundary of array of text lines
'                  ubText%       Upper boundary of array of text lines
'                  i%            Looping index
'                  maxlen%       Length of longest string to display
'                  length%       Length of each array string
'                  row2%         Row number at bottom right corner of window
'                  col2%         Column number at bottom right corner of
'                                window
'                  ul%           Upper left corner border character code
'                  ur%           Upper right corner border character code
'                  ll%           Lower left corner border character code
'                  lr%           Lower right corner border character code
'                  vl%           Vertical border character code
'                  hl%           Horizontal border character code
'                  r%            Index to each line of text
'                  ptr%          Highlighted line pointer
```

(continued)

continued

```
'                       lastPtr%       Last highlighted line
'                       horizontal%    Horizontal mouse mickies
'                       vertical%      Vertical mouse mickies
'                       mickies        Accumulated vertical mickies
'                       choice$        Set of unique characters for each menu line
'                       tmp$           Work string
'                       kee%           Key code returned by InKeyCode% function
'                       leftButton%    Mouse left button state
'                       rightButton%   Mouse right button state
'                       xMouse%        Mouse X position
'                       yMouse%        Mouse Y position
' MODULE LEVEL
'   DECLARATIONS:  SUB Windows (w AS WindowsType, wText$(), wTitle$,
'                       wPrompt$) STATIC
'
  SUB Windows (w AS WindowsType, wText$(), wTitle$, wPrompt$) STATIC
    ' Key code numbers
      CONST DOWNARROW = 20480
      CONST ENTER = 13
      CONST ESCAPE = 27
      CONST UPARROW = 18432

    ' Determine current video page
      VideoState mode%, columns%, page%

    ' Record current cursor location
      cursorRow% = CSRLIN
      cursorCol% = POS(0)

    ' Window will be on the next page, if available
      newpage% = page% + 1
      IF newpage% > 7 THEN
          SCREEN , , 0, 0
          PRINT "Error: Windows - not enough video pages"
          SYSTEM
      END IF

    ' Copy current page to new page
      PCOPY page%, newpage%

    ' Show the current page while building window on new page
      SCREEN , , newpage%, page%
```

(continued)

continued

```
' Determine array bounds
  lbText% = LBOUND(wText$)
  ubText% = UBOUND(wText$)

' Check the text array bounds, lower always 1, upper > 0
  IF lbText% <> 1 OR ubText% < 1 THEN
      SCREEN , , 0, 0
      PRINT "Error: Windows - text array dimensioned incorrectly"
      SYSTEM
  END IF

' Determine longest string in the text array
  maxLen% = 0
  FOR i% = lbText% TO ubText%
      length% = LEN(wText$(i%))
      IF length% > maxLen% THEN
          maxLen% = length%
      END IF
  NEXT i%

' Determine the bottom right corner of window
  row2% = w.row + ubText% + 1
  col2% = w.col + maxLen% + 3

' Check that window is on screen
  IF w.row < 1 OR w.col < 1 OR row2% > 25 OR col2% > columns% THEN
      SCREEN , , 0, 0
      PRINT "Error: Windows - part of window is off screen"
      SYSTEM
  END IF

' Set the edge characters
  SELECT CASE w.edgeLine
  CASE 0
      ul% = 32
      ur% = 32
      ll% = 32
      lr% = 32
      vl% = 32
      hl% = 32
  CASE 1
      ul% = 218
      ur% = 191
      ll% = 192
      lr% = 217
      vl% = 179
      hl% = 196
```

(continued)

continued

```
        CASE 2
            ul% = 201
            ur% = 187
            ll% = 200
            lr% = 188
            vl% = 186
            hl% = 205
        CASE ELSE
            SCREEN , , 0, 0
            PRINT "Error: Windows - Edge line type incorrect"
            SYSTEM
    END SELECT

    ' Draw top edge of the box
    LOCATE w.row, w.col, 0
    COLOR w.fgdEdge, w.bgdEdge
    PRINT CHR$(ul%); STRING$(maxLen% + 2, hl%); CHR$(ur%);

    ' Draw the body of the window
    FOR r% = w.row + 1 TO row2% - 1
        LOCATE r%, w.col, 0
        COLOR w.fgdEdge, w.bgdEdge
        PRINT CHR$(vl%);
        COLOR w.fgdBody, w.bgdBody
        tmp$ = LEFT$(wText$(r% - w.row) + SPACE$(maxLen%), maxLen%)
        PRINT " "; tmp$; " ";
        COLOR w.fgdEdge, w.bgdEdge
        PRINT CHR$(vl%);
    NEXT r%

    ' Draw bottom edge of the box
    LOCATE row2%, w.col, 0
    COLOR w.fgdEdge, w.bgdEdge
    PRINT CHR$(ll%); STRING$(maxLen% + 2, hl%); CHR$(lr%);

    ' Center and print top title if present
    IF wTitle$ <> "" THEN
        LOCATE w.row, (w.col + col2% - LEN(wTitle$) + 1) \ 2, 0
        COLOR w.fgdTitle, w.bgdTitle
        PRINT wTitle$;
    END IF
```

(continued)

continued

```
    ' Center and print prompt if present
    IF wPrompt$ <> "" THEN
        LOCATE row2%, (w.col + col2% - LEN(wPrompt$) + 1) \ 2, 0
        COLOR w.fgdPrompt, w.bgdPrompt
        PRINT wPrompt$;
    END IF

    ' Now make the new page visible and active
    SCREEN , , newpage%, newpage%

    ' Take next action based on action code
    SELECT CASE w.action
    CASE 1

        ' Get a key code number and return it
        DO
            w.returnCode = InKeyCode%
        LOOP UNTIL w.returnCode

    CASE 2

        ' Set choice pointer to last selection if known
        IF w.returnCode > 0 AND w.returnCode < ubText% THEN
            ptr% = w.returnCode
        ELSE
            ptr% = 1
        END IF

        ' Start with last pointer different, to update highlighting
        IF ptr% > 1 THEN
            lastPtr% = 1
        ELSE
            lastPtr% = 2
        END IF

        ' Clear any mouse mickey counts
        MouseMickey horizontal%, vertical%
        mickies% = 0
```

(continued)

continued

```
   ' Create unique key selection string
    choice$ = ""
    FOR i% = 1 TO ubText%
        tmp$ = UCASE$(LTRIM$(wText$(i%)))
        DO
            IF tmp$ <> "" THEN
                t$ = LEFT$(tmp$, 1)
                tmp$ = MID$(tmp$, 2)
                IF INSTR(choice$, t$) = 0 THEN
                    choice$ = choice$ + t$
                END IF
            ELSE
                SCREEN 0, , 0
                PRINT "Error: Windows - No unique character"
                SYSTEM
            END IF
        LOOP UNTIL LEN(choice$) = i%
    NEXT i%

   ' Main loop, monitor mouse and keyboard
    DO

       ' Add the mouse mickies
        MouseMickey horizontal%, vertical%
        mickies% = mickies% + vertical%

       ' Check for enough mickies
        IF mickies% < -17 THEN
            mickies% = 0
            IF ptr% > 1 THEN
                ptr% = ptr% - 1
            END IF
        ELSEIF mickies% > 17 THEN
            mickies% = 0
            IF ptr% < ubText% THEN
                ptr% = ptr% + 1
            END IF
        END IF

       ' Check keyboard
        kee% = InKeyCode%
        IF kee% >= ASC("a") AND kee% <= ASC("z") THEN
            kee% = ASC(UCASE$(CHR$(kee%)))
        END IF
        SELECT CASE kee%
```

(continued)

continued

```
            CASE UPARROW
                IF ptr% > 1 THEN
                    ptr% = ptr% - 1
                END IF
            CASE DOWNARROW
                IF ptr% < ubText% THEN
                    ptr% = ptr% + 1
                END IF
            CASE ENTER
                w.returnCode = ptr%
            CASE ESCAPE
                w.returnCode = -1
            CASE ELSE
                w.returnCode = INSTR(choice$, CHR$(kee%))
                IF w.returnCode THEN
                    ptr% = w.returnCode
                END IF
            END SELECT

        ' Check the left mouse button
            MouseNow leftButton%, rightButton%, xMouse%, yMouse%
            IF leftButton% THEN
                w.returnCode = ptr%
            END IF

        ' Update the highlight if line has changed
            IF ptr% <> lastPtr% THEN
                LOCATE lastPtr% + w.row, w.col + 2, 0
                COLOR w.fgdBody, w.bgdBody
                tmp$ = LEFT$(wText$(lastPtr%) + SPACE$(maxLen%), maxLen%)
                PRINT tmp$;
                LOCATE ptr% + w.row, w.col + 2, 0
                COLOR w.fgdHighlight, w.bgdHighlight
                tmp$ = LEFT$(wText$(ptr%) + SPACE$(maxLen%), maxLen%)
                PRINT tmp$;
                lastPtr% = ptr%
            END IF

        LOOP WHILE w.returnCode = 0

    CASE ELSE
        w.returnCode = 0
    END SELECT

' Reset the cursor position
    LOCATE cursorRow%, cursorCol%

END SUB
```

Subprogram: WindowsPop

Removes the most recently created window from the screen. The SCREEN statement is used to change the apage and vpage parameters simultaneously, resulting in nearly instant removal of the window.

```
' ****************************************************
' **   Name:        WindowsPop               **
' **   Type:        Subprogram               **
' **   Module:      WINDOWS.BAS              **
' **   Language:    Microsoft QuickBASIC 4.00   **
' ****************************************************
'
' Removes last displayed window.
'
' EXAMPLE OF USE:   WindowsPop
' PARAMETERS:       (none)
' VARIABLES:        mode%      Current video mode
'                   columns%   Current number of display columns
'                   page%      Current display page
' MODULE LEVEL
'   DECLARATIONS:   DECLARE SUB WindowsPop ()
'
SUB WindowsPop STATIC
    VideoState mode%, columns%, page%
    IF page% THEN
        SCREEN 0, , page% - 1, page% - 1
    END IF
END SUB
```

WORDCOUN

The WORDCOUN toolbox counts words in a file and contains a function that counts words in a string. Enter a filename on the command line when you run this program.

Name	Type	Description
WORDCOUN.BAS		Demo module
WordCount%	Func	Returns number of words in a string

Demo Module: WORDCOUN

```
' *********************************************
' **   Name:          WORDCOUN                **
' **   Type:          Toolbox                 **
' **   Module:        WORDCOUN.BAS            **
' **   Language:      Microsoft QuickBASIC 4.00 **
' *********************************************
'
' USAGE:         WORDCOUN filename
' .MAK FILE:     (none)
' PARAMETERS:    filename      Name of file to be processed
' VARIABLES:     fileName$     Name of file from the command line
'                sep$          List of characters defined as word separators
'                a$            Each line from the file
'                totalCount&   Total count of words

  DECLARE FUNCTION WordCount% (a$, sep$)

' Assume a filename has been given on the command line
  fileName$ = COMMAND$

' Open the file
  OPEN fileName$ FOR INPUT AS #1

' Define the word-separating characters as space, tab, and comma
  sep$ = " " + CHR$(9) + ","
```

(continued)

continued

```
' Read in and process each line
  DO
      LINE INPUT #1, a$
      totalCount& = totalCount& + WordCount%(a$, sep$)
  LOOP UNTIL EOF(1)

' Print the results
  PRINT "There are"; totalCount&; "words in "; fileName$

' That's all
  END
```

Function: WordCount%

Returns the number of words in a string. Words are defined as groups of characters separated by one or more of the characters in sep$. The WORDCOUN toolbox passes sep$ with a space, a tab, and a comma in it, but you can place any characters in sep$ that you want to use to define the separation of words.

```
' *************************************************
' **  Name:          Wordcount%                   **
' **  Type:          Function                     **
' **  Module:        WORDCOUN.BAS                 **
' **  Language:      Microsoft QuickBASIC 4.00    **
' *************************************************
'
' Returns the number of words in a string.
'
' EXAMPLE OF USE:   WordCount% a$, sep$
' PARAMETERS:       a$         String containing words to be counted
'                   sep$       List of word separation characters
' VARIABLES:        count%     Count of words
'                   flag%      Indicates if scanning is currently inside of a
'                              word
'                   la%        length of a$
'                   i%         Index to each character of a$
' MODULE LEVEL
'   DECLARATIONS:   DECLARE FUNCTION WordCount% (a$, sep$)
```

(continued)

continued

```
FUNCTION WordCount% (a$, sep$) STATIC
    count% = 0
    flag% = 0
    la% = LEN(a$)
    IF la% > 0 AND sep$ <> "" THEN
        FOR i% = 1 TO la%
            IF INSTR(sep$, MID$(a$, i%, 1)) THEN
                IF flag% THEN
                    flag% = 0
                    count% = count% + 1
                END IF
            ELSE
                flag% = 1
            END IF
        NEXT i%
    END IF
    WordCount% = count% + flag%

END FUNCTION
```

PART III

MIXED-LANGUAGE TOOLBOXES

USING MIXED-LANGUAGE TOOLBOXES

Although Microsoft QuickBASIC is a sophisticated and powerful software-development tool, other languages, such as C, FORTRAN, Pascal, and assembly language, have unique strengths. The ability to mix subprograms and functions written in any of these languages lets you use the best features of each. FORTRAN, for example, has extensive mathematics and engineering libraries, and C is a powerful development language. For the fastest running programs, assembly language can't be beat. Once you understand a few concepts, you'll be able to easily combine routines from these languages.

Near and Far Addressing

MS-DOS runs on the 8088, 8086, 80286, and 80386 family of microprocessors found at the heart of IBM Personal Computers and compatibles. These chips use special hardware registers that allow quicker access and shorter instruction when referring to data or procedures located in the same block of 65536 (64 KB) bytes of memory.

From a software point of view, microprocessor instructions can address memory locations by referring to either locations in a currently defined, single block of 64 KB memory addresses or to any possible locations in memory space. These references are called "near" and "far," respectively. Near references require one word, and far references require two words. Normally, high-level languages such as QuickBASIC take care of all these details for you, but when you link subprograms from other languages with QuickBASIC, you need to be sure that references to variables and calls to subprograms and functions all use the same type of near or far addressing.

You can adjust Microsoft QuickC and Microsoft Macro Assembler 5.0 to create programs using a variety of memory models that indicate whether memory locations are referred to by near or far addressing. To be compatible with QuickBASIC's method, you should use Medium Model settings for both compilers. In fact, this is the default setting for QuickC, making it easy for you to write QuickC routines to be called from QuickBASIC.

Passing Variables

Most programming languages, including QuickBASIC and QuickC, let you pass variables to called subprograms, functions, and subroutines by listing them in parentheses as part of the calling statement. This list matches one for one the parameters defined and used in the called routine.

You can pass these parameters to and from a subprogram or function by reference or by value. Some languages pass the address of the referenced variable, and changes made to the variable by the routine modify the contents of memory that this address points to. Other languages pass copies of the values of the variables. Changes to the passed variables don't affect the originals because the changes are made only to the copies.

The important concept is that both the calling routine and the called routine must agree as to how they pass parameters back and forth. For example, QuickBASIC usually passes parameters by reference, and QuickC by value. Fortunately, both languages let you control whether parameters are passed by value or by reference. See the CDECL modifier of the QuickBASIC DECLARE statement for an example of how you can control parameter passing.

Parameter passing can also vary from language to language in the order in which the parameters are pushed onto the stack as well as in the method used to remove these parameters from the stack when the called routine is finished. For example, consider a QuickBASIC program that passes parameters (A, B, C) to a QuickC subprogram. The QuickC routine processes the parameters as (C, B, A). The CDECL modifier in the QuickBASIC DECLARE statement can tell QuickBASIC to reverse the normal order of parameter pushing to be compatible with QuickC.

In most languages, when a subprogram or function is finished, the parameters are removed from the stack before the routine returns to the calling program. QuickC routines expect the calling program to clean up the stack after the return. (This allows passing a variable number of parameters in C.) The CDECL modifier instructs Quick-BASIC to clean up the stack after calling a subprogram or function.

By using standard parameter-passing techniques and by following the examples in this book and in your Microsoft QuickBASIC and Microsoft Macro Assembler manuals, you'll find mixed-language programming easy and convenient.

The routines in Part III of this book demonstrate passing integers, arrays of integers, and string variables. The Microsoft Macro Assembler was used to develop the mouse interface subprogram, and Microsoft QuickC was used to create some bit manipulation and byte-movement routines.

Creating Mixed-Language Toolboxes

In the section "Using QuickBASIC Toolboxes," you will find the steps to follow for using the QuickC and Macro Assembler routines presented in Part III of this book. Please see "Creating MIXED.QLB," beginning on page 22.

In addition to compiling from the system prompt, you can also compile each QuickC toolbox, CTOOLS1.C and CTOOLS2.C, from within the QuickC environment. Run QuickC by typing *QC*, and notice that the environment is very similar in appearance and feel to that of QuickBASIC. Pull down the Files menu and choose Open. Select CTOOLS1.C to load the first toolbox into QuickC. Then pull down the Run menu and choose Compile. A dialog box opens, providing several compiling options. In the Output Options section, select Obj, rather than the default Memory, and then select Compile File, rather than the default Build Program option. You can experiment with the options listed under Miscellaneous, but selecting Optimizations and deselecting the Stack Checking and Debug options generally results in a smaller .OBJ file. QuickC then compiles the CTOOLS1.C source code currently in memory and writes the resulting CTOOLS1.OBJ file to disk. Repeat the process for the CTOOLS2.C file.

Once you have created the object-code files and the MIXED.QLB Quick Library and have loaded MIXED.QLB with QuickBASIC, you can then call any or all of the QuickC and Macro Assembler functions and subprograms from within programs running in the QuickBASIC environment. Be sure to declare the subprogram or function in the module-level code, and then call the routines freely, as though they were part of the standard set of QuickBASIC functions and commands.

Once a program is running as desired in the QuickBASIC environment you may want to compile it into a stand-alone .EXE format file. Simply compile the program from within QuickBASIC and the appropriate .LIB file will be searched. The MIXED.LIB file will automatically pull in the necessary code during the LINK process.

NOTE: You must have QuickC installed to compile CDEMO1 and CDEMO2 into executable files.

Assembly Source-Code Files

The CASEMAP.ASM and MOUSE.ASM source-code files are listed here for your convenience in building both the MIXED.QLB and MIXED.LIB libraries.

The CASEMAP.ASM subprogram is called by TranslateCountry$, a function found in the DOSCALLS module, to translate each character, one at a time.

This routine demonstrates how you can use QuickBASIC's DECLARE statement to pass parameters by value rather than by reference. In this case, the segment- and offset-address parameters for the MS-DOS translation routine are passed by value, resulting in a very efficient branch to the MS-DOS character-translation routine from CaseMap.

```
; **********************************************
; ** CASEMAP.ASM                   MASM 5.0  **
; **                                          **
; ** Assembly subprogram for translating      **
; ** some characters according to the         **
; ** currently loaded MS-DOS country-         **
; ** dependent information.                   **
; **                                          **
; ** Use:  CALL CASEMAP (CHAR%, SEG%, OFS%)   **
; ** Note: CHAR% is passed by reference       **
; **       SEG% and OFS% are passed by value  **
; **********************************************
;
; EXAMPLE OF USE:   CALL CaseMap (char%, seg%, ofs%)
; PARAMETERS:       char%    Character byte to be translated
;                   seg%     Segment of address of MS-DOS translate routine
;                   ofs%     Offset of address of MS-DOS translate routine
; VARIABLES:        (none)
; MODULE LEVEL
;   DECLARATIONS:   DECLARE SUB GetCountry (country AS CountryType)
;                   DECLARE SUB CaseMap (character%, BYVAL Segment%,
;                                       BYVAL Offset%)
;                   DECLARE FUNCTION TranslateCountry$ (a$, country AS CountryType)
```

(continued)

continued

```
.MODEL  MEDIUM
.CODE
        public  casemap

casemap proc

; Standard entry
        push    bp
        mov     bp,sp

; Get CHAR% into AX register
        mov     bx,[bp+10]
        mov     ax,[bx]

; Call the translate function in MS-DOS
        call    dword ptr [bp+6]

; Return translated character to CHAR%
        mov     bx,[bp+10]
        mov     [bx],ax

; Standard exit, assumes three variables passed
        pop     bp
        ret     6

; End of the procedure
casemap endp
        end
```

The MOUSE.ASM subprogram provides a fast and efficient method of interfacing QuickBASIC with the memory-resident mouse-driver software. (See your mouse documentation for information on loading this driver into memory.)

```
; ***********************************************
; **  MOUSE.ASM               Macro Assembler  **
; **                                           **
; **  Assembly subprogram for accessing the    **
; **  Microsoft Mouse from QuickBASIC 4.00     **
; **                                           **
; **  Use:  CALL MOUSE (M1%, M2%, M3%, M4%)    **
; ***********************************************
```

(continued)

continued

```
; EXAMPLE OF USE:  CALL Mouse (m1%, m2%, m3%, m4%)
; PARAMETERS:      m1%         Passed in AX to the mouse driver
;                  m2%         Passed in BX to the mouse driver
;                  m3%         Passed in CX to the mouse driver
;                  m4%         Passed in DX to the mouse driver
; VARIABLES:       (none)
; MODULE LEVEL
;   DECLARATIONS:  DECLARE SUB Mouse (m1%, m2%, m3%, m4%)

.MODEL   MEDIUM
.CODE
         public  mouse

mouse    proc

; Standard entry
         push    bp
         mov     bp,sp

; Get M1% and store it on the stack
         mov     bx,[bp+12]
         mov     ax,[bx]
         push    ax

; Get M2% and store it on the stack
         mov     bx,[bp+10]
         mov     ax,[bx]
         push    ax

; Get M3% into CX register
         mov     bx,[bp+8]
         mov     cx,[bx]

; Get M4% into DX register
         mov     bx,[bp+6]
         mov     dx,[bx]

; Move M2% from stack into BX register
         pop     bx

; Move M1% from stack into AX register
         pop     ax

; Set ES to same as DS (for mouse function 9)
         push    ds
         pop     es
```

(continued)

continued

```
; Do the mouse interrupt
        int     33h

; Save BX (M2%) on stack to free register
        push    bx

; Return M1% from AX
        mov     bx,[bp+12]
        mov     [bx],ax

; Return M2% from stack (was BX)
        pop     ax
        mov     bx,[bp+10]
        mov     [bx],ax

; Return M3% from CX
        mov     bx,[bp+8]
        mov     [bx],cx

; Return M4% from DX
        mov     bx,[bp+6]
        mov     [bx],dx

; Standard exit, assumes four variables passed
        pop     bp
        ret     / 8

; End of this procedure
mouse   endp
        end
```

CDEMO1.BAS AND CTOOLS1.C

The CDEMO1.BAS program is a QuickBASIC program that demonstrates the proper declaration and calling of the QuickC routines presented in the CTOOLS1.C toolbox.

The IsIt[Type]% functions can efficiently determine the classification of any character, given its ASCII numeric value. For example, given c% = ASC("A"), the IsItAlnum%, IsItAlpha%, IsItAscii%, IsItGraph%, IsItPrint%, IsItUpper%, and IsItxDigit% functions all return a true (non-zero) value, and all other functions return zero.

The MovBytes and MovWords subprograms allow movement of bytes or words from any location in memory to any other, using the QuickC movedata function. You can use these subprograms to copy the contents of variables into variables of a different type. The eight bytes of a double-precision number, for example, can be easily extracted from an eight-character string after the data has been moved from the number into the string. Large arrays of data can efficiently be moved into arrays of a different type, and video memory can be stored in a string, as demonstrated by the module-level code of CDEMO1.

Name	Type	Description
CDEMO1.BAS		QuickBASIC program module
CTOOLS1.C		C-language toolbox containing functions/ subprograms
IsItAlnum%	Func	Alphanumeric character determination
IsItAlpha%	Func	Alphabetic character determination
IsItAscii%	Func	Standard ASCII character determination
IsItCntrl%	Func	Control character determination
IsItDigit%	Func	Decimal digit (0–9) determination
IsItGraph%	Func	Graphics character determination
IsItLower%	Func	Lowercase character determination

(continued)

(continued)

Name	Type	Description
IsItPrint%	Func	Printable character determination
IsItPunct%	Func	Punctuation character determination
IsItSpace%	Func	Space character determination
IsItUpper%	Func	Uppercase character determination
IsItXDigit%	Func	Hexadecimal character determination
MovBytes	Sub	Moves bytes from one location to another
MovWords	Sub	Moves blocks of words in memory

Program Module: CDEMO1

```
' *********************************************
' **   Name:       CDEMO1                    **
' **   Type:       Program                   **
' **   Module:     CDEMO1.BAS                **
' **   Language:   Microsoft QuickBASIC 4.00 **
' *********************************************
'
' Demonstrates the QuickC routines presented in
' the file CTOOLS1.C.
'
' USAGE:         No command line parameters
' REQUIREMENTS:  CGA
'                MIXED.QLB/.LIB
' .MAK FILE:     (none)
' PARAMETERS:    (none)
' VARIABLES:     a%(0 TO 1999) Storage space for first text screen
'                b%(0 TO 1999) Storage space for second text screen
'                i%            Looping index
'                sseg%         Word and byte move source segment
'                              part of address
'                soff%         Word and byte move source offset
'                              part of address
'                dseg%         Word and byte move destination segment
'                              part of address
'                doff%         Word and byte move destination offset
'                              part of address
'                nwords%       Number of words to move
'                nbytes%       Number of bytes to move
'                t$            Copy of TIME$
'                quitflag%     Signal to end first demonstration
```

(continued)

continued

```
' Functions
  DECLARE FUNCTION IsItAlnum% CDECL (BYVAL c AS INTEGER)
  DECLARE FUNCTION IsItAlpha% CDECL (BYVAL c AS INTEGER)
  DECLARE FUNCTION IsItAscii% CDECL (BYVAL c AS INTEGER)
  DECLARE FUNCTION IsItCntrl% CDECL (BYVAL c AS INTEGER)
  DECLARE FUNCTION IsItDigit% CDECL (BYVAL c AS INTEGER)
  DECLARE FUNCTION IsItGraph% CDECL (BYVAL c AS INTEGER)
  DECLARE FUNCTION IsItLower% CDECL (BYVAL c AS INTEGER)
  DECLARE FUNCTION IsItPrint% CDECL (BYVAL c AS INTEGER)
  DECLARE FUNCTION IsItPunct% CDECL (BYVAL c AS INTEGER)
  DECLARE FUNCTION IsItSpace% CDECL (BYVAL c AS INTEGER)
  DECLARE FUNCTION IsItUpper% CDECL (BYVAL c AS INTEGER)
  DECLARE FUNCTION IsItXDigit% CDECL (BYVAL c AS INTEGER)

' Subprograms
  DECLARE SUB MovBytes CDECL (sseg%, soff%, dseg%, doff%, nbytes%)
  DECLARE SUB MovWords CDECL (sseg%, soff%, dseg%, doff%, nwords%)

' Make two buffers for the first page of video memory
  DIM a%(0 TO 1999), b%(0 TO 1999)

' Prevent scrolling when printing in row 25, column 80
  VIEW PRINT 1 TO 25

' Create the first page of text
  CLS
  COLOR 14, 4
  FOR i% = 1 TO 25
      PRINT STRING$(80, 179);
  NEXT i%
  COLOR 15, 1
  LOCATE 11, 25
  PRINT STRING$(30, 32);
  LOCATE 12, 25
  PRINT "     -  Calling MovWords  -    "
  LOCATE 13, 25
  PRINT STRING$(30, 32);

' Move the screen memory into the first array
  sseg% = &HB800
  soff% = 0
  dseg% = VARSEG(a%(0))
  doff% = VARPTR(a%(0))
  nwords% = 2000
  MovWords sseg%, soff%, dseg%, doff%, nwords%
```

(continued)

continued

```
' Create the second page of text
CLS
COLOR 14, 4
FOR i% = 1 TO 25
    PRINT STRING$(80, 196);
NEXT i%
COLOR 15, 1
LOCATE 11, 25
PRINT STRING$(30, 32);
LOCATE 12, 25
PRINT "    -   Calling MovBytes   -   "
LOCATE 13, 25
PRINT STRING$(30, 32);

' Move the screen memory into the second array
sseg% = &HB800
soff% = 0
dseg% = VARSEG(b%(0))
doff% = VARPTR(b%(0))
nwords% = 2000
MovWords sseg%, soff%, dseg%, doff%, nwords%

' Set destination to the video screen memory
dseg% = &HB800
doff% = 0

' Do the following until a key is pressed
DO

    ' Move 2000 words from first array to screen memory
    sseg% = VARSEG(a%(0))
    soff% = VARPTR(a%(0))
    nwords% = 2000
    MovWords sseg%, soff%, dseg%, doff%, nwords%

    ' Wait one second
    t$ = TIME$
    DO
        IF INKEY$ <> "" THEN
            t$ = ""
            quitFlag% = 1
        END IF
    LOOP UNTIL TIME$ <> t$
```

(continued)

443

continued

```
        ' Move 4000 bytes from second array to screen memory
        sseg% = VARSEG(b%(0))
        soff% = VARPTR(b%(0))
        nbytes% = 4000
        MovBytes sseg%, soff%, dseg%, doff%, nbytes%

        ' Wait one second
        t$ = TIME$
        DO
            IF INKEY$ <> "" THEN
                t$ = ""
                quitFlag% = 1
            END IF
        LOOP UNTIL TIME$ <> t$

    LOOP UNTIL quitFlag%

    ' Create a table of all 256 characters and their type designations
    FOR i% = 0 TO 255

        ' After each screenful, display a heading
        IF i% MOD 19 = 0 THEN

            ' If not the first heading, prompt user before continuing
            IF i% THEN
                PRINT
                PRINT "Press any key to continue"
                DO WHILE INKEY$ = ""
                LOOP
            END IF

            ' Print the heading
            CLS
            PRINT "Char   Alnum Alpha Ascii Cntrl Digit Graph ";
            PRINT "Lower Print Punct Space Upper XDigit"
            PRINT
        END IF

        ' Some characters we don't want to display
        SELECT CASE i%
        CASE 7, 8, 9, 10, 11, 12, 13, 29, 30, 31
            PRINT USING "###     "; i%;
        CASE ELSE
            PRINT USING "### \ \"; i%, CHR$(i%);
        END SELECT
```

(continued)

444

continued

```
' Display "1" if test is true, "0" otherwise
    PRINT USING "  #  "; 1 + (0 = IsItAlnum%(i%));
    PRINT USING "  #  "; 1 + (0 = IsItAlpha%(i%));
    PRINT USING "  #  "; 1 + (0 = IsItAscii%(i%));
    PRINT USING "  #  "; 1 + (0 = IsItCntrl%(i%));
    PRINT USING "  #  "; 1 + (0 = IsItDigit%(i%));
    PRINT USING "  #  "; 1 + (0 = IsItGraph%(i%));
    PRINT USING "  #  "; 1 + (0 = IsItLower%(i%));
    PRINT USING "  #  "; 1 + (0 = IsItPrint%(i%));
    PRINT USING "  #  "; 1 + (0 = IsItPunct%(i%));
    PRINT USING "  #  "; 1 + (0 = IsItSpace%(i%));
    PRINT USING "  #  "; 1 + (0 = IsItUpper%(i%));
    PRINT USING "  #  "; 1 + (0 = IsItXDigit%(i%))

NEXT i%
END
```

Toolbox: CTOOLS1.C

The CTOOLS1.C toolbox provides access to the efficient QuickC functions for classifying characters and to QuickC's fast memory move functions for copying blocks of bytes or words from any location in memory to any other.

You can determine character types using QuickBASIC code, but the QuickC routines are optimized for speed. Also, adhering to the definitions provided by QuickC guarantees that character classifications will be the same for both languages.

You must add both of the following #include statements at the top of the CTOOLS1.C source-code file, before the function definitions are given. These two statements pull in the contents of header files necessary for correct compilation by QuickC:

```
#include <ctype.h>
#include <memory.h>
```

Function: IsItAlnum%

Determines whether a character is alphanumeric. This function returns a non-zero value if the integer value represents an alphanumeric ASCII character or a zero if the value does not. Alphanumeric characters are in the ranges A through Z, a through z, and 0 through 9.

```
/***********************************************
**    Name:          IsItAlnum%                **
**    Type:          Function                  **
**    Module:        CTOOLS1.C                 **
**    Language:      Microsoft QuickC/QuickBASIC **
************************************************
*
* EXAMPLE OF USE:    result% = IsItAlnum%(c%)
* PARAMETERS:        c%         ASCII character code
* VARIABLES:         (none)
* MODULE LEVEL
*    DECLARATIONS:   #include <ctype.h>         */

int isitalnum (c)
int c;
    {
    return (isalnum(c));
    }
```

Function: IsItAlpha%

Determines whether a character is alphabetic. This function returns a non-zero value if the integer value represents an alphabetic ASCII character or a zero if the value does not. The alphabetic characters are in the ranges A through Z and a through z.

```
/***********************************************
**    Name:          IsItAlpha%                **
**    Type:          Function                  **
**    Module:        CTOOLS1.C                 **
**    Language:      Microsoft QuickC/QuickBASIC **
************************************************
```

(continued)

continued

```
 * EXAMPLE OF USE:    result% = IsItAlpha%(c%)
 * PARAMETERS:        c%         ASCII character code
 * VARIABLES:         (none)
 * MODULE LEVEL
 *   DECLARATIONS:    #include <ctype.h>         */


int isitalpha (c)
int c;
    {
    return (isalpha(c));
    }
```

Function: IsItAscii%

Determines whether a character is standard ASCII. This function returns a non-zero value if the integer value represents an ASCII character or a zero if the value does not. The ASCII character values are in the range 0 through 127.

```
/***********************************************
 **   Name:         IsItAscii%                 **
 **   Type:         Function                   **
 **   Module:       CTOOLS1.C                  **
 **   Language:     Microsoft QuickC/QuickBASIC **
 ***********************************************
 *
 * EXAMPLE OF USE:    result% = IsItAscii%(c%)
 * PARAMETERS:        c%         ASCII character code
 * VARIABLES:         (none)
 * MODULE LEVEL
 *   DECLARATIONS:    #include <ctype.h>         */


int isitascii (c)
int c;
    {
    return (isascii(c));
    }
```

Function: IsItCntrl%

Determines whether a character is a control character. This function returns a non-zero value if the integer value represents a control character or a zero if the value does not. The control characters are in the range 0 through 31, and 127.

```
/************************************************
**    Name:           IsItCntrl%                **
**    Type:           Function                  **
**    Module:         CTOOLS1.C                 **
**    Language:       Microsoft QuickC/QuickBASIC **
*************************************************
*
* EXAMPLE OF USE:    result% = IsItCntrl%(c%)
* PARAMETERS:        c%           ASCII character code
* VARIABLES:         (none)
* MODULE LEVEL
*   DECLARATIONS:    #include <ctype.h>         */

int isitcntrl (c)
int c;
    {
    return (iscntrl(c));
    }
```

Function: IsItDigit%

Determines whether a character is a numeric digit. This function returns a non-zero value if the integer value represents a decimal digit or a zero if the value does not. The digit characters are in the range 0 through 9.

```
/************************************************
**    Name:           IsItDigit%                **
**    Type:           Function                  **
**    Module:         CTOOLS1.C                 **
**    Language:       Microsoft QuickC/QuickBASIC **
*************************************************
```

(continued)

continued

```
*  EXAMPLE OF USE:   result% = IsItDigit%(c%)
*  PARAMETERS:       c%          ASCII character code
*  VARIABLES:        (none)
*  MODULE LEVEL
*    DECLARATIONS:   #include <ctype.h>         */


int isitdigit (c)
int c;
    {
    return (isdigit(c));
    }
```

Function: IsItGraph%

Determines whether a character is graphic. This function returns a non-zero value if the integer value represents a printable character, not including the space character. These character values are in the range 33 through 126.

```
/**********************************************
**   Name:         IsItGraph%                 **
**   Type:         Function                   **
**   Module:       CTOOLS1.C                  **
**   Language:     Microsoft QuickC/QuickBASIC **
***********************************************
*
*  EXAMPLE OF USE:   result% = IsItGraph%(c%)
*  PARAMETERS:       c%          ASCII character code
*  VARIABLES:        (none)
*  MODULE LEVEL
*    DECLARATIONS:   #include <ctype.h>         */


int isitgraph (c)
int c;
    {
    return (isgraph(c));
    }
```

Function: IsItLower%

Determines whether a character is lowercase. This function returns a non-zero value if the integer value represents a lowercase character or a zero if the value does not. The lowercase characters are in the range a through z.

```
/***********************************************
**    Name:          IsItLower%                **
**    Type:          Function                  **
**    Module:        CTOOLS1.C                 **
**    Language:      Microsoft QuickC/QuickBASIC **
************************************************
*
* EXAMPLE OF USE:   result% = IsItLower%(c%)
* PARAMETERS:       c%           ASCII character code
* VARIABLES:        (none)
* MODULE LEVEL
*   DECLARATIONS:   #include <ctype.h>            */

int isitlower (c)
int c;
    {
    return (islower(c));
    }
```

Function: IsItPrint%

Determines whether a character is printable. This function returns a non-zero value if the integer value represents a printable character or a zero if the value does not. The printable characters are in the range 32 through 126.

```
/***********************************************
**    Name:          IsItPrint%                **
**    Type:          Function                  **
**    Module:        CTOOLS1.C                 **
**    Language:      Microsoft QuickC/QuickBASIC **
************************************************
```

(continued)

continued

```
* EXAMPLE OF USE:   result% = IsItPrint%(c%)
* PARAMETERS:       c%          ASCII character code
* VARIABLES:        (none)
* MODULE LEVEL
*   DECLARATIONS:   #include <ctype.h>           */


int isitprint (c)
int c;
    {
    return (isprint(c));
    }
```

Function: IsItPunct%

Determines whether a character is punctuation. This function returns a non-zero value if the integer value represents a punctuation character or a zero if the value does not. The punctuation characters are in the ranges 33 through 47, 59 through 64, 91 through 96, or 123 through 126.

```
/*********************************************
**   Name:       IsItPunct%                   **
**   Type:       Function                     **
**   Module:     CTOOLS1.C                    **
**   Language:   Microsoft QuickC/QuickBASIC  **
***********************************************
*
* EXAMPLE OF USE:   result% = IsItPunct%(c%)
* PARAMETERS:       c%          ASCII character code
* VARIABLES:        (none)
* MODULE LEVEL
*   DECLARATIONS:   #include <ctype.h>           */


int isitpunct (c)
int c;
    {
    return (ispunct(c));
    }
```

Function: IsItSpace%

Determines whether a character is white space. This function returns a non-zero value if the integer value represents a white-space character or a zero if the value does not. The white-space character values are in the range 9 through 13, and 32.

```
/***********************************************
**    Name:          IsItSpace%                **
**    Type:          Function                  **
**    Module:        CTOOLS1.C                 **
**    Language:      Microsoft QuickC/QuickBASIC **
************************************************
*
*  EXAMPLE OF USE:   result% = IsItSpace%(c%)
*  PARAMETERS:       c%           ASCII character code
*  VARIABLES:        (none)
*  MODULE LEVEL
*    DECLARATIONS:   #include <ctype.h>         */

int isitspace (c)
int c;
   {
   return (isspace(c));
   }
```

Function: IsItUpper%

Determines whether a character is uppercase. This function returns a non-zero value if the integer value represents an uppercase character or a zero if the value does not. The uppercase characters are in the range A through Z.

```
/***********************************************
**    Name:          IsItUpper%                **
**    Type:          Function                  **
**    Module:        CTOOLS1.C                 **
**    Language:      Microsoft QuickC/QuickBASIC **
************************************************
```

(continued)

continued

```
*  EXAMPLE OF USE:   result% = IsItUpper%(c%)
*  PARAMETERS:       c%           ASCII character code
*  VARIABLES:        (none)
*  MODULE LEVEL
*    DECLARATIONS:   #include <ctype.h>          */

int isitupper (c)
int c;
    {
    return (isupper(c));
    }
```

Function: IsItXDigit%

Determines whether a character is a hexadecimal digit. This function returns a non-zero value if the integer value represents a hexadecimal character or a zero if the value does not. The hexadecimal characters are in the ranges 0 through 9, a through f, or A through F.

```
/***********************************************
**   Name:       IsItXDigit%                  **
**   Type:       Function                     **
**   Module:     CTOOLS1.C                    **
**   Language:   Microsoft QuickC/QuickBASIC  **
***********************************************
*
*  EXAMPLE OF USE:   result% = IsItXDigit%(c%)
*  PARAMETERS:       c%           ASCII character code
*  VARIABLES:        (none)
*  MODULE LEVEL
*    DECLARATIONS:   #include <ctype.h>          */


int isitxdigit (c)
int c;
    {
    return (isxdigit(c));
    }
```

Subprogram: MovBytes

Calls the QuickC movedata function to quickly copy a block of bytes from any address in memory to any other.

```
/***********************************************
**   Name:         MovBytes                    **
**   Type:         Subprogram                  **
**   Module:       CTOOLS1.C                   **
**   Language:     Microsoft QuickC/QuickBASIC **
************************************************
*
*   Moves bytes from a source segment and offset
*   location in memory to a destination segment and
*   offset location.
*
*   EXAMPLE OF USE:  MovBytes sseg%, soff%, dseg%, doff%, nbytes%
*   PARAMETERS:      sseg%    Source segment address of bytes to be moved
*                    soff%    Source offset address of bytes to be moved
*                    dseg%    Destination segment address of bytes to be moved
*                    doff%    Destination offset address of bytes to be moved
*                    nbytes%  Number of bytes to be moved
* VARIABLES:         (none)
* MODULE LEVEL
*   DECLARATIONS:    #include <memory.h>        */

void movbytes (srcseg, srcoff, destseg, destoff, nbytes)
unsigned int *srcseg, *srcoff, *destseg, *destoff, *nbytes;
   {
   movedata(*srcseg, *srcoff, *destseg, *destoff, *nbytes);
   }
```

Subprogram: MovWords

Moves a block of words from any memory location to any other. This subprogram calls the QuickC movedata function to quickly copy a block of words from any address in memory to any other.

```
/*********************************************
**   Name:        MovWords                  **
**   Type:        Subprogram                **
**   Module:      CTOOLS1.C                 **
**   Language:    Microsoft QuickC/QuickBASIC **
*********************************************
*
* Moves words from a source segment and offset
* location in memory to a destination segment and
* offset location.
*
* EXAMPLE OF USE: MovWords sseg%, soff%, dseg%, doff%, nbytes%
* PARAMETERS:     sseg%     Source segment address of words to be moved
*                 soff%     Source offset address of words to be moved
*                 dseg%     Destination segment address of words to be moved
*                 doff%     Destination offset address of words to be moved
*                 nwords%   Number of words to be moved
* VARIABLES:      (none)
* MODULE LEVEL
*   DECLARATIONS: #include <memory.h>         */


void movwords (srcseg, srcoff, destseg, destoff, nwords)
unsigned int *srcseg, *srcoff, *destseg, *destoff, *nwords;
    {
    unsigned int nbytes;

    nbytes = *nwords + *nwords;
    movedata(*srcseg, *srcoff, *destseg, *destoff, nbytes);
    }
```

CDEMO2.BAS AND CTOOLS2.C

The CDEMO2.BAS program is a QuickBASIC program that demonstrates the proper declaration and calling of the QuickC routines presented in the CTOOLS2.C toolbox.

The MenuString% function creates a horizontal bar menu, similar to the menu line at the top of the display in the QuickBASIC environment. The function call returns the number of the word selected. You can place the menu bar anywhere on the screen, and it can contain any number of one-word choices. The first letter of each word must be uppercase, and no more than two words can have the same first letter.

The BitShiftLeft% and BitShiftRight% functions let you shift all the bits in a string of bytes one position to the left or right. Each function returns the bit shifted off the end of the string and shifts in a zero at the other end.

The NumberOfBits& function returns the number of bits in all the bytes of a string. You could do this by using the bit-shifting functions and adding up the returned values, but the NumberOfBits& function is much faster. The string contents are unchanged by the function.

The PackWord and UnPackWord subprograms let you pack and unpack two byte values (integers in the range 0 through 255) into an integer variable. This can be accomplished using the QuickBASIC math functions (although it gets complicated when dealing with negative numbers), but QuickC has features ideal for performing these types of data manipulations. By declaring a union of a two-byte structure with an integer, the bytes can simply be moved into place instead of calculated.

The TextGet and TextPut subprograms let you quickly save and restore rectangular areas of the text-mode screen. These routines are similar in concept to the QuickBASIC GET and PUT statements that save and restore rectangular areas of graphics-mode screens. Unlike the GET and PUT statements, though, the rectangular area restored can be of a different shape than the area that was saved. The total number of bytes must be identical, but the width and height of the area can differ. The program module first prints a line of text that is saved into a string using TextGet and is then restored in a vertical (one column wide) rectangular area.

Name	Type	Description
CDEMO2.BAS		QuickBASIC program module
CTOOLS2.C		C-language toolbox containing functions/subprograms
BitShiftLeft%	Func	Shifts all bits in a string left one bit
BitShiftRight%	Func	Shifts all bits in a string right one bit
MenuString%	Func	Bar menu and user response function
NumberOfBits&	Func	Determines number of 1 bits in a string
PackWord	Sub	Packs two bytes into an integer value
TextGet	Sub	Saves characters and attributes from area of screen
TextPut	Sub	Restores text from TextGet to screen
UnPackWord	Sub	Unpacks values from high and low bytes

Program Module: CDEMO2

```
' *****************************************
' ** Name:         CDEMO2                **
' ** Type:         Program               **
' ** Module:       CDEMO2.BAS            **
' ** Language:     Microsoft QuickBASIC 4.00 **
' *****************************************
'
' USAGE:         No command line parameters
' REQUIREMENTS:  CGA
'                MIXED.QLB/.LIB
' .MAK FILE:     (none)
' PARAMETERS:    (none)
' VARIABLES:     m$          Menu string
'                word%       Integer to be packed with two bytes
'                hi%         Most significant byte unpacked from an
'                            integer
```

(continued)

continued

```
'       lo%             Least significant byte unpacked from an
'                       integer
'       a$              Workspace for TextGet and TextPut
'       b$              Workspace for TextGet and TextPut
'       n%              Timing constant for TextPut demonstration
'       row%            Row location to put small "window" using
'                       TextPut
'       col%            Column location to put small "window" using
'                       TextPut
'       t0              Timer variable
'       x$              String variable for bit shifting
'       i%              Looping index

' Functions
  DECLARE FUNCTION MenuString% CDECL (row%, col%, a$)
  DECLARE FUNCTION BitShiftleft% CDECL (a$)
  DECLARE FUNCTION BitShiftRight% CDECL (a$)
  DECLARE FUNCTION NumberOfBits& CDECL (a$)

' Subprograms
  DECLARE SUB PackWord CDECL (word%, hi%, lo%)
  DECLARE SUB UnPackWord CDECL (word%, hi%, lo%)
  DECLARE SUB TextGet CDECL (r1%, c1%, r2%, c2%, a$)
  DECLARE SUB TextPut CDECL (r1%, c1%, r2%, c2%, a$)

' Build menu string
  m$ = "Packword Unpackword Textget Textput "
  m$ = m$ + "Bitshiftleft Bitshiftright Numberofbits Quit"

' Let user repeatedly select the demonstrations
  DO
        COLOR 15, 1
        CLS
        PRINT
        PRINT
        PRINT "MenuString function..."
        PRINT
        PRINT "Select one of the CTOOLS2 demonstrations by ";
        PRINT "pressing the Left arrow,"
        PRINT "Right arrow, first letter of the choice, or Enter keys."

    ' Use MenuString to choose demonstrations
        SELECT CASE MenuString%(1, 1, m$)
```

(continued)

continued

```
' PackWord demonstration
  CASE 1

      CLS
      PRINT "PackWord word%, 255, 255  ... word% = ";
      PackWord word%, 255, 255
      PRINT word%
      PRINT "PackWord word%,   0,   1 ... word% = ";
      PackWord word%, 0, 1
      PRINT word%
      PRINT "PackWord word%,   1,   0 ... word% = ";
      PackWord word%, 1, 0
      PRINT word%

      PRINT
      PRINT "Press any key to continue..."

      DO
      LOOP UNTIL INKEY$ <> ""

' UnPackWord demonstration
  CASE 2

      CLS
      PRINT "UnPackWord  -1, hi%, lo%  ... hi%, lo% =";
      UnPackWord -1, hi%, lo%
      PRINT hi%; lo%
      PRINT "UnPackWord   1, hi%, lo%  ... hi%, lo% =";
      UnPackWord 1, hi%, lo%
      PRINT hi%; lo%
      PRINT "UnPackWord 256, hi%, lo%  ... hi%, lo% =";
      UnPackWord 256, hi%, lo%
      PRINT hi%; lo%

      PRINT
      PRINT "Press any key to continue..."

      DO
      LOOP UNTIL INKEY$ <> ""

' TextGet and TextPut demonstration
  CASE 3, 4

    ' TextGet a line of text
      CLS
```

(continued)

continued

```
        PRINT "A Vertical Message"
        a$ = SPACE$(36)
        TextGet 1, 1, 1, 18, a$

    ' TextPut it back, but stretch it vertically
        TextPut 6, 1, 23, 1, a$

    ' Now just a normal line of text at top
        LOCATE 1, 1
        PRINT "TextGet and TextPut - Press any key to stop"

    ' Create first of two colorful text patterns
        COLOR 14, 4
        LOCATE 13, 13, 0
        PRINT CHR$(201); CHR$(205); CHR$(209); CHR$(205); CHR$(187)
        LOCATE 14, 13, 0
        PRINT CHR$(199); CHR$(196); CHR$(197); CHR$(196); CHR$(182)
        LOCATE 15, 13, 0
        PRINT CHR$(200); CHR$(205); CHR$(207); CHR$(205); CHR$(188)
        a$ = SPACE$(30)
        TextGet 13, 13, 15, 17, a$

    ' Create second of two colorful text patterns
        COLOR 10, 1
        LOCATE 13, 13, 0
        PRINT CHR$(218); CHR$(196); CHR$(210); CHR$(196); CHR$(191)
        LOCATE 14, 13, 0
        PRINT CHR$(198); CHR$(205); CHR$(206); CHR$(205); CHR$(181)
        LOCATE 15, 13, 0
        PRINT CHR$(192); CHR$(196); CHR$(208); CHR$(196); CHR$(217)
        b$ = SPACE$(30)
        TextGet 13, 13, 15, 17, b$

    ' Randomly pop up little "windows"
        n% = 0
        DO
            row% = INT(RND * 21 + 3)
            col% = INT(RND * 73 + 4)
            TextPut row%, col%, row% + 2, col% + 4, a$
            row% = INT(RND * 21 + 3)
            col% = INT(RND * 73 + 4)
            TextPut row%, col%, row% + 2, col% + 4, b$
            IF n% < 10 THEN
                n% = n% + 1
                t0 = TIMER
```

(continued)

continued

```
                DO
                LOOP UNTIL TIMER > t0 + (10 - n%) / 10
            END IF
        LOOP UNTIL INKEY$ <> ""

    ' BitShiftLeft demonstration
    CASE 5

        CLS
        x$ = "This string will be shifted left 8 bits"
        PRINT x$
        FOR i% = 1 TO 8
            PRINT "bit ="; BitShiftleft%(x$)
        NEXT i%
        PRINT x$

        PRINT
        PRINT "Press any key to continue..."

        DO
        LOOP UNTIL INKEY$ <> ""

    ' BitShiftRight demonstration
    CASE 6

        CLS
        x$ = "This string will be shifted right 8 bits"
        PRINT x$
        FOR i% = 1 TO 8
            PRINT "bit ="; BitShiftRight%(x$)
        NEXT i%
        PRINT x$

        PRINT
        PRINT "Press any key to continue..."

        DO
        LOOP UNTIL INKEY$ <> ""

    ' BitShiftRight demonstration
    CASE 7

        CLS
        x$ = "The number of bits in this string is ..."
```

(continued)

continued

```
        PRINT x$
        PRINT NumberOfBits&(x$)

        PRINT
        PRINT "Press any key to continue..."

        DO
        LOOP UNTIL INKEY$ <> ""

    ' Must be time to quit
    CASE ELSE
        COLOR 7, 0
        CLS
        END
    END SELECT
LOOP
```

Toolbox: CTOOLS2.C

The CTOOLS2.C toolbox provides a collection of functions and subprograms that perform tasks that QuickC is well suited for.

You must enter the following block of lines into the first lines of the CTOOLS2.C source-code file, immediately before the functions and subprograms. Note that the definition for VIDEO_START should be changed to 0xb0000000 for monochrome operation.

```
#include <ctype.h>
#include <conio.h>

#define VIDEO_START          0xb8000000

#define BLACK_ON_CYAN        48
#define RED_ON_CYAN          52
#define BRIGHT_WHITE_ON_RED  79

#define ENTER                13
#define RIGHT_ARROW          77
#define LEFT_ARROW           75

/* Definition of the QuickBASIC string descriptor structure */
struct bas_str
    {
    int  sd_len;
    char *sd_addr;
    };
```

Function: BitShiftLeft%

Shifts all bits in a QuickBASIC string variable to the left one bit position. The number of bits in a string is eight times the length of the string. The function returns the leftmost bit of the first character of the string.

```
/**********************************************
** Name:       BitShiftLeft%                 **
** Type:       Function                      **
** Module:     CTOOLS2.C                     **
** Language:   Microsoft QuickC/QuickBASIC   **
***********************************************
*
* Shifts all bits in a QuickBASIC string one bit
* to the left. The leftmost bit is returned, and
* the rightmost bit is set to zero.
*
* EXAMPLE OF USE:  bit% = BitShiftLeft%(bit$)
* PARAMETERS:      bit$      String containing a bit pattern
* VARIABLES:       len       Length of the string (number of bytes)
*                  str       Pointer to string contents
*                  i         Looping index to each byte of the string
*                  carry     Bit carried over from byte to byte
*                  the_byte  Working copy of each byte of the string
*
* Definition of the QuickBASIC string descriptor structure
*    struct bas_str
*        {
*        int  sd_len;
*        char *sd_addr;
*        };                                        */

int bitshiftleft (basic_string)
struct bas_str *basic_string;
    {
    int len = basic_string->sd_len;
    unsigned char *str = basic_string->sd_addr;
    int i, carry;
    unsigned int the_byte;
```

(continued)

continued

```
    for (i=len-1, carry=0; i>=0; i--)
        {
        the_byte = *(str + i);
        *(str + i) = (the_byte << 1) + carry;
        carry = the_byte >> 7;
        }
    return (carry);
    }
```

Function: BitShiftRight%

Shifts all bits in a QuickBASIC string variable to the right one bit position. The number of bits in a string is eight times the length of the string. The function returns the rightmost bit of the last character of the string.

```
/************************************************
** Name:         BitShiftRight%              **
** Type:         Function                    **
** Module:       CTOOLS2.C                   **
** Language:     Microsoft QuickC/QuickBASIC **
*************************************************
*
* Shifts all bits in a QuickBASIC string one bit to
* the right.  The rightmost bit is returned, and the
* leftmost bit is set to zero.
*
* EXAMPLE OF USE:   bit% = BitShiftRight%(bit$)
* PARAMETERS:       bit$      String containing a bit pattern
* VARIABLES:        len       Length of the string (number of bytes)
*                   str       Pointer to string contents
*                   i         Looping index to each byte of the string
*                   carry     Bit carried over from byte to byte
*                   the_byte  Working copy of each byte of the string
*
* Definition of the QuickBASIC string descriptor structure
*     struct bas_str
*         {
*         int  sd_len;
```

(continued)

continued

```
*          char *sd_addr;
*       };                                              */
int bitshiftright (basic_string)
struct bas_str *basic_string;
    {
    int len = basic_string->sd_len;
    unsigned char *str = basic_string->sd_addr;
    int i, carry;
    unsigned int the_byte;

    for (i=0, carry=0; i<len; i++)
        {
        the_byte = *(str + i);
        *(str + i) = (the_byte >> 1) + carry;
        carry = (the_byte & 1) << 7;
        }

    if (carry)
        return(1);
    else
        return(0);
    }
```

Function: MenuString%

Creates a horizontal menu bar, highlights the one-word choices, and returns the number of the choice selected when the Enter key is pressed. The menu is highlighted using the same color scheme as the main pull-down menu bars of both the QuickBASIC and QuickC environments.

```
/**********************************************
**  Name:          MenuString%                **
**  Type:          Function                   **
**  Module:        CTOOLS2.C                  **
**  Language:      Microsoft QuickC/QuickBASIC **
***********************************************
*
*  Displays a horizontal bar menu and waits for a
*  response from the user.  Returns the number of
*  the word selected from the string.
```

(continued)

continued

```
 * EXAMPLE OF USE:   choice% = MenuString%(row%, col%, menu$)
 * PARAMETERS:       row%        Row location to display the menu string
 *                   col%        Column location to display the menu string
 *                   menu$       String containing list of words representing
 *                               choices
 * VARIABLES:        len         Length of the menu string
 *                   str         Pointer to string contents
 *                   vidptr      Pointer to video memory
 *                   attribute   Index into string
 *                   character   Character from keyboard press
 *                   both        Combination of a character and its attribute
 *                   i           Looping index
 *                   j           Looping index
 *                   k           Looping index
 *                   c           Looping index
 *                   choice      Menu selection number
 *                   wordnum     Sequential count of each word in the menu string
 *                   refresh     Signals to redraw the menu string
 * #include <ctype.h>
 * #include <conio.h>
 * #define VIDEO_START          0xb8000000
 * #define BLACK_ON_CYAN        48
 * #define RED_ON_CYAN          52
 * #define BRIGHT_WHITE_ON_RED  79
 * #define ENTER                13
 * #define RIGHT_ARROW          77
 * #define LEFT_ARROW           75
 *
 * Definition of the QuickBASIC string descriptor structure
 *     struct bas_str
 *         {
 *         int  sd_len;
 *         char *sd_addr;
 *         };                                              */

int menustring (row, col, basic_string)
int *row, *col;
struct bas_str *basic_string;
    {
    int len;
    char * str;
    int far * vidptr;
    int attribute, character, both;
    int i, j, k, c;
```

(continued)

continued

```c
    int choice, wordnum;
    int refresh;
    void packword();

    /* Initialize variables */
    len = basic_string->sd_len;
    str = basic_string->sd_addr;
    vidptr = (int far *) VIDEO_START + (*row - 1) * 80 + (*col - 1);
    choice = 1;
    refresh = 1;

    /* Loop until return() statement */
    while (1)
        {

        /* Display the string only if refresh is non-zero */
        if (refresh)
            {
            refresh = 0;

            /* Loop through each character of the string */
            for (wordnum = 0, i=0; i<len; i++)
                {

                /* Set the character and default attribute */
                character = str[i];
                attribute = BLACK_ON_CYAN;

                /* Uppercase? */
                if (isupper(character))
                    {
                    wordnum++;
                    attribute = RED_ON_CYAN;
                    }

                /* In the middle of the current selection? */
                if (wordnum == choice && character != ' ')
                    attribute = BRIGHT_WHITE_ON_RED;

                /* Move data to video */
                packword(&both, &attribute, &character);
                vidptr[i] = both;
                }
            }
```

(continued)

continued

```c
        /* Check for any key presses */
    if (kbhit())
        {

        /* Get the key code and process it */
        switch (c = getch())
            {

            /* Return the choice when Enter is pressed */
            case ENTER:
                return (choice);

            /* Highlight next choice if Right arrow is pressed */
            case RIGHT_ARROW:
                if (choice < wordnum)
                    {
                    choice++;
                    refresh = 1;
                    }
                break;

            /* Highlight previous choice if Left arrow is pressed */
            case LEFT_ARROW:
                if (choice > 1)
                    {
                    choice --;
                    refresh = 1;
                    }
                break;

            /* Check for match on first character of each word */
            default:
                c = _toupper(c);
                for (k=0, j=0; j<len; j++)
                    {

                    /* Each choice starts at an uppercase char */
                    if (isupper(str[j]))
                        k++;

                    /* Match if same char and not current choice */
```

(continued)

continued

```
                        if (str[j] == c && k != choice)
                            {
                            choice = k;
                            refresh = 1;
                            break;
                            }
                        }
                    break;
                    }
                }
            }
        }
```

Function: NumberOfBits&

Returns the number of bits in a string without altering its contents.

```
/************************************************
**   Name:        NumberOfBits&              **
**   Type:        Function                   **
**   Module:      CTOOLS2.C                  **
**   Language:    Microsoft QuickC/QuickBASIC **
*************************************************
*
* Counts the 1 bits in a QuickBASIC string.
*
* EXAMPLE OF USE:  count& = NumberOfBits&(a$)
* PARAMETERS:      a$         String containing bits to be counted
* VARIABLES:       len        Length of the string
*                  str        Pointer to string contents
*                  i          Looping index to each byte
*                  the_byte   Working copy of each byte of the string
*                  count      Count of the bits
*
* Definition of the QuickBASIC string descriptor structure
*     struct bas_str
*         {
*         int  sd_len;
*         char *sd_addr;
*         };                                            */
```

(continued)

continued

```
long numberofbits (basic_string)
struct bas_str *basic_string;
    {
    int len = basic_string->sd_len;
    unsigned char *str = basic_string->sd_addr;
    int i,the_byte;
    long count = 0;

    for (i=0; i<len; i++)
        {
        the_byte = *(str+i);
        while (the_byte)
            {
            count += (the_byte & 1);
            the_byte >>= 1;
            }
        }
    return (count);
    }
```

Subprogram: PackWord

Packs two bytes into an integer value. For example, the high and low (most significant and least significant) bytes of the integer value 258 are 1 and 2. QuickBASIC can pack two values into an integer by multiplying the first value by 256 and adding the second. This works well for small byte values but becomes awkward when the high byte is 128 or greater. In such cases, the resulting integer is a negative number.

PackWord uses the QuickC union and structure data definition features to pack the byte values using simple data moves in memory.

```
/*********************************************
**   Name:         PackWord                  **
**   Type:         Subprogram                **
**   Module:       CTOOLS2.C                 **
**   Language:     Microsoft QuickC/QuickBASIC **
**********************************************
*
*  Packs two byte values into the high and low
*  bytes of an integer (word).
```

(continued)

continued

```
* EXAMPLE OF USE:    PackWord hiloword%, hibyte%, lobyte%
* PARAMETERS:        hiloword%   Integer word to pack the two bytes into
*                    hibyte%     Integer value of the most significant byte
*                    lobyte%     Integer value of the least significant byte
* VARIABLES:         both        A union of a two-byte structure and an integer
*                                variable                                    */


void packword (hiloword, hibyte, lobyte)
int *hiloword, *hibyte, *lobyte;
    {
    union
        {
        struct
            {
            unsigned char lo;
            unsigned char hi;
            } bytes;
        int hilo;
        } both;

    both.bytes.hi = *hibyte;
    both.bytes.lo = *lobyte;
    *hiloword = both.hilo;
    }
```

Subprogram: TextGet

Copies a rectangular area of the text screen into a string variable. This is similar in concept to the graphics-oriented GET statement, except that this subprogram copies text-mode screen data. To redisplay the text anywhere on the screen, use the TextPut subprogram.

The string variable must be exactly the right length for the amount of data to be copied, or the call will be ignored. There are two bytes of screen memory for each character displayed (the character and its color attribute), so the string must contain width * height * 2 bytes. For example, to save the area from row 3, column 4, to row 5, column 9, the string length must be 3 * 6 * 2, or 36 characters. The SPACE$ statement is ideal for preparing strings for this call. For example, a$ = SPACE$(36) makes the previous string the correct length.

```
/*********************************************
**   Name:        TextGet                    **
**   Type:        Subprogram                 **
**   Module:      CTOOLS2.C                  **
**   Language:    Microsoft QuickC/QuickBASIC **
**********************************************
*
* Saves characters and attributes from a rectangular
* area of the screen.
*
* EXAMPLE OF USE:  TextGet r1%, c1%, r2%, c2%, a$
* PARAMETERS:      r1%      Pointer to row at upper left corner
*                  c1%      Pointer to column at upper left corner
*                  r2%      Pointer to row at lower right corner
*                  c2%      Pointer to column at lower right corner
*                  a$       String descriptor, where screen contents
*                           will be stored
* VARIABLES:       len      Length of string
*                  str      Pointer to string contents
*                  video    Pointer to video memory
*                  i        Index into string
*                  row      Looping index
*                  col      Looping index
* #define VIDEO_START       0xb8000000
*
* Definition of the QuickBASIC string descriptor structure
*
*   struct bas_str
*       {
*       int  sd_len;
*       char *sd_addr;
*       };                                           */

void textget (r1,c1,r2,c2,basic_string)
int *r1,*c1,*r2,*c2;
struct bas_str *basic_string;
    {
    int len;
    int * str;
    int far * video;
    int i,row,col;

    len = basic_string->sd_len;
    str = (int *) basic_string->sd_addr;
    video = (int far *) VIDEO_START;
```

(continued)

continued

```
    if (len == (*r2 - *r1 + 1) * (*c2 - *c1 + 1) * 2)
        for (row = *r1 - 1, i = 0; row < *r2; row++)
            for (col = *c1 - 1; col < *c2; col++)
                str[i++] = video[row * 80 + col];
}
```

Subprogram: TextPut

Restores a rectangular area of a text screen from a string variable previously used to copy screen contents via the TextGet subprogram. This is similar to the graphics-oriented PUT statement, except that this subprogram copies text-mode screen data.

The string variable must be exactly the right length for the amount of data to be copied onto the screen, or the call will be ignored. There are two bytes of screen memory for each character displayed (the character and its color attribute), so the string must contain width * height * 2 bytes. See the TextGet subprogram for more details on string length requirements.

The shape of the restored area can differ from the original area as long as the total number of bytes is the same. For example, an area three characters wide by four characters high can be copied using TextGet and then placed back on the screen in an area two wide by six high. As long as the width times the height remains constant, TextPut will move the data onto the screen.

```
/************************************************
**   Name:         TextPut                      **
**   Type:         Subprogram                   **
**   Module:       CTOOLS2.C                    **
**   Language:     Microsoft QuickC/QuickBASIC  **
*************************************************
*
* Restores characters and attributes to a rectangular
* area of the screen.
*
* EXAMPLE OF USE:  TextPut r1%, c1%, r2%, c2%, a$
* PARAMETERS:      r1%       Pointer to row at upper left corner
*                  c1%       Pointer to column at upper left corner
*                  r2%       Pointer to row at lower right corner
*                  c2%       Pointer to column at lower right corner
*                  a$        String descriptor where screen contents are stored
```

(continued)

continued

```
* VARIABLES:      len         Length of string
*                 str         Pointer to string contents
*                 video       Pointer to video memory
*                 i           Index into string
*                 row         Looping index
*                 col         Looping index
* #define VIDEO_START          0xb8000000
*
* Definition of the QuickBASIC string descriptor structure
*    struct bas_str
*       {
*       int  sd_len;
*       char *sd_addr;
*       };                                                  */

void textput (r1,c1,r2,c2,basic_string)
int *r1,*c1,*r2,*c2;
struct bas_str *basic_string;
    {
    int len;
    int * str;
    int far * video;
    int i,row,col;

    len = basic_string->sd_len;
    str = (int *) basic_string->sd_addr;
    video = (int far *) VIDEO_START;

    if (len == (*r2 - *r1 + 1) * (*c2 - *c1 + 1) * 2)
        for (row = *r1 - 1, i = 0; row < *r2; row++)
            for (col = *c1 - 1; col < *c2; col++)
                video[row * 80 + col] = str[i++];
    }
```

Subprogram: UnPackWord

Extracts two bytes from a QuickBASIC integer value. For example, the high and low (most significant and least significant) bytes of the integer value 258 are 1 and 2, and the two bytes of −1 are 255 and 255.

This subprogram uses the QuickC union and structure data definition features to unpack the byte values using simple data moves in memory.

```
/************************************************
** Name:         UnPackWord                    **
** Type:         Subprogram                    **
** Module:       CTOOLS2.C                     **
** Language:     Microsoft QuickC/QuickBASIC   **
*************************************************
*
*  Unpacks two byte values from the high and low
*  bytes of an integer (word).
*
* EXAMPLE OF USE:  UnPackWord hiloword%, hibyte%, lobyte%
* PARAMETERS:      hiloword%  Integer word containing the two bytes
*                  hibyte%    Integer value of the most significant byte
*                  lobyte%    Integer value of the least significant byte
* VARIABLES:       both       A union of a two-byte structure and an integer
*                             variable                                    */

void unpackword (hiloword, hibyte, lobyte)
int *hiloword, *hibyte, *lobyte;
    {
    union
        {
        struct
            {
            unsigned char lo;
            unsigned char hi;
            } bytes;
        int hilo;
        } both;

    both.hilo = *hiloword;
    *hibyte = both.bytes.hi;
    *lobyte = both.bytes.lo;
    }
```

PART IV

APPENDIXES

APPENDIX A

REQUIREMENTS FOR RUNNING TOOLBOXES/PROGRAMS

In the following table, the Usage line assumes execution from the system prompt after you compile the .BAS program. From QuickBASIC, modify COMMAND$ and enter any parameters before selecting Run and Start.

CGA–Color Graphics Adapter/Monitor   Sub–Subprogram
EGA–Enhanced Graphics Adapter/Monitor   Func–Function
VGA–Video Graphics Adapter/Monitor

Name	Description
ATTRIB.BAS	Screen/Text Attribute Display Utility Program: 1 Sub Usage: ATTRIB Requirements: CGA
BIN2HEX.BAS	Binary-to-Hex Conversion Utility Program Usage: BIN2HEX *inFileName.ext outFileName.ext* .MAK File: BIN2HEX.BAS PARSE.BAS
BIOSCALL.BAS	ROM BIOS Interrupt Calls Toolbox: 6 Sub with Demo Module Usage: BIOSCALL Requirements: MIXED.QLB/.LIB
BITS.BAS	Bit Manipulation Toolbox: 2 Func/2 Sub with Demo Module Usage: BITS
CALENDAR.BAS	Calendar and Time Routines Toolbox: 19 Func/1 Sub with Demo Module Usage: CALENDAR
CARTESIA.BAS	Cartesian Coordinate Routines Toolbox: 2 Func/2 Sub with Demo Module Usage: CARTESIA

(continued)

continued

Name	Description

CDEMO1.BAS	Demo 1 of C-Language Routines
	Program
	Usage: CDEMO1
	Requirements: CGA
	     MIXED.QLB/.LIB
	     Microsoft QuickC

CDEMO2.BAS	Demo 2 of C-Language Routines
	Program
	Usage: CDEMO2
	Requirements: CGA
	     MIXED.QLB/.LIB
	     Microsoft QuickC

CIPHER.BAS	Cipher File Security Utility Program: 1 Func/1 Sub Usage: CIPHER *filename.ext key* or CIPHER /NEWKEY .MAK File: CIPHER.BAS RANDOMS.BAS

COLORS.BAS	VGA Color Selection
	Utility Program: 1 Func
	Usage: COLORS
	Requirements: VGA or MCGA
	     MIXED.QLB/.LIB
	     Mouse
	.MAK File: COLORS.BAS
	     BITS.BAS
	     MOUSSUBS.BAS

COMPLEX.BAS	Complex Numbers Toolbox: 12 Sub with Demo Module Usage: COMPLEX .MAK File: COMPLEX.BAS CARTESIA.BAS

CTOOLS1.C	C Functions—Characters
	C-Language Toolbox: 12 Func/2 Sub
	Usage: Place in MIXED.QLB and MIXED.LIB
	    after compiling into object files and then run
	    CDEMO1.BAS from QuickBASIC

CTOOLS2.C	C Functions—Text
	C-Language Toolbox: 4 Func/4 Sub
	Usage: Place in MIXED.QLB and MIXED.LIB
	    after compiling into object files and then run
	    CDEMO2.BAS from QuickBASIC

(continued)

APPENDIX A

continued

Name	Description
DOLLARS.BAS	Dollar Formatting Toolbox: 3 Func with Demo Module Usage: DOLLARS
DOSCALLS.BAS	MS-DOS System Calls Toolbox: 6 Func/9 Sub with Demo Module Usage: DOSCALLS Requirements: MIXED.QLB/.LIB MS-DOS 3.3 or later
EDIT.BAS	Editing Toolbox: 5 Sub with Demo Module Usage: EDIT .MAK File: EDIT.BAS KEYS.BAS
ERROR.BAS	Error Message Toolbox: 1 Sub with Demo Module Usage: ERROR
FIGETPUT.BAS	FILEGET and FILEPUT Routines Toolbox: 1 Func/1 Sub with Demo Module Usage: FIGETPUT
FILEINFO.BAS	Directory/File Listing Information Toolbox: 3 Sub with Demo Module Usage: FILEINFO Requirements: MIXED.QLB/.LIB
FRACTION.BAS	Fractions Toolbox: 3 Func/7 Sub with Demo Module Usage: FRACTION
GAMES.BAS	Games Toolbox: 4 Func/2 Sub with Demo Module Usage: GAMES Requirements: CGA

HEX2BIN.BAS	Hex-to-Binary Conversion
	Utility Program
	Usage: HEX2BIN *inFileName.ext outFileName.ext*
	.MAK File: HEX2BIN.BAS
	           PARSE.BAS
	           STRINGS.BAS

(continued)

continued

Name	Description

JUSTIFY.BAS	Paragraph Justification
	Toolbox: 1 Sub with Demo Module
	Usage: JUSTIFY
	.MAK File: JUSTIFY.BAS
	    EDIT.BAS
	    KEYS.BAS
	    PARSE.BAS

KEYS.BAS	Enhanced Keyboard Input Functions Toolbox: 2 Func with Demo Module Usage: KEYS
LOOK.BAS	Text File Display Utility Utility Program Usage: LOOK *filename.ext* .MAK File: LOOK.BAS KEYS.BAS
MONTH.BAS	Three-Month Calendar Utility Program Usage: MONTH .MAK File: MONTH.BAS CALENDAR.BAS

MOUSGCRS.BAS	Custom Graphics Mouse Cursors
	Utility Program
	Usage: MOUSGCRS
	Requirements: CGA
	    MIXED.QLB/.LIB
	    Mouse
	.MAK File: MOUSGCRS.BAS
	    BITS.BAS
	    MOUSSUBS.BAS

MOUSSUBS.BAS	Mouse Subroutines
	Toolbox: 26 Subs with Demo Module
	Usage: MOUSSUBS
	Requirements: CGA
	    MIXED.QLB/.LIB
	    Mouse
	.MAK File: MOUSSUBS.BAS
	    BITS.BAS

(continued)

APPENDIX A

continued

Name	Description
MOUSTCRS.BAS	Text-Mode Mouse Cursor Utility Program Usage: MOUSTCRS Requirements: MIXED.QLB/.LIB 　　　　　　　Mouse .MAK File: MOUSTCRS.BAS 　　　　　　MOUSSUBS.BAS 　　　　　　BITS.BAS 　　　　　　ATTRIB.BAS
OBJECT.BAS	Interactive Graphics Creation Toolbox and Utility Program: 1 Sub Usage: OBJECT Requirements: CGA .MAK File: OBJECT.BAS 　　　　　　KEYS.BAS 　　　　　　EDIT.BAS
PARSE.BAS	Command Line Parsing Toolbox: 2 Subs with Demo Module Usage: PARSE
PROBSTAT.BAS	Probability and Statistical Routines Toolbox: 7 Func with Demo Module Usage: PROBSTAT
QBFMT.BAS	Formatting Utility Utility Program: 3 Subs Usage: QBFMT *filename* [*indention*] .MAK File: QBFMT.BAS 　　　　　　PARSE.BAS 　　　　　　STRINGS.BAS
QBTREE.BAS	Directory/Subdirectory/Files Listing Utility Program Usage: QBTREE [*path*] Requirements: MIXED.QLB/.LIB .MAK File: QBTREE.BAS 　　　　　　FILEINFO.BAS
QCAL.BAS	Command Line Scientific Calculator Utility Program: 1 Func/3 Subs Usage: QCAL [*number*] [*function*] [...] .MAK File: QCAL.BAS 　　　　　　QCALMATH.BAS

(continued)

continued

Name	Description
QCALMATH.BAS	Math Functions Toolbox: 31 Func/2 Sub Usage: loaded by the QCAL program
RANDOMS.BAS	Pseudorandom Numbers Toolbox: 6 Func/1 Sub with Demo Module Usage: RANDOMS
STDOUT.BAS	MS-DOS Standard (ANSI) Output Toolbox: 12 Sub with Demo Module Usage: STDOUT Requirements: MIXED.QLB/.LIB ANSI.SYS
STRINGS.BAS	String Manipulation Toolbox: 18 Func/1 Sub with Demo Module Usage: STRINGS
TRIANGLE.BAS	Triangles Toolbox: 3 Func/1 Sub with Demo Module Usage: TRIANGLE Requirements: CGA .MAK File: TRIANGLE.BAS QCALMATH.BAS
WINDOWS.BAS	Windows Toolbox: 2 Sub with Demo Module Usage: WINDOWS Requirements: MIXED.QLB/.LIB Mouse (optional) .MAK File: WINDOWS.BAS BIOSCALL.BAS BITS.BAS KEYS.BAS MOUSSUBS.BAS
WORDCOUN.BAS	Word Counting Toolbox: 1 Func with Demo Module Usage: WORDCOUN *filename*

APPENDIX B

FUNCTIONS-TO-MODULES CROSS REFERENCE

Function	Module	Description
AbsoluteX#	QCALMATH	Absolute value of a number
Add#	QCALMATH	Sum of two numbers
Angle!	CARTESIA	Angle between X axis and line to x, y point
ArcCosine#	QCALMATH	Arc cosine function of a number
ArcHypCosine#	QCALMATH	Inverse hyperbolic cosine of a number
ArcHypSine#	QCALMATH	Inverse hyperbolic sine of a number
ArcHypTangent#	QCALMATH	Inverse hyperbolic tangent of a number
ArcSine#	QCALMATH	Inverse sine of a number
ArcTangent#	QCALMATH	Inverse tangent of a number
ArithmeticMean#	PROBSTAT	Arithmetic mean of an array of numbers
Ascii2Ebcdic$	STRINGS	Converts string from ASCII to EBCDIC
BestMatch$	STRINGS	Returns best match to input string
Bin2BinStr$	BITS	Integer to 16-character binary string
BinStr2Bin%	BITS	16-character binary string to integer
BitShiftLeft%	CTOOLS2	Shifts all bits in a string left one bit
BitShiftRight%	CTOOLS2	Shifts all bits in a string right one bit
BufferedKeyInput$	DOSCALLS	ASCII string of specified length
Card$	GAMES	Returns name of card given a number from 1 through 52
Ceil#	QCALMATH	Smallest whole number greater than a number
Center$	STRINGS	Centers string by padding with spaces
ChangeSign#	QCALMATH	Reverses sign of a number
CheckDate%	CALENDAR	Validates date with return of TRUE/FALSE
Collision%	GAMES	Returns TRUE or FALSE collision condition
Combinations#	PROBSTAT	Combinations of *n* items, *r* at a time
Comma$	DOLLARS	Double-precision with commas inserted
Cosine#	QCALMATH	Cosine of a number

(continued)

APPENDIXES

continued

Function	Module	Description
Date2Day%	CALENDAR	Day of month number from date string
Date2Julian&	CALENDAR	Julian day number for a given date
Date2Month%	CALENDAR	Month number from date string
Date2Year%	CALENDAR	Year number from date string
DayOfTheCentury&	CALENDAR	Day of the given century
DayOfTheWeek$	CALENDAR	Name of day of the week for given date
DayOfTheYear%	CALENDAR	Day of the year (1 through 366) for given date
DaysBetweenDates&	CALENDAR	Number of days between two dates
Deg2Rad#	TRIANGLE	Converts degree angular units to radians
Detab$	STRINGS	Replaces tab characters with spaces
Dice%	GAMES	Returns total showing for throwing *n* dice
Divide#	QCALMATH	Result of dividing two numbers
DollarString$	DOLLARS	Dollar representation rounded with commas
DOSVersion%	DOSCALLS	Version number of MS-DOS returned
Ebcdic2Ascii$	STRINGS	Converts a string from EBCDIC to ASCII
Entab$	STRINGS	Replaces spaces with tab characters
Exponential#	QCALMATH	Exponential function of a number
Factorial#	PROBSTAT	Factorial of a number
FileGet$	FIGETPUT	Returns a string with contents of file
FilterIn$	STRINGS	Retains only specified characters in string
FilterOut$	STRINGS	Deletes specified characters from string
Fraction2String$	FRACTION	Converts type Fraction variable to a string
FractionalPart#	QCALMATH	Fractional part of a number
GeometricMean#	PROBSTAT	Geometric mean of an array of numbers
GetDirectory$	DOSCALLS	Path to disk directory specified
GetDrive$	DOSCALLS	Current drive string
GetVerifyState%	DOSCALLS	Verify setting (state)
GreatestComDiv&	FRACTION	Returns greatest common divisor
HarmonicMean#	PROBSTAT	Harmonic mean of an array of numbers
HMS2Time$	CALENDAR	Time string for given hour, minute, and second
HypCosine#	QCALMATH	Hyperbolic cosine of a number
HypSine#	QCALMATH	Hyperbolic sine of a number

(continued)

APPENDIX B

continued

Function	Module	Description
HypTangent#	QCALMATH	Hyperbolic tangent of a number
InKeyCode%	KEYS	Returns unique integer for any key pressed
IntegerPart#	QCALMATH	Integer part of a number
IsItAlnum%	CTOOLS1	Alphanumeric character determination
IsItAlpha%	CTOOLS1	Alphabetic character determination
IsItAscii%	CTOOLS1	Standard ASCII character determination
IsItCntrl%	CTOOLS1	Control character determination
IsItDigit%	CTOOLS1	Decimal digit (0–9) determination
IsItGraph%	CTOOLS1	Graphics character determination
IsItLower%	CTOOLS1	Lowercase character determination
IsItPrint%	CTOOLS1	Printable character determination
IsItPunct%	CTOOLS1	Punctuation character determination
IsItSpace%	CTOOLS1	Space character determination
IsItUpper%	CTOOLS1	Uppercase character determination
IsItXDigit%	CTOOLS1	Hexadecimal character determination
Julian2Date$	CALENDAR	Date string from given Julian day number
KeyCode%	KEYS	Waits and returns integer value for key
LeastComMul&	FRACTION	Returns least common multiple
LogBase10#	QCALMATH	Log base 10 of a number
LogBaseN#	QCALMATH	Log base *N* of a number
LogE#	QCALMATH	Natural logarithm of a number
Lpad$	STRINGS	Returns left-justified input string
LtrimSet$	STRINGS	Deletes specified characters from left
Magnitude!	CARTESIA	Distance from origin to x, y point
MDY2Date$	CALENDAR	Date string from given month, day, and year
MenuString%	CTOOLS2	Bar menu and user response function
Modulus#	QCALMATH	Remainder of the division of two numbers
MonthName$	CALENDAR	Name of month for a given date
Multiply#	QCALMATH	Product of two numbers
NewWord$	CIPHER	Creates pseudorandom new word
NextParameter$	QCAL	Extracts number or command from COMMAND$
NumberOfBits&	CTOOLS2	Determines number of 1 bits in a string

(continued)

APPENDIXES

continued

Function	Module	Description
OneOverX#	QCALMATH	Result of dividing 1 by a number
Ord%	STRINGS	Returns byte number for ANSI mnemonic
Permutations#	PROBSTAT	Permutations of *n* items, *r* at a time
QuadraticMean#	PROBSTAT	Quadratic mean of an array of numbers
Rad2Deg#	TRIANGLE	Converts radian angular units to degrees
Rand&	RANDOMS	Long integers
RandExponential!	RANDOMS	Real value with exponential distribution from mean
RandFrac!	RANDOMS	Single-precision positive value < 1.0
RandInteger%	RANDOMS	Integers within desired range
RandNormal!	RANDOMS	Single-precision from mean and standard deviation
RandReal!	RANDOMS	Single-precision value in desired range
Repeat$	STRINGS	Combines multiple copies into one string
Replace$	STRINGS	Replaces specified characters in string
Reverse$	STRINGS	Reverses order of characters in a string
ReverseCase$	STRINGS	Reverses case for each charater in a string
Round#	DOLLARS	Rounding at specified decimal place
Rpad$	STRINGS	Returns right-justified input string
RtrimSet$	STRINGS	Deletes specified characters from right
Second2Date$	CALENDAR	Seconds from last of 1979 to date given
Second2Time$	CALENDAR	Time of day from seconds since last of 1979
Shade&	COLORS	Color value from given red, green, and blue
Shuffle$	GAMES	Randomizes character bytes in string
Sign#	QCALMATH	Sign of a number
Sine#	QCALMATH	Sine of a number
SquareRoot#	QCALMATH	Square root of a number
Subtract#	QCALMATH	Difference between two numbers
Tangent#	QCALMATH	Tangent of a number
Time2Hour%	CALENDAR	Hour number from time string
Time2Minute%	CALENDAR	Minute number from time string
Time2Second%	CALENDAR	Seconds number from time string
TimeDate2Second&	CALENDAR	Seconds from last of 1979 from date/time

(continued)

continued

Function	Module	Description
Translate$	STRINGS	Exchanges characters in string from table
TranslateCountry$	DOSCALLS	Translates string—current country setting
TriangleArea#	TRIANGLE	Calculates area of triangle from three sides
WordCount%	WORDCOUN	Returns number of words in a string
Xsquared#	QCALMATH	Square of a number
YRaisedToX#	QCALMATH	Number raised to the power of a second

APPENDIX C

SUBPROGRAMS-TO-MODULES CROSS REFERENCE

Subprogram	Module	Description
AssignKey	STDOUT	Reassigns a string to a key
Attrib	ATTRIB	Table of color attributes (text mode)
Attribute	STDOUT	Sets screen color (ANSI driver definition)
BitGet	BITS	Value from any bit position in a string
BitPut	BITS	Sets or clears bit at location in a string
BuildAEStrings	STRINGS	Builds ASCII and EBCDIC character translation tables
ClearLine	STDOUT	Clears line from cursor to end of line
ClearScreen	STDOUT	Clears screen
Complex2String	COMPLEX	String representation of a complex number
ComplexAdd	COMPLEX	Adds two complex numbers
ComplexDiv	COMPLEX	Divides two complex numbers
ComplexExp	COMPLEX	Exponential function of a complex number
ComplexLog	COMPLEX	Natural log of a complex number
ComplexMul	COMPLEX	Multiplies two complex numbers
ComplexPower	COMPLEX	Complex number raised to a complex number
ComplexReciprocal	COMPLEX	Reciprocal of a complex number
ComplexRoot	COMPLEX	Complex root of a complex number
ComplexSqr	COMPLEX	Square root of a complex number
ComplexSub	COMPLEX	Subtracts two complex numbers
CrLf	STDOUT	Sends carriage return and line feed
Curschek	MOUSSUBS	Check-mark mouse cursor pattern mask
Cursdflt	MOUSSUBS	Arrow mouse cursor pointing up and left
Curshand	MOUSSUBS	Pointing hand mouse cursor
Curshour	MOUSSUBS	Hourglass mouse cursor

(continued)

APPENDIX C

continued

Subprogram	Module	Description
Cursjet	MOUSSUBS	Jet-shaped mouse cursor
Cursleft	MOUSSUBS	Left arrow mouse cursor
CursorDown	STDOUT	Moves cursor down specified number of lines
CursorHome	STDOUT	Moves cursor to upper left corner of screen
CursorLeft	STDOUT	Moves cursor left specified number of spaces
CursorPosition	STDOUT	Moves cursor to specified row and column
CursorRight	STDOUT	Moves cursor right specified number of spaces
CursorUp	STDOUT	Moves cursor up specified number of lines
Cursplus	MOUSSUBS	Plus sign mouse cursor
Cursup	MOUSSUBS	Up arrow mouse cursor
Cursx	MOUSSUBS	X-mark mouse cursor
DisplayStack	QCAL	Displays final results of the program
DrawBox	EDIT	Creates a double-lined box on the display
Dup	QCALMATH	Duplicates top entry on the stack
EditBox	EDIT	Allows editing in a boxed area of the screen
EditLine	EDIT	Allows editing of string at cursor position
Equipment	BIOSCALL	Equipment/hardware information
ErrorMessage	ERROR	Error message display
FilePut	FIGETPUT	Writes contents of string into binary file
FileRead	LOOK	Reads lines of ASCII files into an array
FileTreeSearch	QBTREE	Recursive directory search routine
FillArray	GAMES	Fills an integer array with a sequence of numbers defined by the bounds
FindFirstFile	FILEINFO	Finds first file that matches parameter
FindNextFile	FILEINFO	Finds next file that matches parameter
FormatTwo	EDIT	Splits string into two strings
FractionAdd	FRACTION	Adds two fractions and reduces
FractionDiv	FRACTION	Divides two fractions and reduces
FractionMul	FRACTION	Multiplies two fractions and reduces
FractionReduce	FRACTION	Reduces fraction to lowest terms
FractionSub	FRACTION	Subtracts two fractions and reduces
GetCountry	DOSCALLS	Current country setting

(continued)

APPENDIXES

continued

Subprogram	Module	Description
GetDiskFreeSpace	DOSCALLS	Disk space format and usage for input drive
GetFileAttributes	DOSCALLS	Attribute bits for given file
GetFileData	FILEINFO	Extracts file directory information
GetMediaDescriptor	DOSCALLS	Drive information for system
GetShiftStates	BIOSCALL	Shift key states
Indent	QBFMT	Performs line indention
InsertCharacter	EDIT	Inserts a character
Justify	JUSTIFY	Adjusts strings to specified widths
MouseHide	MOUSSUBS	Turns off mouse visibility
MouseInches	MOUSSUBS	Sets mouse-to-cursor motion ratio
MouseInstall	MOUSSUBS	Checks mouse availability; resets mouse parameters
MouseLightPen	MOUSSUBS	Mouse emulation of a lightpen
MouseMaskTranslate	MOUSSUBS	Translates pattern/hot spot to binary
MouseMickey	MOUSSUBS	Returns motion increments since last call
MouseNow	MOUSSUBS	Current state/location of the mouse
MousePressLeft	MOUSSUBS	Location of mouse—left button press
MousePressRight	MOUSSUBS	Location of mouse—right button press
MousePut	MOUSSUBS	Moves cursor to the given position
MouseRange	MOUSSUBS	Limits mouse cursor motion to rectangle
MouseReleaseLeft	MOUSSUBS	Location of mouse—left button release
MouseReleaseRight	MOUSSUBS	Location of mouse—right button release
MouseSetGcursor	MOUSSUBS	Sets graphics-mode mouse cursor
MouseShow	MOUSSUBS	Activates and displays mouse cursor
MouseSoftCursor	MOUSSUBS	Sets text-mode attributes (mouse cursor)
MouseWarp	MOUSSUBS	Sets mouse double-speed threshold
MovBytes	CTOOLS1	Moves bytes from one location to another
MovWords	CTOOLS1	Moves blocks of words in memory
OneMonthCalendar	CALENDAR	One-month calendar for given date
PackWord	CTOOLS2	Packs two bytes into an integer value
ParseLine	PARSE	Breaks a string into individual words
ParseWord	PARSE	Parses and removes first word from string

(continued)

continued

Subprogram	Module	Description
Pol2Rec	CARTESIA	Polar to Cartesian conversion
PrintScreen	BIOSCALL	Screen dump
Process	QCAL	Controls action for command line parameters
ProcesX	CIPHER	Enciphers string by XORing bytes
QcalHelp	QCAL	Provides a "Help" display for program
RandShuffle	RANDOMS	Initializes random number generator
Reboot	BIOSCALL	System reboot
Rec2Pol	CARTESIA	Cartesian to polar conversion
SaveObject	OBJECT	Creates graphics "PUT" file source code
Scroll	BIOSCALL	Moves text in designated area of screen
SetCode	QBFMT	Determines indention code by keyword
SetDirectory	DOSCALLS	Sets current directory
SetDrive	DOSCALLS	Sets current disk drive
SetFileAttributes	DOSCALLS	Sets the attribute bits for a given file
SetVerifyState	DOSCALLS	Sets or clears verify state (writing to file)
ShuffleArray	GAMES	Randomizes integers in an array
SplitFractions	FRACTION	Parses fraction problem string
SplitUp	QBFMT	Splits line into major components
StdOut	STDOUT	Sends a string to standard output channel
String2Complex	COMPLEX	Converts string to complex variable
String2Fraction	FRACTION	Converts a string to Fraction variable
SwapXY	QCALMATH	Swaps top two entries on the stack
TextGet	CTOOLS2	Saves characters and attributes from area of screen
TextPut	CTOOLS2	Restores text from TextGet to screen
Triangle	TRIANGLE	Calculates sides and angles of triangle
UnPackWord	CTOOLS2	Unpacks values from high and low bytes
VideoState	BIOSCALL	Mode, column, and page display of current state
Windows	WINDOWS	Creates a pop-up window
WindowsPop	WINDOWS	Removes last displayed window
WriteToDevice	DOSCALLS	Outputs a string to a device

APPENDIX D

Hexadecimal Format (.OBJ) Files

Three assembly-language modules are discussed in this book. The suggested method for creating object-code files is to use the Microsoft Macro Assembler 5.0 on the source-code files. If necessary, however, you can process these files using the HEX2BIN.BAS program to create the desired object-code files. (See the HEX2BIN.BAS program for information about how to make the conversions.)

```
MOUSE.HEX (MOUSE.OBJ)

80 0B 00 09 4D 4F 55 53 - 45 2E 41 53 4D D4 96 24
00 00 06 44 47 52 4F 55 - 50 04 44 41 54 41 04 43
4F 44 45 0A 4D 4F 55 53 - 45 5F 54 45 58 54 05 5F
44 41 54 41 7D 98 07 00 - 48 39 00 05 04 01 D6 98
07 00 48 00 00 06 03 01 - 0F 9A 04 00 02 FF 02 5F
90 0C 00 00 01 05 4D 4F - 55 53 45 00 00 00 D5 88
04 00 00 A2 01 D1 A0 3D - 00 01 00 00 55 8B EC 8B
5E 0C 8B 07 50 8B 5E 0A - 8B 07 50 8B 5E 08 8B 0F
8B 5E 06 8B 17 5B 58 1E - 07 CD 33 53 8B 5E 0C 89
07 58 8B 5E 0A 89 07 8B - 5E 08 89 0F 8B 5E 06 89
17 5D CA 08 00 BC 8A 02 - 00 00 74


INTRPT.HEX (INTRPT.OBJ)

80 0C 00 0A 49 4E 54 52 - 50 54 2E 41 53 4D 7A 88
03 00 80 9E 57 96 25 00 - 00 06 44 47 52 4F 55 50
04 44 41 54 41 04 43 4F - 44 45 05 5F 44 41 54 41
0B 49 4E 54 52 50 54 5F - 54 45 58 54 23 98 07 00
```

(continued)

INTRPT.HEX *continued*

```
48 07 01 06 04 01 06 98 - 07 00 48 00 00 05 03 01
10 9A 04 00 02 FF 02 5F - 90 1E 00 00 01 09 49 4E
54 45 52 52 55 50 54 00 - 00 00 0A 49 4E 54 45 52
52 55 50 54 58 0D 00 00 - 3F 88 04 00 00 A2 01 D1
A0 0B 01 01 00 00 55 8B - EC 83 C4 E2 C7 46 FA 08
00 EB 0B 55 8B EC 83 C4 - E2 C7 46 FA 0A 00 89 76
E4 89 7E E2 8C 5E FC 9C - 8F 46 FE 8B 76 08 8D 7E
E6 8B 4E FA FC 16 07 F3 - A5 55 8B 76 0A 8B 1C 0A
FF 74 03 E9 00 00 80 FB - 25 74 05 80 FB 26 75 0E
B8 08 00 50 B8 02 CA 50 - B8 83 C4 50 EB 07 33 C0
50 B8 CA 06 50 8A E3 B0 - CD 50 0E B8 00 00 50 16
8B C4 05 06 00 50 8B 46 - F4 25 D5 0F 50 8B 46 E6
8B 5E E8 8B 4E EA 8B 56 - EC 8B 76 F0 8B 7E E2 83
7E FA 08 74 14 81 7E F6 - FF FF 74 03 8E 5E F6 81
7E F8 FF FF 74 03 8E 46 - F8 8B 6E EE 9D CB 55 8B
EC 8B 6E 02 9C 8F 46 F4 - FF 76 FE 9D 89 46 E6 89
5E E8 89 4E EA 89 56 EC - 8B 46 DE 89 46 EE 89 76
F0 89 7E E2 8C 5E F6 8C - 46 F8 8E 5E FC 8D 76 E6
1E 07 8B 7E 06 8B 4E FA - FC F3 A5 8B 76 E4 8B 7E
E2 8B E5 5D CA 06 00 8B - 76 0A C7 04 FF FF 8B 76
E4 8B 7E E2 8E 5E FC 8B - E5 5D CA 06 00 0B 9C 0F
00 84 3E 00 01 01 F1 00 - C4 66 00 01 01 A8 00 CC
8A 02 00 00 74
```

CASEMAP.HEX (CASEMAP.OBJ)

```
80 0D 00 0B 43 41 53 45 - 4D 41 50 2E 41 53 4D 5F
96 26 00 00 06 44 47 52 - 4F 55 50 0C 43 41 53 45
4D 41 50 5F 54 45 58 54 - 04 44 41 54 41 04 43 4F
```

(continued)

CASEMAP.HEX *continued*

```
44 45 05 5F 44 41 54 41 - 08 98 07 00 48 14 00 03
05 01 FC 98 07 00 48 00 - 00 06 04 01 0E 9A 04 00
02 FF 02 5F 90 0E 00 00 - 01 07 43 41 53 45 4D 41
50 00 00 00 60 88 04 00 - 00 A2 01 D1 A0 18 00 01
00 00 55 8B EC 8B 5E 0A - 8B 07 FF 5E 06 8B 5E 0A
89 07 5D CA 06 00 E3 8A - 02 00 00 74
```

APPENDIX E

Line-Drawing Characters

You can enter line-drawing characters into QuickBASIC programs by pressing and holding the Alt key while typing up to three decimal digits on the numeric keypad. You can then use QuickBASIC strings to outline screen areas or to draw boxes around text. This chart organizes the line-drawing characters by type rather than by ASCII value.

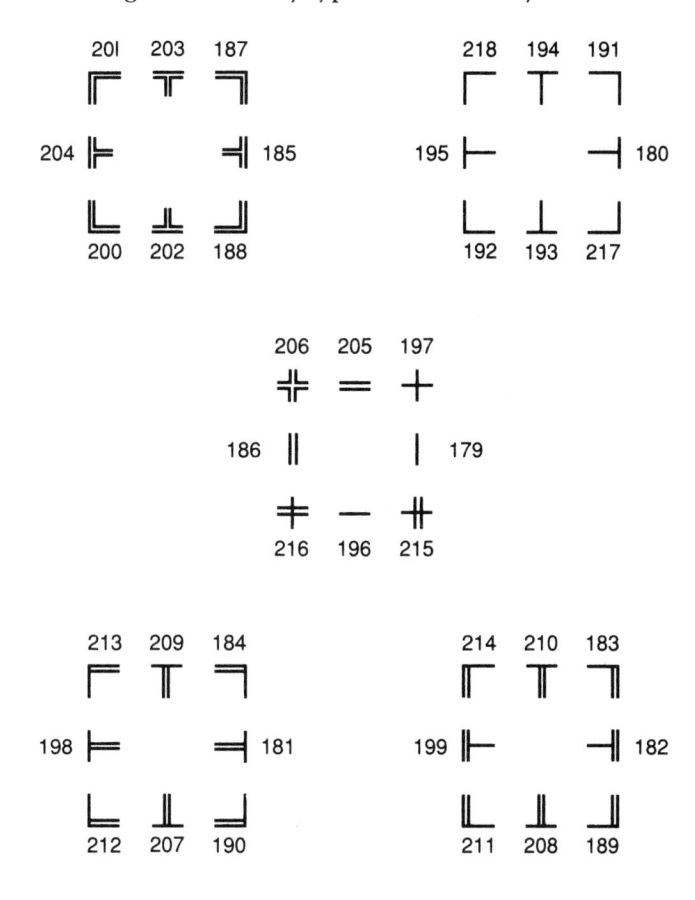

John Clark Craig has written several books on computer programming since 1980, including *True BASIC Programs and Subroutines*. He lives with his family in Eagle River, Alaska, where he is a programmer for ARCO Alaska, Inc.

The manuscript for this book was prepared and submitted to Microsoft Press in electronic form. Text files were processed and formatted using Microsoft Word.

Cover design by Ted Mader and Associates
Interior text design by Darcie S. Furlan
Illustrations by Darcie S. Furlan
Principal typography by Jean Trenary

Text composition by Microsoft Press in Baskerville with display in Baskerville Bold, using the Magna composition system and the Linotronic 300 laser imagesetter.